Reading and Writing Prep for the

SAT®&

ACT®

2nd Edition

Jonathan Chiu and the Staff of The Princeton Review

PrincetonReview.com

Penguin
Random
House

The Princeton Review
110 East 42nd Street, 7th Floor
New York, NY 10017
Email: editorialsupport@review.com

Published in the United States by Penguin Random House LLC, New York, and in Canada by Random House of Canada, a division of Penguin Random House Ltd., Toronto.

The material in this book was previously published as *Reading and Writing Workout for the SAT, 3rd Edition,* a trade paperback published by Random House, an imprint and division of Penguin Random House LLC, in 2016, and *English and Reading Workout for the ACT,* a trade paperback published by Random House, an imprint and division of Penguin Random House LLC, in 2015.

ISBN: 978-0-525-56754-7
ISSN: 2575-6311

Editor: Aaron Riccio
Production Editor: Liz Rutzel
Production Artist: Deborah A. Weber

Printed in the United States of America on partially recycled paper.

10 9 8 7 6 5 4 3 2 1

Second Edition

Editorial

Rob Franek, Editor-in-Chief
Casey Cornelius, VP Content Development
Mary Beth Garrick, Director of Production
Selena Coppock, Managing Editor
Meave Shelton, Senior Editor
Colleen Day, Editor
Sarah Litt, Editor
Aaron Riccio, Editor
Orion McBean, Associate Editor

Penguin Random House Publishing Team

Tom Russell, VP, Publisher
Alison Stoltzfus, Publishing Director
Jake Eldred, Associate Managing Editor
Ellen Reed, Production Manager
Suzanne Lee, Designer

Acknowledgments

The Princeton Review would like to thank the following individuals for their help on this book: Brian Becker, Melissa Hendrix, Kathryn Menefee, Gina Donegan, Susan Swinford, Krissi Taylor Leslie, Lori DesRochers, Cat Healey, Sara Soriano, Stefan Maisnier, Bobby Hood, Joelle Cotham, and Anthony Krupp, as well as Jonathan Chiu, the National ACT & SAT Content Director at The Princeton Review.

The Princeton Review would also like to thank the dedicated production team of Deborah Weber and Liz Rutzel, who have worked so diligently to ensure the quality of this book.

Special thanks to Adam Robinson, who conceived of and perfected the Joe Bloggs approach to standardized tests and many of the other successful techniques used by The Princeton Review.

Contents

Get More (Free) Content

1 Go to **PrincetonReview.com/cracking.**

2 Enter the following ISBN for your book: 9780525567547.

3 Answer a few simple questions to set up an exclusive Princeton Review account. (If you already have one, you can just log in.)

4 Click the "Student Tools" button, also found under "My Account" from the top toolbar. You're all set to access your bonus content!

Need to report a potential **content** issue?

Contact **EditorialSupport@review.com**.
Include:

- full title of the book
- ISBN number
- page number

Need to report a **technical** issue?

Contact **TPRStudentTech@review.com** and provide:

- your full name
- email address used to register the book
- full book title and ISBN
- computer OS (Mac/PC) and browser (Firefox, Safari, etc.)

Once you've registered, you can...

- Take a full-length practice PSAT, SAT, and/or ACT

- Get valuable advice about the college application process, including tips for writing a great essay and where to apply for financial aid

- If you're still choosing between colleges, use our searchable rankings of *The Best 382 Colleges* to find out more information about your dream school

- Check to see if there have been any corrections or updates to this edition

Look For These Icons Throughout The Book

 PROVEN TECHNIQUES

 APPLIED STRATEGIES

 MORE GREAT BOOKS

Chapter 1
Introduction to the Verbal Sections of the SAT & ACT

For more on admissions, see The Princeton Review's *The Best 382 Colleges* or visit our website, PrincetonReview.com.

See The Princeton Review's companion book, *Math and Science Prep for the SAT and ACT, 2nd Edition.*

WELCOME

Standardized tests are an important aspect of college admissions. Most schools require their applicants to submit either SAT or ACT scores, but no school will mandate which particular test to take—they just want to see good scores. For a long time, different schools would accept only one or the other. If you wanted to apply to schools in the Midwest, you took the ACT, but if you wanted to apply to schools on the East or West Coast, you took the SAT.

The good news is that these rules are obsolete. All schools that require a standardized test will take either the ACT or SAT.

This is good news indeed for test-takers. While there are many similarities between the two tests, many students find they do better on one than on the other. The expert advice of The Princeton Review is to take whichever test you do better on. While you can certainly take both, you should focus your efforts on one for substantive score improvement. True improvement takes hard work, and it can be tough to become an expert on both tests. And since schools will accept scores for either one, you won't win any brownie points for punishing yourself.

Since you bought this book, we assume you've already made the decision to boost your ACT or SAT score. This book provides a strategic and efficient way to improve your scores, specifically on Reading and English or Writing and Language. For a more thorough review of content and exhaustive practice, we recommend *Cracking the ACT* and *Cracking the SAT.*

FUN FACT ABOUT THE ACT AND SAT

The ACT and the SAT are nothing like the tests you take in school. In your English class, you may learn grammar, but do you have to fix underlined portions? You may have to read a lot, but do you write papers or take speed tests on comprehension? All the content review and strategies we teach in the following lessons are based on the specific structure and format of the ACT or the SAT. Before you can beat either test, you have to know how it's built.

Structure of the ACT

The ACT is made up of four multiple-choice tests and an optional Writing test.

The five tests are always given in the same order.

English	Math	Reading	Science	Writing
45 minutes	60 minutes	35 minutes	35 minutes	40 minutes
75 questions	60 questions	40 questions	40 questions	1 Essay

Structure of the SAT

The SAT is also made up of 4 multiple-choice tests and an optional essay. In addition, the Math sections have a handful of questions that are free-response. Like the ACT, the sections always appear in the same order.

Reading	Writing and Language	Math: No Calculator	Math: Calculator	Essay
65 minutes	35 minutes	25 minutes	55 minutes	50 minutes
52 questions	44 questions	20 questions	38 questions	1 essay

Scoring on the ACT

When students and schools talk about ACT scores, they mean the composite score, a range of 1–36. The composite is an average of the four multiple choice tests, each scored on the same 1–36 scale. There's no penalty for leaving questions blank or answering them incorrectly, so you can only improve your score by guessing. Neither the Writing test score nor the combined English plus Writing score affect the composite.

Whether you look at your score online or wait to get it in the mail, the biggest number on the page is always the composite. While admissions offices will certainly see the individual scores of all five tests (and their sub-scores), schools will use the composite to evaluate your application, and that's why it's the only one that matters in the end.

The composite is an average: Let the full weight of that sink in. Do you need to bring up all four scores equally to raise your composite? Do you need to be a superstar in all four tests? Should you focus more on your weaknesses than your strengths? No, no, and absolutely not. The best way to improve your composite is to shore up your weaknesses but exploit your strengths as much as possible.

Since 2015, ACT score reports have included subscores in addition to the traditional (1–36) ACT score. These indicators are designed to measure student performance and predict career readiness, as well as competency in STEM (Science, Technology, Engineering, Mathematics) and English language arts. ACT believes that these additional scores will give students better insight into their strengths and how those strengths can be harnessed for success in college and beyond. In addition to the 1–36 score for each of the tests and their composite score, students will now see score breakdowns in the following categories:

- **STEM score:** This score represents students' overall performance on the math and science sections of the ACT. The goal of this score is to help students better understand their strengths in math and science and how they might use those strengths to guide their academic and career goals.

- **Progress Toward Career Readiness Indicator:** This is meant to help students understand the extent to which they are prepared for a future career. It can also help teachers guide their students toward numerous career pathways.

- **English Language Arts Score:** This score measures achievement in the English, reading, and writing portions of the exam (for students who take all three of those sections), and allows students to see how their performance compares with others.

- **Text Complexity Progress Indicator:** This is intended to help students determine how well they understand the kinds of complex texts that they will encounter in college and whether they need to improve. This score is based on a student's performance on all of the writing passages.

As we said before, these changes to the test won't impact how students test or the types of questions they'll need to answer, but rather how their scores are reported and the kind of information they'll be able to gather from their results.

If you do take the Writing test, you will receive an additional score: your Writing subscore, which will range from 2–12. This score is not factored into the composite, so taking the Writing test will not have a direct impact on your composite score. Be sure to check ACT's website to determine whether your target schools want you to take the ACT Writing test. Also, check out Part IV of this book for more information and practice for the revised Writing test.

Scoring on the SAT

When students and schools talk about the SAT score, they mean the total score, a range of 400–1600. The total score is comprised of two area scores: one for Evidence-Based Reading and Writing, and one for Math. The Essay score does not affect the total score. For each question you answer correctly on the SAT, you'll receive one raw point, period. There's no penalty for leaving questions blank or answering them incorrectly, so you can only improve your raw score by guessing.

Your Evidence-Based Reading & Writing (EBRW) section score combines your raw scores from both areas, so out of the 52 Reading questions and 44 Writing and Language questions, you can gain up to 96 raw points. This total raw score is then converted to a scaled score falling between 200 and 800 points. These scores are reported in 10-point increments, so you could score a 510 or a 520, but not a 515. This, in turn, makes up half of your total score. To get that total, simply add your EBRW score to your Math score.

When you receive your scores, you'll notice a number of other scores as well. These are your "test" scores, "cross-test" scores, and "subscores." For Verbal, your test scores refer to the Reading and Writing and Language sections individually and are reported on a scale of 10–40. The two cross-test scores are also reported on a scale of 10–40 but cover questions that fall into the category of "Analysis in Science" or "Analysis of History/Social Studies." These questions can appear in any of the tests, including the Math test. Lastly, the subscores tallied within the Reading and W&L sections are: Expression of Ideas, Standard English Conventions, Words in Context, and Command of Evidence. Each of these is reported on a scale of 1–15.

As with the ACT, the SAT Essay is optional and scored separately. It will not impact your total score. Two graders will read and score the essay on a 1–4 scale in three different categories: Reading, Analysis, and Writing. Each category will receive a total score of 2–8, which is attained by adding the individual 1–4 scores from your two graders. Each task (Reading, Analysis, and Writing) is scored individually, so a high score in one does not guarantee a high score in another. Your final Essay score will be displayed as *x/y/z,* in order, for the Reading, Analysis, and Writing domains. As with the ACT Writing test, start researching your chosen schools now to see if they will require you to take the SAT Essay.

What We Say About the Essay
Your Essay is optional and scored separately, so you don't have to worry about it having an impact on your total.

What's a Good Score?

Simply put, a good score is the one that gets you into the college of your dreams. So, what's your first step to figuring out what's a good score for *you*? Start doing some research! Make a list of the schools you'd most like to attend and look into their average/median scores to get an idea of what you'll need to score to be considered for admission (we're a bit biased, but we've heard **www.princetonreview. com** and *The Best 382 Colleges* are both great resources for college research). From there, take a practice test and start putting a plan in place to hit your goal score. While colleges consider a LOT of factors when making admissions decisions, your ACT or SAT results are a big factor, and can be just what you need to get your foot in the door at the school of your dreams.

Timing on the ACT and SAT

Time is your enemy on the ACT. You have less than a minute per question on either the English or Reading sections. SAT Writing and Language is the same way. The SAT Reading section is a bit more generous with time, but it's not as if there's extra time for reading the passages on any of these sections. The Princeton Review's strategies are all based on this time crunch. You can think of both Reading and English/Writing and Language tests as open-book tests, but you can neither waste all your time reading the whole book nor skip it altogether.

Verbal Content on the ACT and SAT

On the ACT English section, there are 5 prose passages with 15 questions each. These range in topic from historical essays to personal narratives. For the SAT Writing and Language section, there are 4 prose passages with 11 questions each. Topics will include areas such as history, science, social studies, and careers.

The ACT Reading section contains 4 passages with 10 questions each. These are always in the same order: Prose Fiction/Literary Narrative, Social Science, Humanities, and Natural Science. On the SAT Reading section, there are 5 passages, each with 10 to 11 questions. One passage will be a selection of U.S. or World Literature, two will be based on History/Social Studies, and two will be based on Science. The order of these may vary, but Literature is generally first. For both the ACT and SAT Reading sections, expect to see one Dual Passage, with some questions based on both passages.

The two main differences in the verbal content of the two tests is that the SAT will contain a handful of graph questions based on Reading or Writing and Language passages and some paired questions in the Reading section.

Chapter 2
Strategies

STRATEGIES

You don't necessarily have to work harder to raise your ACT or SAT score, though it helps. You do, however, have to be *smarter*, because a smart test-taker is a strategic test-taker. Target specific content to review, apply an effective and efficient approach, and employ the common sense that frequently deserts many of us when we pick up a number 2 pencil. These three things, along with the following strategies, can make a huge difference.

Each test on the ACT or SAT demands a different approach, and even the most universal strategies vary in their applications. The chapters that follow discuss these terms in greater detail, customized to English/Writing and Language and Reading.

Personal Order of Difficulty (POOD)

If time is going to run out, would you rather it run out on the hardest Reading passage or on the easiest? Of course you want it to run out on the points you are less likely to get right. On the English/Writing and Language test, you can't afford to spend too long on questions you find the most time-consuming and never even get to a bunch of questions you'd nail. The trick is to know how to pick your order of passages and questions in Reading, and how to pace yourself in English/Writing and Language to get to as many easy questions as you can.

We'll discuss in greater detail what these mean in the individual lessons, but for now, understand that you have to make smart decisions for good reasons quickly as you move through each test.

The Best Way to Bubble In

Work a page at a time, circling your answers right on the booklet. Transfer a page's worth of answers to the scantron at one time. It's better to stay focused on working questions rather than disrupt your concentration to find where you left off on the scantron. You'll be more accurate at both tasks. Do not wait until the end, however, to transfer all the answers from that test onto your scantron. Go a page at a time.

Now

Does a question look okay? Do you know how to do it? Do it *Now*.

Later

Will this question take a long time to work? Leave it and come back to it *Later*. Circle the question number for easy reference to return.

Never

Test-taker, know thyself. Know the topics that are your worst and learn the signs that flash danger. Don't waste time on questions you should *Never* do. Instead, use more time to answer the Now and Later questions accurately.

Pacing

When you're under the pressure of a timed test, every point counts, but stressing about getting to every single question could actually be the worst thing you can do. When the clock is involved, we somehow seem to find the quickest way to do the "wrongest" thing, the proverbial "careless mistake." And what's worse than coming to an easy question, a question you KNOW you should get right, working through it too quickly, and getting it wrong because you misread it? Is it better to attempt all of the Reading passages if you only get 50% of the questions right, or would it be better to do fewer Reading passages and focus on accuracy to get 75% of those questions correct? Right there, you'd already be scoring 4 or 5 more points doing less work with option #2. And don't forget, there is no penalty for wrong answers! Guessing on that last passage will pick up another extra point or two, meaning that working smarter, rather than harder, actually pays off big!

So pacing is not about figuring out how to get to every question; it's about doing the right number of questions for YOU! Mastering the art of effective pacing takes practice, but it's all about finding the number of questions you need to answer correctly in order to hit your goal score.

For English or Writing and Language, there is no order of difficulty of the passages or their questions. The most important thing is to finish, finding all the Now questions you can throughout the whole test and skipping over the Never questions as you go. Just don't forget to fill in a guess for those Never questions!

Process of Elimination (POE)

Take a look at the following example:

> **1**
>
> What does the word "strategy" mean in the context of the passage?

Kind of tough to answer this question without the context of the passage, isn't it? While test-writers aren't known for fairness, rest assured that you'll never be asked a question like that. But what if I told you that you could still get the question right without the passage? "How?" you might ask. Well, let's take a look at the question again, this time with something test-writers always provide on the Verbal portion of the ACT and SAT, the answers:

What does the word "strategy" mean in the context of the passage?

A) peacocks

B) working smart to improve your test score

C) the Philippines

D) five

It's much easier once you've got the answer choices to consider! You're still unlikely to see a question like this one on the ACT or SAT, but checking the choices is always the first and most important strategy to use if you want to improve your score. It's all about the Process of Elimination. The correct answer is right there in front of you; you just need to get rid of the bad answers. For each and every question on the Verbal portion of the ACT or SAT, there are three incorrect answers, which means that 75% of the test is garbage. Your task: start taking out the trash!

Bad answers are all over the test and they're generally easier to spot than the correct (and often very well hidden) answer. By starting with the answer choices and eliminating the ones that you know are wrong, you increase your chance of getting the question correct. Whenever you see an answer that can't be correct, cross it out with a slash. If it looks right, put a check next to it and keep reading. If it looks like it might be true, but you aren't sure, put a ~ mark next to it. We will refer to these three marks (slash, check, and ~) as POE symbols.

On English/Writing and Language and Reading both, it's more important, and often easier, to know what's wrong and eliminate it rather than try to find out what's right. In fact, on English/Writing and Language, POE is so strong you may find few Never questions.

It's worth the time to eliminate what's wrong and pick from what's left before you move on. On Reading, you may have absolutely no idea what you *have* read, but you'll likely know what you *haven't* and be able to eliminate a few wrong answers. Using POE to get rid of at least one or two wrong answers will substantially increase your odds of getting a question right.

Letter of the Day (LOTD)

Using the Process of Elimination on this test means that, even if you're not 100% sure your answer is the correct one, you're able to make an educated guess and earn a raw point you might not have otherwise earned. But what about those questions that you either aren't able to eliminate any answers on or that are too time-consuming? Since there's no penalty for getting a question wrong on the ACT or SAT, regardless of whether you're able to eliminate any answers or not, always have your **LOTD (Letter of the Day)** at the ready for questions you don't know how to do, don't want to do, or simply don't have time to do.

There is one thing to keep in mind: **Pick one letter for the SAT or a two-letter combo for the ACT and stick to it throughout the test!** For example, always choose (B) on the SAT or choose (A)/(F) or (C)/(H) on the ACT. Since both tests have a mostly-even distribution of answers, by maintaining a consistent guessing pattern, you have a much better chance of picking up a few free raw points than if you were to guess at random. And, let's be honest: if you find yourself running out of time, scoring a few extra points without even reading a question is pretty awesome.

Use Your Pencil

There is no doubt about it: the verbal sections of these tests have their challenges. With so much going on in so little time, you need every tool at your disposal to take down this test. That's why it's imperative that your pencil ALWAYS be moving. Whether it's crossing out bad answers, underlining key information in the passage, or bubbling in answers a passage at a time, it all comes down to keeping you actively engaged in what you are doing. One of the easiest ways to start increasing your ACT or SAT score is to jot things down in the test book, by the questions, in the margins, next to the answer choices, and so on. Don't try to keep everything in your head: That's what the test makers want you to do. Using that pencil to leave reminders or to call out relevant details is a key step for reaching your pacing goals. Every note helps to keep you focused and one step ahead of the test.

Everything about these tests, from the length to the passage selections and the questions and answers, is designed to put you through the wringer. Take control of the test and use everything available to you to make this test a little easier. Remember the Ps and embrace your POE, pacing, POOD, and pencil.

A Change Will Do You Good

The practice in this workbook is designed to help you find the best way for you to take the test. But that means you need to be willing to give new methods a chance, especially if you want your score to change. As the saying goes, doing the same thing over and over again with the expectation of different results is the definition of insanity.

Throughout this book, we will introduce you to all of the question types you'll encounter on the verbal sections of the ACT and SAT and we'll show you how to strategically and systematically approach them to increase your score. Really give these strategies a try; if you don't get it the first time, don't just give up and go back to old habits. You've likely been taking tests for a long time, and it may be hard to approach some of these questions in a different way, but we won't steer you in the wrong direction. Think about learning a new skill to add to something you're already good at: for instance, if you're a golfer learning a new swing or a tennis player learning a new serve. It's not that your old swing or serve didn't serve you well, it got you where you are. But in order to get better, you sometimes need to try things that might seem a little odd. At first, you might not be used to shifting the weight in your hips or adjusting the angle at which your racquet hits the ball, but with practice your new swing or new serve can take you to the next level. It just takes practice.

Be Flexible

The worst mistake a test-taker can make is to throw good time after bad. You read a question, don't understand it, so read it again. And again. If you stare at it really hard, you know you're going to just *see* it. And you can't move on, because really, after spending all that time it would be a waste not to keep at it, right? Actually, that way of thinking couldn't be more wrong.

You can't let one tough question drag you down. Instead, the best way to improve your ACT or SAT score is to follow our advice.

1.   Use the techniques and strategies in the lessons to work efficiently and accurately through all your Now and Later questions.

2.   Know your Never questions, and use your LOTD.

3.   Know when to move on. Use POE, and guess from what's left.

Now move on to the lessons and learn the best way to approach the content.

Part I
Reading and Writing Workout for the SAT

Chapter 3
Reading

EVIDENCE-BASED READING

The reading section is *long*—you have 65 minutes to tackle 5 passages and 52 questions, and the passages aren't exactly drawn from what most would consider a relaxing beach read. That might sound like a recipe for a lot of frantic reading, but it doesn't have to be. Consider the questions below:

5

In line 14, "blotted out" most nearly means

A) blemished

B) obscured

C) extinguished

D) removed

6

The author mentions Sweden and Brazil in order to emphasize which point about the Krakatoa eruption?

A) Although the eruption was devastating in Krakatoa, there were no effects felt in other parts of the word.

B) The volcanic eruption was so powerful that it affected the climate of countries thousands of miles away.

C) Local destruction in Krakatoa was enormous, but the destruction in Europe and South America was, if anything, greater.

D) The explosion would have been even more destructive had it happened today.

Did you notice something super helpful about question 5? Sure enough, the question actually tells you where to look to find the answer! That means that instead of having to read the entire passage in the hopes of finding the answer, you can focus on a much more manageable portion, something that looks more like this:

Line　The eruption of Krakatoa sent clouds of ash and
dust into Earth's atmosphere to a height of 50 miles.
The Sun was blotted out entirely for two days within a
15　100-mile radius of the volcano, and Earth temperatures
as far away as Sweden and Brazil were several degrees
lower than average that year.

Of course, you also might have noticed that question 6 *doesn't* contain a handy line reference. But while there isn't a line reference, question 6 does still provide a way to narrow down your search in the passage: it asks about *Sweden* and *Brazil*, two words that will likely stand out while skimming the passage. In fact, the portion of the passage you read for question 5 also mentions Sweden and Brazil. Even without a line reference, you could attack question 6 by using key words from the question, in addition to the fact that the questions in each passage are asked in roughly chronological order, to look for references to Sweden and Brazil in the portion of the passage after line 14.

In other words, the answers to questions 5 and 6 are located in specific places in the passage, and you don't have to read the entire passage to find the evidence you need to get them right. While the phrase "evidence-based" might *sound* like a lot of extra work, what it actually means is that the answers are in the passage and you can use the questions themselves to help you work efficiently to find the evidence and choose the correct answer.

Your Goal Is to Answer Questions

No matter how much you read, the proctor will not be walking around the examination room, saying, "Ah, Jessica! Excellent reading form. I'm giving you 20 extra points on your Evidence-based Reading score." The only way you get points in SAT Evidence-based Reading is by correctly answering questions.

The sooner you get to the questions, the sooner you start earning points. For example, both of the questions on the previous page could be answered without reading the rest of the passage (which we didn't show you). In question 5, you needed to supply a word that would fit in place of the quoted words "blotted out." The correct answer was (B), "obscured," because the volcanic ash filled the sky to the point that the sun's rays couldn't get through. Even if you had read the entire passage several times and made extensive notes, the answer to this question was based on only one thing: your understanding of this sentence in this paragraph.

The correct answer to question 6, which asked us why the author brought up Sweden and Brazil, was (B). In the context of this paragraph, the two countries were mentioned to show just how powerful the eruption had been. Again, even if you had memorized the entire passage, the only place to find the answer to this question was right here in this paragraph.

These questions are pretty typical of the SAT in that they include either a line reference or an identification of the paragraph in which the answer can be found. Most of the reading questions tell you where to look for the answer because they are arranged in chronological order. The answer to question 16 can be found somewhere between the answers to questions 15 and 17.

They're Too Long!

Many students look at a passage of 500 to 750 words and feel defeated at the thought of trying to keep track of a passage that long—but the situation is much better than they think. Reading passages are actually just a series of paragraphs like the one you just read. You don't need to remember details from the entire passage at once; you just need to focus on the details of one section at a time as you answer the questions dealing with that information. Then you can move on to another section.

THE PASSAGES

Subject Areas

Because everybody's Personal Order of Difficulty is different, it's important that you know what types of passages to expect on the test. This will allow you to use your time as efficiently as possible. The five passages will come from three subject areas and will consist of:

- One **US/World Literature** passage drawn from a classic or more recent work of literature.
- Two **History/Social Studies** passages drawn from fields such as history, economics, sociology, and political science and from primary historical documents.
- Two **Science** passages drawn from work in fields such as earth science, chemistry, and physics and addressing concepts, information, and/or experiments.

Other Features

A couple of the passages will also have additional features that could make them *appear* more intimidating:

The Exception that Proves the Rule
Dual passages, which we'll talk about in a moment, do have some questions that refer to content from both passages. But they also have questions that pertain to each individual passage, and so they can still be tackled, for the most part, in bite-sized chunks.

Dual Passages

One of the History/Social Studies or Science Passages will actually consist of two shorter passages on the same topic. Recent examples of these dual passages have given two views on the subject of mining in space, on the effect of new media on brain development, and on the rights of eighteenth-century women. Whatever the subject matter of the dual passages you encounter, you should tackle them in the following order:

1. Answer the questions that refer only to the first passage.
2. Answer the questions that refer only to the second passage.
3. Answer the questions that refer to both passages.

Charts, Tables, and Graphs

Two passages in the reading section will contain one or two of what the College Board calls *informational graphics,* which are charts, tables, and graphs. That means that two of the four history/social studies and science passages will be accompanied by one or two figures that will provide additional information related to the passages. These passages will include a few questions that ask about the data presented in the graphics, either alone or in relation to the information in the passage. These figures might seem like they'll require more work, but the charts, tables, and graphs provided in the reading section and the questions about them are relatively straightforward.

The bottom line is that neither dual passages nor charts, tables, and graphs should be cause for alarm, and passages that feature them will not necessarily be more difficult than passages that don't.

THE PRINCETON REVIEW METHOD

Once you've chosen and started working on a passage, you want to find the correct answers to the questions as efficiently as possible. Here's how to do that:

Step One, Read the Blurb: The blurb is the introductory sentence or two given before the body of the passage begins. The blurb provides a frame of reference for the content of the passage.

Step Two, Select and Understand a Question:

Remember that questions are presented with general ones first, followed by more specific ones in chronological order. Choose a question whose answer is likely easy to locate—for instance, a question that provides a line reference—and then make sure you understand what the question is asking. Most "questions" on the SAT are not questions at all, but open-ended statements. Rewording the statement as an actual question will help you to better understand how to answer it.

Step Three, Read Just What You Need:

Many questions will provide line numbers or a lead word that tell you where to look for your answer. If you read about five lines above and five lines below the referenced line or lead word, you should have enough information to answer the question. Read to find the particular phrase, sentence, or set of lines that provide the evidence on which the answer will be based. If you work through the specific questions this way, you should find that by the time you tackle the more general questions, you've gained a fairly good understanding of the passage, even if you didn't read it from start to finish.

Step Four, Predict the Correct Answer:

Since the test writers do their best to provide answer choices that look correct, the best way to avoid talking yourself into an appealing but wrong answer is to know exactly what you're looking for before you consider the answer choices. Take the time to answer the question for yourself in terms of the evidence you've found *before* you consider the answer choices. Marking the support for your answer in the passage is a great way to keep track of the information as you move to the next step in the process. It's also important when working with paired questions, which will be discussed in more detail later in the chapter.

Step Five, Use Process of Elimination:

With each wrong answer you cross off, it gets easier to compare the remaining answers and decide which one correctly answers the question. Eliminate answer choices that don't match your prediction and compare the remaining choices to see which is correct.

Notice that what you're *NOT* doing is tackling the passage first, lessening the possibility that your mind will wander or decide to savor the nuances of the passage irrelevant to the task of the SAT questions. Use the questions to guide you, reading sections of the passage as you need the information in them. Remember that the only way to get points on the test is by correctly answering questions. It's not how much you read, then, but how much you answer.

THE QUESTION TYPES

Line Reference and Lead Word Questions

The reading questions will be line reference or lead word questions. In each case, the question will tell you where in the passage to look for the answer.

Line reference questions ask you about a part of the passage and tell you to which lines the question refers. These questions will look like one of the following:

> In paragraph 4, why does the author mention Harry McCallan?
>
> The author cites "many interesting creatures" in lines 34–36 in order to . . .

Sometimes, instead of a line or paragraph number, you will be asked about a proper name or important word that will be pretty easy to find in the passage by running your finger down the passage until you come across it.

In either case, you should look back to the passage and find the lines indicated by the question or the lines in which the lead word can be found. It's important to read a little above and a little below the line number mentioned or the line on which the lead word is, to make sure you understand the line in context. Once you've found the relevant evidence in the passage, predict the answer to the question, and then eliminate any answer choices that do not match your prediction.

From time to time, you will see a question that seems specific, even though it has neither a line reference nor a colorful word to help you find the reference in the passage. It's not a bad idea to skip a question like this until after you've answered the rest of the questions and have a better understanding of the passage. Remember, however, that the questions are arranged chronologically. If you're considering question 6, then the information you need to answer it will probably closely follow the information needed to answer question 5 and come before the information needed to answer question 7.

Vocabulary-In-Context Questions

Vocabulary-in-context questions always include line numbers and ask you to identify the best alternative phrasing for a quoted word or phrase. Here's what one of these questions looks like:

> In line 44, "objective" most nearly means. . .

The thing to bear in mind for these questions is that ETS and the College Board often pick words that have more than one meaning, and the words are generally not being used in their primary sense. For example, ETS and the College Board's answer to the question above about the meaning of the word "objective" was the word "material"—certainly not the first meaning anyone would think of picking.

If you find yourself running out of time as you get to a reading passage, then these are the questions to answer first. Not only do they take the least amount of time, but they also require the smallest amount of overall knowledge of the passage.

General Questions

As you've seen, questions that ask about a specific section of the text are easier to answer without reading the entirety of the passage. The targeted reading you'll do to answer those questions will make you more familiar with the passage overall. This means that once you've answered the more specific questions, you'll be in a good position to tackle the more general questions that you skipped over at first.

The general questions will be easy to recognize because they will ask questions like this:

> The main idea of this passage is to
>
> The primary purpose of the passage is to
>
> The passage is best described as
>
> The passage serves primarily to
>
> The author uses the example of the [Krakatoa eruption] primarily to

Save this type of question for last and you'll save yourself a lot of time.

PAIRED QUESTIONS

ETS and the College Board have added one more wrinkle to the variety of questions you'll see—paired questions. How can you tell if questions are paired? Take a look at this example:

9

Which choice provides the best evidence for the answer to the previous question?

A) Lines 25–27 ("then . . . reading")

B) Lines 31–32 ("It . . . *ate*")

C) Lines 38–40 ("Because . . . actions")

D) Lines 40–44 ("When . . . Nervous")

If somehow there were an error in your test booklet and you couldn't read question 8, would you be able to do anything more than guess on question 9? No, because without question 8, you'd have no idea what kind of evidence you were looking for! Now consider what happens when you can look at question 8 first:

8

The author introduces the "Homeric idea of *ate*" primarily in order to

A) emphasize the difficulty of the books she was reading.

B) suggest that her father had reacted in the same way that Achilles had.

C) provide another way to understand the use of a particular local term.

D) show the relationship between reading Greek literature and feeling anger.

When you have question 8, it's a lot easier to figure out what to do with question 9, which is why we call questions like these *paired questions*. Paired questions are sets of questions in which one question is followed by a second question that asks you to choose which set of lines best supports the answer you chose for the first question.

In this case, questions 8 and 9 are *specific* paired questions, because question 8 asks a specific question and provides strong lead words. To answer this pair of questions, you'd tackle question 8 first, looking in the passage for the phrase "Homeric idea of *ate*" and then searching the lines above and below the phrase to find out why the author introduces that idea. Once you've found and marked the evidence to answer question 8, it's a piece of cake to answer its partner: all you have to do is check which answer choice for question 9 refers to the lines that you used to answer question 8. It's like a two-for-one deal—answer question 8 and you've done the work for question 9 as well!

You will also come across *general* paired questions. In these, answering the first question in the pair requires a sense of the entire passage. Consider the following pair:

33

Of the series of realizations the author describes, the one most significant to his overall understanding of the events is his realization that

A) he has a serious illness.

B) his previous understanding of his genetic history was erroneous.

C) his treatment will be longer and more painful than he'd originally thought.

D) doctors sometimes try to heal a patient's body without taking into account the patient's emotional and intellectual needs.

34

Which choice provides the best evidence for the answer to the previous question?

A) Lines 1–3 ("Modern . . . body")

B) Lines 18–21 ("Thus . . . precocious")

C) Lines 30–32 ("My . . . idea")

D) Lines 47–51 ("Yet . . . phenomenon")

Question 33 is a general question that asks you to identify the most significant of a number of realizations that are discussed throughout the passage. Characteristically, this general question lacks both a line reference and strong key words to help narrow down a search, and the answer choices in question 34 are not concentrated in one part of the passage but are spread throughout the passage.

Though it might seem counterintuitive, the easiest way to tackle general paired questions is to work backward from the second question in the pair, checking the answer choices to see which sets of lines can be connected to any of the answer choices in the first question. If, in this particular instance, lines 1–3 don't refer to any of the realizations identified in the answer choices for question 33, then (A) can be eliminated for question 34. Likewise, if none of the answer choices in 34 support the idea that the author's realization that he has a serious illness is most significant, then (A) can be eliminated from question 33.

To tackle general paired questions, be methodical:

Step One: **Look for connections between the answers**

Check each answer choice in the second question to see if it offers support for an answer choice in the first question. Record any connections you see.

Step Two: **Eliminate any unconnected answers**

Once you have checked all four answers from the second question, cross off any answers in the second question that you can't connect to an answer in the first question. Then cross off any answer in the first question that is not supported by an answer to the second question.

Step Three: **Compare the remaining answers in the first question and POE**

It might take a little practice to make this approach feel more natural, but the practice will definitely pay off!

PACING STRATEGIES FOR READING

The reading section is a long section with five different passages and 52 questions to get through, but the only thing that counts toward your score is how many questions you answer correctly. Thus, it pays to be efficient:

- Don't be afraid to skip over a more challenging passage—even if you've started working on it. Do the passages you find easier first.
- Always look to eliminate wrong answers. Even if you can eliminate only one or two answers, you've still increased your odds of getting the question right.
- Don't stay stuck on a hard question—guess and move on. Once you've made your way through the whole section, you can use any remaining time to return to any questions you found tricky.
- Make sure to bubble in an answer for every question. There's no penalty for guessing, so use the LOTD if you need to.

READING CHECKLIST

1. Read the blurb at the beginning of the passage.
2. Answer specific questions first. These include line-reference, lead-word, and vocabulary-in-context questions, as well as specific paired questions. Use chronology when necessary to help narrow down where to search in the passage for an answer.

3.   Answer the general questions next, including general paired questions.
4.   With dual passages, answer questions relating to the first passage first. Then answer questions relating to the second passage. Save questions that ask about both passages for last.

Keep these techniques in mind as you try the practice passages that follow. First up is a drill using introductory paragraphs to practice techniques. Then you'll have the opportunity to work some passages using the Process of Elimination. Finally, you have four full-length passages so that you can practice thinking about the order in which you tackle the questions, and start identifying the question and passage types that you feel you need more practice with.

Short Passage Drills

Questions 1–2 are based on the following passage.

Ben Jonson, a well-known playwright and seventeenth-century contemporary of John Donne, wrote that while "the first poet in the
Line world in some things," Donne nevertheless "for
5 not keeping of an accent, deserved hanging." Donne's generation admired the depth of his feeling, but was puzzled by his often irregular rhythm and obscure references. It was not until the twentieth century and modern movements
10 that celebrated emotion and allusion that Donne really began to be appreciated. Writers such as T. S. Eliot and W. B. Yeats admired the psychological intricacies of a poet who could one moment flaunt his earthly dalliances with his
15 mistress and the next, wretched, implore God to "bend your force, to break, blow, burn, and make me new."

1

The main idea of the paragraph is that

A) poetry is judged by different standards at different times.

B) Jonson misjudged Donne's worth.

C) Donne's poetry was not fully appreciated until hundreds of years after his death.

D) Donne's rough meter prevented him from being understood in his own lifetime.

2

It can be inferred from the passage that W. B. Yeats was

A) uninterested in meter and rhythm.

B) a modern writer.

C) close to T. S. Eliot.

D) interested in imitating Donne's technique.

Questions 3–4 are based on the following passage.

The term "genetic modification" refers to technology that is used to alter the genes of living organisms. Genetically modified organisms
Line are called "transgenic" if genes from different
5 organisms are combined. The most common transgenic organisms are crops of common fruits and vegetables, which are now grown in more than fifty countries. These crops are typically developed for resistance to herbicides, pesticides,
10 and disease, as well as to increase nutritional value. Some of these transgenic crops currently under development might even yield human vaccines. Along with improving nutrition and alleviating hunger, genetic modification of crops
15 may also help to conserve natural resources and improve waste management.

3

The primary purpose of the paragraph is to

A) establish that transgenic crops are safe.

B) critique the process of genetic modification.

C) overcome opposition to genetically modified foods.

D) provide information about transgenic crops.

4

In line 12, the word "yield" most nearly means

A) produce.

B) surrender.

C) give way.

D) replace.

Questions 5–6 are based on the following passage.

In 1782, philosopher J. Hector St. John de Crèvecoeur became the first to apply the word "melting" to a population of immigrants: "Here
Line individuals of all nations are melted into a new
5 race of men." Crèvecoeur idealized a nation built from individuals who had transcended their origins and embraced a common American ethos: "From involuntary idleness, servile dependence, penury, and useless labour, he has passed to toils
10 of a very different nature, rewarded by ample subsistence. This is an American." While debate raged as to what exactly "melting" meant— diverse peoples coexisting peacefully while maintaining their differences or refashioning
15 themselves to blend indistinguishably into a new, common substance—Crèvecoeur's term was here to stay: America, settled by immigrants, was to have a unified populace.

5

According to the paragraph, "debate raged" (lines 11–12) over whether immigrant groups

A) had the ability to put aside their differences and coexist peacefully.

B) understood what Crèvecoeur originally meant by the term "melting."

C) needed to change their identity to match a common American identity.

D) transcended their humble origins merely by moving to the United States.

6

The phrase "common substance" (line 16) is used to refer to

A) a new, distinctly American cuisine.

B) Crèvecoeur's use of the term "melting pot."

C) a culture and identity shared by all Americans.

D) a unified populace made of many diverse and distinct groups.

Questions 7–8 are based on the following passage.

The goal of plants, or any living organism, is to propagate as much as possible. To this end, many plants in the wild, including wheat's
Line ancestor, have mechanisms that scatter seeds
5 as widely as possible. However, this adaptation makes it difficult to cultivate some plants; it is impossible to farm productively if a crop is spread hither and thither! Wild wheat had a number of other mechanisms that supported its existence
10 in nature but lessened its usefulness in the field. A number of mutations had to take place before wild wheat was a suitable candidate for agriculture. Humans encouraged these mutations by providing a stable environment that favored
15 and nurtured the mutations that would have proven deleterious in the wild.

7

Which choice best summarizes the main idea of the paragraph?

A) Wheat's evolution into a plant that could be farmed productively was shaped by human needs and actions.

B) Wheat is a difficult plant to farm unless a very stable environment is available.

C) The most important mechanism utilized by wild wheat is the means of scattering seeds as widely as possible.

D) All living organisms seek to reproduce as much as possible.

8

Which choice provides the best evidence for the answer to the previous question?

A) Lines 1–2 ("The . . . possible")

B) Lines 2–5 ("To . . . possible")

C) Lines 8–11 ("Wild . . . field")

D) Lines 13–16 ("Humans . . . wild")

Questions 9–10 are based on the following passage.

Perhaps the scientists most excited about reigniting the lunar program are not lunar specialists, but astronomers studying a wide
Line range of subjects. Such scientists would like
5 new missions to install a huge telescope with a diameter of 30 meters on the far side of the moon. Two things that a telescope needs for optimum operation are extreme cold and very little vibration. Temperatures on the moon
10 can be as frigid as 200°C below zero in craters on the dark side. Because there is no seismic activity, the moon is a steady base. Permanent darkness means the telescope can be in constant use. Proponents claim that under
15 these conditions a lunar-based telescope could accomplish as much in seventeen days as the replacement for the Hubble telescope will in ten years of operation.

9

The main idea of the paragraph is most accurately described by which of the following statements?

A) Most astronomers are in favor of re-igniting the lunar program.

B) Some scientists believe the moon is an ideal location for an interplanetary telescope.

C) New lunar missions could discover important new features of the moon.

D) The new lunar telescope will replace the defunct Hubble telescope.

10

As used in line 2, "reigniting" most nearly means

A) restarting.

B) relighting.

C) ruling.

D) gaining control over.

Questions 11–12 are based on the following passage.

Robert Schumann's orchestral music has been underappreciated and misunderstood for many years by critics and audiences alike. The
Line nineteenth-century virtuoso's works for the
5 piano are acknowledged as brilliant masterworks. However, his large scale orchestral works have always suffered by comparison to those of contemporaries such as Mendelssohn and Brahms. Perhaps this is because Schumann's
10 works should be measured with a different yardstick. His works are often considered poorly orchestrated, but they actually have an unusual aesthetic. He treats the orchestra as he does the piano: one grand instrument with a uniform
15 sound. This is so different from the approach of most composers that, to many, it has seemed like a failing rather than a conscious artistic choice.

11

The author's primary purpose in this paragraph is to

A) praise Schumann for his innovative approach.

B) reassess a portion of Schumann's portfolio.

C) re-evaluate the standing of Mendelssohn and Brahms.

D) examine the influence of Schumann's performances.

12

The author of this passage would most likely attribute the underappreciation of Schumann's orchestral music to

A) the poor orchestration of the works.

B) comparisons of Schumann to the greater genius of Mendelssohn and Brahms.

C) Schumann's failure to make the best use of instruments other that the piano.

D) the difference between Schumann's approach to the orchestra and that of many other composers.

SHORT PASSAGE DRILLS: ANSWERS AND EXPLANATIONS

1. **C** The passage states that it was not until the twentieth century "that Donne really began to be appreciated." As Jonson was a "seventeenth-century contemporary" of Donne's, the twentieth-century appreciation of Donne's work was in fact hundreds of years after his death. Thus, (C) is well-supported in the passage, which focuses on a major shift in the way Donne's poetry was perceived. Choice (A) is too broad; it doesn't even mention Donne. Choice (B) is too narrow; the passage is not primarily about Jonson and his opinions. Choice (D) is too narrow; the passage states that several factors hindered Donne's contemporaries from fully appreciating him. Choice (C) is the correct answer.

2. **B** Look to eliminate wrong answers. While the passage states that Yeats admired Donne's "psychological intricacies," there is no evidence that such admiration meant Yeats was not interested in meter and rhythm. Eliminate (A).

   Though T. S. Eliot and Yeats are both mentioned as examples, there's no evidence that their mutual admiration for Donne's work made them "close," just as there's no evidence that Yeats's admiration made him interested in imitating Donne's technique. Eliminate (C) and (D). Eliot and Yeats are identified as writers in the passage and they are mentioned as examples of people who began to really admire Donne's poetry during the twentieth century when "modern movements" changed attitudes. Thus, (B) is well-supported by the text and is the correct answer.

3. **D** The paragraph provides a lot of information without much analysis or interpretation. Eliminate (A), as the paragraph does not address the issue of crop safety. Eliminate (B), since no *critique* of the process is offered. Eliminate (C), as *opposition to genetically modified foods* is not mentioned, let alone overcome. Choice (D) is consistent with the paragraph's focus on providing information and is the correct answer.

4. **A** Return to the indicated sentence and replace the word "yield" with a word or phrase that makes sense in the context. In this sentence, "yield" must mean something like *make* or *give rise to*. Eliminate (B) and (C) because while both are possible meanings of yield, they do not match the sense needed in the sentence. Eliminate (D), as it also does not match the prediction. Choice (A), *produce*, fits the sense of *make* or *give rise to* and is the correct answer.

5. **C** The *debate* mentioned in line 11 is over what the term *melting* means, and the passage offers two alternatives, one in which *diverse peoples* live together peacefully but keep their differences and another in which those differences are refashioned into a new, shared thing. Eliminate (A), which uses language directly from the passage to say something the passage does not say. Eliminate (B), because the debate was not over whether *immigrant groups understood* the term but over how the term itself was interpreted. Eliminate (D), which also uses language from the passage but does not address the debate described in the relevant sentence. Choice (C) does address the question of the degree to which immigrants groups needed to change their identity and thus is the correct answer.

6. **C** Notice how much easier this question is after you have done the work for question 5, which focused on the debate about whether a "melting pot" described *diverse peoples coexisting peacefully while maintaining their differences* or diverse peoples *refashioning themselves to blend indistinguishably into a new, common substance*. This question asks about the phrase "common substance," which is part of the latter option in the pair. Eliminate (A), as the paragraph does not address the issue of *cuisine*. Eliminate (B), as the "common substance" is part of one way to interpret Crèvecoeur's term, not a reference to his *use* of the term. Eliminate (D) since the "common substance" interpretation of the term *melting pot* is the version in which all Americans blend together, not the one in which groups maintain their distinct identities. Choice (C) correctly identifies the "common substance" as a *culture and identity shared by all Americans*, creating a blending that erodes distinctions, and is therefore the correct answer.

7. **A** Questions 7 and 8 are a set of specific paired questions, since question 7 indicates that the answer will be found in a particular paragraph (and not potentially from anywhere within the longer passage in which this paragraph is found). The paragraph introduces the goal of all organisms to *propagate as much as possible* and then discusses the limitation of one means of doing that—scattering seeds—and why this made wild wheat a less productive crop for humans. Noting that a number of mutations had to take place for wheat to evolve into a *suitable candidate for agriculture*, the paragraph ends with its main idea: *Humans encouraged these mutations by providing a stable environment that favored and nurtured the mutations that would have proven deleterious in the wild.* Choice (A) restates this idea effectively, so keep it. Eliminate (B), since the main idea is not that wheat is difficult *to farm* without a stable environment, but that such an environment helped it to evolve. Eliminate (C), as the passage states only that scattering seeds is a mechanism that wild wheat utilized, not that it was the most important one. Eliminate (D), since this idea is too general and does not directly address wheat's development. The correct answer is (A).

8. **D** If, when you worked question 7, you underlined the last sentence in the paragraph as providing evidence to support the claim about the main idea, then this question is basically the bonus of a solve-one-get-one-free set of paired questions. Just skim the answer choices to see that (D) clearly indicates the last sentence. Eliminate (A), (B), and (C). Choice (D) is the correct answer.

9. **B** Check the passage to see if *most* astronomers are in favor of reigniting the lunar program and eliminate (A), since no relative number of astronomers is given. Since the passage overall is about astronomers' interest in the building of a lunar telescope, eliminate (C), which does not mention the lunar telescope and mentions finding new features of the moon, not of the other bodies that could be observed from the moon. A replacement for the Hubble telescope is mentioned, but the proponents of a lunar telescope argue that it could accomplish more than a replacement for the Hubble telescope, not that it would *be* a replacement, so eliminate (D). Choice (B) addresses the desire of some scientists for a lunar telescope to further their study of a wide range of subjects; it is the correct answer.

10. **A** In the context of the passage, *reigniting* has to have something to do with sending out new missions, so the word must mean something like *starting up* or *getting working again*. Between (A) and (B), eliminate (B), which is a more literal synonym that does not work as well as (A) in the context of the sentence. Eliminate (C) and (D), as there's no evidence that the astronomers want to seize control of the program, only that they want it to begin sending out missions to the moon again. The correct answer is (A).

11. **B** The paragraph focuses on what the author considers the *underappreciation* of Schumann's orchestral works. Eliminate (C), since the paragraph is about Schumann, not Brahms and Mendelssohn. Eliminate (D), as Schumann's *performances* are not addressed in the passage. The passage is not as much concerned with *praising* Schumann as it is concerned with the issue of why Schumann's orchestral works have not been as highly regarded as his works for the piano. Eliminate (A). Choice (B) is the correct answer.

12. **D** The paragraph notes that Schumann's *works are often considered poorly orchestrated, but they actually have an unusual aesthetic* and further explains that this aesthetic involves treating the orchestra as *one grand instrument with a uniform sound*. Eliminate (A), as there is no evidence the author agrees with those who think the works are poorly orchestrated. Eliminate (B) because, while there is evidence that Schumann was compared to Brahms and Mendelssohn, there is no evidence to support the claim that author believes those two had *greater genius*. Similarly, while there is evidence that the orchestral works were compared to the works for the piano, there is no evidence to support the idea that the author thinks Schumann's unusual aesthetic resulted in a poor use of the orchestra's instruments. Choice (D) is supported by the paragraph, since the author credits Schumann's *unusual aesthetic,* which might also be characterized as his approach to orchestra, as the cause of the misunderstanding and under-appreciation of Schumann's orchestral works; this is the correct answer.

Predict the Answer and POE: Drill 1

In the passage below, mark the reference window for each question, where appropriate. Then, UNDERLINE (or paraphrase) your predicted answer for each question. Write down the lines you underlined in the space below the question.

The following passage is excerpted from an auto-biographical novel by Maya Angelou and describes an incident from her youth.

One summer afternoon, sweet-milk fresh in my memory, Mrs. Flowers stopped at the Store to buy provisions. Another Negro woman of her
Line health and age would have been expected to carry
5 the paper sacks home in one hand, but Momma said, "Sister Flowers, I'll send Bailey up to your house with these things."

She smiled that slow dragging smile. "Thank you, Mrs. Henderson. I'd prefer Marguerite,
10 though." They gave each other age-group looks.

Momma said, "Well, that's all right then. Sister, go and change your dress. You going to Sister Flowers's."

There was a little path beside the rocky road,
15 and Mrs. Flowers walked in front swinging her arms and picking her way over the stones.

She said, without turning her head, to me, "I hear you're doing very good school work, Marguerite, but that it's all written. The teachers
20 report that they have trouble getting you to talk in class." We passed the triangular farm on our left and the path widened to allow us to walk together. I hung back in the separate unasked and unanswerable questions.

25 "Come and walk along with me, Marguerite." I couldn't have refused even if I wanted to. She pronounced my name so nicely. Or more correctly, she spoke each word with such clarity that I was certain a foreigner who didn't
30 understand English could have understood her.

"Now no one is going to make you talk— possibly no one can. But bear in mind, language is man's way of communicating with his fellow man and it is language alone which separates him
35 from the lower animals." That was a totally new idea to me, and I would need time to think about it.

"Your grandmother says you read a lot. Every chance you get. That's good, but not good enough.
40 Words mean more than what is set down on paper. It takes the human voice to infuse them with the shades of deeper meaning."

She said she was going to give me some books and that I not only must read them, I must read
45 them aloud.

"I'll accept no excuse if you return a book to me that has been badly handled." My imagination boggled at the punishment I would deserve if in fact I did abuse a book of Mrs. Flowers's. Death
50 would be too kind and brief.

The odors in the house surprised me. Somehow I had never connected Mrs. Flowers with food or eating or any other common experience of common people. There must
55 have been an outhouse, too, but my mind never recorded it.

The sweet scent of vanilla had met us as she opened the door.

"I made tea cookies this morning. You see,
60 I had planned to invite you for cookies and lemonade so we could have this little chat."

They were flat round wafers, slightly browned on the edges and butter-yellow in the center. With the cold lemonade they were sufficient
65 for childhood's lifelong diet. Remembering my manners, I took nice little lady-like bites off the edges. She said she had made them expressly for me. So I jammed one whole cake in my mouth and the rough crumbs scratched the insides of my
70 jaws, and if I hadn't had to swallow, it would have been a dream come true.

As I ate she began the first of what we later called "my lessons in living." She said that I must always be intolerant of ignorance but
75 understanding of illiteracy. That some people, unable to go to school, were more educated and even more intelligent than college professors. She encouraged me to listen carefully to what country people called mother wit.

80   When I finished the cookies she brushed off
the table and brought a thick, small book from
the bookcase. I had read *A Tale of Two Cities* and
found it up to my standards as a romantic novel.
She opened the first page and I heard poetry for
85 the first time in my life.

    "It was the best of times and the worst of times
. . ."

    Her voice slid in and curved down through
and over the words. She was nearly singing. I
90 wanted to look at the pages. Were they the same
that I had read? Or were there notes, music, lined
on the pages, as in a hymn book?

    "How do you like that?"

    It occurred to me that she expected a
95 response.

    The sweet vanilla flavor was still on my tongue
and her reading was a wonder in my ears. I had
to speak.

    I said, "Yes ma'am." It was the least I could do,
100 but it was the most also.

    On that first day, I ran down the hill and into
the road (few cars ever came along it). I was liked,
and what a difference it made. I was respected not
as Mrs. Henderson's grandchild or Bailey's sister
105 but for just being Marguerite Johnson.

1.   The narrative point of view of the
passage is that of

2.   In the context of the passage, lines 26-30
("I couldn't . . . her) are primarily meant
to

3.   As used in line 42, "shades" most nearly
means

4.   In the context of the passage, Marguerite's statement "My imagination boggled
at the punishment I would deserve if
in fact I did abuse a book of Mrs. Flowers's" (lines 47-49) is primarily meant to
convey the idea that

5.   According to Mrs. Flowers, which of the
following is a "lesson in living"?

6.   Which choice provides the best evidence
for the answer to the previous question?

7.   Marguerite's statement in lines 82-83
("I had . . . novel") suggests that she initially viewed *A Tale of Two Cities* as

8.   In the context of the passage, Marguerite's question in lines 90-92 ("Were they
. . . book") primarily serves to

9.   Marguerite's attitude toward Mrs.
Flowers in lines 94-100 ("It occurred . . .
also") is best described as one of

10.   According to Mrs. Flowers, which of
the following is enhanced by the human
voice?

11.   Which choice provides the best evidence
for the answer to the previous question?

Now compare each answer choice to your underlined prediction and use POE!

1

The narrative point of view of the passage is that of

A) a woman explaining the importance of reading.

B) a child presenting her opinions on a particular novel.

C) an adult recounting a memorable childhood experience.

D) a writer describing why she chose to write.

2

In the context of the passage, lines 26-30 ("I couldn't . . . her) are primarily meant to

A) recount an anecdote.

B) describe a theory.

C) present an example.

D) note an impression.

3

As used in line 42, "shades" most nearly means

A) shadows.

B) reflections.

C) levels.

D) insights.

4

In the context of the passage, Marguerite's statement "My imagination boggled at the punishment I would deserve if in fact I did abuse a book of Mrs. Flowers's" (lines 47-49) is primarily meant to convey the idea that

A) Mrs. Flowers is known for her strict and unforgiving nature.

B) Mrs. Flowers is overly concerned with the importance of books.

C) Marguerite would fear for her life if harmed one of Mrs. Flowers's books.

D) Marguerite is unlikely to mistreat one of Mrs. Flowers's books.

5

According to Mrs. Flowers, which of the following is a "lesson in living"?

A) Intelligence is not dependent on formal education.

B) Intellectuals are not as clever as many people suppose.

C) Well-educated people lack common sense.

D) Impoverished people are deserving of compassion.

6

Which choice provides the best evidence for the answer to the previous question?

A) Lines 43-45 ("She said . . . aloud")

B) Lines 65-67 ("Remembering my . . . edges")

C) Lines 73-75 ("She said . . . illiteracy")

D) Lines 75-77 ("That some . . . professors")

Marguerite's statement in lines 82-83 ("I had . . . novel") suggests that she initially viewed *A Tale of Two Cities* as

A) original.

B) sentimental.

C) satisfactory.

D) stunning.

In the context of the passage, Marguerite's question in lines 90-92 ("Were they . . . book") primarily serves to

A) imply that Marguerite was bewildered by Mrs. Flowers's unusual speech patterns.

B) show the religious fervor that Mrs. Flowers brought to her reading.

C) indicate that Mrs. Flowers had set the words of the book to music.

D) convey Marguerite's admiration for the eloquence of Mrs. Flowers's reading.

Marguerite's attitude toward Mrs. Flowers in lines 94-100 ("It occurred . . . also") is best described as one of

A) respectful awe.

B) grudging acceptance.

C) relaxed affection.

D) guarded fear.

According to Mrs. Flowers, which of the following is enhanced by the human voice?

A) Words

B) Poetry

C) Education

D) Freedom

Which choice provides the best evidence for the answer to the previous question?

A) Lines 18-21 ("I hear . . . class")

B) Lines 38-42 ("Your grandmother . . . meaning")

C) Lines 67-71 ("She said . . . true")

D) Lines 101-103 ("On that . . . made")

DRILL 1 REVIEW

1. I was able to predict the answer for _____ questions.

2. Compared to the given answer choices, my predicted answers matched _____ times.

3. TRUE / FALSE: I used POE symbols for all answer choices on all questions.

4. Some new vocabulary words that I need to learn from this passage are as follows:

   _____

   _____

   _____

Predict the Answer and POE: Drill 2

In the passage below, mark the reference window for each question, where appropriate. Then, UNDERLINE (or paraphrase) your predicted answer for each question. Write down the lines you underlined in the space below the question.

The following passage is adapted from a 2010 short story about a woman who comes back to the United States after living for four years in Europe.

By the time I was 22, my girlhood home seemed like the real foreign country, not the language or even the people, but that combination of familiarity and fear. In that combination, I
5 sensed my own closed-mindedness and open-heartedness all at once. I had my way of life, and I'd have to learn a new one to come here.

It's said that you can never really be at home in a foreign country, that your national origins are
10 attached to you like fingerprints. And, of course, when people are conversing easily and fluidly in a language you may never perfect, you're on the outside, and they're on the inside.

I definitely know what it means to be on the
15 outside. I was born and raised in a place that could not be more American, but for those four college years, every time I stepped out of my front door, I could feel myself cycling through thousands of different identities. I belonged here
20 as much as anyone else. Like a local, I could assimilate the collection of odd sights on my walk to school: the homeless man with a different dog every day, the park with shards of classical sculpture, and the former government buildings
25 that now sold American electronics at a huge markup.

I embraced the strangeness, walking down the street with my eyes and ears as open as vast doorways. I embraced the way that leaving my
30 apartment, in pursuit of newspapers in soothing, familiar English or breads so light and fluffy they might've been made from clouds, never felt like entering one foreign country, but like entering many of them, with all the world's cultures and
35 races represented in a panoply of storefronts, restaurants, languages, clothing, and people.

Imagine a rainbow with three times as many colors as it normally has.

But my days on the rainbow were short-lived.
40 It was four years altogether, my four years of college, first in London then in Paris, until my school's commencement, which felt like an ironic name when all I could feel was the end. I came back to Virginia that July, and after months of
45 kicking and screaming that I did not belong here anymore, I couldn't help feeling that I had never left. I both loved and hated this feeling. I felt like a stranger in a very familiar land, as if I had been hired to play a difficult role that only I could play.

50 My jetsetter persona from college would be appalled if she knew that this is what waited for her after her travels. I wanted to make the United States, especially my little corner of Virginia, a fond memory, an object of nostalgia rather than
55 a real home, as I spent the rest of my days in Europe. Instead, here I was in the car with my parents, riding in the passenger seat as I had when I was a teenager, and there they all were, behind every familiar door, every address plaque,
60 every twist and turn of the driveways: all the people that I knew from my youth were here and looked oddly the same, but I looked like them, too.

"How does it feel to come back?" asked my
65 father, and after a moment of consideration (a long moment, for my father is never in a hurry), I knew that "come back" had different meanings for the two of us. For him, it was "back home," the place that he and I would always return to,
70 but for me it was "back in time," as I had always imagined my future to be on the other side of the Atlantic Ocean.

My hometown—for that much it surely is— lies just to the west of the Shenandoah Valley.
75 The town is tiny, maybe 500 people altogether, but I learned on our drive back from the airport in Washington, D.C., that my "hometown" has much more capacious borders than I had ever realized. The majestic Shenandoahs tower above
80 the scenery, and you can take them in from many

miles away. Once you leave the D.C. suburbs in Virginia, you can feel the warmth of communities that historically had only their own resources on which to rely. Every trip here was a trip "back"
85 as only a few technological updates made secret changes within a visually unchanged landscape. I was coming back not only to my own home but also to the homes of many others before me.

I wanted to be like all my favorite American
90 expatriates from the 1920s, and maybe I could have been. But my circumstances brought me back here. I should consider it a great privilege rather than an insufferable burden that I had nothing to escape from, so why pretend
95 otherwise? I could've made it in Paris, I think, but now, I finally realize that I can just as well make it here, too. I didn't have to be a foreigner to feel like myself. This community doesn't have to swallow everything that makes me an individual. It can
100 take me in, and in fact, it can give me the freedom to be myself in a way that the hustle and bustle, the true unfamiliarity, of Paris and London never could. At home, I can be a local or a stranger as I please.

12. The central contrast in the passage is between

13. In the passage, the narrator is concerned primarily with

14. As it is used in line 10, the word "finger-prints" is a simile for

15. Paragraphs 3 and 7 are similar in the way they

16. Which choice provides the best evidence for the answer to the previous question?

17. In context, the phrase "my days on the rainbow" (line 39) refers mainly to a time that the narrator was

18. Lines 47-49 ("I both . . . play") are notable for their description of

19. In line 58, the word "they" refers to

20. In line 85, "secret" most nearly means

21. The narrator's description of the "warmth" (line 82) chiefly reveals her

22. In lines 92-95 ("I should … otherwise"), the narrator poses a question that primarily

Now compare each answer choice to your underlined prediction and use POE!

12

The central contrast in the passage is between

A) anger and redemption.

B) foreignness and sophistication.

C) maturity and childishness.

(D)) familiarity and unfamiliarity.

13

In the passage, the narrator is concerned primarily with

A) extending a heated disagreement with her parents.

B) settling reluctantly into a shocking new reality.

C) reminiscing about the most difficult period of her life.

(D)) characterizing her acceptance of a change in life.

14

As it is used in line 10, the word "fingerprints" is a simile for

A) manual labor.

B) criminal proceedings.

(C)) inescapable marks.

D) celebratory gestures.

15

Lines 22-26 ("the homeless . . . markup") are similar to lines 59-60 ("every familiar . . . driveways") in the way they

A) correct a misrecognition.

B) create a fantastic setting.

(C)) describe a scene.

D) evoke a paradox.

16

In context, the phrase "my days on the rainbow" (line 39) refers mainly to a time that the narrator was

(A)) living a pleasantly varied and diverse lifestyle.

B) often flying back and forth between continents.

C) denying the natural beauty of her home state.

D) ignoring her studies for extracurricular activities.

17

Which choice provides the best evidence for the answer to the previous question?

(A)) Lines 37-38 ("Imagine a . . . has")

(B)) Line 39 ("But my . . . short-lived")

C) Lines 43-47 ("I came . . . left")

D) Lines 47-49 ("I felt . . . play")

18

Lines 47-49 ("I both . . . play") are notable for their description of

A) unscrupulous actions.

B) theatrical performances.

C) deep-seated antipathies.

(D)) conflicted feelings.

19

In line 58, the word "they" refers to

A) "travels" (line 52).

B) "days" (line 55).

C) "driveways" (line 60).

(D)) "people" (line 61).

In line 85, "secret" most nearly means

A) unspoken.

B) invisible.

C) embarrassing.

D) shameful.

The narrator's description of the "warmth" (line 82) chiefly reveals her

A) anger.

B) comfort.

C) foreignness.

D) age.

In lines 92-95 ("I should . . . otherwise"), the narrator poses a question that primarily

A) shows her defensive stance.

B) argues for an older way of life.

C) demonstrates her calm acceptance.

D) evokes her international experience.

DRILL 2 REVIEW

1. I was able to predict the answer for _____ questions.
2. Compared to the given answer choices, my predicted answers matched _____ times.
3. TRUE / FALSE: I used POE symbols for all answer choices on all questions.
4. Some new vocabulary words that I need to learn from this passage are as follows:

_____

_____

_____

Predict the Answer and POE: Drill 3

In the passage below, mark the reference window for each question, where appropriate. Then, UNDERLINE (or paraphrase) your predicted answer for each question. Write down the lines you underlined in the space below the question.

The following passage is adapted from Edith Wharton's *The House of Mirth,* a novel set in the early twentieth century. Lily Bart, a New York socialite, is speaking with her friend Lawrence Selden about some of the differences between the lives led by women and men.

Lily sank with a sigh into one of the shabby leather chairs.

"How delicious to have a place like this all
Line to one's self! What a miserable thing it is to
5   be a woman." She leaned back in a luxury of discontent.

Selden was rummaging in a cupboard for the cake.

"Even women," he said, "have been known to
10   enjoy the privileges of a flat."

"Oh, governesses—or widows. But not girls—not poor, miserable, marriageable girls!"

"I even know a girl who lives in a flat."

She sat up in surprise. "You do?"

15   "I do," he assured her, emerging from the cupboard with the sought-for cake.

"Oh, I know—you mean Gerty Farish."
She smiled a little unkindly. "But I said marriageable—and besides, she has a horrid little
20   place, and no maid, and such odd things to eat.
Her cook does the washing and the food tastes of soap. I should hate that, you know."

She began to saunter about the room, examining the bookshelves. Suddenly her
25   expression changed from desultory enjoyment to active conjecture, and she turned to Selden with a question. "You collect, don't you—you know about first editions and things?"

He had seated himself on an arm of the chair
30   near which she was standing, and she continued to question him, asking which were the rarest volumes, whether the Jefferson Gryce collection was really considered the finest in the world, and what was the largest price ever fetched by a single
35   volume.

It was so pleasant to sit there looking up at her, as she lifted now one book and then another from the shelves, fluttering the pages between her fingers, while her drooping profile was outlined
40   against the warm background of old bindings, that he talked on without pausing to wonder at her sudden interest in so unsuggestive a subject. But he could never be long with her without trying to find a reason for what she was doing,
45   and as she replaced his first edition of *La Bruyère* and turned away from the bookcases, he began to ask himself what she had been driving at. Her next question was not of a nature to enlighten him. She paused before him with a smile which
50   seemed at once designed to admit him to her familiarity, and to remind him of the restrictions it imposed.

"Don't you ever mind," she asked suddenly, "not being rich enough to buy all the books you
55   want?"

He followed her glance about the room, with its worn furniture and shabby walls.

"Don't I just? Do you take me for a saint on a pillar?"

60   "And having to work—do you mind that?"

"Oh, the work itself is not so bad—I'm rather fond of the law."

"No; but the being tied down: the routine—don't you ever want to get away, to see new places
65   and people?"

"Horribly—especially when I see all my friends rushing to the steamer."

She drew a sympathetic breath. "But do you mind enough—to marry to get out of it?"

70   Selden broke into a laugh. "God forbid!" he declared.

She rose with a sigh.

"Ah, there's the difference—a girl must, a man may if he chooses." She surveyed him critically.
75   "Your coat's a little shabby—but who cares? It doesn't keep people from asking you to dine. If I were shabby no one would have me: a woman is

asked out as much for her clothes as for herself.
The clothes are the background, the frame, if
80 you like: they don't make success, but they are
a part of it. Who wants a dingy woman? We are
expected to be pretty and well-dressed till we
drop—and if we can't keep it up alone, we have to
go into partnership."

85   Selden glanced at her with amusement: it was
impossible, even with her lovely eyes imploring
him, to take a sentimental view of her case.

    "Ah, well, there must be plenty of capital on
the look-out for such an investment. Perhaps
90 you'll meet your fate tonight at the Trenors.'"

23. Lily's tone at the beginning of the passage is one of

24. Which choice provides the best evidence for the answer to the previous question?

25. In line 11 ("Oh, governesses—or widows"), Lily's comment serves to

26. Lily's remarks in lines 17-22 ("Oh, . . . you know") help to convey her

27. In lines 43-49 ("But he . . . him"), Selden is best described as

28. In line 50, "designed" most nearly means

29. Selden's response to Lily in lines 58-59 ("Don't I . . . pillar") most directly suggests that he

30. Lily's observation in line 75 ("Your coat's . . . cares") serves primarily to

31. Lily's remarks about marriage primarily indicate that she views marriage as a

32. In line 87, "sentimental" most nearly means

33. In line 90, Selden's use of the word "fate" refers to the

Now compare each answer choice to your underlined prediction and use POE!

23

Lily's tone at the beginning of the passage is one of

A) surprise.

B) indignation.

C) delight.

(D) self-pity.

24

Which choice provides the best evidence for the answer to the previous question?

A) Lines 3-4 ("How delicious . . . self")

(B) Lines 4-5 ("What a . . . woman")

C) Line 14 ("She sat . . . surprise")

D) Lines 23-24 (She began . . . bookshelves")

25

In line 11 ("Oh, governesses—or widows"), Lily's comment serves to

A) express anger about a change in social status.

B) bemoan the lack of help in Selden's apartment.

C) call attention to a person's arrogant behavior.

(D) indicate exceptions to a perceived rule.

26

Lily's remarks in lines 17-22 ("Oh, . . . you know") help to convey her

A) dislike of a former friend.

(B) distaste for a certain lifestyle.

C) fear of an uncertain future.

D) concern for a close friend.

27

In lines 43-49 ("But he . . . him"), Selden is best described as

A) irritated by Lily's childish questions about literature.

B) puzzled by Lily's fascination with financial matters.

C) disturbed by Lily's casual treatment of his book collection.

(D) uncertain about the motivation for Lily's actions.

28

In line 50, "designed" most nearly means

A) renovated.

B) charted.

(C) intended.

D) allowed.

29

Selden's response to Lily in lines 58-59 ("Don't I . . . pillar") most directly suggests that he

A) regrets his decision to become a lawyer.

B) wishes to be seen as deeply religious.

C) hopes to move to a wealthier neighborhood.

(D) agrees that wealth has certain advantages.

30

Lily's observation in line 75 ("Your coat's . . . cares") serves primarily to

A) ridicule a character.

B) dismiss a belief.

(C) highlight a discrepancy.

D) voice a concern.

Lily's remarks in the passage indicate that she views marriage as a

A) natural result of a prolonged courtship.

B) happy coincidence that cannot be counted on.

C) distant dream for the average person.

D) practical necessity for a young woman.

In line 87, "sentimental" most nearly means

A) melodramatic.

B) nostalgic.

C) sympathetic.

D) subjective.

In line 90, Selden's use of the word "fate" refers to the

A) possibility that Lily will meet a potential suitor.

B) likelihood that Lily will be forced to remain single.

C) conviction that people's lives are largely predetermined.

D) probability that a business venture will be profitable.

DRILL 3 REVIEW

1. I was able to predict the answer for _____ questions.
2. Compared to the given answer choices, my predicted answers matched _____ times.
3. TRUE / FALSE: I used POE symbols for all answer choices on all questions.
4. Some new vocabulary words that I need to learn from this passage are as follows:

   _____

   _____

   _____

Predict the Answer and POE: Drill 4

In the passage below, mark the reference window for each question, where appropriate. Then, UNDERLINE (or paraphrase) your predicted answer for each question. Write down the lines you underlined in the space below the question.

The following is an adaptation of an essay published by a journalist in a collection of essays on the cultural history of newspapers.

There was a time when journalists were rogue heroes who showed society's hidden workings and did so fearlessly. While the rogue journalist
Line may still exist, our own news-media landscape
5 has altered, and we are necessarily much worse-informed because of it. Particularly on television news, the copywriters have all become editors. That is to say, those who were previously tasked with dredging up the cold, hard facts
10 are now much more likely to provide viewers with predetermined opinions and personal perspectives.

One possible cause for this shift is the increasingly vicious fight for viewers and readers.
15 Not only are there hundreds of channels on the television, there are now literally millions of attention-grabbing options on computers, tablets, and smartphones. After a long, hard day at the office, the average viewer wants an easy time
20 at home, not a mental challenge (life provides enough of those) but a comfortable retelling of the day's events. That retelling can be made most comfortable when it is delivered in an entertaining package by people whose view of the
25 world will basically square with the viewer's own.

A crucial historical example offers the comforting reminder that things were not always this way. Joseph Pulitzer was born in Mako, Hungary, in 1847. In his younger years, Pulitzer
30 wanted to be a soldier. He was turned away from the Austrian Army, but in Germany, he was eventually recruited to fight as a mercenary in the U.S. Union Army. After the Civil War ended, Pulitzer made his way to St. Louis, where he
35 began to study English and law. A chance meeting with two German newspaper owners led to Pulitzer's first job as a copywriter.

Pulitzer was a tireless and innovative journalist. He worked doggedly to write high-
40 quality stories and to increase the circulation of his papers. At the shockingly young age of 31, Pulitzer was the owner of the English-language St. Louis Post-Dispatch, where he oversaw all aspects of the newspaper's publication. In this
45 era, Pulitzer became particularly interested in championing the causes of the common man. His paper commonly featured exposes of the corruption of the rich and powerful. Circulation of the Post-Dispatch rose to such heights, in
50 fact, that Pulitzer was able to purchase the much larger New York World in 1883. Pulitzer's same commitment to exposing corruption and educating his underrepresented public created what has been called a "one-man revolution" in
55 the World's editorial policies and in newspaper publishing more generally.

One of the most vicious circulation battles of Pulitzer's career came from 1896 to 1898, the period of the Spanish-American War. This
60 war famously stretched the limits of journalistic objectivity, and Pulitzer's main competitor, William Randolph Hearst, famously said to one of his photographers, "You supply the pictures, and I'll supply the war." In the context of Pulitzer's
65 larger career, it is especially unfortunate that Pulitzer was equally guilty of these kinds of fabrications, though the battled soured him on this kind of sensationalist journalism for the remainder of his career.
70 With Hearst at the forefront of this new "yellow journalism," newspapers became the mouthpieces for the ideologies of their editors, not for the hard realities of common men. Pulitzer withdrew from this method of
75 journalism, and in time, the New York World became a more nuanced newspaper. With the paper's help and at its prodding, the U.S. government protected American business by passing new antitrust legislation and by

80 regulating an increasingly out-of-control
insurance industry.

Pulitzer's name is best-known today because
of its association with the Pulitzer Prize, awarded
every year to works ranging from journalism to
85 drama. The prize, especially the prize awarded
for journalism, serves as a constant reminder
that journalism is most valuable when it at its
most honest. Pulitzer explained his journalistic
credo this way: "An able, disinterested, public-
90 spirited press, with trained intelligence to know
the right and courage to do it, can preserve that
public virtue without which popular government
is a sham and a mockery." He would surely be
disappointed in the direction that journalism has
95 taken today, and we should be, too. We can only
hold out the hope that someone with Pulitzer's
courage and perseverance can come along to
restore journalism to its rightful place as teller of
things as they really are. Only then can we begin
100 to change those things to how they really should
be.

34. The primary purpose of the passage is to

35. The author's attitude toward the journalists described in the first paragraph is
best characterized as

36. Which choice provides the best evidence
for the answer to the previous question?

37. The information in lines 28-37 ("Joseph
Pulitzer . . . copywriter") serves primarily to

38. The information in lines 41-44 ("At the . . .
publication") reveals Pulitzer's

39. The misfortune referred to in lines 64-69
("In the . . . career") is that

40. The author's comment in lines 93-95
("He would . . . too") is best described as

41. The "hope" referred to in line 96 is that

42. Which of the following, if true, is the
author most likely to see as an unfortunate consequence of modern journalistic
practices?

43. Which choice provides the best evidence
for the answer to the previous question?

Now compare each answer choice to your underlined prediction and use POE!

34

The primary purpose of the passage is to

A) detail the contributions of immigrants to contemporary journalism.

B) garner support for the return of print in place of electronic media.

C) blame the reading public for its lack of interest in current events.

D) draw the reader's attention to an issue in contemporary news reporting.

35

The author's attitude toward the journalists described in the first paragraph is best characterized as

A) confused.

B) obstinate.

C) open-minded.

D) disapproving.

36

Which phrase provides the best evidence for the answer to the previous question?

A) Lines 1-3 ("There was . . . fearlessly")

B) Lines 3-6 ("While the . . . it")

C) Lines 6-7 ("Particularly on . . . editors")

D) Lines 8-12 ("That is . . . perspectives")

37

The information in lines 28-37 ("Joseph Pulitzer . . . copywriter") serves primarily to

A) explain the reasons behind Pulitzer's change in career.

B) sketch the early career of a historical figure.

C) preview the conflicts outlined in the following paragraph.

D) decry the state of contemporary journalism and media.

38

The information in lines 41-44 ("At the . . . publication") reveals Pulitzer's

A) apathy.

B) humbleness.

C) kindness.

D) precociousness.

39

The misfortune referred to in lines 64-69 ("In the . . . career") is that

A) Pulitzer stopped competing with Hearst for readers and lost the circulation battle.

B) Pulitzer built the remainder of his career on a series of dubious journalistic practices.

C) a career built on journalistic integrity should be compromised by this particular lapse.

D) many journalists used sensationalist tactics to gain an edge in circulation.

40

The author's comment in lines 93-95 ("He would . . . too") is best described as

A) an overstatement.

B) a critique.

C) a hypothesis.

D) a concession.

41

The "hope" referred to in line 96 is that

A) journalists will stop listening to the corporate interests of their editors.

B) a brave individual will come along and change the face of journalism forever.

C) news reporting will free itself from sensationalism and return to an era of purer objectivity.

D) journalistic integrity will be recognized as the true way to produce social change.

42

Which of the following, if true, is the author most likely to see as an unfortunate consequence of modern journalistic practices?

A) A rural journalist accepts a higher salary to transfer to a popular newspaper published in an urban area.

B) A newspaper editor is reluctant to state his political views because he fears doing so may decrease the popularity of his paper.

C) A newspaper receives public scrutiny for uncovering the details of corruption within a state government.

D) A television news station that claims to be fair to all political ideologies represents the viewpoints of only one political perspective.

43

Which choice provides the best evidence for the answer to the previous question?

A) Lines 8-12 ("That is . . . perspectives")

B) Lines 41-44 ("At the . . . publication")

C) Lines 64-69 ("In the . . . career")

D) Lines 93-95 ("He would . . . too")

DRILL 4 REVIEW

1. I was able to predict the answer for _____ questions.
2. Compared to the given answer choices, my predicted answers matched _____ times.
3. TRUE / FALSE: I used POE symbols for all answer choices on all questions.
4. Some new vocabulary words that I need to learn from this passage are as follows:

_____

_____

_____

PREDICT AND POE: ANSWERS AND EXPLANATIONS

Drill 1

1. **C** The question asks for the narrative point of view, which means that the correct choice will refer to what the author's perspective is for the entire passage. General questions such as this should be done after all of the specific questions; also be sure to check the blurb, which indicates that *the following passage is excerpted from an autobiographical novel by Maya Angelou and describes an incident from her youth.* Based on the blurb, the correct answer will say something about an adult woman remembering a childhood memory. Choice (A) matches *Maya Angelou*, but the perspective is not one that explains *the importance of reading,* so eliminate (A). Choice (B) says the point of view is a child's, which is incorrect; eliminate (B). Choice (D) accurately describes Ms. Angelou, but the passage does not explain *why she chose to write,* so eliminate (D). Choice (C) is the correct answer.

2. **D** Context questions ask why an author used a specific word or phrase. Return to the passage and read the necessary window around lines 26-30 to predict the correct answer. From the phrase *she pronounced my name so nicely. Or more correctly, she spoke each word with such clarity,* it can be predicted that the author intended to show the reader how impressed Marguerite was by how Mrs. Flowers spoke. The phrase in question involves neither *a theory* nor *an example,* so eliminate (B) and (C). Marguerite is neither retelling nor recounting a story or anecdote; eliminate (A). The author does share Marguerite's *impression* with the reader within lines 26-30. Choice (D) is the correct answer.

3. **C** The question asks what *shades most nearly* means, so this is a Vocab-in-Context question. Remember to cross out the word in quotation marks and substitute an alternative word. Then, rely on Process of Elimination. In this case *degrees* would be a good synonym to explain how *deeper meaning* was being infused by the voice. Of the answer choices, only *levels* has a similar meaning to the prediction *degrees.* Choice (C) is the correct answer.

4. **D** Context questions ask why an author used a specific word or phrase. Return to the passage and read the necessary window around lines 47-49 to predict the correct answer. Since Marguerite is the main subject of this paragraph, you can predict that the answer will be referring to her, so eliminate (A) and (B), which talk about Mrs. Flowers. The key phrase required to choose between the remaining options (C) and (D) comes in the sentence after the quoted phrase: *death would be too kind and brief.* Since this is an autobiography, it can be predicted that the author was being hyperbolic to show the reader how much she did not want to return a book that *has been badly handled.* Choice (D) is the correct answer.

5. **A** Note that the following question is a best evidence question, so this question and Q6 can be answered in tandem. Detail questions ask for information regarding a key word or line reference. In this case there is no line reference for Q5, but by skimming for the lead words *lesson in living,* it can be determined that the evidence will be around line 68. Look at the answers for Q6 first. The

lines in (6A) and (6B) are outside of the window, so eliminate both. *She said that I must always be intolerant of ignorance but understanding of illiteracy* is within the window, so look to see if those words support any of the answers in Q5. None of the Q5 choices refer to illiteracy or ignorance, so (6C) can be eliminated. Now evaluate (6D), which says *that some people, unable to go to school, were more educated and even more intelligent than college professors.* From this it can be predicted that a *lesson in living* could be that some people who did not go to school were smarter than some that went to college. Choice (5A) accurately matches this prediction, so keep it. Choice (5B) questions the cleverness of intellectuals, but Mrs. Flowers only mentions those *unable to go to school;* she does not attack the intelligence of intellectuals; eliminate (5B). Choice (5C) may be eliminated for the same reason. *Impoverished people* are not mentioned, so eliminate (5D). Choices (5A) and (6D) are the correct answers.

6.   **D**   (See explanation above)

7.   **C**   The question asks how Marguerite initially viewed *A Tale of Two Cities.* Line 83 indicates that she *found it up to (her) standards,* so the prediction could simply be "standard." Because *original, sentimental,* and *stunning* do not match this prediction, eliminate (A), (B), and (D). Choice (C) is the correct answer.

8.   **D**   Context questions ask why an author used a specific word or phrase. Return to the passage and read the necessary window before lines 90-92 to predict the correct answer. Marguerite is listening to Mrs. Flowers read *A Tale of Two Cities* in this section, so it can be predicted that the answer will be referring to Marguerite listening to Mrs. Flowers. Marguerite does not find any patterns unusual, so eliminate (A). Marguerite's reference to a *hymn book* illustrates how melodic the reading was, not that it was literally set to music, nor that *religious fervor* played any role; eliminate (B) and (C). Choice (D) is the correct answer.

9.   **A**   Attitude questions ask how an author or character feels regarding something in a passage—in this case how Marguerite feels about Mrs. Flowers. From reading the window of lines 94-100, specifically *her reading was a wonder in my ears,* it can be predicted that Marguerite was impressed. Only *respectful awe* captures this sentiment. Choice (A) is the correct answer.

10.   **A**   Note that the following question is a best evidence question, so this question and Q11 can be answered in tandem. Detail questions ask for information regarding a key word or line reference. In this case there is no line reference for Q10, but by skimming for the lead words *human voice,* it can be determined that the evidence will be around line 38. Look at the answers for Q11 first. Only answer (11B) is even close to the reference window found by skimming for the words *human voice,* so evaluate this choice first. Q10 asks what is enhanced by the human voice and according to the excerpt in (11B), words are infused by *the human voice* with *shades of deeper meaning,* which matches (10A). Nowhere in the passage are *poetry, education, or freedom* mentioned in tandem with *the human voice,* so eliminate (10B), (10C), and (10D). Choices (10A) and (11B) are the correct answers.

11.   **B**   (See explanation above)

Vocab Check

Here is a list of challenging words from Drill 1. If you don't know the definitions, look them up to learn them!

impoverished   anecdote   incomprehensible   eloquence   fervor   sentimental

Drill 2

12. **D**   General questions such as this should be done after all of the specific questions. Also be sure to check the blurb, which indicates that *the following passage is adapted from a 2010 short story about a woman who comes back to the United States after living for four years in Europe.* This blurb does not provide enough information to make much of a prediction, so this question should be left for last. After reading the passage and completing all of the specific questions, it becomes clear that the prediction concerning the central contrast could be something similar to what the author knows and what she doesn't. There is no reference to the author's *anger* or *maturity*, so eliminate (A) and (C). Choice (B) references the *foreignness* that the author feels, but she finds foreign places to be sophisticated, so eliminate (B). *Familiarity and unfamiliarity* match the prediction. Choice (D) is the correct answer.

13. **D**   General questions such as this should be done after all of the specific questions. Then, it becomes clear that the narrator is concerned with accepting changes in her life. Words such as *heated disagreement, shocking,* and *most difficult* are too extreme to be supported by the passage; eliminate (A), (B), and (C). Choice (D) is the correct answer.

14. **C**   The question asks what *fingerprints is a simile for*, so this is a Vocab-in-Context question. Remember to cross out the word in quotation marks and substitute an alternative word. Then, use POE. In this case *ink stains* would be a good synonym to explain how *fingerprints are attached to you.* Of the answer choices, only *inescapable marks* would share characteristics with the prediction. Choice (C) is the correct answer.

15. **C**   The question asks how the two phrases are similar, so read the reference windows and provide a prediction of how they are similar. In this case they both provide a description of what the narrator sees. These scenes are not a *misrecognition, a fantastic setting,* or *a paradox,* so eliminate (A), (B), and (D). Choice (C) is the correct answer.

16. **A**   Note that the following question is a best evidence question, so this question and Q17 can be answered in tandem. Context questions ask why an author used a specific word or phrase. Return to the passage and read the necessary window around line 39 to predict the correct answer. From the two sentences before the phrase referenced in Q16, it can be predicted that the narrator believed that her experience was positively diverse. Look at the answers for Q16 first. Choice (17B) is the phrase from Q16 itself, so eliminate (17B). Lines 40-49 are negative in tone; eliminate (17C) and (17D). Only answer (17A) captures the positive tone of the prediction. Return to Q16 and seek

an answer that is equally positive. Choice (16A) also matches the tone of the prediction. Choices (16A) and (17B) are the correct answers.

17. **B** (See explanation above)

18. **D** The question asks for a detail regarding the description provided in lines 47-49, so read the reference window to make a prediction. The window indicates that the narrator was providing a scene to show how she was conflicted because she *both loved and hated this feeling*. Only (D) provides an accurate portrayal of this conflict. Choice (D) is the correct answer.

19. **D** The question asks what "they" *refers to*, so this is a context question. Context questions ask why an author used a specific word or phrase. The colon in the sentence is a good clue. After that point in the sentence, it can be predicted that the narrator is referring to *all the people that (she) knew*. Choice (D) is the correct answer.

20. **B** The question asks what "secret" *means*, so this is a Vocab-in-Context question. Remember to cross out the word in quotation marks and substitute an alternative word. Then, use POE. In lines 85–86 it is clear that these *secret changes* exist *within a visually unchanged landscape*. The choices *unspoken*, *embarrassing*, and *shameful* do not match *visually unchanged*. Choice (B) is the correct answer.

21. **B** The question asks what the word *warmth* reveals about the author, so this is a context question. Context questions ask why an author used a specific word or phrase. The overall tone in this paragraph, as with the passage as a whole, is positive. Therefore, warmth is a positive term. The words *anger*, *foreignness*, and *age* are not even marginally positive terms; eliminate (A), (C), and (D). Choice (B) is the correct answer.

22. **C** The question asks why the author poses the question in lines 92-95, so this is a context question. Context questions ask why an author used a specific word or phrase. The narrator answers the question *I should consider it a great privilege rather than an insufferable burden that I had nothing to escape from, so why pretend otherwise?* by asserting that she *could've made it in Paris*, but she *can just as well make it here too*. This shows that she accepts how her life has played out; she is not *defensive* and it cannot be said that she *argues*, so eliminate (A) and (B). While Paris involved an *international experience*, she does not ask the question to evoke this experience, so eliminate (D). Choice (C) is the correct answer.

Vocab Check

Here is a list of challenging words from Drill 2. If you don't know the definitions, look them up to learn them!

paradox   irony   allusion   singularity   unscrupulous   antipathy

Drill 3

23. **D** Note that the following question is a best evidence question, so this question and Q24 can be answered in tandem. This question asks about *Lily's tone*. For specific detail questions without a line reference, find the reference window based on lead words and make a prediction based on what is supported by the passage. From the phrase *Lily sank with a sigh,* which begins the passage, through Lily saying *poor, miserable, marriageable girls* in line 12 it is shown that *Lily's tone* is an unhappy one. Look at the answers for Q24 first: two are outside of the reference window, so eliminate (24C) and (24D). Choice (24A) references *how delicious to have a place like this all to one's self,* while *what a miserable thing it is to be a woman* captures the unhappy tone predicted. Return to Q23 and find an answer that matches this negativity. Neither *surprise* nor *delight* match *unhappy;* eliminate (23A) and (23C). Choice (23B) *indignation* is negative, but connotes anger, whereas Lily is more *miserable* and sunken, so eliminate (23B). Choices (23D) and (24B) are the correct answers.

24. **B** (See explanation above)

25. **D** The question asks what *Lily's comment serves to* do in line 11, so this is a context question. Context questions ask why an author used a specific word or phrase. Lily's comment *oh, governesses—or widows. But not girls—not poor, miserable, marriageable girls* is made to counter Selden's comment that *women have been known to enjoy the privileges of a flat,* so it can be predicted that her response was to counteract a position. Lily's statement is made in response to Selden's comment, not anything about Selden himself, so eliminate (B) and (C). Lily references social status, but hers has not changed; eliminate (A). Indicating *exceptions* is a way to counter a statement. Choice (D) is the correct answer.

26. **B** The question asks what *Lily's remarks* in lines 17-22 convey, so this is a context question. Context questions ask why an author used a specific word or phrase. Lily's comment *she has a horrid little place, and no maid, and such odd things to eat… I should hate that you know* shows that Lily dislikes how Gerty Farish lives, so a good prediction will match this information. Lily's main point was not personally about Gerty Farish, so eliminate (A) and (D). Lily is not discussing her future in this sentence; eliminate (C). Choice (B) is the correct answer.

27. **D** The question asks for specific details about how Selden is described, so read the reference window to make a prediction. In lines 46-47 Selden asks *himself what she had been driving at,* so an accurate prediction will deal with him having questions about Lily. Selden is questioning of Lily, but he is neither *irritated* nor *disturbed* by her; eliminate (A) and (C). Choice (B) accurately identifies Selden as *puzzled,* but this is not regarding *Lily's fascination with financial matters.* Choice (D) is the correct answer.

28. **C** The question asks what "designed" *most nearly* means, so this is a Vocab-in-Context question. Remember to cross out the word in quotation marks and substitute an alternative word. Then, use POE. In this case *meant* would be a good replacement word. Of the answer choices, only *intended* has a similar meaning to the prediction *meant.* Choice (C) is the correct answer.

29. **D** The question asks what *Selden's response* in lines 58-59 *most directly suggests*, so this is a context question. Context questions ask why an author used a specific word or phrase. Selden's comment *Don't I just? Do you take me for a saint on a pillar?* is in direct response to Lily's question *don't you ever mind not being rich enough to buy all the books you want?* It can therefore be predicted that Selden's negative response means he does in fact mind not being rich enough, which means that for him *wealth has certain advantages*. While Selden might not mind being rich, there is no reference to him desiring a new *wealthier neighborhood*; eliminate (C). There is no mention of Selden's religion or occupation, so eliminate (A) and (B). Choice (D) is the correct answer.

30. **C** The question asks about what *Lily's observation* in line 75 *serves* to do, so this is a context question. Context questions ask why an author used a specific word or phrase. Lily's comment *Your coat's a little shabby—but who cares?* directly follows Lily's claim that a man may choose to marry, but *a girl must*. It can be predicted Lily brought up the coat to highlight this difference between a man and a girl. Both *ridicule* and *dismiss* are the opposite of this prediction, so eliminate (A) and (B). Lily is concerned with her current state of affairs, but this specific observation is not related to her concerns; eliminate (D). The word *discrepancy* means difference. Choice (C) is the correct answer.

31. **D** The question asks about Lily's view of marriage in the passage. By completing the other specific detail questions first, it is easier to complete this general question. Line 73 also lends a prediction that Lily believes *a girl must* marry, which means it is a *practical necessity,* as indicated in (D). It is clear throughout the passage that Lily has a negative opinion of marriage and regards it neither as a *happy coincidence* nor a *dream*, so eliminate (B) and (C). Lily never mentions a *prolonged courtship*; eliminate (A). Choice (D) is the correct answer.

32. **C** The question asks what "sentimental" *most nearly means*, so this is a Vocab-in-Context question. Remember to cross out the word in quotation marks and substitute an alternative word. Then, use POE. In this case, based on the phrase *her lovely eyes, lovingly* would be a good replacement word. Of the answer choices, only *sympathetic* has a similar meaning to the prediction *lovingly*. Choice (C) is the correct answer.

33. **A** The question asks what "fate" *refers to*, so this is a Vocab-in-Context question. Remember to cross out the word in quotation marks and substitute an alternative word. Then, use POE. Throughout the passage Lily is talking about her marriage prospects, so it could be predicted that she is seeking her *future husband*. There is nothing to indicate it is likely Lily *will be forced to remain single* or *that people's lives are largely predetermined*, so eliminate (B) and (C). Choice (D) is a trap answer, but there is no indication that Lily is actually a businesswoman. Only (A) matches the prediction. Choice (A) is the correct answer.

Vocab Check

Here is a list of challenging words from Drill 3. If you don't know the definitions, look them up to learn them!

indignation   discrepancy   melodramatic   nostalgic   subjective

Drill 4

34. **D** The question asks for *the primary purpose of the passage*, so this is a general question. General questions such as this should be done after all of the specific questions, but also be sure to check the blurb, which indicates that *the following passage is an adaptation of an essay published by a journalist in a collection of essays on the cultural history of newspapers*. Based on the blurb, the prediction should say something about *the history of newspapers*. The passage neither argues for the return of print nor blames the reading public for anything, so eliminate (B) and (C). While Pulitzer was an immigrant, there is no discussing the *contributions of immigrants to contemporary journalism*; eliminate (A). Choice (D) is the correct answer.

35. **D** Note that the following question is a best evidence question, so this question and Q36 can be answered in tandem. This question asks about *the author's attitude toward journalists*. For detail questions, find the reference window based on lead words and make a prediction based on what is supported by the passage. The author yearns for *a time when journalists were rogue heroes*, so the prediction should be a negative one. Look at the answers for Q36 first. The opening three sentences describe the change that has occurred in the news business, not how the author feels about this change; eliminate (36A), (36B), and (36C). In the concluding sentence of the opening paragraph, the author prefers *those who were previously tasked with dredging up the cold, hard facts* over today's journalists who *are more likely to provide viewers with predetermined opinions and personal perspectives*. Return to Q35 and find an answer that match this preference for the old over the new. Because *confused, obstinate,* and *open-minded* do not match this preference, eliminate (36A), (36B), and (36C). Choice (36D) *disapproving* reflects the author's preference for how journalists used to be. Choices (35D) and (36D) are the correct answers.

36. **D** (See explanation above)

37. **B** The question asks about what the biographical information about Joseph Pulitzer in lines 28-37 *serves to do*, so this is a context question. Context questions ask why an author used a specific word or phrase. It can be predicted from the phrase *at the shockingly young age* in the subsequent paragraph that this information is intended to introduce the reader to what Joseph Pulitzer had been doing previously. The prediction is centered around Pulitzer, not *conflicts* nor *contemporary journalism,* so eliminate (C) and (D). Choice (A) is a trap answer, for while it uses Pulitzer's name, the lines in question do not explain his *change in career*. Choice (B) is the correct answer.

38. **D** The question asks what specific details lines 41-44 reveal about Pulitzer, so read the reference window to make a prediction. The prediction will refer to his *shockingly young age*. Only *precociousness* matches this prediction, so eliminate (A), (B), and (C). Choice (D) is the correct answer.

39. **C** The question asks what the specific *misfortune* is in lines 64-69, so read the reference window to make a prediction. According to the passage, the *misfortune soured him on this kind of sensationalist journalism*, so the prediction should show that the misfortune was uncharacteristic in terms of

Pulitzer's overall career. There is no reference to Pulitzer having *lost the circulation battle*, so eliminate (A). Choice (B) is the opposite of the prediction, so eliminate it. The *misfortune* was Pulitzer's, not *many journalists'*; eliminate (D). Choice (C) is the correct answer.

40. **B** The question asks for a description of the comment in lines 93-95, so read the reference window to make a prediction. The prediction can be determined by the word *disappointed,* which shows that there is a criticism. There is only a statement, not theory or hyperbole; eliminate (A) and (C). The author also is not conceding anything, so eliminate (D). Choice (B) is the correct answer.

41. **C** The question asks what *the hope* refers to, so this is a context question. Context questions ask why an author used a specific word or phrase. The prediction will match the author's desire to *restore journalism to its rightful place as teller of things.* There is no reference to *corporate interests* or *societal change,* so eliminate (A) and (D). The author speaks about journalism and reporting as an industry, not just *a brave individual*; eliminate (B). Choice (C) is the correct answer.

42. **D** Note that the following question is a best evidence question, so this question and Q43 can be answered in tandem. This question asks what *the author (is) most likely to see as an unfortunate consequence of modern journalistic practices,* so the prediction must have to do with current affairs in journalism. Look at the answers for Q43 first. Choice (43B) is simply a biographical note about Pulitzer, so eliminate (43B). Choice (43C) also refers to a historical occurrence, not *modern journalistic practices;* eliminate (43C). *He would surely be disappointed* indicates that it is the perspective of Pulitzer, which is not possible, so eliminate (43D). The notion that *those who were previously tasked with dredging up the cold hard facts are now much more likely to provide viewers with predetermined opinions and personal perspectives* addresses a contemporary issue, so keep (43A). Return to Q42 and find an answer that matches the concern over *predetermined opinions.* There is no contrast between rural and urban, so eliminate (42A). In addition, no reference to popularity or *public scrutiny* is made; eliminate (42B) and (42C). If a journalistic entity *claims to be fair to all political* ideologies but *represents the viewpoints of only one political perspective,* its opinions are in fact predetermined. Choices (42D) and (43A) are the correct answers.

43. **A** (See explanation above)

Vocab Check

Here is a list of challenging words from Drill 4. If you don't know the definitions, look them up to learn them!

obstinate   decry   precociousness   critique   objectivity

Reading Practice Passage 1

Questions 1–10 are based on the following passage.

Many articles and books have been written proposing a major revamping of the nation's school system. In this excerpt, the author presents his own views on this subject.

When nearly everybody agrees on something, it probably isn't so. Nearly everybody agrees: It's going to take a revolution to fix America's public
Line schools. From the great national think tanks to
5 the neighborhood PTA, the call to the barricades is being trumpeted. Louis V. Gerstner Jr., head of RJR Nabisco and one of the business leaders in education reform, proclaims the Noah Principle: "No more prizes for predicting rain. Prizes only
10 for building arks. We've got to change whole schools and the whole school system."

But it isn't so; most of that is just rhetoric. In the first place, nobody really wants a revolution. Revolution would mean junking the whole
15 present structure of education overnight and inventing a new one from scratch, in the giddy conviction that anything must be an improvement—no matter what it costs in terms of untaught kids, wrecked careers, and doomed
20 experiments. What these folks really want isn't revolution but major reform, changing the system radically but in an orderly fashion. The changes are supposed to be tested in large-scale pilot programs—Gerstner's "arks"—and then installed
25 nationally.

But even that is just a distant gleam in the eye and a dubious proposition too. There's nothing like a consensus even on designing those arks, let alone where they are supposed to come to
30 ground. And anyone who has watched radical reforms in the real world has to be wary of them: Invariably, they take a long time and cost a great deal, and even so they fail more often than they succeed. In organizations as in organisms,
35 evolution works best a step at a time. The best and most natural changes come not in wholesale gulps, but in small bites.

What the think-big reformers fail to acknowledge is that schools all over the
40 country are changing all the time. From Head Start programs to after-school Big Brother/ Big Sister projects to self-esteem workshops, it's precisely these small-scale innovations and demonstration programs that are doing the job,
45 in literally thousands of schools. Some of these efforts are only partly successful; some fail; some work small miracles. They focus varyingly on children, teachers, and parents, on methods of administration and techniques of teaching, on
50 efforts to motivate kids and to teach values and to mobilize community support. Some are relatively expensive; others cost almost nothing. But all of them can be done—and have been done.

The important thing is that local schools aren't
55 waiting for a revolution, or for gurus to decree the new model classroom from sea to shining sea. They are working out their own problems and making their own schools better. And anyone— teachers, parents, principals, school board
60 members—anyone who cares enough and works hard enough can do the same.

1

The primary purpose of the passage is to

(A) present an alternative view of a widely-held belief.

B) refute the notion that change is needed.

C) describe several plans to implement an educational revolution.

D) uncover and analyze new flaws in an old system.

2

The quotation in lines 9–10 ("No more . . . arks") can best be interpreted to mean that Gerstner believes that

A) the present educational system is functioning adequately.

B) the focus should shift from describing problems to finding solutions.

C) trying to make predictions about what will happen is always counterproductive.

D) fixing the educational system requires financing new school buildings.

3

In line 12, "rhetoric" most nearly means

A) the art of persuasive speaking.

B) language that sounds good but has little content.

C) the use of figures of speech.

D) the tendency to question the truth.

4

The author uses the phrase "come to ground" (lines 29–30) to

A) extend an existing metaphor in order to complicate the way a situation has been portrayed.

B) point out how little common ground educational reformers and students share.

C) highlight the difficulty of establishing a timeline for school reform.

D) raise a question about where and how new schools will be built.

5

In line 36, "wholesale" most nearly means

A) cheap.

B) intended for institutions.

C) on a large scale.

D) unnatural.

6

Which best summarizes the idea of "small bites" (line 37)?

A) Changing the system radically but in an orderly fashion

B) Making the system gradually look more like it did in the past

C) Allowing children to choose from a variety of small classroom settings

D) Using modest innovations to improve schools

7

Which choice provides the best evidence for the answer to the previous question?

A) Lines 2–4 ("Nearly . . . schools")

B) Lines 20–22 ("What . . . fashion")

C) Lines 40–45 ("From . . . schools")

D) Lines 47–51 ("They . . . support")

8

The programs mentioned in lines 40–42 are examples of

A) small-scale programs that make it possible for graduates to earn jobs.

B) "arks" that Louis V. Gerstner Jr. would approve of.

C) after-school projects that are only partly successful.

D) ways that local schools are finding solutions to educational problems.

The last paragraph of the passage develops a contrast between

A) conventional classrooms and those that incorporate natural elements.

B) those who call for revolution and those who find small steps to fuel the evolution of education.

C) caring about education and working hard to get an education.

D) waiting for change and decreeing how it will be achieved.

The author of this passage would most likely agree with which of the following statements?

A) Success in business does not qualify someone to make educational policy.

B) Very few people are qualified to improve the educational system.

C) A comprehensive national curriculum is an important step in improving the educational system.

D) Examples of effective educational reform already exist.

Reading Practice Passage 2

Questions 11–20 are based on the following passage.

This passage describes the first detailed observations of the surface of the planet Mars—observations that indirectly led some to the mistaken belief that intelligent life existed there.

The summer of 1877 had been an exceptional time for observing Mars. Every 26 months the slower-moving Mars comes especially close to
Line Earth, creating the most favorable opportunity
5 for observations—or, in the space age, for travel to the planet. Sometimes these opportunities are better than others. Because of the large ellipticity* of the Martian orbit, the distance between Mars and Earth at the closest approach of opposition
10 (when Mars is on the opposite side of Earth from the Sun) varies from as near as 35 million miles to as far as 63 million. The closest of these oppositions occurs approximately every 15 years, and 1877 was one of those choice viewing times.
15   Among the astronomers taking advantage of the opportunity was Giovanni Virginio Schiaparelli, director of Milan's Brera Observatory and a scientist highly esteemed, particularly for his research concerning meteors
20 and comets. While examining Mars with a relatively small 8-inch telescope, Schiaparelli saw faint linear markings across the disc. Earlier observers had glimpsed some such streaks, but nothing as prominent and widespread as those
25 Schiaparelli described seeing. His drawings of Mars showed the dark areas, which some took to be seas, connected by an extensive network of long straight lines. Schiaparelli called the lines *canali.*
30   In Italian, the primary meaning of *canali* is "channels" or "grooves," which is presumably what Schiaparelli intended in the initial announcement of his discovery. He said that they "may be designated as *canali* although we
35 do not yet know what they are." But the word can also mean "canal," which is how it usually was translated. The difference in meanings had tremendous theoretical implications.

"The whole hypothesis was right there in the
40 translation," science writer Carl Sagan has said. "Somebody saw canals on Mars. Well, what does that mean? Well, canal—everybody knows what a canal is. How do you get a canal? Somebody builds it. Well, then there are *builders* of canals on
45 Mars."
    It may be no coincidence that the Martian canals inspired extravagant speculation at a time when canal-building on Earth was a reigning symbol of the Age of Progress. The Suez Canal
50 was completed in 1869, and the first efforts to breach Central America at Nicaragua or Panama were being promoted. To cut through miles of land and join two seas, to mold imperfect nature to suit man—in the nineteenth-century way of
55 thinking, this was surely how intelligent beings met challenges, whether on Earth or on Mars.
    Schiaparelli seemed to be of two minds about the markings. Of the canal-builders' interpretation he once remarked, "I am careful
60 not to combat this suggestion, which contains nothing impossible." But he would not encourage speculation. At another time, Schiaparelli elaborated on observations suggesting to him that the snows and ice of the Martian north pole
65 were associated with the canals. When snows are melting with the change of season, the breadth of the canals increases and temporary seas appear, he noted, and in the winter the canals diminish and some of the seas disappear. But he saw a
70 thoroughly natural explanation for the canals. "It is not necessary to suppose them to be the work of intelligent beings," he wrote in 1893, "and notwithstanding the almost geometrical appearance of all of their system, we are now
75 inclined to believe them to be produced by the evolution of the planet, just as on Earth we have the English Channel."
    His cautionary words had little effect. Those who wanted to believe in a system of water canals
80 on Mars, built by intelligent beings, were not to be discouraged—or proven wrong—for another 70 years.
    * *Ellipticity* refers to an oval (rather than a perfectly round) orbit around the sun.

11

Which choice best describes the developmental pattern of the passage?

A) A long-held but erroneous belief is introduced and debunked.

B) The circumstances that led to an incorrect interpretation of reported data are presented.

C) An example of the consequences of jumping to conclusions too quickly is provided as a warning.

D) An astronomical phenomenon is detailed and its potential consequences are explored.

12

Which of the following dates was likely to be the best for viewing Mars?

A) 6 months prior to the summer of 1877

B) 26 months after the summer of 1877

C) 15 years after the summer of 1877

D) 26 months before the summer of 1877

13

In line 14, "choice" most nearly means

A) designated.

B) optional.

C) excellent.

D) favorite.

14

The passage indicates that which of the following is the definition of "*canali*" that Schiaparelli most likely intended?

A) Extensive networks

B) Dark sea-like areas

C) Long canals

D) Channels or grooves

15

Which choice provides the best evidence for the answer to the previous question?

A) Lines 25–28 ("His drawings . . . lines")

B) Lines 30–33 ("In Italian . . . discovery")

C) Lines 35–37 ("But . . . translated")

D) Lines 41–43 ("Somebody . . . canal")

16

The author quotes Carl Sagan in lines 39–45 primarily to

A) introduce a modern writer's views into the discussion.

B) illustrate the thought process that led to a particular interpretation.

C) call into question Schiaparelli's observations.

D) indicate how difficult it is to translate scientific observations into another language.

17

As it is used in line 51, "breach" most nearly means

A) make a gap in.

B) rise through the surface of the water in.

C) bring together.

D) amass troops in.

Which statement best summarizes the point made in the fifth paragraph?

A) The sightings of the Mars canals in 1877 led to a surge of canal-building on Earth.

B) The Suez Canal's completion in 1869 set in motion another canal-building project that ultimately became the Panama Canal.

C) Canal-building in the nineteenth century was a feat of engineering with significant cultural implications.

D) The readiness to believe that the *canali* were constructed by intelligent beings may have come from a general fascination with canal-building at the time.

In line 57, "of two minds" is used to indicate that Schiaparelli was

A) skeptical.

B) tentative.

C) undecided.

D) changeable.

To what did Schiaparelli attribute the periodic changes in appearance of the Martian canals described in the sixth paragraph?

A) Melted ice from the north pole flowing into the canals during some seasons, enlarging them

B) The ellipticity of the Martian orbit exerting a tidal pull on the water in the canals

C) The visual distortion of Schiaparelli's relatively small telescope not allowing Schiaparelli to see the Martian surface clearly

D) Changes in the distance between Earth and Mars making objects appear larger or smaller

Reading Practice Passage 3

Questions 21–30 are based on the following passage.

The following passage gives a critical overview of the work of Frank Lloyd Wright, one of America's most famous architects. It has been adapted from "Frank Lloyd Wright—Twenty Years After His Death," published in *The New York Times,* April 15, 1979.

It is 30 years since Frank Lloyd Wright died at 91, and it is no exaggeration to say that the United States has had no architect even roughly
Line comparable to him since. His extraordinary
5 72-year career spanned the shingled Hillside Home School in Wisconsin in 1887 to the Guggenheim Museum built in New York in 1959.

His great early work, the prairie houses of
10 the Midwest in which he developed his style of open, flawing spaces and great horizontal planes, and integrated structure of wood, stone, glass, and stucco, were mostly built before 1910. Philip Johnson once insulted Wright by calling him
15 "America's greatest nineteenth-century architect." But Mr. Johnson was then a partisan of the sleek, austere International Style that Wright abhorred. Now, the International Style is in disarray, and what is significant here is that Wright's reputation
20 has not suffered much at all in the current antimodernist upheaval.

One of the reasons that Wright's reputation has not suffered too severely in the current turmoil in architectural thinking is that he
25 spoke a tremendous amount of common sense. He was full of ideas that seemed daring, almost absurd, but which now in retrospect were clearly right. Back in the 1920s, for example, he alone among architects
30 and planners perceived the great effect the automobile would have on the American landscape. He foresaw "the great highway becoming, and rapidly, the horizontal line of a new freedom extending from ocean to ocean,"
35 as he wrote in his autobiography of 1932. Wright wrote approvingly of the trend toward decentralization, which hardly endears him to today's center-city-minded planners—but if

his calls toward suburban planning had been
40 realized, the chaotic sprawl of the American landscape might today have some rational order to it.

Wright was obsessed with the problem of the affordable house for the middle-class
45 American. It may be that no other prominent architect has ever designed as many prototypes of inexpensive houses that could be mass-produced; unlike most current high stylists, who ignore the boredom of suburban tract
50 houses and design expensive custom residences in the hope of establishing a distance between themselves and mass culture, Wright tried hard to close the gap between the architectural profession and the general public.

55 In his modest houses or his grand ones, Wright emphasized appropriate materials, which might well be considered to prefigure both the growing preoccupation today with energy-saving design and the surge of interest
60 in regional architecture. Wright, unlike the architects of the International Style, would not build the same house in Massachusetts that he would build in California; he was concerned about local traditions, regional climates, and
65 so forth. It is perhaps no accident that at Taliesin, Wright's Scottsdale, Ariz., home and studio, which continues to function, many of the younger architects have begun doing solar designs, a logical step from Wright's work.

21

The main purpose of the passage is to

A) argue that Frank Lloyd Wright has never received sufficient appreciation.

B) draw attention to a little known but remarkable American architect.

C) assess a prolific career some years after its end.

D) highlight the errors made by Frank Lloyd Wright's detractors.

22

In the passage, the author anticipates which of the following objections to a point made in the passage about Wright's career?

A) The consequences of decentralization were not entirely positive.

B) Prairie houses are not appropriate for many regions of America.

C) Homebuyers are uncomfortable with the idea of inexpensive, mass-produced housing.

D) The gap between the architectural profession and mass culture cannot and perhaps should not be closed.

23

Which choice provides the best evidence for the answer to the previous question?

A) Lines 9–13 ("His great . . . 1910")

B) Lines 13–17 ("Philip . . . abhorred")

C) Lines 36–38 ("Wright . . . planners")

D) Lines 43–48 ("Wright . . . mass-produced")

24

Philip Johnson's quotation about Wright (line 15) was an insult because

A) Johnson felt Wright was responsible for much of the disarray of the antimodernist upheaval.

B) Johnson's remark implies that Wright's contributions to twentieth-century architecture were not as noteworthy as his earlier contributions.

C) urban and suburban space constraints rendered the open, flawing space of prairie houses obsolete in the twentieth century.

D) Johnson did not believe the automobile would have a positive effect on American architecture.

25

As used in line 16, "partisan" most nearly means

A) modernist.

B) critic.

C) weapon.

D) proponent.

26

The main purpose of the third paragraph (lines 22–42) is to

A) assess Wright's role in the early development of suburban planning.

B) assert and illustrate a claim about why Wright's reputation has not greatly declined.

C) bemoan the mistakes made by those who did not heed Wright's warnings.

D) contextualize some of Wright's more outdated ideas about architecture.

27

The author includes the reference to "high stylists" (line 48) primarily in order to

A) contrast Wright's practices with those of contemporary architects of comparable theoretical conviction.

B) decry the practices of some of the architects who have worked since Wright's death.

C) show the extent to which many other architects share Wright's obsession with affordable middle-class American housing.

D) distinguish between architects who design original structures and those who remodel existing buildings.

It can be inferred that the architects of the International Style would

A) resent the way Wright's reputation has not suffered to the extent theirs have.

B) never use mass-produced or inexpensive materials.

C) regret the extent to which architecture has become less sleek and more focused on an aesthetics of messiness.

D) regard style as determined by factors other than the particulars of a proposed building site.

Which choice provides the best evidence for the answer to the previous question?

A) Lines 1–4 ("It is . . . since")

B) Lines 18–21 ("Now . . . upheaval")

C) Lines 48–54 ("unlike . . . public")

D) Lines 60–65 ("Wright . . . forth")

It can be inferred from the passage that "appropriate materials" (line 56) are materials that

A) can be mass-produced.

B) are suitable based on a site's climate, history, and resources.

C) incorporate resource-conserving features such as solar panels and xeriscape design.

D) reflect the prairie and desert landscapes that inspired Wright's greatest work.

Reading Practice Passage 4

Questions 31–40 are based on the following passage.

In the following adapted excerpt from Anne Tyler's "Dinner at the Homesick Restaurant," Pearl, an elderly woman, is speaking to her son.

Pearl opened her eyes when Ezra turned a page of his magazine. "Ezra," she said. She felt him grow still. He had this habit—he had always
Line had it—of becoming totally motionless when
5 people spoke to him. It was endearing but also in some ways a strain, for then whatever she said to him ("I feel a draft," or "the paper boy is late again") was bound to disappoint him, wasn't it? How could she live up to Ezra's expectations? She
10 plucked at her quilt. "If I could just have some water," she told him.

He poured it from the pitcher on the bureau. She heard no ice cubes clinking; they must have melted. Yet it seemed just minutes ago that he'd
15 brought in a whole new supply. He raised her head, rested it on his shoulder, and tipped the glass to her lips. Yes, lukewarm—not that she minded. She drank gratefully, keeping her eyes closed. His shoulder felt steady and comforting.
20 He laid her back down on the pillow.

"Dr. Vincent's coming at ten," he told her.
"What time is it now?"
"Eight-thirty."
"Eight-thirty in the morning?"
25 "Yes."
"Have you been here all night?" she asked.
"I slept a little."
"Sleep now. I won't be needing you."
"Well, maybe after the doctor comes."
30 It was important to Pearl that she deceive the doctor. She didn't want to go to the hospital. Her illness was pneumonia, she was almost certain; she guessed it from a past experience. She recognized the way it settled into her back. If
35 Dr. Vincent found out he would take her out of her own bed, her own house, and send her off to Union Memorial, tent her over with plastic. "Maybe you should cancel the doctor altogether," she told Ezra. "I'm very much improved, I
40 believe."

"Let him decide that."
"Well, I know how my own self feels, Ezra."
"We won't argue about it just now," he said.
He could surprise you, Ezra could. He'd let a
45 person walk all over him but then display, at odd moments, a deep and rock-hard stubbornness. She sighed and smoothed her quilt. Wasn't it supposed to be the daughter who came and nursed you? She knew she should send him away
50 but she couldn't make herself do it. "I guess you want to get back to that restaurant," she told him.
"No, no."
"You're like a mother hen about that place," she said. She sniffed. Then she said, "Ezra, do
55 you smell smoke?"
"Why do you ask?" he said (cautious as ever).
"I dreamed the house burned down."
"It didn't really."
"Ah."
60 She waited, holding herself in. Her muscles were so tense, she ached all over. Finally she said, "Ezra?"
"Yes, Mother?"
"Maybe you could just check."
65 "Check what?"
"The house, of course. Check if it's on fire."

31

Which choice best summarizes the passage?

A) A woman makes stilted conversation with her son, all the while wishing her daughter could be with her.

B) A mother and son make small talk while pretending they are not concerned about a rash of arson attempts in the neighborhood.

C) A mother asks her son questions to try to discover the extent to which he is deceiving her.

D) A woman awakens and talks to her son while she is preoccupied by concerns that she does not express directly to him.

32

Pearl's attitude toward Ezra can best be described as

A) covert hostility.

B) condescension concealed by passivity.

C) apathetic resignation.

D) affection mixed with discomfort.

33

The action described in the passage takes place

A) in the apartment above the restaurant Ezra owns.

B) in a nursing home.

C) in Pearl's house.

D) in a rural hospital of limited means.

34

As used in line 6, "strain" is closest in meaning to

A) great pull.

B) source of tension.

C) injury caused by overexertion.

D) kind.

35

In the second paragraph, the issue of ice cubes is important to Pearl primarily because

A) she is grateful they have melted to produce water she can drink.

B) she dislikes cold water.

C) their absence makes her aware that time has passed.

D) they give her an excuse to ask Ezra for his help.

36

It can be inferred from the passage that it is "important to Pearl that she deceive the doctor" (lines 30–31) because

A) she is reluctant to go on the camping trip her family has planned.

B) she is feeling much better after her sleep.

C) previous experience with pneumonia has taught her to distrust doctors.

D) she does not want to be put in the hospital.

37

Which choice provides the best evidence for the answer to the previous question?

A) Lines 21–29 ("Dr. Vincent's . . . comes")

B) Lines 31–37 ("She . . . plastic")

C) Lines 38–40 ("Maybe . . . believe")

D) Lines 41–46 ("Let . . . stubbornness")

38

The statement, "He could surprise you, Ezra could" serves primarily to

A) highlight Pearl's sense that she knows Ezra very well and yet does not fully understand him.

B) draw attention to the narrator's lack of omniscience.

C) reinforce the characterization of Ezra as volatile.

D) show that Pearl has never really understood her son at all.

39

The references to the quilt in lines 10 and 47 primarily serve to

A) highlight the waning of Pearl's strength during her illness.

B) suggest her mental unrest is echoed by her movements.

C) inject physical activity to offset the slow nature of the conversation that makes up so much of the passage.

D) suggest Pearl is dissatisfied with the bedding now that she cannot do her own laundry.

The parenthetical observation "cautious as ever" in line 56 functions in the context of the passage to

A) reflect the way Pearl perceives Ezra as she interacts with him.

B) hint at Ezra's guilt about the fire he'd set the previous night.

C) reveal the extent to which Ezra is worried that his mother is losing her grip on reality.

D) reinforce that Pearl's fears about fire are justifiable.

READING PRACTICE: ANSWERS AND EXPLANATIONS

Reading Practice Passage 1

1. **A**   Answer this question after work on the specific questions has provided a sense of the passage over-all. The passage begins by observing that when *nearly everybody agrees on something, it probably isn't so*, which sets up the passage's main purpose of exposing the fallacies of what *everybody agrees* about regarding America's public schools. The passage does not refute the idea that *change* is needed—it refutes the idea that *revolution* is needed—so eliminate (B). The main idea relates to the fact that there is more than one way to envision and affect change in the school system, but the focus is not on describing several implementation plans, so eliminate (C). Since the passage is focused on exist-ing ways to address problems, (D) can be eliminated. Choice (A) matches the prediction and is the correct answer.

2. **B**   In the context of the Noah story, *predicting rain* would be predicting that something bad was coming, while *building arks* would be taking action to respond to the situation. In the context of Gerstner's entire comment, then, building *arks* must mean something like *change whole schools and change the whole school system*. Eliminate (A), since this is the opposite of what Gerstner believes. Eliminate (C), since Gerstner is commenting in particular on the situation regarding education and there's no evidence he thinks that making predictions is *always* counterproductive. Eliminate (D), which is too literal a reading of *building arks*, since there's no evidence that changing whole schools and the whole school system requires new school buildings to be built. Choice (B) matches the prediction and is the correct answer.

3. **B**   The word *rhetoric* is used in a sentence that is dismissing Gerstner's claims as untrue, so in context, *rhetoric* must mean something like *things that aren't true*. While (A) and (C) do offer actual defi-nitions of *rhetoric*, those definitions do not fit the context, so they can be eliminated. Choice (D) raises the question of truthfulness, but it is the author who is questioning the validity of Gerstner's claims, whereas when *rhetoric* is used in the sentence, the word is describing Gerstner's claims themselves. Choice (B) does touch on the idea that the content of Gerstner's claim is questionable, and as Gerstner is articulating what *almost everybody believes*, the ideas must be persuasive even if incorrect. The correct answer is (B).

4. **A**   Question 2 asked about Gerstner's articulation of what the author calls *the Noah Principle*. Ger-stner's description uses the ideas of *predicting rain* and *building arks* to describe his assessment of how problems in the educational system must be addressed; the passage's author continues to use the metaphor in the second and third paragraphs' discussion of the problems with Gerstner's claims. Eliminate (B), since there's no evidence on how the backgrounds of educational reformers and students compare. Eliminate (D), which interprets *ground* too literally. Since the extension of

Gerstner's metaphor is used in two paragraphs that elaborate on why what Gerstner said *isn't so*, (C) identifies a challenge that proponents of revolution face, but does not get at the main reason for extending the metaphor as (A) does. Eliminate (C); the correct answer is (A).

5. **C** The word *wholesale* appears in the assertion that the *best and most natural changes come not in wholesale gulps, but in small bites*. The opposition between *wholesale gulps* and *small bites* suggests that *wholesale* must mean *not small* or *large*. Eliminate (A) and (B), which play on uses of *wholesale* that are not relevant in this context. Eliminate (D), which uses language from the sentence but does not reflect the sense of the word suggested by context. Choice (C) matches the prediction well and is the correct answer.

6. **D** The sentence containing the mention of *small bites* is preceded by and further develops the assertion that *in organizations as in organisms, evolution works best a step at a time*. It may be clear from this context that in terms of the overall passage, *wholesale gulps* must refer to the revolution that some reformers are demanding and *small bites* must be the smaller-scale attempts to solve educational issues. Because the options in question 7 are found throughout the passage, these two questions can be worked as a set of general paired questions. Choice (7A) notes that a lot of people think the school system needs revolutionary change, which has some connection to (6A). Choice (7B) contradicts (6A) and does not support any other answers in (6), so (7B) can be eliminated. Choice (7C) provides examples of *small-scale innovations* that are *doing the job* and thus supports (6D). Choice (7D) does not support any of the choices in (6) and can be eliminated. Since the support that (7A) provides for (6A) only addresses the *radical* aspect but not the *orderly* aspect of the change, (7A) and (6A) are weaker answers and they also describe the side of the revolutionaries, not the side of those taking small steps: Both can be eliminated. The correct answer for question 6 is (D), and the correct answer for question 7 is (C).

7. **C** See the explanation for question 6.

8. **D** The sentence in which the examples are given provides the explanation that *these small-scale innovations and demonstration programs* are *doing the job*. Context reveals that *the job* must be changing the public school systems and these programs are doing that job in small ways that nevertheless work toward solutions. Eliminate (A), as the first part of the answer looks good, but there's no evidence that these programs help graduates earn jobs. Eliminate (B), since Gerstner's "arks" are the opposite of the kinds of programs mentioned in the examples. Eliminate (C), as the emphasis is on the small-scale nature of the programs, rather than the fact that not all are successful. Choice (D) matches the prediction and is the correct answer.

9. **B** The overall passage is contrasting the popular wisdom that problems with the educational system require revolutionary solutions to the actual experience of people who are attempting to address problems through small-scale and local fixes. The final paragraph sums up this idea, noting that *the important thing* is that local schools are doing what they can rather than waiting for large-scale revolution. Eliminate (A), as the idea of natural elements in classrooms is not addressed in the

paragraph or passage. Eliminate (C), as the contrasting groups in the passage both care about education; additionally, the passage discusses the education system, not the work that students do to get an education. Eliminate (D), for while those calling for revolution might be portrayed as making decrees, the other side is *not* waiting for change. Choice (B) best matches the prediction and is the correct answer.

10. **D** After answering the other specific questions, question 10 should be relatively straightforward to answer. The author of the passage is most likely to agree with a point that he or she makes in the passage, so check the answer choices to see which statement best matches what the passage actually says. Eliminate (A), (B), and (C), as there is no evidence in the passage to support these claims. Choice (D) makes a claim that the author has already made and is thus the correct answer.

Reading Practice Passage 2

11. **B** Answer this question after work on the specific questions has provided a sense of the passage overall. The passage is informative in tone and describes the circumstances of Schiaparelli's observations and how they came to be interpreted. Eliminate (C), which is too broad; there's no evidence that the author is primarily interested in making an example of the circumstances described. Eliminate (D), since the passage focuses on the process of interpreting astronomical observations, not on the consequences of the phenomenon itself. While the passage does discuss the origins of a *long-held but erroneous belief*, the author is more interested in discussing how the interpretation arose than in debunking it, so eliminate (A). Choice (B) matches the prediction and is the correct answer.

12. **C** The words "summer of 1877" appear in every answer choice and so can function as lead words that, along with chronology, indicate the answer is likely to be found in the first paragraph. This question is tricky, though, because it requires you read the whole of the first paragraph as the window. The first paragraph states that the summer of 1877 was *an exceptional time for viewing Mars* and that *every 26 months* the movement of Mars creates *the most favorable opportunity for observations*, but adds that some of *these opportunities are better than others*. Since the closest oppositions— or best viewing times—occur *approximately every 15 years* and 1877 was one of them, (A), (B), and (D) can be eliminated. The correct answer is (C).

13. **C** The phrase "choice viewing times" describes the best opportunities to observe Mars from Earth, so "choice" must mean something like *best* or *very good*. Eliminate (A), (B), and (D), which do not match this prediction. Choice (C) is the best match for the prediction and is the correct answer.

14. **D** The word *"canali"* appears first on lines 29 and 30. The first sentence of the third paragraph states that *the primary meaning of* canali *is "channels" or "grooves," which is presumably what Schiaparelli intended*. Eliminate (A), (B), and (C), which do not match the prediction. Choice (D) restates precisely what the passage says and is the correct answer.

15. **B** This question is the second in a specific paired set. In answering question 14, you should have underlined the exact place in the passage where you found the evidence to support your answer. That information is contained in lines 30–33, which matches (B). Eliminate (A), (C), and (D). Choice (B) is the correct answer.

16. **B** The quotation from Sagan makes up the bulk of the fourth paragraph. The third paragraph ends with the assertion that the *difference in meanings had tremendous theoretical implications*. Sagan's quote serves to illustrate how one translation—canals—led to *the whole hypothesis* about life on Mars. Since Sagan's comments don't refer to Schiaparelli's observations themselves, eliminate (C). Since the focus is on the implications of a particular translation rather than the difficulty of making such translations generally, eliminate (D). Sagan *is* a modern writer, but the *primary* purpose of quoting his comments is to show the implications of the translation, not to provide modern commentary, so eliminate (A). Choice (B) best matches the prediction and is the correct answer.

17. **A** The word *breach* is used in a sentence that discusses *the first efforts to breach Central America at Nicaragua or Panama*. Since this action was *promoted* after the Suez Canal was completed, it seems likely that the action in Central American was inspired by and similar to the completion of the Suez Canal. The next sentence expands on the idea of "to breach" as *to cut through miles of land and join two seas*, which means that *breach* must mean something like *to cut through* or *to make a hole in*. Eliminate (B), (C), and (D), which do not match this prediction. Choice (A), *make a gap in*, does, and is the correct answer.

18. **D** The fifth paragraph marks a shift from explaining the logic that led people from a translation of Schiaparelli's *canali* as canals to speculation about the makers of those canals. The first sentence of the fifth paragraph offers further context to explain why such logic may have taken hold: Schiaparelli's observations of Mars occurred *at a time when canal building on Earth was a reigning symbol of the Age of Progress*. The examples that follow further develop this context. Eliminate (A), as it is the canal-building that may have led to the interest in the canals on Mars, rather than the reverse. Eliminate (B), as there is no evidence that the building of one canal caused the building of the other, and the relationship between the two canals is not the main idea of the paragraph. Eliminate (C), which is a statement that may be true, but which is not the main point of the paragraph. Choice (D) matches the prediction and is the correct answer.

19. **C** The referenced sentence notes that *Schiaparelli seemed to be of two minds about the markings*. The sentences that follow note that he was *careful* not to deny the validity of the canal-builders theory but would not encourage such speculation. Since he was reluctant to endorse the canal-building theory and could envision other causes of the observed phenomenon but yet would not speak against the canal-building theory, *of two minds* must means something like *unwilling or unable to commit to a side*. The answer that most closely matches this prediction is (C), *undecided*. Choice (D) can be eliminated because there's no evidence that he changed his mind, but rather that he did not decide at all. Though Schiaparelli might have been *skeptical* of one side of the debate, *of two minds* suggests that he did not choose a side, and says little of the manner in which he approached the debate; eliminate (A). Similarly, while Schiaparelli might have been *tentative* in approaching

the hypotheses, the phrase *of two minds* is linked by evidence to the fact that he did not endorse either, so eliminate (B). Choice (C) matches the prediction and is the correct answer.

20. **A** The last question focused on the fact that Schiaparelli did not choose a side in the debate about the origin of the canals on Mars, as described at the start of the sixth paragraph. Looking immediately after where that answer was found shows that the author also states that at another time, Schiaparelli noted that the changes in the canals were consistent with what might be the melting of snow and ice at the Martian north pole during changes of seasons. This prediction matches well with (A), so keep it. The sixth paragraph does not mention the ellipticity of the Martian orbit (which is discussed in the first paragraph, so eliminate (B). There's no evidence that the size of Schiaparelli's telescope produced poor quality observations, so eliminate (C). There's also no evidence that Schiaparelli thought the distance between Earth and Mars affected his perception of the canals, so eliminate (D). The correct answer is (A).

Reading Practice Passage 3

21. **C** The blurb states that the passage is a *critical overview* of Wright's work, and the passage opens with the claim that *the United States has had no architect even roughly comparable to him* since his death 30 years before the passage's publication. The rest of the passage offers support for that claim by pointing out remarkable things about Wright's career. Eliminate (D), since the passage focuses on Wright's career, not on the arguments of his detractors. Eliminate (A) and (B), as there is no evidence in the passage that Wright *never* received sufficient appreciation or that he was *little known* during his career or after his death. Choice (C) matches the prediction well and is the correct answer.

22. **A** This is a general question followed by a "best evidence" question, so questions 22 and 23 can be answered together as a set of general paired questions. Question 2 asks for an objection the author thinks might be raised about Wright's career—that's a tricky question that becomes much easier when the questions are worked together. Choice (23A) does not raise any of the objections mentioned in the choices for question 22, so eliminate (23A). Choice (23B) contains Johnson's insult (and it would be a stretch to call this an objection), but the lines do not support any of the objections in the answers for question 22, so eliminate (23B). Choice (23C) refers to *decentralization*, noting both Wright's approval of the trend and that this approval *hardly endears him to today's center-city-minded planners*, so (23C) seems to support (22A). Choice (23D) contains phrases that appear in (22C), but neither the cited lines nor the passage as a whole addresses an objection based on the feelings of *homebuyers*. Eliminate (23D), and then eliminate (22B), (22C), and (22D), since none of those are supported by evidence from an answer choice in question 23. The correct answer for question 22 is (A), and the correct answer for question 23 is (C).

23. **C** See the explanation for question 22.

24. **B** Johnson insulted Wright by calling him *America's greatest nineteenth-century architect,* a remark that might sound a lot like a compliment. The most likely way for the words to function as an insult would be either that the term *architect* was insulting or that *nineteenth-century* was insulting. Since the passage also refers to Wright as an architect, the former seems unlikely, but the passage notes that Wright's career spanned from 1887 to 1959, so Johnson's comment could have been an insult if it was meant to signal that Wright's twentieth-century work was not also great. Eliminate (A) and (C), which both use words from the passage but make claims for which there is no evidence. Eliminate (D), since Johnson does not figure in the third paragraph, which is where the discussion of the effects of the automobile occurs. Choice (B) matches the prediction well and is the correct answer.

25. **D** The word *partisan* is used in the sentence, *But Mr. Johnson was then a partisan of the sleek, austere International Style that Wright abhorred.* Since this statement follows the report of Johnson's remark about Wright and seems to be offered as context for the insult, it seems likely that, as Wright really disliked the International Style, Johnson probably liked it a lot. In context, *partisan* must mean something like *supporter* or *fan.* Eliminate (A), (B), and (C), since none of these match the prediction. Choice (D), *proponent,* has the sense of *advocate* or *someone who speaks on behalf of a theory or idea,* so it matches the prediction well and is the correct answer.

26. **B** The third paragraph begins with the assertion that one of the reasons Wright's reputation has not suffered too much is that *he spoke a tremendous amount of common sense.* The rest of the paragraph expands on that claim and then illustrates it with the example of Wright's ideas about the effects of cars on the American landscape. Eliminate (A), which is too specific; the purpose of the paragraph is to make and support a larger claim about Wright's reputation, not to focus on Wright's role in suburban planning. Eliminate (C), as the paragraph does not focus on *bemoaning* anything and the emphasis is not on the mistakes of others. Eliminate (D), as the paragraph highlights how many of Wright's ideas *in retrospect were clearly right,* not how they are *outdated.* Choice (B) matches the prediction well and is the correct answer.

27. **A** The words *high stylists* occur in the phrase, *unlike most current high stylists,* which signals that Wright is being compared to some current architects. Wright was a *prominent architect* who did focus on middle-class housing while, according to the passage, many current comparable architects *ignore the boredom of suburban tract houses.* Thus, the phrase *high stylists* is used to set up a comparison between Wright's work and the work of some current architects. Eliminate (B), since the purpose of referring to the other architects is highlighting an aspect of Wright's work, not *decrying* the practices of others. Eliminate (C), which contradicts the information in the passage. Eliminate (D), as there's no evidence that the *high stylists* are remodeling existing buildings. Choice (A) matches the prediction well and is the correct answer.

28. **D** This question asks what must be true based on what the passage says about architects of the International Style, so it could be treated as a lead word question. It is followed by a "best evidence" question whose answer choices are drawn from throughout the passage, though, so the two questions can be effectively answered by treating them as a set of general paired questions. Choice

(29A) could be seen as a weak support for (28A), since the lines assert that no other architect has had a comparable career, but there's no support for the claim that any architects, of the International Style or otherwise, *resent* Wright, so eliminate (29A). Some of the language in and around (29B) is echoed in (28C), but (28C) depends on a too literal reading of the referenced lines. Eliminate (29B). The phrase *mass-produced* in (29C) might seem to connect to (28B), but the lines do not support the extreme statement in (28B) or the claims in any of the other answers, so eliminate (29C). Choice (29D) states that Wright was *concerned about local traditions, regional climates,* and other factors that meant he *would not build the same house in Massachusetts that he would build in California.* Since this makes him *unlike the architects of the International Style,* those architects must have been willing to ignore or not pay attention to those factors. Thus (29D) supports (28D), since Wright's focus on regional architecture was not shared by the International Style architects. Eliminate (28A), (28B), and (28C), as none is well supported by evidence offered in the answers to question 29. The correct answer to question 28 is (D), and the correct answer to question 29 is (D).

29. **D**   See the explanation for question 28.

30. **B**   The passage connects Wright's emphasis on *appropriate materials* with contemporary concerns about *energy-saving design* and *regional architecture,* as well as *local traditions* and *regional climates.* In this context, *appropriate materials* must be materials that are local to an area and that reflect the area's history, tradition, and climate. Eliminate (A), as the reference to mass production does not occur in the relevant window. Keep (B), since it matches the prediction very well. Eliminate (C), as *resource-conservation* is only one aspect of what makes the materials appropriate, and (B) provides those aspects more fully. Eliminate (D), since *appropriate materials* would reflect the site in which a building were being constructed, rather than an area that was significant to Wright. Choice (B) matches the prediction well and is the correct answer.

Reading Practice Passage 4

31. **D**   The overall passage details exchanges between a woman and her son as she wakes up after a night that he has spent sitting at her bedside. The passage provides many details of her thoughts during their exchanges but does not reveal details of the son's inner thoughts. Eliminate (A), as there is no evidence that Pearl wishes her daughter were present, only that she is thinking that the situation she finds herself in is one that usually involves a daughter taking on Ezra's responsibilities. Eliminate (B), since the fact that Pearl had a dream about the house being on fire does not support the idea that any arson attempts have occurred, let alone a number of them. Eliminate (C) because, while Ezra may surprise Pearl on occasion and while Pearl does wish to deceive the doctor, there is no evidence to suggest that Pearl thinks Ezra is deceiving her. Choice (D) matches the prediction well, as it reflects the fact that the narrator provides details of Pearl's preoccupations as well as the conversation between the pair; (D) is the correct answer.

32. **D**   Pearl thinks that Ezra's habit of stilling himself when people speak to him is *endearing but also in some ways a strain,* and this tension between her love for him and the stress that his presence causes

is reflected throughout the passage. Thus she also *knows that she should send him away* but cannot make herself do it, and she shows evidence of having observed him very closely and with affection, even though she does not fully understand him and cannot fully speak her mind to him. Eliminate (A), as there is no evidence that she is *hostile* toward her son. Eliminate (B), as her action when she sniffs in line 54 is not a reaction to him but rather a sign of her concern about fire after her dream; there's no evidence that Pearl looks down on Ezra. Eliminate (C), as there is no evidence that Pearl does not care about Ezra or that she has given up trying to influence her interactions with him. Choice (D) matches the prediction well and is the correct answer.

33. **C** Lead words found in the answer choices—*hospital, house,* and *restaurant*—point to the paragraph from lines 30–40 as a likely source of evidence for this question. Within this paragraph, Pearl thinks that if Dr. Vincent *found out, he would take her out of her own bed, her own house, and send her off to Union Memorial.* Since the evidence clearly indicates that she is in *her own bed* when the action takes place, eliminate (A), (B), and (D). Choice (C) matches the prediction and is the correct answer.

34. **B** The word *strain* appears in Pearl's observation that Ezra's habit of stilling himself to listen is *endearing but also in some ways a strain.* This observation is followed by Pearl's recognition that the strain results from her sense that *whatever she said to him* was *bound to disappoint him.* Thus, *strain* must mean something like *a cause of tension or discomfort.* Eliminate (A), (C), and (D), each of which provides a valid definition of *strain* but not a definition that is appropriate in this context. Choice (B) matches the prediction and is the correct answer.

35. **C** The lead words *ice cubes* appear in the second paragraph, where it is noted that Pearl *heard no ice cubes clinking.* She realizes that they must have melted, even as she thinks that it seems like very little time has passed since Ezra brought fresh ice cubes in. When she drinks the water and finds that it is *lukewarm,* this confirms her theory that more time has passed than she'd thought—time enough for the ice cubes to melt and the water to become warmer. Eliminate (A), as there's no evidence that the ice cubes had to melt before Pearl had access to water and the emphasis in the paragraph is on her recognition that time has passed. Eliminate (B), since the fact that in this case Pearl does not mind that the water is lukewarm suggests that normally she might prefer cold water. Eliminate (D), as Pearl has already asked Ezra for a drink of water before she notices the absence of the ice cubes. Choice (C) matches the prediction well and is the correct answer.

36. **D** This is a specific question that is followed by a "best evidence" question, so questions 16 and 17 can be worked as a set of specific paired questions. The sentence referenced in question 16 is the first sentence of a paragraph and is immediately followed by the statement *She didn't want to go to the hospital.* Pearl believes that she has pneumonia and thinks that *if Dr. Vincent found out he would take her out of her own bed, her own house, and send her off to Union Memorial.* Thus, Pearl wants to deceive Dr. Vincent to keep him from realizing that she has pneumonia, so that she can avoid going to the hospital. Eliminate (A), since the reference to *tent* in the paragraph refers to putting a cover over her hospital bed and not a tent intended for camping, so there is no support for (A) in the passage. Eliminate (B), as the evidence suggests that Pearl tells Ezra that she is feeling better

in order to get him to cancel the doctor's arrival; if she were actually feeling better, she would not need to deceive the doctor. Eliminate (C) because while there is evidence that Pearl has had pneumonia before, there is no evidence that the result was a distrust of doctors. Choice (D) matches the prediction well and is the correct answer.

37. **D** Since this is the second question in a set of specific paired questions, look for the answer choice that contains the evidence used to support the answer in question 16. Eliminate (A), (B), and (C). Choice (D) contains the lines that provide the evidence for why Pearl needs to deceive the doctor and is therefore the correct answer.

38. **A** Aside from the dialogue, most of the information presented in the passage reflects Pearl's thoughts and perspective, as no explanations are offered as to what Ezra is thinking or feeling during the passage. The referenced statement—*He could surprise you, Ezra could*—is followed by the observation that Ezra would *let a person walk all over him but then display, at odd moments, a deep and rock-hard stubbornness*. This suggests that Pearl has observed and thought about her son often, since it is clear here and elsewhere in the passage that she knows how he tends to behave, though she cannot always fully predict what he will do in a particular circumstance. Keep (A), as it matches the prediction. Eliminate (B), since the statement reveals more about Pearl's thinking than about the narrator's perspective. Eliminate (C), as there is no evidence in the passage that Ezra is *volatile*. Eliminate (D), which is too extreme: Ezra may surprise Pearl at times, but that does not mean she has *never understood him at all*. The correct answer is (A).

39. **B** Both references to the quilt follow a moment in which Pearl is thinking about Ezra's personality. In the first, she *plucks* at the quilt after thinking about the strain that she sometimes feels in trying to live up to Ezra's expectations. In the second, she *smoothes* the quilt after thinking about the fact that sometimes Ezra can be surprisingly stubborn, as when he insists on the doctor's visit. In both instances, there's evidence that Pearl is feeling some unease in relation to her thoughts, which suggests that her interactions with the quilt reflect her inner restlessness or unease. Eliminate (A), as there's no evidence linking physical weakness to the actions with the quilt. Keep (B), as it matches the prediction well. Eliminate (C), as this answer does not match the prediction as well as (B) does and the actions with the quilt do not do much to insert physical activity into the scene. Eliminate (D), as there is no evidence that Pearl cannot do her own laundry or that she is dissatisfied with the bedding. The correct answer is (B).

40. **A** The phrase *cautious as ever* modifies the description of Ezra's manner of speaking to Pearl. Most of the narration in the passage reflects Pearl's thoughts and impressions about her current situation: all of Ezra's other actions are seen from Pearl's perspective, not his, so the observation here is also likely to reflect Pearl's perspective. Keep (A), because it matches the prediction. Choices (B) and (C) both suggest that the phrase might reveal Ezra's feelings, but there is no evidence in the passage to support the idea that Ezra is feeling *guilt* or that he is worried about his mother's *grip on reality*: eliminate (B) and (C). Similarly, the passage suggests that Pearl's fear of fire is based on a dream, not that it is a justifiable concern, so eliminate (D). Choice (A) is the correct answer.

Chapter 4
Reading
Practice Test

Reading Test

65 MINUTES, 52 QUESTIONS

Turn to Section 1 of your answer sheet to answer the questions in this section.

Questions 1–10 are based on the following passage.

The following passage is an excerpt from a memoir written by writer John Burke, about the novelist Joseph Heller.

I became a fan of Joseph Heller's writing while I was a student in high school in the 1970s. His most famous book, *Catch-22*, was practically an anthem for
Line my friends and me. We had dissected it, sitting in the
5 park outside school, reciting certain key passages aloud and proclaiming to anyone who would listen that this was quite possibly the best book ever written. Nearly twenty years later I am not sure that we were wrong.

Heller created a modern-day anti-hero who was
10 a soldier trying to stay sane in the midst of a war in which he no longer believed. This spoke to my generation, growing up as we did during the turmoil of Vietnam, and—however you felt about the issue—his ideas were considered important.

15 I had spent many hours imagining what the man who had created the savage wit and brilliant imagery of that book would be like in person. I was soon to find out. To this day, I have no idea how it was arranged, but somehow an invitation to speak at my high school
20 was extended and duly accepted.

On the day, I made sure to be near the gate of the school to see him arrive. I was looking for a limousine, or perhaps an entourage of reporters surrounding the man whose dust-jacket picture I had scrutinized so
25 often. But suddenly, there he was, completely alone, walking hesitantly toward the school like just a normal person. He walked by me, and I was amazed to see that he was wearing rather tattered sneakers, down at the heel.

30 When he began speaking in the auditorium, I was dumbfounded, for he had a very heavy speech impediment.

"That can't be him," I whispered loudly to a friend. "He sounds like a dork."

35 My notions of a brilliant man at that time did not extend to a speech impediment—or any handicap whatsoever. Ordinary people were handicapped, but not men of brilliance. There was, in fact, a fair amount of whispering going on in the auditorium.

40 And then somehow, we began to listen to what he was saying. He was completely brilliant. He seemed to know just what we were thinking and articulated feelings that I had only barely known that I had. He spoke for forty minutes and held us all spellbound. I
45 would not have left my seat even if I could.

As I listened, I began to feel awaken in me the possibility of being more than I had supposed that I could be. With some difficulty I managed to get to the school gate again and waited for twenty minutes while
50 I suppose he signed autographs and fielded questions inside the auditorium. Eventually, he came out, as he had come in, alone.

I screwed up all my courage and called to him, "Mr. Heller."

55 He almost didn't stop but then he turned around and came over to me.

"I just wanted to say how much I enjoyed your book. "

CONTINUE

He looked down at me in my wheelchair, smiled
60 as if it was the most normal thing in the world and
shook my hand. I think that day may have been very
important in the future direction of my life.

1

The main purpose of the passage is to

A) illustrate that authors do not make as much
money as people may expect.

B) describe an event that may have changed the
author's perception of himself.

C) prove that *Catch-22* is the best book ever written.

D) provide insight into the contrast between how
people expect the famous to behave and how they
actually do.

2

Which choice provides the best evidence for the
answer to the previous question?

A) Lines 4–7 ("We . . . written")

B) Lines 22–25 ("I was . . . often")

C) Lines 41–42 ("He was . . . . thinking")

D) Lines 61–62 ("I think . . . life")

3

Based on the information the passage provides about
Heller's novel, *Catch-22* can best be described as

A) a provocative book that appealed almost
exclusively to young men.

B) a memoir whose appeal depended on readers'
proximity to the events that had influenced its
creation.

C) a novel whose brilliance might appeal to people
who were not directly affected by U.S. involvement
in Vietnam.

D) an inspiring and realistic account of one soldier's
valor.

4

The author uses the phrase "however you felt about
the issue" (line 13) to signal

A) that not all critics agreed with the author's
assessment of *Catch-22*'s excellence.

B) that the book was valued by the author and his
friends because of its ability to stir up debate.

C) that the Vietnam War was the subject of much
debate.

D) that books can generate strong emotional
responses in readers.

5

The author quotes his own comment to his friend in
lines 33–34 primarily in order to

A) emphasize the strength of his initial reaction to
Heller's speech.

B) suggest that the reason Heller almost didn't stop
as he was leaving was that he had overheard this
comment.

C) highlight the author's suspicion that Heller had
sent a stand-in to deliver his speech.

D) inject some humor to counterbalance the overall
somber nature of the passage.

6

The author describes Heller's speech (lines 30–45)
primarily in order to

A) show that the students' initial skepticism was
overcome by their interest in what he was saying.

B) illustrate the powerful effect a good speaker can
have.

C) provide a warning not to judge people by how
they speak.

D) respond to charges that Heller's work is overrated.

7

Which choice provides the best evidence for the answer to the previous question?

A) Lines 30–32 ("When . . . impediment")

B) Lines 38–39 ("There . . . auditorium")

C) Lines 40–41 ("And then . . . brilliant")

D) Lines 43–44 ("He . . . spellbound")

8

In the context of the passage as a whole, it can be inferred that the most likely cause of the "difficulty" (line 48) the author had in returning to the school gate was the

A) effect of the emotions Heller's speech had generated.

B) crowd of other students who were waiting to see Heller's departure.

C) injury the author had sustained in the Vietnam War.

D) fact that he has limited physical mobility.

9

In line 50, "fielded" most nearly means

A) answered.

B) evaded.

C) asked.

D) caught.

10

It can be inferred from the passage that the most likely reason the author had to "screw up all [his] courage" was that

A) he was embarrassed about his own speech impediment.

B) he greatly admired Heller.

C) he was afraid Heller would not respond to him.

D) he thought Heller would be annoyed to deal with another student.

CONTINUE

Questions 11–21 are based on the following passage.

The following two passages present two views of the funeral industry in the United States. The first passage is an excerpt from a book written in 1963 by a journalist and takes a hard look at funeral practices at the time. The second passage was written in the 1980s by a member of the funeral business and looks at the changes in the industry since the first book appeared.

Passage 1

Oh death, where is thy sting? O grave, where is thy victory? Where, indeed. Many a badly stung survivor faced with the aftermath of some relative's
Line funeral has ruefully concluded that the victory has
5 been won hands down by a funeral establishment—in disastrously unequal battle.

Much has been written of late about the affluent society in which we live, and much fun poked at some of the irrational "status symbols" set out like golden
10 snares to trap the unwary consumer at every turn. Until recently, little has been said about the most irrational and weirdest of the lot, lying in ambush for all of us at the end of the road—the modern American funeral.

If the dismal traders (as an eighteenth-century
15 English writer calls them) have traditionally been cast in a comic role in literature, a universally recognized symbol of humor from Shakespeare to Dickens to Evelyn Waugh, they have successfully turned the tables in recent years to perpetrate a huge, macabre, and
20 expensive practical joke on the American public. It is not consciously conceived of as a joke, of course; on the contrary, it is hedged with admirably contrived rationalizations.

Gradually, almost imperceptibly, over the years,
25 the funeral men have constructed their own grotesque cloud-cuckoo-land where the trappings of Gracious Living are transformed, as in a nightmare, into the trappings of Gracious Dying. The same familiar Madison Avenue language has seeped into the funeral
30 industry.

So that this too, too solid flesh might not melt, we are offered "solid copper—a quality casket which offers superb value to the client seeking long-lasting protection," or the "colonial Classic Beauty—18 gauge
35 lead-coated steel, seamless top, lap-jointed welded body construction." Some caskets are equipped with foam rubber, some with innerspring mattresses. One company actually offers "the revolutionary Perfect-Posture bed."

Passage 2

40 In the past 20 years, many of the questionable excesses of the funeral trade have been curbed: legislation and self-policing by funeral home associations have brought some measure of regulation to an industry that was at one time sadly deficient. And
45 yet, if the sharp practices of shoddy morticians are no longer cause for customers to "whirl in their urns," as Jessica Mitford once put it so trenchantly, I fear that we may have somehow tilted too far in the other direction.

True, the costs of funerals in the 1960s were
50 escalating out of all proportion to real value, but I am convinced that in our search for economy and avoidance of discomfort we have weakened a very important family rite. Consider the case of one funeral "park" in Southern California that has instituted
55 "drive-in" funerals. Believe it or not, you can view the remains, attend the chapel service, and witness the interment—all without leaving your car.

To the extent that measures such as these have cut costs, I would applaud, but in my opinion these
60 measures have also produced a disconnection from the real purposes of a funeral. The process of spending time mourning the dead fills a real need for the bereaved. There is a purpose to each of the steps of a funeral, and if there is a commensurate cost to those
65 steps, then so be it. These days it is possible to have a funeral without a service for friends and family to gather, without a graveside interment, even without a casket. More frequently now, families will ask that contributions to charity be made in lieu of flowers and
70 wreaths—without recognizing that buying flowers provides a chance for friends and relatives to show their concern in a more tangible way than a gift to charity.

Let us not forget that feelings are as important as
75 economy.

CONTINUE

11

The first paragraph suggests that the "sting" referred to in the question, "Oh death, where is thy sting?" (line 1) is

A) the suffering from which the dead are released.

B) the consequence of the bitterness when heirs fight over an inheritance.

C) the challenges and costs of dealing with the funeral industry.

D) the painful recognition of all that the dying leave behind.

12

It can be inferred from the passage that the "dismal traders" (line 14) are

A) undertakers.

B) shopkeepers.

C) famous writers.

D) practical jokers.

13

The phrase "Madison Avenue language" is used by the author of passage 1 to describe language aimed at

A) distracting mourners from the pain of their losses.

B) persuading people to buy things they don't need.

C) evoking the nightmarish aftermath of sudden death.

D) helping people to live graciously even in their suffering.

14

The examples provided in the last paragraph of passage 1 primarily serve to

A) illustrate how many different casket options are available.

B) demonstrate that modern undertakers have a sense of humor.

C) point to some ironies in the way modern funeral trappings are marketed.

D) highlight the extent to which some caskets will delay the decaying of a corpse.

15

The primary purpose of the second passage is to

A) condemn some new practices as ineffective in terms of addressing the escalating costs of funerals.

B) speculate on how Jessica Mitford might respond to the recent changes in the funeral industry.

C) argue that recent cost-cutting measures have had a detrimental effect on how funerals serve the mourners.

D) suggest that the purposes of each step in a funeral be spelled out more clearly.

16

Which choice provides the best evidence for the answer to the previous question?

A) Lines 40–41 ("In the . . . curbed")

B) Lines 49–53 ("True . . . rite")

C) Lines 55–57 ("Believe . . . car")

D) Lines 68–70 ("More . . . wreaths")

17

In line 41, "curbed" most nearly means

A) brought under control.

B) made public.

C) eliminated.

D) allowed to proliferate.

CONTINUE

18

According to the second passage, the excesses of the funeral trade have been changed for the better as a result of the

A) passage of time.

B) institution of services such as drive-in funerals.

C) elimination of flowers and wreaths at services.

D) actions of legislators and trade associations.

19

The author of passage 2 cites the example of "drive-in funerals" (line 55) in order to

A) illustrate the kind of practices that are detrimental to an essential function of funerals.

B) condemn people who consent to mourn this way.

C) demonstrate the ways the funeral industry has changed for the better.

D) rebut claims that the funeral industry has failed to change in the past twenty years.

20

The phrase "in lieu of" (line 69) most nearly means

A) instead of.

B) as well as.

C) because of.

D) in the form of.

21

The authors of both passages are likely to agree that the funeral industry

A) preys on the suffering of the bereaved.

B) is unlikely to change.

C) engages in widespread shoddy practices.

D) was in a troubled state in the 1960s.

Questions 22–31 are based on the following passage.

Scientists, theologians, and lay persons have debated the origins of life on Earth for hundreds of years. The following passage presents one scientist's explanation.

How did the earliest, most primitive, forms of life begin? Let's start with the formation of Earth 4.5 billion years ago. We can allow the first few hundred
Line million years to pass while Earth settles down to more
5 or less its present state. It cools down and squeezes out an ocean and an atmosphere. The surrounding hydrogen is swept away by the solar wind, and the rain of meteors out of which Earth was formed dwindles and virtually ceases.
10 Then, perhaps 4,000 million years ago, Earth is reasonably quiet and the period of "chemical evolution" begins. The first live molecules are small ones made up of two to five atoms each—the simplest form of life we can imagine—a single-strand RNA
15 molecule.

Different scientific theories have been proposed as to how this molecule first came into being. In 1908 the Swedish chemist Svante August Arrhenius theorized that life on Earth began when spores (living, but
20 capable of very long periods of suspended animation) drifted across space for millions of years, perhaps until some landed on our planet and were brought back to active life by its gentle environment.

This is highly dramatic, but even if we imagine
25 that Earth was seeded from another world, which, long, long before, had been seeded from still another world, we must still come back to some period when life began on some world through spontaneous generation—and we may as well assume that this
30 generation began on Earth.

Why not? Even if spontaneous generation does not (or, possibly, cannot) take place on Earth now, conditions on the primordial Earth were so different that what seems a firm rule now may not have been so
35 firm then.

What won't happen spontaneously may well happen if energy is supplied. In the primordial Earth, there were energy sources—volcanic heat, lightning, and most of all, sunshine. At that time, Earth's atmosphere
40 did not contain oxygen, or its derivative, ozone, and the Sun's energetic ultraviolet rays would reach Earth's surface undiluted.

In 1954 a chemistry student, Stanley Lloyd Miller, made a fascinating discovery that shed light on the
45 passage from a substance that is definitely unliving to one that is, in however simple a fashion, alive. He began with a mixture of water, ammonia, methane, and hydrogen (materials he believed to have been present on Earth at its beginning). He made sure his mixture
50 was sterile and had no life of any kind in it. He then circulated it past an electric discharge (to mimic the energy sources roiling the planet at that time). At the end of a week, he analyzed his solution and found that some of its small molecules had been built up to larger
55 ones. Among these larger molecules were glycine and alanine, the two simplest of the twenty amino acids. This was the first proof that organic material could have been formed from the inanimate substances that existed on Earth so long ago.

22

Which choice best reflects the overall sequence of events in the passage?

A) A theory is proposed, tested, and proved to be impossible; an alternative theory is then presented.

B) A difficult question is introduced and the reasons why the question is difficult to answer definitively are explored in some detail.

C) The assertion is made that a scientific conundrum is impossible to answer and several experiments are described as illustration of the futility of tackling the problem.

D) A challenging question is introduced, a theory is set forth, and its key limitation is raised before a second theory is put forward and a related experiment is described.

CONTINUE

23

The author's assertion that "we can allow the first few hundred million years to pass" (lines 3–4) primarily reflects the author's sense that

A) humans have no way to fully measure or comprehend the long history of Earth.

B) it would take far too long to describe to describe the history of Earth in detail.

C) the most relevant aspects of Earth's history for the purposes of the passage are those that emerged about 4 billion years ago.

D) time and tide wait for no man.

24

The author most likely views the theories of Svante August Arrhenius as

A) innovative and daring.

B) dramatic but too elaborate.

C) interesting but unlikely.

D) illogical and impossible.

25

The word "generation" in line 30 most nearly means

A) creation.

B) reproduction.

C) offspring.

D) forebears.

26

It can be inferred that the fact that in primordial times "Earth's atmosphere did not contain oxygen" (lines 39–40) is significant to the author's explanation primarily because

A) without oxygen, human life could not exist.

B) all energy sources produce more intense heat in the absence of oxygen.

C) the question of how oxygen made its way into Earth's atmosphere has not been answered definitively.

D) without oxygen, the atmosphere lacked ozone to block some of the Sun's rays.

27

According to the passage, the "energy" mentioned in lines 36–42 may have been important for which of the following reasons?

A) Sources of energy found at that time produced the oxygen in Earth's atmosphere, which made life possible.

B) This energy may have helped to promote spontaneous generation.

C) It was more powerful than volcanic heat and ultraviolet rays at that time.

D) It mimicked exactly the energy of electric discharge.

28

In line 42, the word "undiluted" most nearly means

A) purified.

B) not weakened.

C) watered down.

D) condensed.

29

The author uses the example of Stanley Lloyd Miller's experiment primarily to

A) introduce the idea that laboratory confirmation of a theoretical possibility exists.

B) suggest the need for further research in the field.

C) speculate about the materials that were present when the Earth was first created.

D) highlight the significance of amino acids in understanding the origins of life.

CONTINUE

Which choice provides the best evidence for the answer to the previous question?

A) Lines 43–46 ("In 1954 . . . alive")

B) Lines 46–49 ("He . . . beginning")

C) Lines 52–55 ("At the . . .ones")

D) Lines 55–56 ("Among . . . acids")

The author's conclusion at the end of the last paragraph would be most directly supported by additional information concerning

A) what other chemical materials were present on Earth 4 billion years ago.

B) what factors might have kept life from emerging earlier.

C) whether other scientists were able to re-create Miller's experiments and achieve similar results.

D) whether the addition of other chemicals into Miller's initial mixture changed the experiment's outcome.

CONTINUE

Questions 32–42 are based on the following passage.

The following passage relates some conclusions the author draws after listening to a seminar speaker denounce some modern conveniences for their negative effects on people's personal lives.

Several weeks ago, when the weather was still fine, I decided to eat my lunch on the upper quad, an expanse of lawn stretching across the north end
Line of campus and hedged in by ancient pine trees on
5 one side and university buildings on the other. Depositing my brown paper lunch bag on the grass beside me, I munched in silence, watching the trees ripple in the wind and musing over the latest in a series of "controversial" symposiums I had attended
10 that morning. The speaker, an antiquated professor in suspenders and a mismatched cardigan, had delivered an earnest diatribe against modern tools of convenience like electronic mail and instant messaging programs. I thought his speech was interesting, but
15 altogether too romantic.

My solitude was broken by two girls, deep in conversation, who approached from behind and sat down on the grass about ten feet to my left. I stared hard at my peanut butter sandwich, trying to not
20 eavesdrop, but their stream of chatter intrigued me. They interrupted each other frequently, paused at the same awkward moments, and responded to each other's statements as if neither one heard what the other said. Confused, I stole a glance at them out
25 of the corner of my eye. I could tell that they were college students by their style of dress and the heavy backpacks sinking into the grass beside them. Their body language and proximity also indicated that they were friends. Instead of talking to each other, however,
30 each one was having a separate dialogue on her cell phone.

As I considered this peculiar scene, this morning's bleary-eyed lecturer again intruded into my thoughts. His point in the symposium was that, aside from the
35 disastrous effects of emails and chatting on the spelling, grammar, and punctuation of the English language, these modern conveniences also considerably affect our personal lives. Before the advent of electronic mail, people wrote letters. Although writing out words by
40 hand posed an inconvenience, it also conferred certain

important advantages. The writer had time to think about his message, about how he could best phrase it in order to help his reader understand him, about how he could convey his emotions without the use of dancing
45 and flashing smiley face icons. When he finished his letter, he had created a permanent work of art to which a hurriedly typed email or abbreviated chat room conversation could never compare. The temporary, impersonal nature of computers, Professor Spectacles
50 concluded, is gradually rendering our lives equally temporary and impersonal.

And what about cell phones? I thought. I have attended classes where students, instead of turning off their cell phones for the duration of the lecture, leave
55 the classroom to take calls without the slightest hint of embarrassment. I have sat in movie theaters and ground my teeth in frustration at the person behind me who can't wait until the movie is over to give his colleague a scene-by-scene replay. And then I watched
60 each girl next to me spend her lunch hour talking to someone else instead of her friend. Like the rest of the world, these two pay a significant price for the benefits of convenience and the added safety of being in constant contact with the world. When they have a
65 cell phone, they are never alone, but then again, *they are never alone.*

They may not recognize it, but those girls, like most of us, could use a moment of solitude. Cell phones make it so easy to reach out and touch someone
70 that they have us confused into thinking that being alone is the same thing as being lonely. It's all right to disconnect from the world every once in a while; in fact, I feel certain that our sanity and identity as humans necessitate it. And I'm starting to think that
75 maybe the Whimsical Professor ranting about his "technological opiates" is not so romantic after all.

CONTINUE ►

32

The structure of the passage overall can best be characterized as

A) a narrative that traces the development of the author's ideas on a topic that is raised by someone the author encounters during the events described.

B) a balanced assessment of a theory that is introduced, considered, and ultimately debunked.

C) a short anecdote followed by the introduction of a theory and the presentation of evidence related to that theory.

D) a consideration of several sides of an issue that is generally understood to be outdated, followed by a conclusion that redefines the terms under discussion.

33

The author's ultimate attitude toward the symposium speaker can best be described as

A) assent tinged with irreverence.

B) puzzlement tinged by scorn.

C) disagreement coupled with dislike.

D) affection bolstered by nostalgia.

34

Which choice provides the best evidence for the answer to the previous question?

A) Lines 10–14 ("The speaker . . . programs")

B) Lines 32–33 ("As I . . . thoughts")

C) Lines 48–51 ("The temporary . . . impersonal")

D) Lines 74–76 ("And I'm . . . all")

35

In the context of the overall passage, the details about the setting in which the author sat to eat lunch serve primarily to

A) paint a picture in the reader's mind.

B) raise the question of whether the same conclusion would have been reached if the author had encountered the two girls in a busier, urban setting.

C) contribute to the author's growing awareness that there is some validity to what is initially portrayed as the speaker's antiquated or overly romantic viewpoint.

D) evoke a sense of an idyllic college campus.

36

The author's decision to use quotation marks around the word "controversial" in line 9 and to italicize the phrase "they are never alone" in lines 65–66 can best be described as

A) a variation in techniques that is intended to keep the reader's interest by avoiding too much repetition.

B) an inconsistency that might have been pointed out by a copyeditor.

C) a matter of personal preference that reinforces the author's whimsical approach to the material.

D) a desire to call the use of one term into question and to suggest an alternative interpretation of the other.

37

The main purpose of the third paragraph is to

A) link the symposium speaker's outdated argument to his age and fatigue.

B) contrast the modern attitudes of the girls on their phones with the antiquated ideas of the symposium speaker.

C) relate the events that occurred after the author encountered the two girls on their cell phones.

D) explain the main points of the symposium speaker's address.

CONTINUE ➡

38

Based on the information in the passage, with which of the following statements about the "dancing and flashing smiley face icons" mentioned in lines 44–45 is the symposium speaker most likely to agree?

A) The use of such icons in anything but the most informal message is inappropriate.

B) The use of such icons might result in less reflection and less attention to the finer points of language selection.

C) Such icons have no place in a work of art.

D) The tendency of such icons to both dance and flash illustrates the exaggerated nature of most computer-facilitated communication.

39

The author provides the instances listed in lines 52–61 primarily as examples of

A) pet peeves that the author believes many other people can relate to.

B) experiences in the author's life that offer support to the symposium speaker's thesis.

C) rude behavior that the previous generation would not have tolerated.

D) occasions that reveal the need for a new etiquette guide to be written for the digital age.

40

What is the "significant price" (line 62) that is paid by the two girls the author observes during lunch?

A) The relatively higher phone bills they pay for using so much data

B) The confusion caused by trying to carry on a phone conversation when surrounded by other people

C) The sacrifice of opportunities for introspection and solitude

D) The awkward pauses that sometimes emerge in phone conversations when one of the participants is distracted

41

Which of the following would be the best title for a speech countering the arguments of the "Whimsical Professor" (line 75)?

A) "The Romance of Written Communication"

B) "Ties That Bind: How Electronic Communication Brings Us Together"

C) "Spelling Reform for the Computer Age"

D) "Too Convenient?: Benefits and Costs of Instant Communication"

42

As used in lines 15 and 76, the word "romantic" most nearly means

A) concerned with expressions of affection and love.

B) having an academic interest in the Romantic period.

C) not directly or practically applicable to current circumstances.

D) not platonic.

CONTINUE

Questions 43–52 are based on the following passage.

Adapted from Bradley J. Phillips, Coronal Mass Ejections: New Research Directions. *Journal of Solar Research, 2009.*

The idea that the sun has an almost unambiguously benign effect on our planet appears, on the surface, to be an incontrovertible one. Few people realize,
Line
however, that certain events on the sun can have
5 disastrous consequences for life here on Earth. The geomagnetic storm is one such phenomenon. These storms begin on the surface of the sun when a group of sunspots creates a burst of electromagnetic radiation. These bursts thrust billions of tons of ionized gas,
10 known as plasma, into space; scientists refer to these solar projections as coronal mass ejections (CMEs). After this initial explosion, the CME gets caught up in a shower of particles, also known as a "solar wind," that continuously rains down on the Earth from the sun.

15 The last recorded instance of a major CME occurred in 1989, when the resulting geomagnetic storm knocked out an entire electrical power grid, depriving over six million energy consumers of power for an extended period. As we become increasingly
20 dependent on new technologies to sustain ourselves in our day-to-day activities, the potential havoc wrought by a major CME becomes even more distressing. Scientists conjecture that a "perfect storm" would have the potential to knock out power grids across the globe
25 and create disruptions in the orbit of low-altitude communication satellites, rendering such satellites practically useless.

What troubles scientists most about these "perfect storms" is not only their potential for interstellar
30 mischief, but also the fact that they are so difficult to forecast. For one thing, remarkable though these solar occurrences might be, they are still a relatively rare phenomenon, and the few existing records regarding major CMEs provide researchers with scant
35 information from which to draw conclusions about their behavior. Solar storm watchers are frustrated by yet another limitation: time. CMEs have been known to travel through space at speeds approaching 5 million miles per hour, which means they can cover the 93
40 million miles between the sun and the Earth in well under 20 hours. (Some have been known to travel the same distance in as little as 14 hours.) The difficulties created by this narrow window of opportunity are compounded by the fact that scientists are able to
45 determine the orientation of a CME's magnetic field only about 30 minutes before it reaches the atmosphere, giving them little or no time to predict the storm's potential impact on the surface.

Some world governments hope to combat this
50 problem by placing a satellite in orbit around the sun to monitor activity on its surface, in the hopes that this will buy scientists more time to predict the occurrence and intensity of geomagnetic storms. In the meantime, many energy providers are responding to the CME
55 threat by installing voltage control equipment and limiting the volume of electricity generated by some power stations.

CONTINUE

Geomagnetic Storm Activity as Measured by Change in Disturbance Storm index (DST)

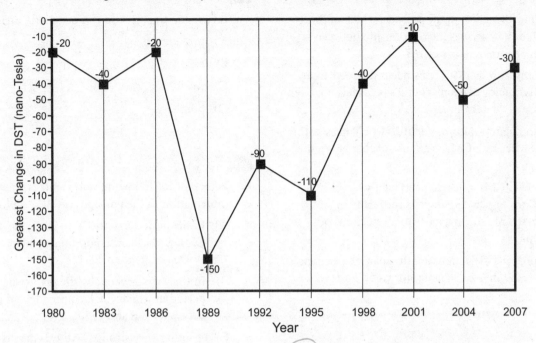

43

Over the course of the passage, the focus shifts from

A) detailing the more positive aspects of an astronomical phenomenon to enumerating the counterbalancing costs of the phenomenon.

B) describing a phenomenon in layman's terms to explaining the same phenomenon in scientific language.

C) introducing a relatively unknown danger to explaining the more challenging aspects of trying to address that danger.

D) warning of the dangers of a new phenomenon to celebrating the steps taken by governments to combat the dangers of that phenomenon.

44

The phrase "almost unambiguously benign" in lines 1–2 describes

A) the effect of the sun on the surface of Earth.

B) a failure to understand the effects of ultraviolet rays.

C) most people's understanding of the effects of the sun on Earth.

D) solar projections that are referred to as coronal mass ejections.

45

With which of the following statements would the author of the passage be most likely to agree?

A) If more people knew about the harm that CMEs might cause, governments would be better able to implement their plans to offset the dangers.

B) The negative effects of CMEs on humans are likely to continue to worsen.

C) Scientists will not be able to overcome the challenges created by the great speed at which CMEs travel.

D) The term *perfect storm* is fittingly ironic when applied to a storm that can cause such immense damage.

46

Which choice provides the best evidence for the answer to the previous question?

A) Lines 3–5 ("Few . . . Earth")

B) Lines 19–22 ("As we . . . distressing")

C) Lines 23–27 ("Scientists . . . useless")

D) Lines 37–41 ("CMEs . . . hours")

CONTINUE

47

Based on information in the passage, which of the following best describes the relationship between CMEs and geomagnetic storms?

A) Scientists know that CMEs occur daily, whereas the frequency of geomagnetic storms has not been accurately determined.

B) A geomagnetic storm is defined by changes in the DST, whereas a CME is a cause of changes in the DST.

C) The term CME refers to particularly large ejections of plasma, whereas the term geomagnetic storm applies to all ejections of plasma.

D) Coronal mass ejections are the solar phenomena that result in geomagnetic storms on Earth.

48

As used in line 44, "compounded by" most nearly means

A) derived from.

B) undone by.

C) combined with.

D) worsened by.

49

According to the passage, some governments seek to address the challenges of predicting when and how a CME will affect Earth by

A) developing a coordinating network of solar storm watchers to ensure that every CME is spotted as soon as it occurs.

B) moving as much as possible of the electrical power grid infrastructure underground.

C) placing a satellite in orbit around the sun.

D) installing voltage control equipment and increasing the volume of electricity generated by some power stations.

50

As used in line 52, "buy" most nearly means

A) provide.

B) earn.

C) waste.

D) purchase.

51

Which of the following statements is consistent with information in the passage and the graph?

A) In the period from 1980 to 2007, the most major CME and its correspondingly bad geomagnetic storm occurred in 2001.

B) In the years covered by the graph, the 6-year period in which CMEs most affected Earth was between 1980 and 1986.

C) Another very strong CME was due to occur in the years between 2007 and 2010.

D) The DST measure is inversely proportional to the strength of geomagnetic storm activity.

52

Which statement is best supported by the data presented in the graph?

A) One troubling aspect of CMEs is the difficulty in predicting when one will occur.

B) CMEs travel through space at speeds that approach 5 million miles per hour.

C) Only a storm as massive as the one that occurred at the end of the 1980s could wreak major havoc on the United States.

D) Scientists are currently able to determine the orientation of a CME's magnetic field less than an hour before the storm reaches Earth's atmosphere.

Chapter 5
Reading Practice Test: Answers and Explanations

READING PRACTICE TEST ANSWERS

44/52

1.	B		27.	B
2.	D		28.	B
3.	C		29.	A
4.	C		30.	A
5.	A		31.	C
6.	A		32.	A
7.	C		33.	A
8.	D		34.	D
9.	A		35.	C
10.	B		36.	D
11.	C		37.	D
12.	A		38.	B
13.	B		39.	B
14.	C		40.	C
15.	C		41.	B
16.	B		42.	C
17.	A		43.	C
18.	D		44.	C
19.	A		45.	B
20.	A		46.	B
21.	D		47.	D
22.	D		48.	D
23.	C		49.	C
24.	C		50.	A
25.	A		51.	D
26.	D		52.	A

EXPLANATIONS FOR THE READING PRACTICE TEST

Passage 1

1. **B**   Question 1 is a general question and is followed by a "best evidence" question, so questions 1 and 2 should be worked together after the specific questions have been tackled. Choice (2A) could support (1C), but the passage overall focuses on the effect of Heller's visit, so the passage does not work to prove the author's estimation of the book. Eliminate (2A). Choice (2B) offers some support for (1D), but the lines do more to note a difference between expectations and reality than to provide *insight* into the contrast. Eliminate (2B). Choice (2C) describes the impression Heller made when he spoke to the students and does not support any of the choices in question 1. Eliminate (2C). Choice (2D) supports (1B), and both reflect the emphasis in the passage on the idea that Heller's visit had an impact on the author. Eliminate (1A), (1C), and (1D), as they are not supported by an answer choice in question 2. The correct answer for question 1 is (B), and the correct answer for question 2 is (D).

2. **D**   See the explanation for question 1.

3. **C**   This question is a little tricky; the key is to eliminate answers that contain details for which no evidence can be located. The description of *Catch-22* is primarily found in the first two paragraphs, so check the answer choices against the details found there. The author does note that the book was *practically an anthem* for his friend and him, but there is no evidence to support the more extreme claim that the book appealed *almost exclusively* to young men (or even that the author's friends were all male). Eliminate (A). The author does note that the book *spoke* to his generation, as they had grown *during the turmoil of Vietnam*, but there is no evidence that Heller's book is a *memoir*, nor does the author explicitly say that *Catch-22* was inspired by the Vietnam War. Eliminate (B). Heller's book features a *modern-day anti-hero* whose action during the book is described as *trying to stay sane in the midst of a war*; there is not additional evidence to show that this action is described realistically or that the main character demonstrates *valor*, so eliminate (D). While (C) might not seem like a strong answer, there is plenty of evidence that the author thinks Heller's novel is brilliant. His conviction 20 years later that his initial assessment of the book was not off base suggests that the book's appeal is not necessarily limited to those directly experiencing the effects of the war. Choice (C) is the correct answer.

4. **C**   The indicated phrase is set off by dashes and, in the context of the sentence, functions as a further commentary on the topic that is mentioned right before the first dash, *the turmoil of Vietnam*. Eliminate (A) and (B), since the phrase is not making reference to the responses of critics or of the author and his friends to *Catch-22*. Eliminate (D) as too broad and also addressing reactions to books rather than reactions to the war. Choice (C) is the only answer that is consistent with the prediction that the indicated phrase comments on the nature of the Vietnam War. Choice (C) is the correct answer.

5. **A**   The quoted lines come at the beginning of the account of Heller's speech and immediately follow the author's explanation that he was *dumbfounded* because Heller had *a very heavy speech impediment*. In the context of the description of the speech, the words serve to emphasize the strength of the author's initial reaction by contrasting his admiration for Heller's book with his sense that Heller was *a dork*. Eliminate (B), as there's no evidence that Heller could overhear the author's comment. Eliminate (C), as there's no evidence in the passage to support the idea that the author's first sentence—*That can't be him*—should be taken literally. The author's comments might add humor as (D) suggests, but a stronger case can be made for (A), which matches the prediction. Eliminate (D). Choice (A) is the correct answer.

6. **A**   This question is the first in a set of specific paired questions, so look in the indicated lines to answer question 6 first. Lines 30–45 describe the adverse initial reaction the author and others in the auditorium had when Heller began speaking. After describing that reaction and the reasons the author reacted as he did, the author describes how the audience's perception shifted: *And then somehow, we began to listen to what he was saying. He was completely brilliant*. The description of the occasion of the speech works to highlight this in attitude. Eliminate (B) as too broad; the author is interested in the effect of Heller's speech, not in the effect of good speakers generally. Choice (C) is also too broad, and there's no evidence elsewhere that the author is trying to *provide a warning*. Eliminate (C). Eliminate (D), as the author is discussing the reaction to Heller's speech, not his book. Choice (A) is consistent with the prediction and is the correct answer.

7. **C**   This question is the second in a set of specific paired questions. The evidence for the answer to question 6 was found in lines 40–41. Choice (C) includes these lines. Eliminate (A), (B), and (D). The correct answer is (C).

8. **D**   This question is tricky and might be easier if saved until questions 9 and 10 have been answered, as the process of answering those questions will provide a better sense of "the passage as a whole." While the author says that he and the rest of the audience were *spellbound* during Heller's speech, there's no evidence that the author's response to the speech made it difficult to move to the gate. Eliminate (A). The author speculates that Heller was held up as he *signed autographs and fielded questions inside the auditorium*, but there's no evidence that others have come out to the gate. Eliminate (B). The author is still in high school when Heller comes to speak, and there's no evidence he served in Vietnam at any time. Eliminate (C). The author says of Heller's speech *I would not have left my seat even if I could*, and that statement coupled with the fact that he is in a wheelchair while he waits for Heller's exit supports the idea that the author was wheelchair-bound. Choice (D) is the correct answer.

9. **A**   The word *fielded* appears in the phrase *signed autographs and fielded questions*. Since the author supposes this is what Heller did after his speech, *fielded* must mean something like *answered* or *responded to*. Choice (A) matches the prediction very well. Eliminate (B), (C), and (D) as there's no evidence that Heller did anything other than interact with his audience as speakers generally do after giving a speech. The correct answer is (A).

10. **B** To answer an inference question, look for the answer that must be true based on what the passage says. There's no evidence that the author had a speech impediment, only that Heller did. Eliminate (A). There's no evidence that the author was afraid that Heller wouldn't respond or that the author anticipated that Heller would not want to deal with another student. Eliminate (C) and (D). There is ample evidence that the author greatly admired both Heller and his book, so (B) is most consistent with what the passage says and is the correct answer.

Passage 2

11. **C** The *sting* referred to in the opening question is echoed in the assertion later in the first paragraph that *many a badly stung survivor faced with the aftermath of some relative's funeral has concluded* that the funeral industry has won the battle. Thus the author is identifying the *sting* of death as the unpleasant aspects of dealing with the funeral industry. Eliminate (A) and (D), as these both refer to the experience of the dying, not the mourners of the dead. While (B) does explicitly mention *heirs*, it focuses on a struggle for inheritance among survivors, not a struggle with the funeral industry. Eliminate (B). Choice (C) matches the prediction and is the correct answer.

12. **A** This question is a bit tricky. The author does not spell out her meaning here, but the blurb notes that the passage is from a book that *takes a hard look at funeral practices* in the 60s. The second paragraph also ends with a reference to the *modern American funeral* and the fourth paragraph begins with a reference to the *funeral men*, so (A), *undertakers*, is most consistent with the structure and subject of the passage overall. The term *traders* could seem to connect with *shopkeepers*, but as *undertakers* also have goods and services to sell, (A) is stronger than (B), and (B) can be eliminated. While three famous authors are mentioned, their names are used as examples of writers who have cast the *dismal traders* in a *comic role in literature*. Eliminate (C). Similarly, while the passage says the dismal traders have perpetrated a practical joke, it also says that this joke is not *consciously conceived of as a joke*, so eliminate (D). The correct answer is (A).

13. **B** This question is also tricky, as it asks about one of the several allusions that the author makes in this passage. The reference to *Madison Avenue* may not trigger any associations, so check the passage to see what characteristics of *Madison Avenue language* are provided. The language is implicated in the creation of a *grotesque cloud-cuckoo-land* (whatever that is) that emphasizes the *trappings of Gracious Dying*. The fifth paragraph provides several illustrations of the kind of language the author is referring to, and the quotations are all examples of appealing language that describes things that are not really necessary. The dead do not need either *long-lasting protection* or elaborate mattresses, and particularly not mattresses intended to address posture issues. While this language might be *distracting* if mourners focused on it, there's no evidence that the language is intended to distract, so eliminate (A). There's no evidence that *sudden* death is of particular concern here, so eliminate (C). The language describes items that one uses only after death, not while dying, so eliminate (D). Choice (B) matches the prediction and is the correct answer.

14. **C**   The work done to answer question 13 helps here. The illustrations in the last paragraph are all examples of items that sound appealing but that are not really necessary. The author signals at the end of the fifth paragraph that she is interested in showing how *Madison Avenue language has seeped into the funeral industry*, which means she's more interested in *how* the items are described than in the range of items available. Eliminate (A). While the descriptions might be funny, there's no evidence the author believes that the funeral industry intends to be funny, so eliminate (B). The issue of delaying decay is raised in some but not all of the examples, so eliminate (D) as not addressing the examples overall. Choice (C) is consistent with the idea demonstrated by all of the examples, which do highlight the strangeness of describing funeral items in terms of benefits that the dead will never need. The correct answer is (C).

15. **C**   This is a general question followed by a "best evidence" question, so treat the questions together as specific paired questions. Choice (16A) does not support any of the choices in question 15, so eliminate (16A). In the lines given in (16B), the author of passage 2 asserts *that in our search for economy and avoidance of discomfort we have weakened a very important family rite*. This works well to support (15C), so keep it. Choices (16C) and (16D) do provide examples of practices that the author raises questions about, but neither is an example of measures that are *ineffective* in addressing escalating funeral costs. Since (16C) and (16D) do not support any of the choices in question 15, they can be eliminated. The only answer choice in 15 that is supported by an answer in 16 is (15C). Eliminate (15A), (15B), and (15D). The correct answer for question 15 is (C), and the correct answer for question 16 is (B).

16. **B**   See the explanation for question 15.

17. **A**   The word *curbed* appears in the statement that *many of the questionable excesses of the funeral trade have been curbed*. This statement is followed by a colon and the explanation that *legislation and self-policing* have brought *some measure of regulation* to the funeral industry. Thus *curbed* must mean something like *reduced* or *made less excessive*. Eliminate (B), (C), and (D), which do not match this prediction. The correct answer is (A).

18. **D**   The work for question 17 makes this question pretty straightforward to answer, since the phrase *questionable excesses of the funeral trade* appears in the lines that were used to answer question 17. The sentence explains that these excesses were curbed by *legislation and self-policing by funeral home associations*. Eliminate (A), (B), and (C), as these choices do not match the prediction; there's no reference to *the passage of time* as a factor, and, while the examples from (B) and (C) are mentioned in the passage, they do not address how the excesses were brought under control. The correct answer is (D).

19. **A**   The author says to *consider the case of one funeral "park"* that offers *drive-in funerals*. The example is provided to illustrate the claim made immediately before it that the *search for economy and avoidance of discomfort* has *weakened a very important family rite*. Choice (A) matches this prediction well. Eliminate (B), as it is not supported in the text and is a potentially offensive answer that a member of the funeral business is especially unlikely to make. The author does acknowledge that

some positive changes have occurred in the funeral industry, but such changes are not being discussed in this paragraph. Eliminate (C). No claims that the funeral industry has not changed are mentioned in the passage, so the author is not *rebutting* them. Eliminate (D). The correct answer is (A).

20. **A** The referenced phrase occurs in the statement that *families will ask that contributions to charity be made in lieu of flowers and wreaths*, which is followed by the point that this occurs without the recognition *that buying flowers provides a chance for friends and relatives to show their concern in a more tangible way than a gift to charity*. Since this opportunity to show tangible concern is not being acknowledged as important, friends and relatives must not have the opportunity to buy flowers and wreaths, so *in lieu of* must mean something like *instead of*. Eliminate (B), (C), and (D), as they do not match this prediction. Choice (A) is the correct answer.

21. **D** The authors of both passages are most likely to agree on a point that each of them makes separately. Look at the answer choices so that you can look for support for the most likely candidate first. Choices (A) and (C) seem unlikely, as a member of the funeral industry is unlikely to make such strong claims, both of which are also inconsistent with the tone of the second passage. Choice (B) can also be eliminated, as the fact that the funeral industry has changed is essential to the argument made in the second passage. Choice (D) seems to be the most likely point upon which both authors agree, and evidence can be found in both passages when the information offered in the blurb is also considered—in the first passage because the author is writing about the negative aspects of the funeral industry in 1963, and in the second because the passage is from the 1980s and the author acknowledges that *many of the questionable excesses of the funeral trade have been curbed* in the last twenty years. Eliminate (A), (B), and (C). Choice (D) is the correct answer.

Passage 3

22. **D** This general question is easier to answer after the more specific questions have been tackled. The passage begins by introducing the question of how life began and noting that numerous theories have been proposed to answer the question. Svante August Arrhenius's proposal is considered and the point is made that the solution ultimately leaves the central question unanswered. A second theory is introduced and Stanley Lloyd Miller's related experiment is described. Eliminate (A), as neither theory that is discussed is *proved to be impossible*. Eliminate (B), as it does not account for the discussion of the two theories. Eliminate (C), as the passage does not state that the question under consideration is *impossible to answer*, only one experiment is described, and that experiment is shown to *shed light* on the origin of life. Choice (D) best matches the prediction and is the correct answer.

23. **C** The passage focuses on the question of how life on Earth arose, and since this occurred *perhaps 4,000 million years ago*, the larger details of the Earth's history prior to this point are less important than the details of what follows. Choices (A) and (B) present ideas that may be true but are not the

primary reason the author does not feel the need to detail the earliest years of Earth's development too thoroughly. Eliminate (D) because while this aphorism may be true, it's not directly relevant to the choices the author makes in terms of how detailed the presented history is. Choice (C) matches the prediction well and is the correct answer.

24. **C** The author presents Arrhenius's theory and then explains why, even if it is true, it still leaves open the question of how life began before it traveled to Earth. While Arrhenius's theory is described as *dramatic*, there is no evidence that the author thinks the theory is *innovative* or *daring*, so eliminate (A). Similarly, (B) can be eliminated, because while *dramatic* is supported, *too elaborate* is not. The author does not rule out the possibility that Arrhenius's theory is valid, so eliminate (D). The author chooses to highlight Arrhenius's theory from among several different theories that have been proposed, which suggests that the author finds the theory *interesting*. The phrase *even if we imagine that the Earth was seeded from another world* suggests that the author does not find the possibility particularly likely, however. Further, the author moves fairly quickly from Arrhenius's theory to another that is more fully elaborated on and that the author seems to find more relevant to the discussion, so the structure of the passage suggests that the author does not find Arrhenius's theory very likely. Choice (C) is best supported by the passage and is the correct answer.

25. **A** The word *generation* appears in the phrase *some period when life began on some world through spontaneous generation*. Since the passage is discussing how life arose from non-living things, the thing that happens spontaneously must be the *creation or beginning of life*. Eliminate (C) and (D), as they refer to a different sense of the word *generation*. Eliminate (B) because if life did not yet exist, it could not be *reproduced*, only *produced*. Choice (A) matches the prediction and is the correct answer.

26. **D** The best evidence for the answer to an inference question is what the passage actually says on the topic. The second half of the sentence that notes that *Earth's atmosphere did not contain oxygen* is the explanation that the lack of oxygen also meant the absence of oxygen's derivative, ozone, and thus that *the Sun's energetic ultraviolet rays would reach Earth's surface undiluted*. Choice (A) might be true, but it does not identify the reason specifically given in the passage, so eliminate it. Choice (B) is extreme and there's no evidence that *all* energy sources produce more heat without oxygen, so eliminate it. Whether (C) is true or not, the issue it addresses is not discussed in the passage, so it, too. Choice (D) matches the prediction well and is the correct answer.

27. **B** The question asks about the energy mentioned in the sixth paragraph, the first sentence of which suggests that something that *won't happen spontaneously may well happen if energy is supplied*. Look to the previous paragraph to see that this is referring to *spontaneous generation*. Eliminate (A), since there's no evidence in the passage that the energy *produced* oxygen. Eliminate (C), as the paragraph states that the energy of the primordial period *included* volcanic heat and ultraviolet rays, not that it was more powerful than those sources. The sixth paragraph does not mention *the energy of electric discharge* at all, so eliminate (D). Choice (B) matches the prediction and is the correct answer.

28. **B** The word *undiluted* appears in the statement that *the Sun's energetic ultraviolet rays would reach Earth's surface undiluted*. Since the reason the Sun's rays reached Earth in this state is that Earth's atmosphere did not contain ozone, the rays reached Earth without being blocked by ozone in the atmosphere. Thus, *undiluted* must mean something like *not blocked* or *unreduced*. Eliminate (A), (C), and (D), as none of them match this prediction. Choice (B), *not weakened*, matches the prediction and is therefore the correct answer.

29. **A** Miller's experiment is discussed in the seventh paragraph and all the answer choices in question 30, a "best evidence" question, come from that paragraph, so the two questions can be treated as specific paired questions. The seventh paragraph opens with the claim that Miller made a discovery that *shed light on the passage from a substance that is definitely unliving to one that is, in however simple a fashion, alive*. This is another way of saying that Miller's discovery showed how life arose from non-living substances. The paragraph's concluding sentence notes that Miller's work was *the first proof that organic material could have been formed from inanimate substances*. Since that formation is the central concern of the passage as a whole, this is likely to be the reason the author discusses Miller's work. Choice (A) best fits with this prediction. Choices (B), (C), and (D) all touch on issues that may be relevant to the topic overall, but not as centrally as (A), which names the primary concern of the passage, so eliminate them. Choice (A) is the correct answer.

30. **A** This is the second question in a set of specific paired questions. The support for the answer in question 29 was found in the first and last sentences of the seventh paragraph. No answer choice covers the last sentence, but (A) does include the first sentence. Eliminate (B), (C), and (D). The correct answer is (A).

31. **C** The author's conclusion at the end of the passage is that Miller's experiment was *the first proof* that the conditions on Earth long ago could have been conducive to the spontaneous generation of life. The best support for the author's conclusion would also backup this *proof*, and that would entail either confirming or expanding upon Miller's findings. Choice (C) directly addresses that issue—if Miller's results were duplicated by others, a conclusion based on Miller's work would be better supported. The other answer choices offer options that might generate interesting information, but they do not equally reinforce the evidence upon with the conclusion is based. Eliminate (A), (B), and (D). Choice (C) is the correct answer.

Passage 4

32. **A** This general question is easier to answer after the more specific questions have been tackled. The passage takes the form of an extended story that traces the author's actions upon reconsidering the author's response to a recently heard speaker. Choice (A) matches this prediction, so keep it. Eliminate (B), as the author ends up thinking that the symposium speaker's argument might have some validity after all, so the theory is not *debunked*. There is no introductory anecdote, as the entire passage is a story of the author's experiences and the thoughts they give rise to, so eliminate (C).

The passage does not have a conclusion that *redefines the terms under discussion*, so eliminate (D). The correct answer is (A).

33. **A** The question asks for the author's *ultimate* attitude toward the symposium speaker, so this and question 34 can be treated as a set of specific paired questions, in which the answer to question 33 will probably be found in the latest mention of the speaker in the passage. (Alternatively, since the answer choices in 34 span the entire passage, these two questions could be worked as a set of general paired questions.) The latest reference to the symposium speaker—both in terms of the development of the author's attitudes and in the layout of the passage—comes in the last line of the passage: *And I'm starting to think that maybe the Whimsical Professor ranting about his "technological opiates" is not so romantic after all*. As before in the passage, the author gives the speaker a nickname that seems gently mocking but which also acknowledges some validity to the speaker's arguments. Choice (A) matches this prediction well. Eliminate (B), as there is no evidence the author is puzzled or feels a negative emotion as strong as scorn. Eliminate (C), since the author no longer rejects the speaker's ideas as absurd and there's no evidence the author dislikes the speaker. Eliminate (D), since the author does not exhibit a sense of nostalgia about the speaker or anything else in the passage. Choice (A) is the correct answer.

34. **D** Since this is the "best evidence" question that pairs with the specific question in 33, look for the answer choice in 34 that includes the lines that were used to predict the answer for 33. This refers to the last sentence of the passage, which is (D); the other three choices can be eliminated.

35. **C** This is a tricky question. Since it asks about the primary purpose of the details *in the context of the overall passage*, the correct answer is likely to be one that shows how those details contribute to the development of the main idea of the passage. Eliminate both (A) and (D), as these answers are more general and there is no indication in the answers of how *painting a picture in the reader's mind* or *evoking a sense of an idyllic college campus* would further the author's development of the main idea. Eliminate (B), since this explanation suggests that the author's main insight could be simply a product of a particular place rather than a generally applicable idea. Choice (C) suggests how the details in the first paragraph might contribute to the main idea overall, and even if it seems like a weak answer choice, it is more readily supported by the text than any other choice. The correct answer is (C).

36. **D** Consider the roles that punctuation and italics play in the referenced lines. Since there is no indication in line 10 that the quotation marks around *controversial* are intended to signal that the word is a quotation, the most likely explanation is that the author is using the term with reservation—that is, that the author did not actually think the symposium was actually controversial. This idea is reinforced by the summation, *I thought the speech was interesting, but altogether too romantic*. The second referenced line has a structure that suggests that two opposing ideas will be presented, as in *they are never very happy, but then again, they are never very sad either*. Since the two ideas that are presented are actually the same phrase used twice, the italics are likely intended to indicate that the second use of the phrase *they are never alone* is different from the first. Eliminate (A) and (B), since the prediction provides a better explanation for the use of both quotation marks and italics than

the need for variation or an error. Choice (C) also does not match the prediction, as there's no evidence that the author has a *whimsical* attitude toward the passage's main idea. Choice (D) matches the prediction and is the correct answer.

37. **D** The third paragraph is devoted to an account of the symposium speaker's argument. Eliminate (A), as the only details that relate to the speaker's *age and fatigue* come in the first sentence, so this answer doesn't account for the whole paragraph. Also eliminate (B), for while a contrast may exist between the speaker and the girls on their cell phones, the passage is devoted to detailing the speaker's ideas, not contrasting those ideas with the attitudes of the girls on their cell phones. Eliminate (C), as the author listened to the speaker in the morning and encountered the girls while eating lunch afterward, so the answer reverses the order of events. Choice (D) accounts for the whole paragraph, matches the prediction, and is the correct answer.

38. **B** When the task is to identify with which statement someone will most likely agree, the answer that repeats or rephrases something the person actually said will be the best supported choice. Check the answers against the comments that are attributed to the symposium speaker to see which best matches what the symposium speaker said. Eliminate (A), since there is no evidence the speaker distinguished between appropriate and inappropriate use of the icons. Eliminate (C) as extreme, since the speaker does not make such a strong proclamation about the use of icons. Eliminate (D), since the speaker does not remark on the separate functions of dancing and flashing. Choice (B) is consistent with the speaker's assertion that a letter-writer had *time to think about his message* and *about how to phrase it*. The correct answer is (B).

39. **B** The beginning of the fourth paragraph—*And what about cell phones? I thought*—signals a transition from the summation of the symposium speaker's ideas to the author's own efforts to consider personal experiences in light of the speaker's larger claims. Eliminate (C), as there's no evidence the author believes people from a generation ago would not have tolerated the behavior. Eliminate (D), as there's no evidence the author believes a new etiquette book should be written. Eliminate (A), as this answer does not provide a connection to the ideas the speaker raised. Choice (B) matches the prediction and is the correct answer.

40. **C** The author's point in the referenced sentence is spelled out in the first sentence of the fifth paragraph: *those girls, like most of us, could use a moment of solitude*. The *significant price* the girls pay is that *they are never alone*, which, the author elaborates, contributes to the confused thinking that *being alone is the same thing as being lonely*. The author also asserts that *disconnecting* from the world for a while is necessary for *our sanity and our identity as humans*. Eliminate (A), (B), and (D), as these are too literal interpretations of the downsides of using cell phones frequently, in public, and while doing other things. Choice (C) is most consistent with the prediction and is the correct answer.

41. **B** *The Whimsical Professor* is one of the nicknames the author bestows on the symposium speaker. The speaker's argument is summarized in the third paragraph, which offers the speaker's conclusion as: *The temporary, impersonal nature of computers is gradually rendering our own lives equally temporary*

and impersonal. The best counter to the speaker's claim would need to show why computers are not, in fact, rendering our own lives equally temporary and impersonal. Eliminate (A), as a speech with this title might actually reinforce the speaker's ideas. Eliminate (C), since no indication is given of how a speech with that title would address the issue of spelling nor that a decline in spelling standards makes our lives *temporary and impersonal.* Eliminate (D), since that title suggests that both sides of the debate will be addressed in a speech of that title; by contrast, the title in (B) clearly signals that the positive aspects of computer use will be discussed. Choice (B) matches the prediction by countering the speaker's negative conclusion with a positive thesis and is therefore the correct answer.

42. **C** The initial portrayal of the speaker, whose ideas are characterized by the author as *altogether too romantic,* suggests the speaker is out-of-step with the world around him—he is *antiquated,* wears mismatched clothes, rails *earnestly* against modern conveniences, and even uses the clunky-sounding *electronic mail* instead of its more common shorter form, email. By the end of the passage, when the term *romantic* is used again, the speaker has come to believe that the speaker is *not so romantic after all,* which reinforces the idea that the author uses *romantic* to mean *not fully relevant* or *not very applicable to modern life.* Eliminate (A), (B), and (D) as accepted definitions of *romantic* that do not fit this particular context. Choice (C) matches the prediction well and is the correct answer.

Passage Five

43. **C** This is a general question, and as such is probably easier to answer after the more specific questions have been tackled. The passage begins by asserting that few people *realize that certain events on the sun can have disastrous consequences* on Earth. After explaining how the events or CMEs can affect life on Earth, the passage addresses the difficulty in forecasting CMEs and how some on Earth are responding to the problems associated with them. Eliminate (A), as the passage does not *detail* the positive effects of CMEs. While the passage does say that CME is the term used by scientists to denote solar projections, it does not explain the phenomenon twice using two different kinds of terms; eliminate (B). There's no evidence in the passage that CMEs are *new* or that the author is issuing a warning, so eliminate (D). Choice (C) matches the prediction well and is the correct answer.

44. **C** The indicated phrase occurs in the first paragraph in a sentence that might require a little untangling. The sentence that immediately follows the referenced line can provide useful context, as it is more straightforward: *Few people realize, however, that certain events on the sun can have disastrous consequences for life here on Earth.* The *however* indicates that the idea that the sun can have disastrous effects on Earth contrasts with the information provided in the first sentence, so the first sentence must indicate that people don't usually think the sun affects the Earth adversely. This suggests that the phrase *almost unambiguously benign* refers to the opinion most people have of the effects of the sun on Earth. Eliminate (B) and (D), as neither addresses the issue of what people think of the sun. When (A) and (C) are compared, (C) is the stronger answer that better matches

the prediction; (A) incorporates a misreading of the phrase *on the surface*, which functions like the phrase *at first glance* in this context and does not literally refer to Earth's surface. Eliminate (A). The correct answer is (C).

45. **B** This question is a general question that is followed by a "best evidence" question whose answer choices are drawn from the whole of the passage, so questions 45 and 46 can be worked as a set of general paired questions. Choice (46A) does address the issue of how many people know about the potential that CMEs have to cause problems on Earth, but the indicated lines do not address governmental plans. Eliminate (46A) or mark its connection to (45A) as weak. Choice (46B) explicitly connects increasing dependence on new technologies to an increase in the potential havoc a major CME could cause. This answer offers strong support for (45B). Choice (46C) explains what scientists conjecture about a *perfect storm*, but the author does not draw attention to any ironies that might exist in the application of the term; thus while (46C) might offer some support to (45D), the support is not as strong as that offered by (46B) for (45B). Eliminate (46C). Choice (46D) does explain the high speeds at which CMEs travel but there is no indication the author believes the difficulties caused by such speeds will not be overcome at any point in the future. Eliminate (46D). Eliminate (45A), (45C), and (45D), as none is as well-supported as (45B) is by (46B). The correct answer for question 45 is (B), and the correct answer for question 46 is (B).

46. **B** See the explanation for the previous question.

47. **D** The term *geomagnetic storm* can be used as a lead word to locate the introduction of that the term in line 6; CMEs are explained later in the first paragraph, so look there to see which answer choice is supported by the passage. There is no mention of the frequency of either phenomenon, so eliminate (A). The relationship between DST and CMEs is not addressed, so eliminate (B). The passage does not clarify if the relative size of plasma ejections affects which term is applied when, so eliminate (C). The passage explains that CMEs are ejections of plasma from the sun's surface and the first sentence of the second paragraph refers to the *last major CME* and explains the effects of *the resulting geomagnetic storm*. These details are consistent with the explanation offered in (D). Thus, the correct answer is (D).

48. **D** The words *compounded by* occur in the following phrase: *The difficulties created by this narrow window of opportunity are compounded by the fact that....* The rest of the sentence goes on to describe a second factor that severely limits the time scientists have to analyze and formulate responses to a major CME. Thus *compounded by* must mean something like *complicated by* or *made even more difficult by*. Eliminate (A) and (B), which do not match the prediction at all, and (C), which does not match the prediction as well as (D) does. Choice (D) is the correct answer.

49. **C** Chronology and the use of *governments* as a lead word help to locate the reference to how some *world governments hope to combat this problem by placing a satellite in orbit around the sun* at the start of the final paragraph. The previous paragraph describes the challenges of trying to predict a geomagnetic storm's impact, so the problem the governments want to use a satellite to combat

is the problem specified in the question. Eliminate (A) and (B), as these options do not match the prediction and are not discussed anywhere in the passage. Eliminate (D) because while the attempted solutions described are mentioned in the passage, these are steps taken—by *energy providers*—to minimize the effects of a CME, not steps taken to provide more time in which to analyze and respond to a CME. Choice (C) matches the prediction and is the correct answer.

50. **A** The word *buy* occurs in the phrase *in the hopes that this will buy scientists more time to predict the occurrence and intensity of geomagnetic storms.* Since a major difficulty with geomagnetic storms is the very short window in which scientists can try to analyze a CME once it occurs, the benefit of placing a satellite in orbit around the sun would be that data about the CME would be available earlier in that window. Thus in this context, *buy* must mean something like *offer to* or *gain*. Eliminate (C) as it is not relevant in this context. Eliminate (D) as a too literal definition of *buy* that also does not fit in this context. Between (A) and (B), (A) better matches the prediction, while (B) introduces a suggestion of *deserving* or *being entitled to* that does not suit the context as well. Eliminate (B). The correct answer is (A).

51. **D** The question asks for the answer that is *consistent* with information in the passage and graph, so check the answer choices to determine which one doesn't contradict the passage and graph. Choice (A) might initially seem consistent with the graph, since the year 2001 features the highest plotted point on the graph (at −10). The start of the second paragraph, however, refers to the *last recorded instance of a major CME,* which *occurred in 1989* and resulted in a geomagnetic storm that caused very large-scale problems. Furthermore, if 1989 contained such a significant CME, then it seems very unlikely that a relatively high value on the vertical axis signals a great deal of geomagnetic storm activity. Eliminate (A), since the last major CME occurred in 1989, not 2001. Eliminate (B), since lower, not higher, relative values on the vertical axis seem to indicate greater geomagnetic storm activity. Eliminate (C), as the start of the third paragraph notes that *perfect storms,* or storms with the potential to cause massive disruptions on Earth, are *difficult to forecast,* so the graph is unlikely to provide any basis for making a prediction about when the next major CME would occur. Choice (D) is consistent with the passage and graph, which together suggest an inverse relationship between DST measure and the strength of geomagnetic storm activity. Choice (D) is the correct answer.

52. **A** The question asks which statement is best supported by the data in the graph, so look for an answer choice that agrees with or at least does not contradict the graph. Choice (A) is consistent with the apparently random pattern of activity that the graph shows, so keep it. Choice (B), like (A), paraphrases information provided in the passage; however, the speed of CMEs is not addressed by the graph, so eliminate (B). The graph also does not support the extreme claim made in (C), nor does it address the factors that result in a storm causing damage. Eliminate (C). Choice (D) also paraphrases information given in the passage, but the timeframe for determining the orientation of a CME's magnetic field is not addressed by the graph. Eliminate (D). Choice (A) is the correct answer.

Chapter 6
Writing and Language

GRAMMAR

Quick—identify the correlative conjunction in the nonrestrictive clause in the following sentence:

1. Just kidding!

You can relax now; the grammar tested on the SAT is not going to be that difficult. Instead, the writing and language section requires you to know only a few basic rules. ETS and The College Board will test these rules with two basic types of questions: Proofreader questions and Editor questions.

Proofreader Questions

Proofreader questions on the SAT look like this:

The history of 1 language although it may sound like a boring subject, is a treasure trove of historical, cultural, and psychological insights.

1

A) NO CHANGE

B) language, although it may sound like a boring subject

C) language, although it may sound, like a boring subject,

D) language, although it may sound like a boring subject,

Most students make the mistake of reading the sentence four times, with each of the answers substituted in, and trying to figure out what sounds wrong. However, this is not a very safe or efficient way of tackling these problems. Notice how all of the answers are virtually identical. The ONLY difference is in the placement of commas. So, rather than reading the sentence over and over again, go straight to the answers! Ask yourself, "What's changing?" (In case you're curious, (D) is the answer.)

Note that about 25 percent of these questions require "NO CHANGE" and generally don't have a question stem.

Editor Questions

Editor questions on the SAT look like this:

The problem has certainly gained a good deal of traction in public debates. The fact that it has gained such traction makes us wonder why isn't there more significant action to combat the gender pay gap. **2**

2

Which of the following gives the best way to combine these two sentences?

A) The problem has certainly gained a good deal of traction in public debates; the fact that it has gained such traction makes us wonder why isn't there more significant action to combat the gender pay gap.

B) The problem has certainly gained a good deal of traction in public debates, which raises the question of why more isn't being done to combat the gap.

C) The problem has certainly gained a good deal of traction in public debates: this fact of more public attention raises a serious question of why more isn't being done to close that gap.

D) The problem has certainly gained a good deal of traction in public debates. Why isn't more being done to combat the gap?

While Proofreader questions have an implied question, Editor questions actually do have a question stem. This one asks us to combine the two sentences. Choice (B) is correct. It combines the sentences and shortens them a bit, unlike (A) and (C), which combine the sentences but don't really do much beyond changing the punctuation, and (D), which doesn't combine the sentences at all.

THE PRINCETON REVIEW METHOD

Step One

Familiarize yourself with the most commonly tested grammatical errors. The College Board tests only a handful of errors. Once you learn these rules and become comfortable with them, keep your eyes peeled for them on the test.

Step Two

Make aggressive use of the Process of Elimination. If you're not sure what the right answer is, find and eliminate any answers you know to be wrong. Learn what the College Board considers "good" writing.

COMMON GRAMMATICAL ERRORS

Pronoun Errors

Pronouns are one of the College Board's favorite grammar subjects to test. When you see a pronoun underlined, check to see if it is **consistent** with the noun it replaces.

Remember: The following pronouns are always singular:

> Any pronoun ending in -one (anyone, someone, everyone)
>
> Any pronoun ending in -body (anybody, nobody, somebody)
>
> Any pronoun ending in -thing (anything, nothing, something)
>
> each
>
> much

Also check pronouns for **ambiguity**. The following sentence is grammatically incorrect:

Successful athletes pay attention to their coaches because they know the value of experience.

Who does "they" refer to, the coaches or the athletes? If you can't tell, then the pronoun is ambiguous.

The College Board might test pronoun **case**, especially who vs. whom. This topic isn't nearly as difficult as you think. Here's a simple rule:

Whenever you would normally use *he*, *she*, or *they*, use *who*.

Example: Who stole my car keys? (She stole my car keys.)

Whenever you would normally use *him*, *her*, or *them*, use *whom*.

Example: To whom should I mail this letter? (I should mail this letter to him.)

Quick Quiz #1

If it is raining on Sunday, each of the children will bring **1** their umbrella to the picnic.

1

A) NO CHANGE
B) his or her
C) one's
D) our

Many photographers are coming to believe **2** that color prints are as artistic as black and white ones because they reveal new definitions of art.

2

A) NO CHANGE

B) which color prints are as artistic as black and white ones because they reveal new definitions of art.

C) that color prints are as artistically as black and white ones because the black and white prints reveal new definitions of art.

D) that color prints are as artistic as black and white ones because color prints reveal new definitions of art.

Roller blades [3] may or may not be superior to roller skates; after all, they've been providing fun and exercise to generations of skaters since the 1860s.

[3]

A) NO CHANGE

B) may or might not be superior to roller skates; after all, they've been providing fun and exercise to many skaters

C) may or may not be superior to roller skates, after all, they've been providing fun and exercise to generations of skaters

D) may or may not be superior to roller skates; after all, roller skates have been providing fun and exercise to generations of skaters

While many cooking experts hold that the only proper way to bake a potato is in a conventional oven, others contend that cooking [4] them in a microwave is a perfectly acceptable alternative.

[4]

A) NO CHANGE

B) it

C) they

D) those

If school is cancelled on Wednesday, we can't decide with [5] who Sheila should spend her day.

[5]

A) NO CHANGE

B) whom

C) that

D) she

Answers and Explanations: Quick Quiz #1

1. **B** Always check underlined pronouns for ambiguity and consistency errors. The issue here is **pronoun consistency**. "Each" is always singular, which means that you need the singular pronoun "his or her" instead of "them."

2. **D** This is a pronoun **ambiguity** question because "they" could refer to photographers, color prints, or black and white prints. Only (D) clarifies this ambiguity. Choice (C) is wrong because of the misuse of "artistically."

3. **D** **Ambiguity** again. "They" could refer to roller blades or roller skates. Only (D) clarifies that roller skates have been around for such a long time.

4. **B** Remember to check pronouns for **consistency** with the nouns they replace. The pronoun "them" (plural) refers to the noun "potato" (singular). You can't EVER mix a singular with a plural. The singular form we need is "it."

5. **B** Sheila should spend her day with *him* (not *he*), so *whom* is the proper substitute.

Verb Errors

When you see a verb underlined, check to make sure it is **consistent** with its subject. Also, make sure all the verbs in the sentence are in the proper **tense**.

Quick Quiz #2

Last year, as in years past, the majority of candidates **1** are dropping out of the race before the actual election because they no longer had the funds or the will to campaign.

1

A) NO CHANGE

B) is dropping

C) dropped

D) drop

Restrictions on one of the committees that **2** monitors corporate waste disposal were revoked, allowing the committee to levy fines on violators of the disposal laws.

2

A) NO CHANGE

B) monitor

C) monitoring

D) will monitor

3 The Lipizzaner, a breed of horses that nearly went extinct at the end of World War II, are featured in performances at the Hofburg Palace in Vienna.

3

A) NO CHANGE

B) The Lipizzaner, a breed of horses that nearly went extinct at the end of World War II, is featured

C) Lipizzaners, a breed of horses that nearly went extinct at the end of World War II, is featured

D) The Lipizzaner, a breed of horses that nearly went extinct at the end of World War II; as such it is featured

Answers and Explanations: Quick Quiz #2

1. **C** The sentence is in the past **tense**, as indicated by "last year." The remaining answers are wrong because they are in the present tense.

2. **A** **Consistency**: The verb "monitors" is singular, while "one" of the committees, the subject of the verb, is also singular. Please note that prepositional phrases such as "of the committees" are almost always irrelevant and are designed to trick your ear!

3. **B** **Consistency**: The subject in the original is "Lipizzaner," which takes a singular verb but is paired here with "are." Eliminate (A). Choice (C) changes the verb from "are" to "is," but it also changes the subject from "The Lipizzaner" to "Lipizzaners," which makes for an incorrect subject-verb pairing. Eliminate (C). Choice (D) has the right subject-verb pairing but incorrectly introduces a semi-colon, so eliminate (D). Choice (B) is the correct answer, as it pairs "The Lipizzaner" with "is" and the singular subject matches well with the phrase "a breed" that refers back to it.

Other Common Errors

Misplaced Modifiers

A misplaced modifier is a phrase that modifies something other than what is intended. Take a look at the following sentence:

Running down the street, a brick fell on my head.

In this sentence, the modifier is "running down the street," but the noun directly after it is "a brick." It appears that the brick is running down the street, not the person. Make sure your modifiers refer to the correct noun.

This sentence should be rewritten as something like this:

As I was running down the street, a brick fell on my head.

Parallel Construction

When making a list of items, make sure all parts of the list are in the same form. The following sentence is incorrect:

Ricky wanted to finish his homework, take a walk, and to be in bed by ten o'clock.

The correct form would be the following:

Ricky wanted to finish his homework, take a walk, and be in bed by ten o'clock.

If you are making a **comparison**, make sure the two things being compared are similar.

John's drumming style is more explosive than Keith.

This sentence is incorrect because it compares John's drumming style to Keith. You should compare John's drumming style to Keith's drumming style.

Quick Quiz #3

Highly sociable animals living in pods that are fairly fluid, dolphin interactions with dolphins from other pods is fairly common.

1

A) NO CHANGE

B) dolphins commonly interact with dolphins from other pods.

C) dolphins interacts commonly with dolphins from other pods.

D) dolphin interactions with dolphins from other pods are a common phenomenon.

Signed in Mexico City on February 2,1848, 2 the boundaries of the United States were extended by The Treaty of Guadalupe Hidalgo.

2

A) NO CHANGE

B) the United States boundaries were extended by the Treaty of Guadalupe Hidalgo

C) the United States extended its boundaries by the Treaty of Guadalupe Hidalgo

D) the Treaty of Guadalupe Hidalgo extended the boundaries of the United States

The language of the West Virginians in Appalachia is almost nothing like 3 New Yorkers or even other West Virginians.

4 Covered with colorful flowers, one of the other visitors noticed my fascination with Monet's *Water Lilies – Setting Sun*.

3
A) NO CHANGE
B) the language of New Yorker's or even other West Virginian's.
C) that of New Yorkers or even other West Virginians.
D) people from New York or from West Virginia.

4
A) NO CHANGE
B) Another visitor covered with colorful flowers, noticed my fascination with Monet's *Water Lilies – Setting Sun*.
C) Another visitor covered with colorful flowers noticed my fascination with Monet's *Water Lilies – Setting Sun*.
D) Another visitor noticed my fascination with Monet's *Water Lilies – Setting Sun*, a painting whose whole canvas was covered with colorful flowers.

Answers and Explanations: Quick Quiz #3

1. **B**   The original sentence contains a **misplaced modifier**; dolphin interactions are not highly sociable animals, and "interactions" is plural, so the verb "are" (not "is") should be used. Choice (D) repeats the misplaced modifier error, so eliminate it. In (C), while the modifier issue is resolved, "interacts" is the incorrect verb to pair with "dolphins." The correct answer is (B).

2. **D**   **Misplaced modifier**: In this sentence, the modifying phrase is "Signed in Mexico City on February 2, 1848." However, the noun directly following it is "the boundaries of the United States." Clearly, the boundaries weren't signed in 1848. Eliminate (A), (B), and (C). The correct answer is (D). (Give yourself a pat on the back if you noticed (B)'s lack of an apostrophe after "United States.")

3. **C**   Look at what's changing in the answer choices. It looks like the main change is between the nouns—New Yorkers or even other West Virginians—and the language. When nouns are changing in the answer choices, make sure those nouns are **consistent** with other nouns in the sentence. In this case, the nouns are being **compared**. The language of Appalachia is being compared with the language of New Yorkers and West Virginians. Choices (A) and (D) suggest that the language is being compared with the people, so these are inconsistent. Choice (B) contains some incorrect apostrophes, which leaves (C) as the correct answer.

4. **D**   This time, the changes in the answer choices pertain to the placement of "covered with colorful flowers." This refers to Monet's painting, not another visitor, so (D) is the only logical choice. Remember, when it comes to **misplaced modifiers** or bad comparisons, the location of the phrase is crucial: it must be next to whatever it's describing.

Now let's take a closer look at some other grammar issues that you will be sure to see in Writing and Language questions:

PUNCTUATION

When you are linking ideas,

STOP
- Period
- Semicolon
- Comma + FANBOYS
- Question mark
- Exclamation Mark

HALF-STOP
- Colon
- Long dash

GO
- Comma
- No punctuation

FANBOYS stands for **F**or, **A**nd, **N**or, **B**ut, **O**r, **Y**et, and **S**o.

STOP punctuation can link *only* complete ideas.

HALF-STOP punctuation must be *preceded* by a complete idea.

GO punctuation can link anything *except* two complete ideas.

Jonah, the valedictorian of his senior class, believes that only one factor contributed to his success in school; his commitment to hard work.

A) NO CHANGE
B) school; and it was
C) school:
D) school: being

As always, check what's changing in the answer choices. In this case, the words vary somewhat, but notice the types of punctuation that are changing: STOP and GO.

Now, when you see STOP punctuation changing in the answer choices, you can do a little something we like to call the Vertical Line Test.

Draw a line where you see the punctuation changing—in this case, between the words *school* and *his*. Then, read up to the vertical line: *Jonah believes that only one factor contributed to his success in school.* That's complete. Now, read after the vertical line: *his commitment to hard work.* That's NOT complete.

So let's think; we do not have two complete ideas here. What kind of punctuation is WRONG? STOP. Eliminate (A) and (B). In (D), the word *being* is unnecessary and wordy. Choice (C) is the correct answer.

Let's try another:

It was a top priority for Jonah to do well in **2** school by his love of friends, family, and sports were just as important.

2

A) NO CHANGE

B) school, but his

C) school: his

D) school, whereas

Check the answer choices. What's changing? Punctuation, except this time it does not appear in the original sentence. Sometimes we need to consider the meaning of the sentence in addition to STOP and GO.

It was a top priority for Jonah to do well in school is complete. Then, *his love of friends, family, and sports were just as important* is complete, too. Therefore, because we have one complete idea (the first) and another complete idea (the second), we can use STOP or HALF-STOP punctuation. (Remember the FANBOYS!)

So, what's the real difference between the answers? Notice that the two ideas in this sentence are competing (school vs. other pursuits). So we need a word that provides a clear transition between the two concepts. Only (B) does this.

Let's see one more:

Admittedly, advanced planning and time management, two necessary characteristics of high **3** achievers, have also been the cornerstones of Jonah's high school success story.

3

A) NO CHANGE

B) achievers—

C) achievers;

D) achievers

The punctuation is changing in the answer choices, and there's some STOP punctuation, so let's use the Vertical Line Test. Put the line between *achievers* and *have*. The first idea, *Admittedly, advanced planning and time management, two necessary characteristics of high achievers*, is incomplete, and the second idea, *have also been the cornerstones of Jonah's high school success story* is incomplete. Therefore, we can't use STOP (which needs two complete ideas) or HALF-STOP (which needs a complete idea before the punctuation), thus eliminating (B) and (C). Do you need the comma after *achievers*? Since achievers is part of the phrase *two necessary characteristics of high achievers* and that phrase is NOT necessary to the sentence, you'll need commas surrounding it. When ideas do not add necessary meaning to the sentence, always separate them with two commas or dashes. Therefore, (A) is the correct answer.

COMMAS

On the SAT, there are only four reasons to use a comma:

- in STOP punctuation, with one of the FANBOYS
- in GO punctuation, to separate incomplete ideas from other ideas
- in a list of three or more things
- in a sentence containing unnecessary information

If you can't cite a reason to use a comma, *don't use one.*

We've already seen the first two concepts, so let's look at the other two.

Try this one.

Environmentalists,

4 consumers; and government officials are all working together to develop new solutions to pollution problems.

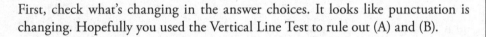

A) NO CHANGE

B) consumers: and

C) consumers, and

D) consumers, and,

First, check what's changing in the answer choices. It looks like punctuation is changing. Hopefully you used the Vertical Line Test to rule out (A) and (B).

The grammatical rule you need to know here is that the SAT expects a comma after every item in a series. That's because there is a potential for ambiguity when this punctuation isn't used:

I went to the park with my parents, my cat Violet and my dog Stuart.

If there's no comma, how do we know that this sentence isn't supposed to say his parents are *my cat Violet and my dog Stuart?* The only way to clear things up would be to add a comma like this:

I went to the park with my parents, my cat Violet, and my dog Stuart.

Keep that in mind as we try to crack number 4. In this problem, *Environmentalists, consumers, and government officials* form a list, so they should be set off by commas as they are in (C). You almost never use a comma after *and*, so eliminate (D).

Let's try another:

5 Jonah, the valedictorian of his senior class believes that only one factor contributed to his success in school: his commitment to hard work.

5
A) NO CHANGE
B) Jonah the valedictorian of his senior class,
C) Jonah, the valedictorian of his senior class,
D) Jonah, the valedictorian, of his senior class

First, check what's changing in the answer choices. Just commas, and those commas seem to be circling around the words *the valedictorian of his senior class*. When you've got a few commas circling around a word, phrase, or clause like this, the question is usually looking to see if there's unnecessary information.

A good way to test whether an idea is necessary to the meaning of the sentence is to take it out. Read the original sentence again. Now read this one: *Jonah believes that only one factor contributed to his success in school: his commitment to hard work.*

Is the sentence still complete? Yes. Has the meaning of the sentence changed? No, we just lost an extra detail. Therefore, the idea is *unnecessary* to the meaning of the sentence and should be set off with commas as it is in (C). Answer (D) has an unnecessary comma. Remember, if you can't find a reason to use a comma, don't!

APOSTROPHES

As with commas, if you can't cite a reason to use an apostrophe, don't use one. There are only two reasons to use apostrophes on the SAT:

- Possessive nouns (NOT pronouns)
- Contractions

Let's see some examples.

Commercial farming often results in excess fertilizer use, which **6** can pollute nearby ponds, resulting in an overgrowth of algae.

6
A) NO CHANGE
B) can pollute nearby pond's,
C) could have polluted nearby ponds,
D) has polluted nearby pond's,

Check what's changing in the answer choices. There are a few shifts in tense, but for the most part, the apostrophes are what are changing. Remember: We don't want to use apostrophes at all if we can't cite a good reason to do so.

Does anything belong to *ponds*? No! Is this supposed to be a contraction, like *pond is?* No! Therefore, there's no reason to use apostrophes, so eliminate (B) and (D). Choice (C) changes the tense, and thus the meaning, of the sentence, so it's also wrong, leaving (A) as the correct answer.

In this case, the College Board is testing whether you can spot unnecessary punctuation. Sometimes they will check the opposite: that is, when apostrophes are necessary.

The first time I visited the museum, I couldn't wait to view **7** painter, Andrew Wyeth's, *Christina's World.*

7

A) NO CHANGE

B) painter, Andrew Wyeths

C) painter Andrew Wyeths

D) painter Andrew Wyeth's

Check what's changing in the answer choices. The main changes have to do with apostrophes and commas.

Andrew Wyeth's needs an apostrophe: It's his painting. So, get rid of (B) and (C). As for the comma, remember the rule about necessary information. If *Andrew Wyeth's* is removed from the sentence, we lose a crucial part of the meaning. Therefore, do NOT use commas around this phrase. Choose (D).

Transition Words

When the College Board underlines a conjunction, they are testing you on the meaning of two different sentences or clauses and are expecting you to choose the transition word that best joins the two ideas together, either by keeping the ideas similar or showing a contrast. Here is a list of some common conjunctions:

Keeps the ideas similar:	*Shows a contrast:*
And	Although / Though / Even though
Since	However
In fact	Yet
Therefore	But
Thus	Rather
So	In contrast to
Also	Despite
As well as	Unlike
Moreover	Instead
Consequently	Nevertheless
Hence	Nonetheless
Finally	Notwithstanding
Subsequently	Alternatively
In addition	
Likewise	

Try this example:

Dark chocolate contains less sugar and fewer calories than milk chocolate. **8** Also, because it contains more antioxidants, it may help to prevent heart disease.

8

A) NO CHANGE

B) However,

C) Although,

D) For example,

It sounds like dark chocolate is pretty wonderful, right? Less sugar and fewer calories are both positive things. Reading what comes after the conjunction, we see that dark chocolate also contains antioxidants that may prevent heart disease, another positive. We need something that keeps the flow of ideas similar. Both (B) and (C) would indicate a shift or contrast, and (D) doesn't make sense, so eliminate those three and you're left with the correct answer, (A).

NUANCES

The College Board may also test your knowledge of a few other grammatical instances. If you don't spot a pronoun, verb, or punctuation error, check for the following.

Idioms

Idioms are specific arrangements of words that convey a certain meaning. For example, the phrase "responsible for" is an idiom; you wouldn't say "responsible of." If you see a preposition underlined, check to see if it's used idiomatically.

Diction

Diction errors are errors in word choice. These are not hard to spot, because you will see single words with similar meanings. Your job is to choose the word with the best **precision** given the meaning of the sentence.

For a specific list of tricky words and phrases to look out for, please see the Appendix on Prepositions and Idioms at the back of the book.

Commonly Misused Words

Their is possessive (*their* house).
There indicates location (my cat is over *there*).
They're means *they are*.

Its is possessive (the dog wags *its* tail).
It's means *it is*.

Than is used for comparison (greater *than*, less *than*).
Then is used for time (and *then* we).

Concision

If you were to ask for directions, which answer would you rather receive?

Turn right at Main Street and walk four blocks.

or

Since this street, Elm Street, is facing in a northerly direction, and your destination is due northeast, go east when you arrive at the intersection of Elm and Main. Going east will entail making a right turn in quite that easterly direction. After having made this turn and arrived on the perpendicular street....

The first one is obviously preferable. That's because concision is key when you want to communicate meaning. Really, as long as everything else is in order—as long as the grammar and punctuation are good to go—the best answer will almost always be the shortest.

Let's see an example.

The warming trend environmentalists observed in the 1990s may repeat 9 itself again, with harmful long-term effects on various species throughout the planet.

9

A) NO CHANGE

B) itself,

C) itself, with much damage and

D) itself possibly,

We should immediately be drawn to (B) because it is the most concise choice. Now let's look at the other words in the answers and decide if they provide any necessary meaning to the sentence. In (A), *again* is simply an echo of the word *repeat*, just as (D), *possibly,* is a rehash of *may*, so eliminate both. In (C), *damage* is unnecessary, as the sentence already contains the word *harmful*. Choose (B).

Common Questions to Look Out For

Here is one Editor-type question that shows up on every test:

The question of unequal pay for women draws on many other broader social issues. 10

10

The writer is considering deleting the phrase *of unequal pay for women* from the preceding sentence. Should this phrase be kept or deleted?

A) Kept, because it contains a crucial piece of information.

B) Kept, because it reminds the reader of social injustice in the modern world.

C) Deleted, because it wrongly implies that there is a disparity between what women and men are paid.

D) Deleted, because it gives information that has no bearing on this particular text.

This question asks whether we should keep or delete the phrase *of unequal pay for women*. Without that phrase, the sentence reads, *The question draws on many other broader social issues*. Because nothing in this sentence or any of the previous ones specifies what this *question* might be, we should keep the phrase. We want to be as precise as possible!

And, as (A) says, we want to keep the phrase because it is crucial to clarifying precisely what *the question* is. Choice (B) is a little too grandiose a reason to keep the phrase, especially when the whole passage is about the particular injustice of the gender pay gap. Choice (A) is therefore the best answer.

Here is another common question:

The gender disparities persist in areas other than pay. It is a kind of open secret, for instance, that women have had the right to vote in the United States for less than a century. There is a long history of misogyny written into the very cultural and social fabric of the United States.

11

At this point, the writer is considering adding the following true statement:

> The year that women's suffrage became legal in the United States was also the year that the American Football League was formed under the leadership of Jim Thorpe.

Should the writer make this addition here?

A) Yes, because it gives a broader context to the achievement of women's suffrage.

B) Yes, because it helps to ease some of the political rhetoric in the rest of the passage.

C) No, because it does not contribute in a significant way to the discussion of the gender pay gap.

D) No, because the question of gender pay is irrelevant when all football players are men.

The proposed sentence does contain an interesting bit of information, but that piece of information has no clear place either in these few sentences or in the passage as a whole. Therefore, it should not be added, thus eliminating (A) and (B).

Then, because it does not play a significant role in the passage, the sentence should not be added for the reason stated in (C). While (D) may be true in a way, it does not reflect anything clearly relating to the role the sentence might play in the passage as a whole. Read literally, and answer as literally and precisely as you can.

Quick Quiz #4

Clothing can be made from many different types of substances. There are two main groups of fibers: natural and man-made. Some natural fibers are cotton, wool, and linen, and some man-made fibers are polyester, rayon, and nylon; the difference depends on look and feel.

Many people prefer to wear natural fibers because they feel more natural against the skin. [1] You sweat and perspire less because the cloth is organic and breathes.

[2] Artificial fibers tend to make a person sweat more because they are composed of a plastic base. Plastic does not breathe very well; think of a plastic rain poncho. But because plastic is man-made, it is easier to manipulate than natural cloth. Because we don't like wrinkly clothes, we make artificial fabrics that stay and remain wrinkle-free.

[1] So if one wants to look ironed and crisp all day, wear man-made clothes. [2] But if one prefers the comfort and feel of aeration and a perspiration-free feeling, choose natural fibers. [3] Determining whether you're a style or a texture person determines which fabrics you'll prefer. [4] If you cannot decide, try a blend! [3]

1

A) NO CHANGE
B) The wearer perspires less because the organic cloth breathes.
C) The cloth ends up sweating and perspiring because it is organic and breathes.
D) Organic, breathing cloth prevents sweating and perspiring.

2

In context, which of the following sentences placed here best connects the second paragraph to the third?

A) Unlike natural fabrics, man-made fabrics wrinkle less, but they do not feel as pleasant on the body.
B) Cotton and linen are not man-made fibers and, consequently, behave differently.
C) Nevertheless, all fibers have their advantages, especially man-made fibers.
D) Some fibers encourage perspiration, a healthy, cleansing process of the skin.

3

The best placement for Sentence [3] (reproduced below) would be

Determining whether you're a style or a texture person determines which fabrics you'll prefer.

A) where it is now.
B) before sentence [1].
C) before sentence [2].
D) after sentence [4].

Answers and Explanations: Quick Quiz #4

1. **B** When revising sentences, first make sure that there are no grammatical errors. Then pick the answer that is **concise** and does not change the meaning of the sentence. The previous sentence mentioned "many people," while the NO CHANGE sentence uses the inconsistent pronoun "you." Eliminate (A). Choices (C) and (D) change the meaning of the sentence. (Choice (C) also has a slightly ambiguous pronoun ("it").) Take those out. You're left with (B), the correct answer.

2. **A** For **transition** questions, go back to the passage and read the sentences before and after the one you're going to work with. Determine what direction the sentences are going in—do they maintain the same flow of ideas or does the topic change from one sentence to the next? When adding a transition, do not go off-topic or add any new information. The end of the second paragraph discusses a benefit of natural fibers. The start of the third paragraph addresses artificial fibers. Since this marks a change of direction, look for the choice that addresses this topic shift. Choice (A) serves as an effective transition between the characteristics of natural fibers and those of artificial fibers. Choice (A) is correct.

3. **B** Some questions require you to work more with the content of the essay. You may need to rearrange sentences or provide a title for the essay. Read only as much as you need to answer these questions. Take a look at sentence [3]. What is it about? Now, read the sentences in the answer choices and use the Process of Elimination to get rid of answers that aren't similar in topic. Putting sentence [3] before [2] makes little sense; it separates the two examples. How about before sentence [1]? That works. Sentence [3] discusses two considerations: style and texture. Sentences [1] and [2] then give example of these two considerations; thus, (B) is correct.

Now that you've learned all the rules, try some of these Problem Sets:

PROOFREADER PROBLEM SET #1

The teacher noted that the inspired writing Joe displayed on his homework was incompatible **1** with the prosaic prose he produced in class.

1

A) NO CHANGE

B) about

C) for

D) to

The well-manicured lawns, the marble columns, and the **2** fountains that were impressive indicated this was no ordinary summer cottage.

2

A) NO CHANGE

B) impressive fountains indicating that

C) impressive fountains indicated that

D) fountains that were impressive indicating

Considering the blinding snowstorm and ice-covered roads, you and **3** her is lucky to arrive here safely.

3

A) NO CHANGE

B) she was

C) her has been

D) she were

Although **4** its flavor is derided by connoisseurs, the popularity of milk chocolate is far greater than that of dark chocolate.

4

A) NO CHANGE

B) its flavor is derided by connoisseurs the popularity of milk chocolate is far greater than

C) the flavor of milk chocolate is derided by connoisseurs, its popularity is far greater than that of

D) the flavor of milk chocolate is derided by connoisseurs, the popularity of it is far greater than

Eager to reach the widest audience possible, the popular group ABBA recorded songs not only in **5** their native Swedish but also in a number of other languages.

5

A) NO CHANGE
B) they're
C) its
D) it's

To celebrate the town's bicentennial, classes from each local school **6** attended a grand fireworks display and, having never seen such a sight, was amazed by the beauty.

6

A) NO CHANGE
B) attended a grand fireworks display and, having never seen such a sight, were amazed
C) attends a grand fireworks display and, having never seen such a sight, was amazed
D) attending a grand fireworks display and, having never seen such a sight, were amazed

ANSWERS AND EXPLANATIONS: PROOFREADER PROBLEM SET #1

1. **A**   **Idioms** are sneaky, but they usually relate to choosing the correct preposition for the word. You either know them or you don't. If you got this one wrong, add it to the list of idioms you should memorize! The correct idiom here is "incompatible with."

2. **C**   This sentence contains a **parallelism** error. Remember to check that any items in a list are consistent—the same part of speech—and if the list contains verbs, then check that those verbs are in the same tense. Because the sentence lists "well-manicured lawns" (an adjective and noun) and "marble columns" (an adjective and noun), the phrase "fountains that were impressive" (noun, verb, and adjective) is not parallel. The phrase correctly written would be "…and the impressive fountains…."

3. **D**   This sentence contains a **verb consistency** error. The use of the pronoun "her" is incorrect, but even if you did not know that, you can still use POE. "You and she/her" is a plural subject and the only plural verb is "were."

4. **C**   This is a **pronoun ambiguity** question because "its" could refer to popularity, milk chocolate, or dark chocolate. Because you don't know which is correct, the pronoun is ambiguous. We also have a potential **bad comparison** in (D). Its popularity is not literally greater than dark chocolate; its popularity is greater than the popularity of dark chocolate (*that of*).

5. **C**   The pronoun "their" (plural) refers to the collective noun ABBA (singular). Remember to check **pronouns** for **consistency** with the noun they replace. Watch out for (D). *It's* means *it is*.

6. **B**   Ignore the extra information in the middle of the sentence when checking for **subject-verb consistency**. The verb "was amazed" is singular, but the subject is "classes," which is plural. Eliminate (A) and (C). Now we're looking at more consistency (**parallelism**). "Attended" is consistent with "amazed." Choose (B).

PROOFREADER PROBLEM SET #2

Visitors to the zoo have often **1** looked into exhibits designed for lions and seen ducks or crows eating treats or enjoying water intended for the large cats.

1

A) NO CHANGE

B) looked into exhibits designed for lions, and seen

C) looked into exhibits designed for lions; and seen

D) looked into exhibits designed for lions: and seen

Before the sun **2** rose yesterday, Rebecca has already awoken and begun her morning regimen of activities.

2

A) NO CHANGE

B) rose yesterday, Rebecca had already awoken and begun

C) had arisen yesterday, Rebecca has already awoken and begun

D) rose yesterday, Rebecca had already awoken and begin

Jill knows that she performs worse on multiple-choice tests than on short answer **3** tests; where she is required to show her understanding in writing.

3

A) NO CHANGE

B) tests; whereby

C) tests, also

D) tests, wherein

Each member of the audience told the director that the thriller was the scariest movie that **4** they had ever seen.

4

A) NO CHANGE

B) they have

C) he had

D) she have

In the summer, the Ruddy Duck [5] male, who lives in marshes, have chestnut colored plumage and its bill is blue, but in the winter, the male is brown with a creamy colored face.

5

A) NO CHANGE

B) male was living in marshes and has

C) male that lives in marshes, it has

D) male, which lives in marshes, has

To be a good psychologist, one must [6] be trustworthy, be kind, and a patient listener, or else one's clients will not feel comfortable.

6

A) NO CHANGE

B) be trusted, kind, and be patiently listening,

C) be trustworthy, kind, and patient,

D) be trusted, have kindness, and also be patient,

ANSWERS AND EXPLANATIONS: PROOFREADER PROBLEM SET 2

1. **A** This is about **punctuation**. Use the Vertical Line Test. The first part of the sentence, up to *lions*, is complete. The second part of the sentence, after *and*, is incomplete. No STOP punctuation is allowed. (Remember that a comma + FANBOYS is STOP.) As for (D), there is no good reason to take a pause after *lions*. NO CHANGE is necessary.

2. **B** The verb "has already awoken" is in the present perfect **tense**, but the sentence is referring to something that happened in the past, before yesterday's sunrise. The past perfect tense, "had already awoken," is required, and (D) is incorrect because it switches tense by using "begin" instead of "begun."

3. **D** Use the Vertical Line Test for **punctuation** changes. Choices (A) and (B) are incorrect, since STOP punctuation cannot be used with incomplete ideas. In (C), using the word *also* creates two complete ideas. (Note: Use the word "where" only to refer to places; in this sentence it incorrectly refers to "short answer tests.")

4. **C** **Pronoun consistency:** The pronoun "they" (plural) incorrectly refers to the pronoun *each* (singular). *He* and *she* are singular, but *have* is plural, so rule out (D).

5. **D** Choice (A) incorrectly uses "who" to refer to an animal and contains a **subject-verb consistency** error; (B) incorrectly mixes past **tense** with present tense; and (C) uses GO punctuation between two complete ideas.

6. **C** In a list of three or more things, always check for **parallelism**. Choice (C) is the most consistent and concise, providing a list of three adjectives. Choice (A) is not consistent because it uses "be" on only the first and second items in the list. Choice (B) is not consistent because it uses "be" on only the first and third items in the list, and the adjective forms are also inconsistent. Choice (D) is not consistent because it switches from "be" to "have" and is also less **concise** than (C).

PROOFREADER PROBLEM SET #3

1 Accept for chocolate desserts in restaurants, I generally avoid eating sugar, cake, and candy in order to stay healthy.

1

A) NO CHANGE
B) Except for
C) Accepting
D) In spite of

Although pennies seem to be cheap and inconsequential donations, charities agree that **2** it adds up to a significant sum.

2

A) NO CHANGE
B) it does add
C) they add
D) they added

3 Against the advice of its coach, who has led many teams to victory, this year's baseball team attended more parties than practices and had an especially disappointing season.

3

A) NO CHANGE
B) Against the advice of their coach
C) As opposed to the advice of their coach
D) Against the advice of it's coach

The ongoing costs associated with feeding so many tigers and the difficulties caused by meddling neighbors **4** has not been considered prior to purchasing the land and building the animal sanctuary.

4

A) NO CHANGE
B) were not considered
C) was not considered
D) has not been in consideration

5 Impractical for cold climates, Ashley decided against packing her flip-flops for her vacation in Alaska.

5

A) NO CHANGE

B) Because she was impractical for cold climates,

C) They are impractical, since the climate is cold, so

D) Because they are impractical for cold climates,

Manny's mother always has snacks on hand, **6** unlike those of Nick's father.

6

A) NO CHANGE

B) unlike Nick's father.

C) unlike the father of Nick's.

D) unlike that of Nick's father.

ANSWERS AND EXPLANATIONS: PROOFREADER PROBLEM SET 3

1. **B**   Here, the author uses incorrect **diction**. The word "accept" means "to receive" something offered. The author should have chosen "except," which means "to the exclusion of."

2. **C**   This **pronoun consistency** question has the singular word "it" referring to the plural words "pennies" and "donations." Don't choose (D); that one changes the tense.

3. **A**   **Pronoun Consistency:** The "team" is singular. "Its" is its singular match. *Their* is plural. *It's* means *it is.*

4. **B**   The **verb** "has not been considered" is singular, but it should stay **consistent** with the plural subject "costs… and difficulties." Only *were* is plural in these options. Kudos if you also noticed that *prior to purchasing* means we need the past tense.

5. **D**   **Parallelism:** The sentence intends to say that flip-flops are impractical for cold climates, so Ashley didn't pack hers. Choice (D) uses the plural pronoun "they," which correctly refers to "flip-flops." Choice (A) has an introductory phrase with no subject, so it makes "Ashley" the thing that is impractical for cold climates. Choice (B) also makes Ashley the impractical element. Choice (C) is awkwardly arranged and lacking **concision**.

6. **B**   The comparison is being made between Manny's mother and Nick's father. Choices (A) and (D) introduce "those of" or "that of" unnecessarily, since the sentence compares one person to another, not Manny's mother to something belonging to Nick's father. Eliminate (A) and (D). Eliminate (C), which incorrectly adds an apostrophe and "s" to "Nick." Choice (B) is the correct answer.

PROOFREADER PROBLEM SET #4

The United States and the Philippines **1** is the top choice for a mining contract.

1

A) NO CHANGE

B) are the top choice

C) is the top choices

D) are the top choices

Anyone seeking to get in shape, regardless of age or ability, can benefit from having a personal trainer show **2** them the best approach.

2

A) NO CHANGE

B) one

C) you

D) him or her

Though popular mainly as a device that played music, Edison's phonograph **3** is originally created as an educational tool to teach spelling and allow deaf people to hear recordings of books.

3

A) NO CHANGE

B) was originally created as

C) will be originally created as

D) have been originally created as

4 Notwithstanding having spent several hours in meetings with each other and with an arbitrator, the parties were unable to reach an agreement.

4

A) NO CHANGE

B) Although the parties spend several hours

C) Nonetheless several hours to be spent—

D) Throughout the spending of several hours

Once considered revolutionary and controversial, the movements of impressionism and abstract expressionism [5] have steadily gained popularity; its images can now be found on drugstore postcards.

Alien species piggybacking on human travelers to new countries [6] are wreaking havoc on planet Earth, though they live for only a short time.

[5]

A) NO CHANGE

B) have steadily gained popularity; impressionist images can now be found on drugstore postcards

C) has steadily gained popularity; and so images can now be found on drugstore postcards

D) has steadily gained popularity, and its images can now be found on drugstore postcards

[6]

A) NO CHANGE

B) are wreaking havoc on planet Earth, though they are living for only a short time.

C) are wreaking havoc on planet Earth, though the alien species live for only a short time.

D) are wreaking havoc on planet Earth and though the species live for only a short time.

ANSWERS AND EXPLANATIONS: PROOFREADER PROBLEM SET 4

1. **D** The subject is *The United States and the Philippines* and uses the plural verb *are*. Two countries are plural and thus *choices* is most **consistent**.

2. **D** The pronoun "them" (plural) is not **consistent** with the pronoun "anyone" (singular). Remember to check pronouns for agreement with the nouns they replace.

3. **B** The changes in these answers pertain to verb **tense**. To match the past tense established and used elsewhere in the sentence ("played," "created"), the past tense "was" is needed.

4. **A** Although "notwithstanding" sounds like a clumsy **transition**, there is no error in the sentence as written. Try not to eliminate answers just because they "sound bad." Look for identifiable errors. Choices (B), (C), and (D) are in the wrong **tense**.

5. **B** The sentence is **ambiguous**; "its images" could refer to the images of abstract expressionism or impressionism. Choice (B) clarifies the ambiguity. Choices (C) and (D) incorrectly use a singular verb (the subject is "movements").

6. **C** The original sentence contains an **ambiguous pronoun**; it is unclear who "they" is referring to. Choice (B) repeats this error; eliminate it. Choice (D) clears up the ambiguity but in doing so creates a sentence fragment.

EDITOR PROBLEM SET #1

In these days of pollution, one must clean one's car with something other than rain. There are many car washing techniques available and they each have their pluses and minuses.

[1] First, one type of car wash is the touch-free car wash that a lot of people like because it doesn't scratch the paint on one's car. Basically it's a stream of water at a really high force like a fire hose's pressure. But not everybody likes touch-free because it might not get off really tough dirt and stains. Sometimes scrubbing is necessary.

[2] The traditional car wash with the waving strips of cloth that touch the exterior have the risk of scratching the car, especially if the cloth strips have bits of dirt or gravel from the last car. But the strips can rub the stains out more successfully [3] with friction and water and soap instead of just water and soap.

[1]

A) NO CHANGE
B) Many people prefer the touch-free car wash because it does not scratch car paint.
C) Because the touch-free car wash scratches car paint, many people prefer it.
D) First, people who do not like scratched car paint will like the touch-free car wash because it does not scratch car paint.

[2]

In context, which of the following sentences placed here best connects the second paragraph to the third?

A) For a scrubbing function, do not use a touch-free car wash.
B) Nevertheless, a touch-free car wash has other advantages.
C) Because a stream of water is never enough to cut through dirt, one should avoid a touch-free car wash.
D) For tougher dirt, one should use a car wash that physically scrubs the car.

[3]

A) NO CHANGE
B) with friction and soap instead of just water
C) with soap added to friction instead of just water
D) with friction added to the standard soap and water mixture

The best type of car wash is done by hand. [4] Although this can take [5] a couple hours of your time, you can [6] get out all the dirt without scratching your car if [7] one is careful and thorough [8] in your work.

4

A) NO CHANGE

B) Because

C) Since

D) However

5

The writer is considering deleting the underlined phrase. Should the writer do this?

A) Yes, because it provides unnecessary information.

B) Yes, because your should be spelled you're.

C) No, because it provides important detail as to the quantity of time needed.

D) No, because it supports the main idea of the paragraph.

6

All of the following are valid substitutions for the underlined portion EXCEPT

A) remove

B) take off

C) eliminate

D) transfer

7

A) NO CHANGE

B) you are

C) your

D) they are

8

The writer is considering deleting the underlined phrase. Should the phrase be kept or deleted?

A) Kept, because it provides a detail that supports the main topic of the paragraph.

B) Kept, because it sets up the main topic of the sentence that follows.

C) Deleted, because it adds an unnecessary detail.

D) Deleted, because it repeats a word that has been provided earlier in the paragraph.

Of course, even the best of methods can have its drawbacks. When you wash a car by hand, you might end up getting soapy or wet as you work. That makes hand washing a much better idea in the summer—if you try it in the winter, you just might freeze! **9**

The writer's main rhetorical purpose of the essay is to

A) explore the advantages and disadvantages of different car washing methods.

B) establish that touch-free is the best type of car wash because it does not scratch a car's paint.

C) show how to wash a car quickly and well by hand.

D) illustrate that hand washing is the superior form of car washing during the winter.

ANSWERS AND EXPLANATIONS: EDITOR PROBLEM SET #1

1. **B** Choices (A) and (D) are not **concise**. Choice (C) changes the meaning of the original sentence. Choice (B) is the best choice because it retains the full meaning of the sentence while conveying the thought concisely.

2. **D** Choice (C) changes the **meaning** of the paragraphs. Choices (A) and (B) focus too much on the touch-free car wash. A sentence added to the beginning of the third paragraph should lead into the topic of that paragraph: the traditional car wash. Because (D) focuses more on the traditional car wash, it is the best choice.

3. **D** Choices (B) and (C) alter the **meaning** of the original sentence. Choice (A) looks appealing, but it still has a lot of repetition. Choice (D) is the best option because it is the most concise without the redundancy problem.

4. **A** With **conjunctions**, check to see whether the sentence is flowing the same direction or in different directions. In this case, we see a contrast, so rule out (B) and (C). "However" can show a contrast, but in this case, it actually creates an incomplete thought.

5. **C** Does the phrase provide necessary **meaning** to preserve the precision of the sentence? Yes, since there is a specific and necessary difference between "time" and "a couple hours of your time." Eliminate (A) and (B). The main idea of the paragraph is not about the amount of time, though, so rule out (D). Note: *your* is the correct spelling in this context.

6. **D** If the goal is to "get out" the dirt, then *transfer*ring it would not *eliminate* or *remove* it, only move it to another place.

7. **B** A change needs to be made to fix an incorrect switch from the second person pronoun "you" to the third person pronoun "one." Always keep **pronouns consistent**! *Your* is incorrect, since it shows possession (*your book*).

8. **C** If it doesn't add **precision**, delete it!

9. **A** Choice (B) states that the author prefers touch-free car washing; however, the essay refutes this claim. Choice (C) is incorrect because the author explains that one cannot hand wash a car well without time. Choice (D) is disproved by the last sentence. Choice (A) is best because it encompasses the whole essay.

EDITOR PROBLEM SET #2

I don't think that people living near an active volcano should be forced to move to a safer home. Let me explain why they should be permitted to keep their homes.

[1] First of all, many people think a volcano is a dangerous place **1** to live but there are plenty of active volcanoes in the world with whole cities around them and plenty that haven't exploded in centuries. [2] Sometimes an active volcano just drizzles out lava. [3] **2** Other places have their own potential problems. [4] Living on the coast is dangerous for hurricanes, living in the Midwest is dangerous for tornados, and living in lower elevated areas is dangerous for flash flooding. [5] People should learn to **3** face their fears because they can never move to a truly safe place. **4**

1

A) NO CHANGE
B) to live; accordingly, there are many active volcanoes surrounded by cities that have not exploded in centuries.
C) to live, including the quiet, citified ones.
D) to live. Many of the world's active volcanoes, however, are surrounded by cities and have remained quiet for centuries.

2

Which of the following words should be placed at the beginning of this sentence?

A) Furthermore,
B) Consequently,
C) Although
D) Subsequently

3

Which of the following would be a valid substitute for the underlined word?

A) view
B) state
C) address
D) represent

4

In the context of paragraph 2, where would be the best place to insert the following sentence?

> Slow, predictable lava flow is not much of a hazard.

A) After sentence 1
B) After sentence 2
C) After sentence 3
D) After sentence 4

Secondly, people should be allowed to live where they choose. Perhaps those who dare to live beside a volcano do so because they have a good view or a fertile garden. Maybe they live near their families and friends. Maybe they have a house that has been in their family for generations. **5** The government should not force them to move because of the possibility of disaster. They have something precious that is worth sustaining all these scary possibilities for: a home. **6**

5

In context, which words should be placed at the beginning of this sentence?

A) Despite these realities,

B) For all these reasons,

C) Misunderstanding their excuses,

D) Against these justifications,

6

The writer's main rhetorical purpose of the essay is to

A) advocate for the rights of those who choose to live on volcanoes.

B) urge the government to instate stricter housing regulations on and around volcanoes.

C) support the idea that home is a state of mind rather than a geographic location.

D) suggest that daredevils abandon dangerous places to live.

ANSWERS AND EXPLANATIONS: EDITOR PROBLEM SET #2

1. **D** Choice (A) is not **concise**. Choices (B) and (C) say that the second half of the sentence is a continuation of the first half. However, in the original sentence, the second half opposes the first.

2. **A** Choices (B) and (D) mean that this sentence agrees with the concepts of the previous ones. However, this sentence does not directly follow the idea of drizzling lava, so (B) and (D) can be eliminated. Choice (C) implies that the two ideas are contrasting, which is not the case since they both aid the author's main point. Choice (A) provides a continuation transition word and is therefore the correct choice.

3. **C** Choices (A), (B), and (D) have different meanings from *face*. Therefore, (C) is the correct answer.

4. **B** This new sentence relates to why people do not need to fear living near a volcano. Sentence 1 gets at that, but it's not until Sentence 2 that lava is mentioned (*an active volcano just drizzles out lava*). By following that, the new sentence most explicitly makes the point that some volcanoes are not very dangerous. Sentence 3 changes topic to talk about other types of natural disasters and Sentence 4 focuses on facing one's fears; neither is as connected to the topic as (B).

5. **B** Choices (A), (C), and (D) incorrectly state that this sentence will be different from the previous sentences. Therefore, (B), which incorporates the earlier sentences, is correct.

6. **A** Choices (B) and (D) oppose the main point of the essay. Choice (C) makes assumptions not stated in the essay. Choice (A) best summarizes the gist of the essay.

Chapter 7
Writing and Language
Practice Test

Writing and Language Test

35 MINUTES, 44 QUESTIONS

Turn to Section 2 of your answer sheet to answer the questions in this section.

DIRECTIONS

Each passage below is accompanied by a number of questions. For some questions, you will consider how the passage might be revised to improve the expression of ideas. For other questions, you will consider how the passage might be edited to correct errors in sentence structure, usage, or punctuation. A passage or a question may be accompanied by one or more graphics (such as a table or graph) that you will consider as you make revising and editing decisions.

Some questions will direct you to an underlined portion of a passage. Other questions will direct you to a location in a passage or ask you to think about the passage as a whole.

After reading each passage, choose the answer to each question that most effectively improves the quality of writing in the passage or that makes the passage conform to the conventions of standard written English. Many questions include a "NO CHANGE" option. Choose that option if you think the best choice is to leave the relevant portion of the passage as it is.

Questions 1–11 are based on the following passage.

Adventures in Cooking

"Turn off the stove!" I told my sister in a panicked voice, lifting the overflowing pot of water off the hot stove. I had never cooked dinner before, and it was much more difficult than I thought it would be. Already I had burned the dinner **1** rolls dropped an egg, on the floor, and now **2** I had let the water boil over. Cooking was not the first household chore I struggled to do.

1

A) NO CHANGE
B) rolls, dropped an egg, on the floor and
C) rolls, dropped an egg on the floor, and
D) rolls, dropped an egg on the floor and,

2

A) NO CHANGE
B) this.
C) the water boils over.
D) I made another mistake.

CONTINUE

When I began high **3** school, my parents gave me a choice, I could cook dinner every evening after school, or I could do the laundry. I tried to do the laundry, with disastrous results. Somehow a red sock ended up in a load of white clothes, and as a result my entire family had to contend with blotchy, stained pink shirts. **4**

5 [1] The evidence was clear; it appeared that I did not speak this cryptic language called "cooking." [2] After that catastrophic first dinner, **6** when I decided that I needed to learn more about cooking. [3] First, I read my grandmother's cookbooks, but the recipes directed me to do mysterious things such as "blanch" and "sauté." [4] Additionally, I could not identify many ingredients: What are shallots and navy beans?

3

A) NO CHANGE
B) school, my parents gave me a choice
C) school, my parents gave me a choice:
D) school my parents gave me a choice.

4

Which of the following sentences would best provide a logical transition from paragraph 2 to Paragraph 3?

A) Pink is my favorite color, so I was not too upset.
B) Following that debacle, I was reassigned to the kitchen.
C) I decided to stop doing laundry.
D) I cannot do yard work properly, either.

5

For the sake of the unity and coherence of this paragraph, Sentence 1 should be placed:

A) where it is now.
B) after sentence 2.
C) after sentence 3.
D) after sentence 4.

6

A) NO CHANGE
B) at which
C) then
D) DELETE the underlined portion.

For a few weeks, my family suffered through my unsuccessful attempts at spaghetti, tacos, **7** and hamburgers. **8** "I hope you don't aspire to be a chef!" my older brother joked.

Then one evening, I began watching a television show called "Iron Chef." The show was from Japan, **9** which is an island country, but the voices were dubbed over in English. "Iron Chef" portrayed a contest between two skilled chefs.

10 He was given one hour to create multiple dishes, all of which had to contain the "ingredient of the day." Sometimes the ingredient was a common food, such as chicken. More often, however, the ingredient was something unusual, like yams, eggplant, or kiwi. Each chef was **11** also allowed to use other ingredients, but had to include the ingredient of the day.

The announcers on "Iron Chef" could have been sports commentators because their remarks were enthusiastic, well-informed, and interesting. "Iron Chef" was amusing, and it taught me how to cook. Never again did I serve burned, bland pasta.

7

A) NO CHANGE

B) and I burned the

C) after that

D) and making

8

The writer wants to add a sentence in this spot to further describe the way in which the meals were badly prepared. Which of the following sentences would most successfully achieve this effect?

A) Hamburgers are not healthy.

B) I do not think I will attend cooking school.

C) Everything I cooked was burned and tasteless.

D) It is difficult to cook hamburgers properly, but I needed to learn.

9

A) NO CHANGE

B) which I learned is an island country,

C) which is a country composed of islands,

D) DELETE the underlined portion.

10

A) NO CHANGE

B) Each was

C) Each were

D) The chef was

11

Which of the following placements for the underlined portion would be LEAST acceptable?

A) Where it is now

B) After the word "chef"

C) After the word "allowed"

D) After the word "other"

CONTINUE ➡

Questions 12–22 are based on the following passage.

Getting Dirty

A woman staggers into the classroom and, with evident relief, drops a bulging box onto a stool **12** standing inside the room. Without a word, she reaches inside and pulls out a handful of moist terracotta clay and tosses it onto the table in front of you. **13** As you eye her grubby hands, she doles out the remaining **14** clay that she instructs the class to "get to know."

A) NO CHANGE

B) resting inside the room.

C) inside the room.

D) DELETE the underlined portion and end the sentence with a period.

A) NO CHANGE

B) Next you

C) At that time you

D) You now

A) NO CHANGE

B) clay she

C) clay, which she

D) clay, whom she

CONTINUE

You stare suspiciously at the brown lump sitting on the table in front of you. You could handle watercolors, but you have no intention of risking your fresh manicure playing with glorified dirt. **15** However, you are repulsed by your neighbors' animated squishing of their own balls of clay, which reminds you of your cousins' frequent mud fights. **16**

[1] Crossing your arms, you sink back into your chair. **17** [2] For better or for worse, you're stuck in Art 1B. [3] You **18** wish, you had signed up for Journalism or even **19** chosen Band instead. [4] Is it too late to request a schedule change? [5] You imagine pleading your case before the harried guidance counselor and immediately reject the idea.

15

A) NO CHANGE

B) Moreover,

C) Although

D) Nevertheless,

16

The writer wants to end this paragraph with a sentence that emphasizes the narrator's growing squeamishness about the clay. Which of the following sentences would best achieve this effect?

A) You never did get along very well with your cousins.

B) Several years ago, your cousin managed to grind a handful of mud into your hair.

C) You cringe at this disgusting association.

D) You manage to rationalize that artists have been sculpting with clay for ages.

17

For the sake of unity and coherence, Sentence 2 should be placed:

A) where it is now.

B) after Sentence 3.

C) after Sentence 4.

D) after Sentence 5.

18

A) NO CHANGE

B) wish you

C) wish, and you

D) wish, that you

19

A) NO CHANGE

B) choose

C) have chosen

D) chose

CONTINUE →

20 You touch the mass gently. It's pleasantly firm and cool, not sludgy like you had expected. You pick up the clay and begin to knead it between your two palms. With every turn it becomes softer and warmer. You don't even mind the reddish stain that appears on your skin. Not really, anyway.

Growing more adventurous, you begin to shape the ball into an oval. You carefully push the clay around with your fingertips, forming soft indentations and mounds until the clay takes on a vaguely human form. You continue to tweak the growing sculpture, adding in more detail with the point of a pencil until it takes on a recognizable shape.

You prop the clay head up on your desk and gaze into **21** it's lopsided eyes. The sculpture is certainly an improvement over the cold clod of earth it once was. **22** Though your fingernails are now encrusted with drying clay, an overwhelming feeling of creativity more than makes up for such a minor inconvenience.

20

The writer wishes to indicate the narrator's reluctance to handle the clay at this point in the essay. Which of the following choices would most successfully achieve this effect?

A) NO CHANGE

B) You prod the mass with a single finger.

C) You hurriedly press down on the mass.

D) You touch the mass with your outstretched hand.

21

A) NO CHANGE

B) its

C) it is

D) its'

22

The writer wants to insert a sentence that indicates that the narrator is pleased with her creation. Which of the following sentences would most successfully achieve this effect?

A) Your neighbor's clay has never really progressed beyond this clod stage.

B) You laugh at the thought of your initial reaction to the clay.

C) A small smile escapes your lips as you lean back in your chair.

D) Your teacher glances over and gives you thumbs up.

CONTINUE

Questions 23–33 are based on the following passage.

Esperanto: a Communications Solution?

Is world peace an unobtainable ideal? Since thousands of languages are [23] spoken aloud across the globe, communication among different populations is often strained. [24] While English is growing as an international language, non-native [25] speakers, who feel that they are at a linguistic or cultural disadvantage, often resent its status as a *lingua franca*.

The desire for an [26] affective, and neutral means of international communication struck Dr. L. L. Zamenhof, who in the late nineteenth century developed the language Esperanto [27] over a hundred years ago.

23

A) NO CHANGE
B) in verbal use
C) communicated orally
D) spoken

24

A) NO CHANGE
B) Nonetheless,
C) However,
D) In addition,

25

A) NO CHANGE
B) speakers who feel
C) speakers, who feel,
D) speakers who feel,

26

A) NO CHANGE
B) effective and
C) affective and
D) effective, and

27

A) NO CHANGE
B) over a century ago.
C) more than one hundred years ago.
D) DELETE the underlined portion and end the sentence with a period.

CONTINUE

Zamenhof **28** has designed the language to be easily learned. Features of **29** Esperanto include: completely regular forms, simple grammar, and a rich root system. Much of the vocabulary is eerily familiar to those with some knowledge of Western European languages.

Though Esperanto is not currently widespread enough to be a realistic solution to world communication problems, it is potentially another step towards global harmony. Esperanto is the most successful constructed language to date. Estimates of the total number of speakers range from 100,000 to 1.6 million. **30** There are even as many as two thousand native speakers across the globe! There is no shortage of material in Esperanto for learners of the language to enjoy. Although most of the quarter million books published in Esperanto have been translated, there are hundreds of original works in print. Esperanto's reach has even penetrated the world of film: a 1965 movie starring William Shatner, *Incubus*, was filmed entirely in Esperanto. **31** Shatner is perhaps most famous for his role as Captain Kirk on "Star Trek."

28

A) NO CHANGE
B) had designed
C) designed
D) was designing

29

A) NO CHANGE
B) Esperanto include,
C) Esperanto include
D) Esperanto:

30

A) NO CHANGE
B) (Do NOT begin new paragraph) There is
C) (Begin new paragraph) There is
D) (Begin new paragraph) There are

31

The writer is considering deleting the underlined sentence. Should the writer do this?

A) Yes, because this information is already found in another paragraph.
B) Yes, because it supplies unnecessary information.
C) No, because it supports the main argument of the passage as introduced in the first paragraph.
D) No, because it continues the explanation of how Esperanto has influenced film.

CONTINUE ▶

Though opponents have voiced their skepticism about the language, the community of Esperantists continues to grow. **32** Knowledge of the language provides a link for people who would otherwise have a difficult time speaking with one another. Hundreds of international conferences and other get-togethers are held each year. In fact, one of the perks of learning Esperanto is access to the publication *Pasporta Servo*, which lists the addresses of those willing to host traveling Esperanto speakers for free.

This promise of international cooperation is what keeps many Esperantists motivated. Only time will tell, however, whether Esperanto will help achieve this goal. **33**

32

The writer is considering deleting the first clause of the preceding sentence and beginning the sentence with the word "The." If the writer did this, the paragraph would primarily lose

A) an acknowledgement that there are critics of the Esperanto movement.

B) an effective transition from the preceding paragraph.

C) an example of how the Esperanto community is growing.

D) a detail that undermines the predominant argument of the essay.

33

The writer wishes to conclude the essay with a sentence that refers to the main theme of the essay. Which of the following choices would best accomplish this goal?

A) With any luck it won't fail!

B) As of now, however, its prospects are dismal.

C) So grab your copy of *Incubus* and make a toast to Esperanto's creator, Dr. Zamenhof!

D) Until then, pacon! Peace!

CONTINUE

Questions 34–44 are based on the following passage.

International Politics and the Birth of the Atomic Bomb

The history of the atomic bomb is marked by strange intersections of international politics [34] yet astounding science. Marie Curie was born in Poland at a time when it was [35] under Russian occupation. She earned her advanced physics and math degrees in France, where she coined the word "radioactivity."

[36] Nevertheless, thirty years later, in 1938, German scientists Otto Hahn and Fritz Strassman [37] discovered that they could split the nucleus of a uranium atom. This "fission," as it was named a year later, released extra neutrons that could in turn split other radioactive atoms. [38] With war looming on the horizon, some members of the worldwide scientific community began to suspect that the energy released in this chain reaction could, in theory, be harnessed to create a bomb with unprecedented power.

34

A) NO CHANGE

B) but

C) as well as

D) DELETE the underlined portion.

35

A) NO CHANGE

B) beneath

C) below

D) doomed to

36

A) NO CHANGE

B) Despite this, some thirty years later,

C) A mere thirty years later,

D) It then took almost thirty years

37

A) NO CHANGE

B) puzzled over

C) tripped over

D) had a lucky accident to know

38

A) NO CHANGE

B) War loomed on the horizon,

C) As the war, which loomed on the horizon,

D) The war that was looming on the horizon would make

Leo Szilard, the son of a Hungarian Jewish civil engineer, studied under Albert Einstein in Germany. After Hitler came to [39] power, he fled Germany for England, and there published his views on the possibility of a neutron chain reaction. [40] In anticipation of the outbreak of World War II, Szilard fled to New York City, where he became a professor at Columbia University [41] in 1938 in that same fateful year of Hahn and Strassman's discovery. Szilard studied Hahn and Strassman's results and the work of other German scientists, which [42] suggested that a few pounds of uranium could have the same explosive and destructive power as many thousands of pounds of dynamite. Szilard contacted Einstein about the potential threat this posed, and in August 1939 succeeded in encouraging Einstein to write to President Franklin D. Roosevelt with a warning that Germany was attempting to develop a nuclear weapon and that the United States should preempt the threat by developing one first.

[39]

A) NO CHANGE
B) power he fled
C) power, Szilard fled
D) power Szilard fled,

[40]

The writer is considering adding the following true statement in this place:

> Szilard had left Germany in 1933 to escape Nazi persecution and continue his work in other parts of Europe.

Should the writer make the addition at this point?

A) Yes, because it indicates that some scientists felt compelled to leave Germany for their safety as well as to avoid lending their knowledge to the Nazi's side.

B) Yes, because it helps explain why Germany would not be pursuing nuclear weapons.

C) No, because it detracts from the flow of the passage, and where Szilard fled is not as important as the fact that he left Nazi Germany.

D) No, because Hitler did not win a majority vote and he was not able to challenge important scientists at this time.

[41]

A) NO CHANGE
B) around the same time as
C) at about the time
D) DELETE the underlined portion.

[42]

A) NO CHANGE
B) would suggest
C) could have suggested
D) suggests

CONTINUE ➡

In September 1941, two of the most knowledgeable atomic scientists met to discuss the recent attempts of making the theory of atomic power a militaristic reality **43** at a meeting in Nazi-occupied Copenhagen, Denmark. German physicist Werner Heisenberg, who had continued his work in Nazi Germany, sought out his former mentor, the Danish scientist Nils Bohr. Bohr had pioneered atomic theories but his work had been impeded by the persecution of the Nazi forces occupying his country. Although it was supposed to be secret, the meeting was almost certainly compromised due to the wartime surveillance Bohr endured, and thus, the men were exceedingly nervous. Unable to speak freely, Heisenberg talked in an indirect manner. Heisenberg spoke so vaguely because he feared charges of treason for giving up German secrets.

In 1943, Bohr made the momentous choice to refuse to work on the German atomic bomb, and he fled to Sweden, then to London, and eventually ended up in the United States.

43

A) NO CHANGE
B) while attending a meeting
C) while in attendance at a meeting
D) attending a meeting

CONTINUE

This decision may have determined the course of the war. The most world-renowned physicists were gathered in the U.S. to work on the Manhattan Project, **44** which had begun in response to Einstein's letter to Roosevelt. These esteemed scientists considered Bohr the sage of the group: The side that had Bohr was the side that would have the bomb.

44

Which of the following statements, if substituted for the underlined portion, would most accurately and effectively represent the information in the graph?

A) a project that has cost U.S. taxpayers more than any other in history.

B) a project that cost more to administer than even the Apollo space program.

C) a project that costs far less than comparable energy programs.

D) a project that received annual funding from 1942 to 1946.

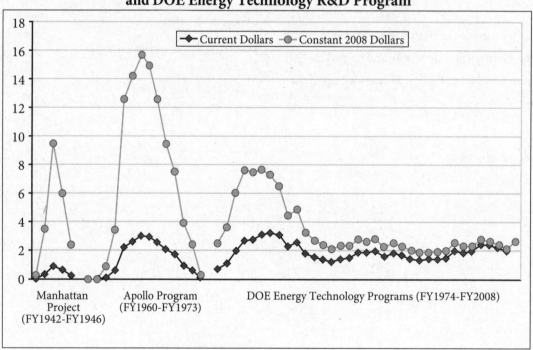

Annual Funding for Manhattan Project, Apollo Program, and DOE Energy Technology R&D Program

Chapter 8
Writing and Language Practice Test: Answers and Explanations

WRITING AND LANGUAGE PRACTICE TEST ANSWERS

1.	C	24.	A
2.	B	25.	A
3.	C	26.	B
4.	B	27.	D
5.	D	28.	C
6.	D	29.	C
7.	A	30.	A
8.	C	31.	B
9.	D	32.	A
10.	B	33.	D
11.	D	34.	C
12.	D	35.	A
13.	A	36.	C
14.	C	37.	A
15.	B	38.	A
16.	C	39.	C
17.	D	40.	C
18.	B	41.	D
19.	A	42.	A
20.	B	43.	B
21.	B	44.	D
22.	C		
23.	D		

WRITING AND LANGUAGE TEST EXPLANATIONS

1. **C** The placement of the commas is changing in the answer choices, so the question is testing comma rules. The underlined portion is part of a list, so the rule here is that there should be a comma after every item in the list. The first item is "burned the dinner rolls" which should then be followed by a comma. Eliminate (A). The second item is "dropped an egg on the floor," which should be followed by a comma. Eliminate (B) and (D). Choice (C) is the correct answer.

2. **B** Notice that the underlined portion is the last item in a list. In order to keep the items in the list consistent, there should not be a subject in the underlined portion. Eliminate (A) and (D). Choices (B) and (C) both refer to the water boiling over, but (B) uses the pronoun "this" which is more concise. Therefore, (B) is the correct answer.

3. **C** The first change in the answer choices is the presence of the comma after "school," which means comma rules are being tested. Because "When I began high school" is an introductory idea, it needs to be followed by a comma. Eliminate (D). The next change in the answers is the punctuation after "choice." "When I began high school, my parents gave me a choice" is a complete idea, and the second piece, "I could cook dinner every evening after school, or I could do the laundry" is also complete. Because complete ideas need to be separated by a period or its equivalent, eliminate (A) and (B). Therefore, (C) is the correct answer.

4. **B** Paragraph 2 ends with an anecdote about the narrator's experience doing laundry, and paragraph 3 starts with information about the narrator's experience cooking. Both (A) and (C) only relate to paragraph 2, so eliminate both. Choice (D) is unrelated and can also be eliminated. Only (B) effectively transitions from one idea to the next by referring back to the failed laundry experience and introducing the cooking experience. Therefore, (B) is the correct answer.

5. **D** When deciding where to best place Sentence 1, start by reading Sentences 2, 3, and 4. Notice that Sentence 1 mentions a "cryptic language"; this refers to the cookbook introduced in Sentence 3. However, don't just hastily answer (C); the transition word "Additionally" suggests that Sentence 4 immediately follows Sentence 3, which means that Sentence 1 actually follows Sentence 4, (D).

6. **D** One of the answer choices is to delete the underlined portion, so this question is testing concision. Since the sentence is complete and the meaning is clear without the underlined portion, delete that portion. (This also has the added benefit of making the sentence grammatically correct.) Choice (D) is the correct answer.

7. **A** The wording of the last item in a list is changing in the answer choices, so the question is testing consistency. In order to make the list consistent, the last item should be a noun. Choices (B), (C), and (D) are not consistent with the previous two items in the list: spaghetti and tacos. Choice (A) is the correct answer.

8. **C** The question is specifically asking for a sentence related to the bad preparation of the meals. Neither (A) nor (B) is about the preparation. Eliminate (A) and (B). Choice (D) is about proper preparation, but (C) is consistent with the goal of describing how the meals were badly prepared. Therefore, (C) is the correct answer.

9. **D** The primary change in the answer choices is the inclusion of extra words, so this question is testing concision. Choices (A), (B), and (C) contain no grammatical errors, but the fact that Japan is an island is unnecessary information. In order to make the sentence concise, delete the underlined portion. Choice (D) is the correct answer.

10. **B** The subject and the verb are changing in the answer choices, so the question is testing subject verb agreement and precision. Choice (A) uses the pronoun "he" when there are two chefs, so the use of the pronoun is not precise. Eliminate (A). Choice (D) can be eliminated for the same reason: "the chef" refers to only one of the two chefs. Both (B) and (C) use the subject "each," which is singular, but only (B) keeps the verb consistent with the subject. Choice (B) is the correct answer.

11. **D** The answer choices give other options for the placement of the word "also." As it is used in the sentence currently, the meaning is clear. Choice (A) is acceptable. The meaning of the sentence would remain consistent if "also" were placed after "chef" or "allowed," so (B) and (C), both acceptable, can also be eliminated. When placed after "other," the meaning is no longer clear. Choice (D) is not acceptable. Therefore, (D) is the correct answer.

12. **D** The primary change in the answer choices is the inclusion of extra words, so this question is testing concision. Looking back at the sentence, it is already noted that the woman is in the classroom. It is, therefore, unnecessary to mention that information again. Therefore, (D) is the correct answer.

13. **A** The wording of the beginning of the sentence is changing in the answer choices, so you need to find the answer that is consistent with the remainder of the sentence. The underlined portion is part of an introductory idea. Choices (B) and (D) include the subject "you," which would turn the underlined portion into a complete idea. Because this is not consistent with the comma that follows, eliminate (B) and (D). Choices (A) and (C) are similar in meaning, but (A) is more concise and is therefore the correct answer.

14. **C** The answer choices deal with the inclusion of a comma, so the question is testing punctuation. The clause "she instructs the class to 'get to know'" is not necessary to the meaning of the sentence, so it should be preceded by a comma. Eliminate (A) and (B). Choices (C) and (D) use "which" and "whom" to refer to the clay, respectively. Because clay is not a person, "whom" is incorrect. Eliminate (D). Choice (C) is the correct answer.

15. **B** The transition word is changing in the answer choices, so determine whether you need to transition in the same direction or to change direction. Both sentences express negative ideas about the dirt, so you need to transition in the same direction. Eliminate (A), (C), and (D). Choice (B) is the correct answer.

16. **C**   The question asks for the sentence that best emphasizes squeamishness. Eliminate (A), (B) and (D) because they have no relation to squeamishness. Choice (C) contains the word "cringe," which is a reaction associated with squeamishness. Therefore, (C) is the correct answer.

17. **D**   The answer choices are offering other placements for the underlined sentence. Because the sentence discusses being "stuck" in the class, it is logical to place it after Sentence 5, a sentence about rejecting a potential way out of the class. Therefore, (D) is the correct answer.

18. **B**   The placement of the comma is changing in the answer choices, so this question is testing comma rules. Because "You wish you had signed up for Journalism" is one clause; there should not be a comma anywhere within it. Eliminate (A), (C), and (D). Choice (B) is the correct answer.

19. **A**   Notice the verb changing in the answer choices. The question is testing verb tense. The verb used previously in the sentence is "had signed," so to keep the verbs consistent you need "had chosen." Choice (A) works because the word "had" that is already in the sentence can apply to both "signed" and "chosen." Eliminate (B), (C), and (D) because they are not consistent with "had signed." Therefore, (A) is the correct answer.

20. **B**   The question seeks a sentence that reflects reluctance to handle the clay. Therefore, look for an answer choice that includes a word or phrase related to reluctance. Neither (A) nor (D) include such a phrase, so eliminate both. Choice (C) says "hurriedly" which is the opposite of reluctance, so eliminate it. Choice (B) includes the phrase "with a single finger," which could be related to reluctance, and is therefore the correct answer.

21. **B**   Notice the answer choices are changing the form of the word "it's." The form used in (A) is a contraction for "it is," which is not consistent with the meaning of the sentence. Eliminate (A) and (C). Choice (D) isn't actually a word, and can be eliminated. Choice (B) is the possessive pronoun form of the word, which is consistent with the intended meaning in the sentence. Therefore, (B) is the correct answer.

22. **C**   The question asks for a sentence that reflects the narrator's pleasure about her creation. Therefore, look for an answer choice that includes a word or phrase related to being pleased. Choice (A) is about a neighbor's clay. Eliminate (A). Choice (B) mentions a laugh, but it is in reference to the feeling about the clay rather than the finished creation. Eliminate (B). Choice (C) mentions the narrator's smile. Keep (C). Choice (D) mentions the teacher's reaction rather than the narrator's. Eliminate (D). Choice (C) is the correct answer.

23. **D**   The primary change in the answer choices is the inclusion of extra words, so this question is testing concision. The meaning in each answer choice is consistent with the intended meaning of the sentence. However, "spoken aloud" is redundant because speaking is implicitly something done aloud, so eliminate (A). From the remaining choices, (D) is the most concise. Therefore, (D) is the correct answer.

24. **A** Notice the transition word and the comma changing in the answer choices. The question is testing the use of transition words and commas. If a comma is used, the transition word is an introductory idea that should be followed by a complete idea, which is not consistent with the sentence that follows. Eliminate (B), (C), and (D) because they include commas. Choice (A) is the correct answer.

25. **A** The comma placement is changing in the answer choices, so the question is testing comma rules. The clause "who feel that they are at a linguistic or cultural disadvantage" is an extra detail that is not necessary to the overall meaning of the sentence, so it should be offset with commas both before and after. Eliminate (B) and (D). The comma after "feel" separates two parts of the same clause, so it cannot be included. Eliminate (C). Choice (A) is the correct answer.

26. **B** The word "affective" is changing in the answer choices, so the question is testing the difference between "affective" and "effective." The word "effective" is used to describe an object or action that successfully produces a desired effect while the word "affective" is related to moods and emotions. The former is the meaning that is consistent with the sentence here, so eliminate (A) and (C) because they use "affective." The next change is the inclusion of a comma. Because you cannot use a comma with "and" in this instance, eliminate (D). Choice (B) is the correct answer.

27. **D** The primary change in the answer choices is the inclusion of extra words, so this question is testing concision. "Over a hundred years ago" is a reference to the time period, but because this is already stated by the phrase "in the late nineteenth century," the underlined portion is redundant and should be deleted. Choice (D) is the correct answer.

28. **C** Notice the verb tense changing in the answer choices. To stay consistent with the information in the previous sentence, use simple past tense. Choice (C) is the correct answer.

29. **C** Notice the punctuation changing after the word "include." Choices (A) and (D) use a colon, which must follow a complete idea. Because that's not the case here, eliminate (A) and (D). Choice (B) includes a comma before a list, but commas should come between every item in a list, not before the list. Eliminate (B). Choice (C) is the correct answer.

30. **A** The paragraph break and "is" and "are" are changing in the answer choices, so the question is testing paragraph breaks and subject verb agreement. Because the sentence that follows is a continuation of the discussion in the preceding sentence, do not start a new paragraph. Eliminate (C) and (D). The subject of the verb is "speakers," which is plural, so the verb should be "are." Eliminate (B). Choice (A) is the correct answer.

31. **B** The question is asking if the underlined portion should be deleted. The other information in this paragraph is all related to the widespread nature of the language Esperanto, and this sentence is not consistent with that topic. Therefore, the sentence should be deleted. Eliminate (C) and (D). Additionally, the information is not found in another paragraph, so eliminate (A). Choice (B) is the correct answer.

32. **A** The question is asking what would be lost if the clause "Though opponents have voiced their skepticism about the language" were deleted. This information is unrelated to the preceding paragraph.

Eliminate (B). The remaining portion of the sentence is related to the growth of the language, not the clause in question, so eliminate (C). This information does not undermine the essay. Eliminate (D). Choice (A) is the correct answer.

33.　**D**　The question is asking which sentence best refers to the main theme of the essay, which discusses the creation of a simple language intended to help improve global communication and therefore help foster global harmony. Choices (A), (B), and (C) do not make any references to the simplicity or the goal of global harmony. Choice (D) addresses the goal of peace, while also demonstrating the use of common roots to make the language easy to learn (the root "pac" means peace). Therefore, (D) is the correct answer.

34.　**C**　The conjunction is changing in the answer choices, so the question is testing the use of conjunctions. The words "yet" and "but" are used with items in contrast, which is not consistent with the meaning of the sentence. Eliminate (A) and (B). Because the conjunction is necessary, we cannot delete the underlined portion. Eliminate (D). Choice (C) is the correct answer.

35.　**A**　The wording is changing in the answer choices, so the question is testing word choice. While "under," "beneath," and "below" can have similar meanings, the word choice must be consistent with the word that follows, "occupation." Choices (B) and (C) do not meet this requirement. Eliminate (B) and (C). The use of the phrase "doomed to Russian occupation" would be in reference to future events, which is also not consistent with the meaning of the sentence. Choice (A) is the correct answer.

36.　**C**　Notice the wording changing in the answer choices. Because the information in this sentence is a continuation of previous information, do not use a direction changing transition. Eliminate (A) and (B). Choice (D) would make the start of the sentence, "It then took almost thirty years in 1938," which is not consistent with the intended meaning. Therefore, (C) is the correct answer.

37.　**A**　Notice the wording changing in the answer choices. Because the sentence discusses the scientists learning something new, (B) and (C) are not consistent with the intended meaning of the sentence. Eliminate those choices. In (D), the word "accident" changes the meaning and is not consistent with the intended meaning of the sentence. Eliminate (D). Choice (A) is the correct answer.

38.　**A**　Notice the wording and comma placement changing in the answer choices. The question is testing concision and punctuation. In (B) there are two complete ideas separated by a comma. Since stop punctuation is required to separate two complete ideas, eliminate (B). Choice (C) results in an incomplete sentence, so eliminate it. Choice (D) uses the verb "would make," which is not consistent with the verb "began" later in the sentence. Eliminate (D). Choice (A) is the correct answer.

39.　**C**　The first change in the answer choices is the deletion of a comma, so comma rules are being tested. "After Hitler came to power" is an introductory idea that must be followed by a comma. Eliminate (B) and (D). The next change is the use of the pronoun "he" or the name "Szilard." The name "Szilard" is more precise than "he," which could refer to either Szilard or Hitler. Eliminate (A). Choice (C) is the correct answer.

40. **C** The question is asking if the addition of information about where Szilard fled would benefit the passage. Because the previous sentence already mentions Szilard leaving Germany, this information is not necessary. Eliminate (A) and (B). Choice (D) has nothing to do with the text in question, and can also be eliminated. Choice (C) is therefore the correct answer.

41. **D** The primary change in the answer choices is the inclusion of extra words, so this question is testing concision. In the non-underlined portion of the sentence, there is already mention of the timing of these events, so (A), (B), and (C) are redundant. In order to make the sentence the most concise, eliminate the underlined portion. Therefore, (D) is the correct answer.

42. **A** The verb tense is changing in the answer choices so the question is testing verb tense rules. In order to remain consistent with the rest of the passage, use past tense. Eliminate (B), (C), and (D). Choice (A) is the correct answer.

43. **B** Notice the wording changing in the answer choices in regard to the scientists attending the meeting. Choice (A) sounds like the theories about making atomic power a militaristic reality are occurring at a particular meeting, and (D) sounds like a militaristic reality is attending a meeting. These misplaced modifiers should be eliminated. The addition of the word "while" clarifies that the scientists are the ones attending the meeting. While (B) and (C) are similar in meaning, (B) is more concise. Therefore, (B) is the correct answer.

44. **D** The question is asking for the statement that most accurately represents the information in the graph. Choices (A) and (B) state that the Manhattan Project was the most expensive project in history, but the graph indicates that the Apollo project was more expensive. Choice (C) says the Manhattan Project cost less than comparable energy programs, but this does not reflect information in the graph. Therefore, (D) is the correct answer.

Chapter 9
The Essay

THE SAT ESSAY: WHAT YOU NEED TO KNOW

The SAT includes an optional rhetorical analysis essay. Your job is to read a text (typically a speech or editorial of some sort) and discuss how the author effectively builds an argument. This might be a familiar task if you've done it in school. If not, don't worry. The format is straightforward, and with some practice, you can learn how to write a good SAT essay. In this chapter we'll look at the three tasks you'll need to complete for the essay—reading, analysis, and writing—and show you how to approach each task in the most effective way possible.

THE "OPTIONAL" ESSAY

The Essay used to be a required part of the SAT Writing test, counting for about a third of the Writing score. Some colleges found the writing score to be helpful, while others did not, so when the College Board rolled out the new SAT, they made the Essay "optional." The Essay score is now completely separate from your total score, so the essay has no effect on your 200–800 score. Notice how we're using quotation marks whenever we say the Essay is "optional," though? There's a reason for that: You should consider the Essay to be optional for colleges, but *not* optional for you.

That's because some schools require the Essay and others don't, and you can't take the Essay independently of the rest of the SAT. In other words, if you opt out of the Essay and later you realize you need it for your application, you must retake the entire SAT. So go ahead and write the Essay. You've already killed a Saturday morning and you're sitting in the testing room. Just write it. Also, as we'll show you in this chapter, it's not so ridiculously challenging to prepare for the Essay that you'll gain a lot of time from skipping it.

In short, the Essay can make your college application look more attractive. This score appears on every report you send to colleges. So regardless of whether the schools you apply to look at your essay, they'll at least see that you took the initiative to write the Essay, which is a good thing.

YOUR ESSAY MISSION

The SAT provides you with 50 minutes in which to read a text and write a logical, well-constructed analysis of that text's argument. The thing to remember here is that the College Board is **not asking you for your opinion on a topic or a text**. Your essay will be an **objective** analysis of a speech or argument.

Although the source material changes from test to test, the prompt tends to look something like this:

As you read the passage below, consider how the author uses

- evidence, such as facts or examples, to support claims.
- reasoning to develop ideas and to connect claims and evidence.
- stylistic or persuasive elements, such as word choice or appeals to emotion, to add power to the ideas expressed.

Write an essay in which you explain how [the author] builds an argument to persuade [his/her] audience that [author's claim]. In your essay, analyze how [the author] uses one or more of the features listed above (or features of your own choice) to strengthen the logic and persuasiveness of [his/her] argument. Be sure that your analysis focuses on the most relevant aspects of the passage.

Your essay should not explain whether you agree with [the author's] claims, but rather explain how the author builds an argument to persuade [his/her] audience.

In the Essay section, you will have to

- carefully read a text.
- understand how an author appeals to a reader's logic, emotions, or morals.
- write a logical analysis of an argument.
- explain how style choices can affect an author's persuasiveness.

In the Essay, you will NOT need to

- give your opinion about a text.
- memorize examples from history or literature.
- have previous experience with the text.

Two graders will read and score the essay on a 1–4 scale in three different categories: Reading, Analysis, and Writing.

> 4 = Advanced
>
> 3 = Proficient
>
> 2 = Partial
>
> 1 = Inadequate

Essay Scoring

Each category will receive a total score of 2–8, which is attained by adding the individual 1–4 scores from your two graders.) Each task (Reading, Analysis, and Writing) is scored individually, so a high score in one does *not* guarantee a high score in another. Your final Essay score will be displayed as *x/y/z*, in order, for the Reading, Analysis, and Writing domains.

TASK 1: READING

In order to write an essay that analyzes a source text, you must first read the text. Unlike with the Reading passages, there are no tricks to shorten your reading time or cut out pieces of the text. However, knowing what to look for as you read can help streamline the reading process and give you a good start on the second task of analysis.

According to the College Board and ETS, your Reading score will be based on your

- comprehension of the source text.
- understanding of central ideas, important details, and their relationship.
- accuracy in representation of the source text (i.e., no errors of fact or interpretation introduced).
- use of textual evidence (quotations, paraphrases, or both) to demonstrate understanding of the source text.

When you start the Essay task, the very first thing you have to do is read the text. Obvious, right? But reading for the Essay is more than just pleasure reading, where all you need to worry about is, say, whether Katniss is going to make it. As you read your Essay prompt, you need to consider the central idea (SOAPS) and important details that support that idea (types of appeals and style elements).

SOAPS—Like in the Tub?

SOAPS is an acronym to help you remember the five things you need to look for in order to establish the central idea of a passage or argument.

Speaker
Occasion
Audience
Purpose
Subject

Speaker: Who is speaking or writing?

Knowing whose voice you are reading is a very important part of understanding the text. It will help you understand the author's motivations as well as the reason he or she is speaking or writing in the first place.

Occasion: What happened that requires this speech or text?

The event that caused the author to want to express his or her thoughts is an integral part of analyzing the work. It might be as simple as the type of event in which the speech was given or it could be something larger such as a significant time in a war. You will need to think about the historical context of the text.

For instance, at a wedding, a minister is likely to be optimistic and cheerful; at a funeral, a minister is more likely to be solemn and comforting. The occasion makes all the difference. Taking note of the occasion will help you understand why the author uses a certain tone and what motivates it.

Audience: Who is the intended audience?

Considering your audience is critical when you are writing a speech. Therefore, it is critical that you consider who the author's audience is in order to understand the text. What do you know about him or her? What's the relationship between the speaker/author and the intended audience? What sort of values or prior ideas might the audience have? How might that affect their perception of the speaker/author?

A principal is more likely to be more informal in tone with experienced teachers and provide less detailed information than with new teachers, with whom it's important to make a good impression and establish a position of supportive authority. With new teachers, the principal will need to give clear information and perhaps repeat that information while filling them in on things that didn't need to be said to the more experienced group.

Audience can entirely change a work! When reading your source text for the essay, make sure to consider who the audience is and how that affected how the author built his or her argument.

Qualifications
You should always consider what makes a person credible as an author; for instance, an avid vegetarian might have some bias in writing about the five foods you should never eat. However, on the SAT, you will never read something from an unqualified author.

Purpose: What is the author or speaker's intention?

Occasion, Subject, and Audience all contribute to Purpose. What is the author trying to accomplish with this work? Is it an attack? Defense? Persuasion? Does it aim to give praise or blame? Is its goal to teach or is it something else?

Subject: What is the main idea?

Of course, you need to know what the work is about. What is the topic? What is the author's main point? What are the main lines of reasoning used?

Appeals

A rhetorical appeal is a persuasive strategy that authors and speakers use to support their claims (or, in a debate, to respond to opposing arguments). When a speaker or author wants to convince an audience of something, there are three main types of rhetorical appeals that can be used.

Appeal to Credibility: "Why Should I Believe You?"

This is the author's way of establishing trust with the audience. We tend to believe people whom we respect, and a good writer knows this! One of the central tasks of persuasion is to project an impression to the reader that the author is someone worth listening to, as well as someone who is likable and worthy of respect. Remember in SOAPS when we talked about the credibility of the speaker? This is how an author might use that to his or her benefit.

Appeal to Emotion: "Gee, That Made Me Feel All Warm and Fuzzy"

This is when the author tries to appeal to the reader's emotions. This allows an author or speaker to connect with an audience by using fear, humor, happiness, disgust, and so on. Imagery and language choice are often big components of appeals to emotions.

Appeal to Logic: "Well, This Just Makes Sense!"

This connects with an audience's reason or logic. This isn't logic like the formal logic in math, philosophy, or even computer science; it is the consistency and clarity of an argument as well as the logic of evidence and reasons.

Once you find all the SOAPS points and examples of appeals, you've got what you need for the Reading task. Remember, for the Reading task, the College Board and ETS wants to see that you understand the text, can identify the central idea/theme of the text, and know how details and examples support that central idea.

TASK 2: ANALYSIS

Remember: a good score on one task does not guarantee a good score on another. Doing a good job explaining the main idea of the speech and the details that support that main idea will get you a good Reading score, but now we need to talk about the Analysis Task.

For the Analysis task, you'll have to determine the pieces of evidence, stylistic elements, or logical reasoning the author uses to effectively achieve his or her objective.

According to the College Board and ETS, your Analysis score will be based on your ability to

- analyze the source text and understand the analytical task.
- evaluate the author's use of evidence, reasoning, and/or stylistic and persuasive elements, and/or features chosen by the student.
- support claims or points made in the response.
- focus on features of the text most relevant to addressing the task.

For the second task, you will need to explain the author's use of specific elements in the essay. It's not enough to say, "The author uses a quote to appeal to the audience's reason." You have to explain *how* the quote appeals to the audience's reason. This task is all about the *how* and *why*. Look for facts, evidence, literary devices, persuasive elements, and other elements the author has used to form his or her argument.

Here are some common style elements that may show up in the text.

Style Detail	Definition	Example
Allusion	A brief reference to a person, thing, or idea from history, literature, politics, or something with cultural significance.	"Don't ask him for a donation; he's a total Scrooge." "Chocolate was her Kryptonite."
Comparisons	Comparing two distinct things; the author/speaker makes a connection between them	"Juliet is the sun." "My love is like a red rose."
Diction	The author's choice of words.	"Skinny" instead of "slender" sounds less flattering. Slang or vernacular gives a text an informal feel, while a professional vocabulary makes a text feel more formal.
Hyperbole	Exaggeration not meant to be taken literally	"I'm so hungry I could eat a horse."
Imagery	Using language that appeals to our senses. Visual representation of an object or idea is a common perception of imagery, but imagery actually can create ideas that appeal to all five senses.	"The woman walked by, trailing a thick, cloying cloud of perfume." "The percussive thump of the large drums vibrated in her chest as the band marched by."
Juxtaposition	Placing two ideas side-by-side in order for the audience to make a comparison or contrast	"It was the best of times, it was the worst of times…"
Repetition	Deliberate repetition of a letter, word, or phrase to achieve a specific effect.	"We shall not flag or fail. We shall go on to the end. We shall fight in France, we shall fight on the seas and oceans, we shall fight with growing confidence and growing strength in the air…"
Statistics or quotes	A writer or speaker may add credibility to his or her argument by adding data or quotes from a respected/recognized source.	A quote from the American Academy of Pediatrics in a speech about best practices for carseat use.
Syntax	How words are put together to achieve a certain effect. First and last words of an idea can be particularly important.	An author who wants to convey a message quickly or urgently might choose to use short, direct sentences, while an author who wants to deliberately slow down a text may use longer, more convoluted sentences.
Tone	The attitude of the author/speaker toward the subject	Sarcastic, professional, critical

Note: These devices are deliberately used by the author/speaker for a specific purpose. You will need to know the purposes of the devices and their effects on a text, but you will not need to know the specific names.

Spot the Element

Let's read the following pieces of text and then identify the rhetorical device used in each.

1. "In our kitchen, he would bolt his orange juice (squeezed on one of those ribbed glass sombreros and then poured off through a strainer) and grab a bite of toast (the toaster a simple tin box, a kind of little hut with slit and slanted sides, that rested over a gas burner and browned one side of the bread, in stripes, at a time), and then he would dash, so hurriedly that his necktie flew back over his shoulder, down through our yard, past the grapevines hung with buzzing Japanese-beetle traps, to the yellow brick building, with its tall smokestack and wide playing fields, where he taught."

   —John Updike, "My Father on the Verge of Disgrace"

   Rhetorical device:_____

2. "Five score years ago, a great American, in whose symbolic shadow we stand today, signed the Emancipation Proclamation. This momentous decree came as a great beacon light of hope to millions of Negro slaves who had been seared in the flames of withering injustice. It came as a joyous daybreak to end the long night of their captivity."

   —Martin Luther King, Jr., "I Have a Dream"

   Rhetorical device:_____

3. "When he lifted me up in his arms I felt I had left all my troubles on the floor beneath me like gigantic concrete shoes."

   —Anne Tyler, Earthly Possessions

   Rhetorical device:_____

4. "Well now, one winter it was so cold that all the geese flew backward and all the fish moved south and even the snow turned blue. Late at night, it got so frigid that all spoken words froze solid afore they could be heard. People had to wait until sunup to find out what folks were talking about the night before."

   —"Paul Bunyan and Babe the Blue Ox"

   Rhetorical device:_____

5. "I was not born in a manger. I was actually born on Krypton and sent here by my father, Jor-el, to save the Planet Earth."

—Senator Barack Obama, speech at a fund-raiser for Catholic charities, October 16, 2008

Rhetorical device:_____

Answer Key

1. Imagery (visual)
2. Metaphor (beacon of light)
3. Simile
4. Hyperbole
5. Allusion

SOAPS AND APPEALS DRILL #1

See if you can identify the SOAPS and rhetorical devices used in the following prompts:

(John F. Kennedy. September 12, 1962. Rice Stadium, Houston, TX)

1   We set sail on this new sea because there is new knowledge to be gained, and new rights to be won, and they must be won and used for the progress of all people. For space science, like nuclear science and all technology, has no conscience of its own. Whether it will become a force for good or ill depends on man, and only if the United States occupies a position of pre-eminence can we help decide whether this new ocean will be a sea of peace or a new terrifying theater of war. I do not say that we should or will go unprotected against the hostile misuse of space any more than we go unprotected against the hostile use of land or sea, but I do say that space can be explored and mastered without feeding the fires of war, without repeating the mistakes that man has made in extending his writ around this globe of ours.

2   There is no strife, no prejudice, no national conflict in outer space as yet. Its hazards are hostile to us all. Its conquest deserves the best of all mankind, and its opportunity for peaceful cooperation many never come again. But why, some say, the moon? Why choose this as our goal? And they may well ask why climb the highest mountain? Why, 35 years ago, fly the Atlantic? Why does Rice play Texas?

3   We choose to go to the moon. We choose to go to the moon in this decade and do the other things, not because they are easy, but because they are hard, because that goal will serve to organize and measure the best of our energies and skills, because that challenge is one that we are willing to accept, one we are unwilling to postpone, and one which we intend to win, and the others, too.

4   It is for these reasons that I regard the decision last year to shift our efforts in space from low to high gear as among the most important decisions that will be made during my incumbency in the office of the Presidency…

5   To be sure, we are behind, and will be behind for some time in manned flight. But we do not intend to stay behind, and in this decade, we shall make up and move ahead.

6   The growth of our science and education will be enriched by new knowledge of our universe and environment, by new techniques of learning and mapping and observation, by new tools and computers for industry, medicine, the home as well as the school. Technical institutions, such as Rice, will reap the harvest of these gains.

7 And finally, the space effort itself, while still in its infancy, has already created a great number of new companies, and tens of thousands of new jobs. Space and related industries are generating new demands in investment and skilled personnel, and this city and this State, and this region, will share greatly in this growth. What was once the furthest outpost on the old frontier of the West will be the furthest outpost on the new frontier of science and space. Houston, your City of Houston, with its Manned Spacecraft Center, will become the heart of a large scientific and engineering community. During the next 5 years the National Aeronautics and Space Administration expects to double the number of scientists and engineers in this area, to increase its outlays for salaries and expenses to $60 million a year; to invest some $200 million in plant and laboratory facilities; and to direct or contract for new space efforts over $1 billion from this Center in this City...

8 Many years ago the great British explorer George Mallory, who was to die on Mount Everest, was asked why did he want to climb it. He said, "Because it is there."

9 Well, space is there, and we're going to climb it, and the moon and the planets are there, and new hopes for knowledge and peace are there. And, therefore, as we set sail we ask God's blessing on the most hazardous and dangerous and greatest adventure on which man has ever embarked.

Thank you.

S: President John F. Kennedy

O: speaking in favor of expanded space travel

A: Rice University and Houston, Texas

P: to persuade the audience to be enthusiastic about space travel

S: difficult goals are still worth pursuing

(John F. Kennedy. September 12, 1962. Rice Stadium, Houston, TX)	**Appeal to Authority:** *He's the President!* **Audience:** *Rice students, faculty, Houston residents*
We set sail on this new sea because there is new knowledge to be gained, and new rights to be won, and they must be won and used for the progress of all people.	**Purpose**
Why does Rice play Texas?	**Audience/Allusion:** *Rice has an athletic rivalry with the University of Texas. Kennedy is showing that some challenges are inspiring.*
We choose to go to the moon. We choose to go to the moon in this decade and do the other things, not because they are easy, but because they are hard, because that goal will serve to organize and measure the best of our energies and skills, because that challenge is one that we are willing to accept, one we are unwilling to postpone, and one which we intend to win, and the others, too.	**Subject**
I regard the decision to shift our efforts in space from low to high gear as among the most important decisions made during my incumbency in the office of the Presidency…	**Occasion** **Appeal to Authority**
And finally, the space effort itself, while still in its infancy, has already created a great number of new companies, and tens of thousands of new jobs. Space and related industries are generating new demands in investment and skilled personnel, and this city and this State, and this region, will share greatly in this growth. What was once the furthest outpost on the old frontier of the West will be the furthest outpost on the new frontier of science and space. Houston, your City of Houston, with its Manned Spacecraft Center, will become the heart of a large scientific and engineering community. During the next 5 years the National Aeronautics and Space Administration expects to double the number of scientists and engineers in this area, to increase its outlays for salaries and expenses to $60 million a year; to invest some $200 million in plant and laboratory facilities; and to direct or contract for new space efforts over $1 billion from this Center in this City…	**Appeal to Logic/Audience:** *Here, Kennedy is giving us the rational reasons to support the space industry: it creates jobs. We know that the audience values education and the furthering of science because JFK discusses the benefit to the scientific community as well as the medical community.*
ask God's blessing	**Audience:** *many Texans in the 1960s would be religious people who would appreciate this reference.*

SOAPS AND APPEALS DRILL #2

Read the following prompt and underline anything that references SOAPS points. Look for rhetorical devices.

Excerpt(s) from THE RAREST OF THE RARE: VANISHING ANIMALS, TIMELESS WORLDS by Diane Ackerman, 1995. Used by permission of Random House, an imprint and division of Penguin Random House LLC. All rights reserved.

1   Leafing idly through *The Home Planet*, I stop at a picture of Earth floating against the black velvet of space. Africa and Europe are visible under swirling white clouds, but the predominant color is blue. This was the one picture from the Apollo missions that told the whole story—how small the planet is in the vast sprawl of space, how fragile its environments are. Seen from space, Earth has no national borders, no military zones, no visible fences. Quite the opposite. You can see how storm systems swirling above a continent may well affect the grain yield half a world away. The entire atmosphere of the planet—all the air we breathe, all the sky we fly through, even the ozone layer—is visible as the thinnest rind. The picture eloquently reminds us that Earth is a single organism. For me, the book contains visual mnemonics of how I feel about nature. At some point, one asks, "Toward what end is my life lived?" A great freedom comes from being able to answer that question. A sleeper can be decoyed out of bed by the sheer beauty of dawn on the open seas. Part of my job, as I see it, is to allow that to happen. Sleepers like me need at some point to rise and take their turn on morning watch, for the sake of the planet, but also for their own sake, for the enrichment of lives. From the deserts of Namibia to the razor-backed Himalayas, there are wonderful creatures that have roamed Earth much longer than we, creatures that not only are worthy of our respect but could teach us about ourselves.

2   Some of those wilds I know personally, at the level of sand, orchid, wingless fly, human being. So each photograph is an album, a palimpsest, a pageant. There is Torishima, the little island south of Tokyo, which is the final stronghold of short-tailed albatrosses. There is French Frigate Shoals, the last refuge of the Hawaiian monk seal. There is Antarctica, home to vast herds of animals. While I look at a photograph of the Hawaiian Islands—puddles of ink on a bright copper sea—I remember the sound and rumble of humpback-whale song cresting over me as I swam. Humpback whales have had a civilization without cities, a kind of roaming culture, for many ages. They live in the ocean as in a wide blue cave. They pass on an oral tradition, teach one another their songs, abandon old versions, use rhyme. Our recordings of them go back to 1951, but after more than forty years, the whales haven't returned to their original songs of the fifties. Just imagine the arias, ballads, and cantatas of ancient days

that have filled the oceans with song, then died out, never to be heard again. Today we can visit the campfires of a few remaining tribes of Stone Age people and hear the stories they tell, stories marvelous, imaginative, and rich with wonder. But we will never know all the lost stories of the cave people. The same may be true of humpback whales. As I page through the book, I feast on habitats far-flung and dizzying. Life haunts every one of them, no matter how distant, dry, hot, salty, or sunless. The photograph of Africa reminds me of the giant animals caged forever in the past. The large animals we associate with Africa—elephants, giraffes, hippos, ostriches, and others—are dwindling remnants of the massive creatures that once flourished…. When I look at the photographs of Borneo, Brazil, and New Guinea, I remember how the dynamic well of the rain forests has generated new life-forms. Our genetic safety net is woven from their biodiversity.

Write an essay in which you explain how Diane Ackerman builds an argument to persuade her audience. In your essay, analyze how Ackerman uses one or more of the features in the directions that precede the passage (or features of your own choice) to strengthen the logic and persuasiveness of her argument. Be sure that your analysis focuses on the most relevant features of the passage.

Your essay should not explain whether you agree with Ackerman's claims, but rather explain how Ackerman builds an argument to persuade her audience.

S: Ackerman appears to be a naturalist, though we cannot be sure that she is a scientist.

O: mankind's current place within environmental history

A: general audience

P: to inspire serious concern regarding mankind's prospects for extinction

S: We are not special in the grand scheme of history; we, too, are vulnerable.

Leafing idly through *The Home Planet*, I stop at a picture of Earth floating against the black velvet of space. Africa and Europe are visible under swirling white clouds, but the predominant color is blue.	***Imagery***: *While not a developed story, Ackerman's experience leafing through a book of photographs introduces her inspiration for the essay and personalizes her points. The description she gives of the planet Earth has poetic flourishes, indicating its beauty in the eyes of the author. Throughout this piece of writing, Ackerman's depictions of the Earth's beauty shows her reader what is at stake if humans are inattentive.*
This was the one picture from the Apollo missions that told the whole story—how small the planet is in the vast sprawl of space, how fragile its environments are. Seen from space, Earth has no national borders, no military zones, no visible fences. Quite the opposite. You can see how storm systems swirling above a continent may well affect the grain yield half a world away. The entire atmosphere of the planet—all the air we breathe, all the sky we fly through, even the ozone layer—is visible as the thinnest rind.	***Imagery and Depth of Observation***: *Ackerman makes several observations here about how small the Earth is relative to space, and how fragile it is; she also notes that Earth from this distance has no political markings.*
The picture eloquently reminds us that Earth is a single organism.	***Claim/Comparison***: *Ackerman's prior statements describing the lack of visible divisions on the face of the Earth lead up to this claim about the Earth's unity and likening it to a single organism.*
For me, the book contains visual mnemonics of how I feel about nature. At some point, one asks, "Toward what end is my life lived?" A great freedom comes from being able to answer that question. A sleeper can be decoyed out of bed by the sheer beauty of dawn on the open seas.	***Appeal to Emotion***: *Ackerman shares her feelings as she looks at the photos, as well as a profound question that people ask themselves.*
Part of my job, as I see it, is to allow that to happen. Sleepers like me need at some point to rise and take their turn on morning watch, for the sake of the planet, but also for their own sake, for the enrichment of lives.	***Comparison***: *Ackerman here implies that people, including herself, need to take responsibility for the planet's wellbeing not only for it but for themselves. She refers to herself and others as "sleepers," asserting that we need to "wake up."*
From the deserts of Namibia to the razor-backed Himalayas, there are wonderful creatures that have roamed Earth much longer than we, creatures that not only are worthy of our respect but could teach us about ourselves.	***Evidence and claim***: *Ackerman gives examples of the various landscapes and their inhabitants to which we should be attentive; she reiterates her claim that people need to respect nature and in turn learn about themselves.*

SOAPS AND APPEALS DRILL #3

Again read the prompt looking for SOAPS and rhetorical devices.

> **Excerpted from *Who grows your food? (And why it matters)*,
> an article by Bob Schildgen that originally appeared in the
> November/December 2004 issue of Sierra magazine.
> www.sierramagazine.org.**

1   We [environmentalists] criticize farmers for the use of polluting
pesticides and fertilizers; for robbing wildlife of water by pulling
it from rivers and aquifers for irrigation; for damaging streams
and causing erosion through bad grazing practices; and for
erasing wildlife habitat. We condemn agriculture for poisoning
wells in the Midwest and California's Central Valley, and blame
it for the dead zone in the Gulf of Mexico, where the Mississippi
dumps toxic runoff from a third of the U.S. landmass.

2   Such criticism usually doesn't sit too well with the farmers
themselves. After all, they are feeding us, and doing it as
efficiently as they know how. It often sounds as if we're yelling at
them across a cultural gap.

3   Fortunately, some farmers are now bridging this gap, with help
from those environmentalists who support sustainable agriculture.
Farmers like the Dubas family from eastern Nebraska… are trying
environmentally friendly methods and selling their products
locally. They're running a diversified operation, rotating crops,
keeping plenty of land in pasture, and raising their livestock
without routinely dosing them with antibiotics.

4   The history of the Dubas family is one that has played out across
rural America. Ron Dubas's father made a living on 200 to 300
acres. Today, the family runs 2,000 acres and struggles to keep
afloat. Four hundred miles northeast, on the northern edge of the
corn belt in Wisconsin's unglaciated prairie, my grandparents got
by on 80 acres. Now farms up there are often five times that size.
The number of real producing farms nationwide has shrunk from
3.3 million in 1950 to 750,000 today.

5   What explains this decline? Price, mainly. You can't afford to
stay in business if your costs exceed what you're paid for your
product. In 1998, for example, hog prices plummeted—from 45
cents a pound to less than 10 cents a pound, only one-fourth the
cost of production. Customers in the supermarket had no way of
noticing: The price of a pork chop fell by only pennies.

6   What's this got to do with the environment? Well, farmers can
cope by producing more, in the hope that volume will make
up for low prices. Or they can switch to other commodities,
but they'll likely raise them in high volume to cover previous
losses. Either way, they're forced to resort to more intensive

cultivation and more irrigation, fertilizers, and pesticides. They have long been encouraged to do this by the agricultural establishment. Universities supplied the research and technical assistance to ramp up production, lending agencies the capital, and government the subsidies. For years the mantra was "Get big or get out," and Richard Nixon's agriculture secretary exhorted, "Plant fencerow to fencerow."

7   But this "efficiency" has a high cost. As production soared, prices generally dropped, encouraging more production. The math is simple. Consider corn. In 1955, a farmer got $1.43 a bushel. Adjusted for inflation, that bushel should be worth over $9 today, but the price hovers around $2 or $3. Although the yield has almost tripled since the 1950s, this increase hasn't kept pace with rising expenses, like taxes, mortgages, fertilizers, and pesticides. Moreover, half of that increased yield, according to research at Purdue University, has come from increased use of nitrogen fertilizers, a major source of pollution.

8   The biggest beneficiaries of the farmers' cornucopia are the agribusiness corporations that absorb the glut of cheap raw material and turn it into our dazzlingly diverse (and dangerously unhealthy) supply of processed foods. Take soft drinks made with cheap corn sweeteners. Sixty years ago, each American consumed an average of 60 12-ounce servings of soda a year. Today, we're guzzling almost ten times that much. Yesterday's occasional treat has exploded into a regular diet of 64-ounce Double Gulps.

9   As food-processing profits have grown, the farmer's average share of food income has shrunk. In 1950, farmers got 50 cents out of every retail food dollar; now they receive less than 20 cents. The rest goes to processing, distribution, and marketing. While thousands of farmers take outside jobs to survive, advertisers spend $28 billion a year just to promote food products. To illustrate the triumph of marketing over honest toil: The corn in a one-pound, $4 box of cornflakes costs about four cents. The retailer is paid eight cents to process a coupon for this box. Yes, the farmer gets half as much as the coupon shufflers.

S: an environmentalist

O: the state of agriculture in the modern Western world

A: other environmentalists

P: to explain how farmers have been disadvantaged by modern industrial farming practices and to inspire understanding; also, to show hope for the future (Dubas family)

S: Environmentalists and farmers need a greater understanding of each other's priorities and challenges. Modern industrial agriculture does not benefit farmers economically and may slow the development of more sustainable methods.

We [environmentalists] criticize farmers for the use of polluting pesticides and fertilizers; for robbing wildlife of water by pulling it from rivers and aquifers for irrigation; for damaging streams and causing erosion through bad grazing practices; and for erasing wildlife habitat. We condemn agriculture for poisoning wells in the Midwest and California's Central Valley, and blame it for the dead zone in the Gulf of Mexico, where the Mississippi dumps toxic runoff from a third of the U.S. landmass.

Audience: Schildgen establishes right away that his audience already agrees with a few of the claims in paragraph 1. He is speaking to environmentalists. He is establishing common ground with the audience, but he will later raise issues they may not have considered.

Such criticism usually doesn't sit too well with the farmers themselves. After all, they are feeding us, and doing it as efficiently as they know how.

Appeal to Emotion

yelling at them across a cultural gap
Farmers like the Dubas family from eastern Nebraska... are trying environmentally friendly methods and selling their products locally. They're running a diversified operation, rotating crops, keeping plenty of land in pasture, and raising their livestock without routinely dosing them with antibiotics.

Metaphor

Anecdote: The example of the Dubas family helps to persuade the reader that environmentally-friendly changes to agriculture are possible.

Ron Dubas's father made a living on 200 to 300 acres. Today, the family runs 2,000 acres and struggles to keep afloat. Four hundred miles northeast, on the northern edge of the corn belt in Wisconsin's unglaciated prairie, my grandparents got by on 80 acres. Now farms up there are often five times that size. The number of real producing farms nationwide has shrunk from 3.3 million in 1950 to 750,000 today.

Appeal to Logic: Through specific examples and statistical data, the author persuades us that farming has changed.

In 1998, for example, hog prices plummeted-from 45 cents a pound to less than 10 cents a pound, only one-fourth the cost of production.

Appeal to Logic

The math is simple. Consider corn. In 1955, a farmer got $1.43 a bushel. Adjusted for inflation, that bushel should be worth over $9 today, but the price hovers around $2 or $3. Although the yield has almost tripled since the 1950s, this increase hasn't kept pace with rising expenses, like taxes, mortgages, fertilizers, and pesticides.

Appeal to Logic: statistics and comparing time periods to show a general trend

Double Gulps

Allusion: to point out the absurdity of the modern food industry?

As food-processing profits have grown, the farmer's average share of food income has shrunk. In 1950, farmers got 50 cents out of every retail food dollar; now they receive less than 20 cents. The rest goes to processing, distribution, and marketing. While thousands of farmers take outside jobs to survive, advertisers spend $28 billion a year just to promote food products. To illustrate the triumph of marketing over honest toil: The corn in a one-pound, $4 box of cornflakes costs about four cents. The retailer is paid eight cents to process a coupon for this box. Yes, the farmer gets half as much as the coupon shufflers.

Appeal to Logic: statistics and more time comparisons to invoke sympathy for the plight of farmers

TASK 3: WRITING

The final task of the Essay test is to actually write the essay. According to the College Board, this requires you to

- make use of a central claim.
- use effective organization and progression of ideas.
- use varied sentence structures.
- employ precise word choice.
- maintain consistent, appropriate style and tone.
- show command of the conventions of standard written English.

This is also where you show your grader that you have read, understood, and analyzed the text.

Essay Template

Introduction

Your introduction needs to do three things:

1. Describe the text. This is where you'll bring in the SOAPS points. This can be done in one sentence.
2. Paraphrase the argument. This is where you'll show your grader that you understand the text by concisely summing up the main points and the overall message of the text. The Reading score comes from your demonstration of comprehension of the text.
3. Introduce the examples you will be discussing in the body paragraphs. You will establish a framework in your introduction that you should then follow for the rest of the essay.

Body Paragraphs

The body paragraphs will focus on different appeals or style elements the author uses to effectively communicate the argument. Each body paragraph will need to do the following:

1. Name and explain the rhetorical device or appeal.
   a. Where is it in the text?
   b. Use short, relevant quotes to show you understand the text and the rhetorical device, but do not rely on long excerpts from the passage. In order to get a high score, you need to use your words to explain what's going on.

2. Identify the effects of the author's rhetorical choices.
   a. Explain the connection between the rhetorical device/appeal and the text, and your argument in general. Do not simply quote chunks of text and then briefly paraphrase. Your goal is to answer the question, "How does this contribute to the author's argument?"
   b. For example:
      i. Do not simply say, "This is an example of imagery."
      ii. Explain why the imagery is effective. Perhaps the author's descriptions of the beautiful sunset effectively draw in the reader, creating an emotional connection between the author and her audience. This connection may make the audience more sympathetic to the author's subsequent points because there is an emotional connection now.
   c. Explaining how the device or appeal works is how you show your grader your ability to analyze the text.

Conclusion

1. Restate the goal of the text and briefly paraphrase the elements you discussed in your essay.
2. Be concise and accurate.

ESSAY CHECKLIST

Check your essay for

1. An introductory paragraph.
   Does your introductory paragraph contain a strong topic sentence, one that lets the reader know what the paper will discuss? Does your introductory paragraph mention what examples your paper will include?

2. Body paragraphs.
   Does each body paragraph contain a nice clear transition sentence? Does each body paragraph develop one or multiple similar examples? Did you include short quotes?

3. A conclusion.
   Your essay has a conclusion, right? Did you restate your main ideas? Did you summarize how your quotes are relevant?

WRITING TIPS!

- Maintain a formal style and objective tone. Avoid "I" and "you." No slang.
- Use varied sentence structure.
- Write neatly.
- Use clear transitions.
- Use short, relevant quotes from the text.
- Don't worry about official terms for things. "Appeal to the emotions" is fine instead of specifically referencing "pathos," and "comparison of two things" is okay instead of referring to a metaphor. If you *do* know the official terms, though, feel free to use them!

PACING

You have 50 minutes for the essay. Spend the first five to ten minutes reading the prompt and brainstorming examples.

Use the next 40-45 minutes to write your essay. Aim for a five or six paragraph essay, with an introduction, three to four body paragraphs, and a conclusion. Stay focused on the topic, and keep things simple.

Take the last five minutes to proofread your essay. Watch out for grammar mistakes—one or two may be okay, but too many of them will hurt your Writing score. If you're unsure how to spell a word, choose a different one.

The visual appearance of your essay is important, as well. While you should avoid double-spacing or otherwise puffing up your essay, it helps to indent your paragraphs, neatly erase any mistakes, and write as legibly as you can manage. If you make the reader's job easier, you're more likely to get a better score.

Chapter 10
Miscellaneous

PREPOSITION LIST

Prepositions are everywhere in our language, but you don't need to know every preposition in the world to do well on the SAT. In fact, there are really only a handful of prepositions that are regularly tested, but keep your eyes peeled for these, as seeing one could mean a prepositional phrase or an idiom.

- about
- above
- after
- against
- among
- around
- as
- at
- before
- behind
- below
- beneath
- beside(s)
- between
- beyond
- but
- by
- despite
- down
- during
- except
- for
- from
- in
- inside
- into

- like
- of
- off
- on
- onto
- outside
- over
- per
- regarding
- since
- than
- through
- to
- toward
- towards
- under
- underneath
- unlike
- until
- up
- upon
- versus
- with
- within
- without

IDIOM LIST

Here's a list of the idioms tested most frequently on the SAT. Learn them!

About

Worry...about

If you **worry** too much **about** the SAT, you'll develop an ulcer.

As

Define...as

Some people **define** insanity **as** repeating the same action but expecting a different outcome.

Regard...as

Art historians **regard** the *Mona Lisa* **as** one of the greatest works of art.

Not so...as

He is **not so** much smart **as** cunning.

So...as to be

She is **so** beautiful **as to be** exquisite.

Think of...as

Think of it more **as** a promise than a threat.

See...as

Many people **see** euthanasia **as** an escape from pain.

The same...as

Mom and Dad gave **the same** punishment to me **as** to you.

As...as

Memorizing idioms is not **as** fun **as** playing bingo.

At

Target...at

The commercials were obviously **targeted at** teenage boys.

For
Responsible for
You are **responsible for** the child.

From
Prohibit...from
He was **prohibited from** entering the public library after he accidentally set the dictionary on fire with a magnifying glass.

Different...from
There are some who argue that Chicago's deep-dish pizza is not so **different from** New York City's pan pizza.

Over
Dispute over
The men had a **dispute over** money.

That
So...that
He was **so** late **that** he missed the main course.

Hypothesis...that
The **hypothesis that** aspartame causes brain tumors has not been proven yet.

To be
Believe...to be
His friends do not **believe** the ring he bought at the auction **to be** Lady Gaga's; they all think he was tricked.

Estimate...to be
The time he has spent impersonating Elvis is **estimated to be** longer than the time Elvis himself spent performing.

To
Forbid...to
I **forbid** you **to** call me before noon.

Ability…to

If you take the test enough times, you might develop the **ability to** choose the credited responses without reading the questions.

Attribute…to

Many amusing quips are **attributed to** Anna Kendrick.

Require…to

Before you enter the house you are **required to** take off your hat.

Responsibility…to

Reporters have a **responsibility to** accurately relay the news.

Permit…to

I don't **permit** my children **to** play with knives in the living room.

Superior…to

My pasta sauce is far **superior to** my mother-in-law's.

Try…to

Try to stay awake during the essay section of the test.

With

Credit…with

Many people **credit** Christopher Columbus **with** the discovery of America, but Native Americans were here first.

Associate…with

Most politicians prefer not to be **associated with** the Mafia.

Contrast…with

My father likes to **contrast** my grades **with** my brother's.

No preposition

Consider…(nothing)

Art historians **consider** the *Mona Lisa* one of the greatest works of art.

More than one preposition

Distinguish…from

I can't **distinguish** day **from** night.

Distinguish between...and

I can **distinguish** between black **and** white.

Native (noun)...of

Russell Crowe is a **native of** Australia.

Native (adjective)...to

The kangaroo is **native to** Australia.

Comparisons and links

Not only...but also

She is **not only** beautiful, **but also** smart.

Not...but

The review was **not** mean-spirited **but** merely flippant.

Either...or

I must have **either** chocolate ice cream **or** carrot cake to complete a grand meal.

Neither...nor

Because Jenny was grounded, she could **neither** leave the house **nor** use the telephone.

Both...and

When given the choice, I choose **both** ice cream **and** cake.

More...than; Less...than

The chimpanzee is much **more** intelligent **than** the orangutan.

As vs. like

As is used to compare actions.

Like is used to compare nouns.

He did not vote for the Libertarian Party, **as** I did.

Her coat is just **like** mine.

Like vs. such as

Like means *similar to*.

Such as means *for example*.

The mule, **like** the donkey, is a close relative of the horse.

Many of my favorite ice cream flavors, **such as** chocolate chip and strawberry, are also available as frozen yogurt.

The more…the -er

The **more** you ignore me, the **louder** I get.

From…to

Scores on the SAT range **from** 400 **to** 1600.

Just as…so too

Just as I crossed over to the dark side, **so too** will you, my son.

Miscellaneous

Each vs. all or both

Use *each* when you want to emphasize the separateness of the items.

Use *both* (for two things) or *all* (for more than two things) when you want to emphasize the togetherness of the items.

Each of the doctors had his own specialty.

Both of the women went to Bryn Mawr for their undergraduate degrees.

All of the letters received before January 15 went into the drawing for the $10 million prize.

Whether vs. if

Use *whether* when there are *two possibilities*.

Use *if* in *conditional statements*.

Eduardo wasn't sure **whether** he could make it to the party.

If Eduardo comes to the party, he will bring a bag of chips.

Yes, These are Real Words

Sometimes the SAT likes to use big words to frighten you. If you see these in an Improving Sentences or Improving Paragraphs question, see if ETS and the College Board have given you an option to use a simpler, more direct word.

Furthermore	Nonetheless
Heretofore	Notwithstanding
Hereinafter	Ought
Inasmuch	Ongoing
Insofar	Therefore
Likewise	Thereby
Moreover	Whereas
Nevertheless	Whereby

Part II
English and
Reading
Workout for
the ACT

Chapter 11
The ACT
English Test

The English test is not a grammar test. It's also not a test of how well you write. In fact, it tests your editing skills: your ability to fix errors in grammar and punctuation and to improve the organization and style of five different passages. In this chapter, you'll learn the basic strategy of how to crack the passages and review three of the most heavily tested concepts—commas, apostrophes, and strategy questions.

FUN FACTS ABOUT THE ENGLISH TEST

Before we dive into the details of the content and strategy, let's review what the English test looks like. Remember, the five tests on the ACT are always given in the same order, and English is always first.

There are five prose passages on topics ranging from historical essays to personal narratives. Each passage is typically accompanied by 15 questions for a total of 75 questions that you must answer in 45 minutes. Portions of each passage are underlined, and you must decide if these are correct as written or if one of the other answers would fix or improve the selection. Other questions will ask you to add, cut, or re-order text, while still others will ask you to evaluate the passage as a whole.

WRITING

While the idea of English grammar makes most of us think of persnickety, picky rules long since outdated, English is actually a dynamic, adaptive language. We add new vocabulary all the time, and we let common usage influence and change many rules. Pick up a handful of style books and you'll find very few rules that everyone agrees upon. This is actually good news for studying for the ACT: You're unlikely to see questions testing the most obscure or most disputed rules. However, few of us follow ALL of even the most basic, universally accepted rules when we speak, much less when we e-mail, text, or tweet.

The 4 C's: Complete, Consistent, Clear, and Concise

ACT test writers will never make you name a particular error. But with 75 questions, they can certainly test a lot of different rules—and yes, that's leaving out the obscure and debated rules. You would drive yourself crazy if you tried to learn, just for the ACT, all of the grammar you never knew in the first place. You're much better off with a common sense approach. That's where the 4 C's come in.

Good writing should be in *complete* sentences; everything should be *consistent*; the meaning should be *clear*. The best answer, free of any errors, will be the most *concise*.

Grammar Review

The 4 C's make sense of the rules you should specifically study. Focus your efforts on heavily tested topics that you can identify and know (or can learn) how to fix. In *Cracking the ACT*, we focus on the use of punctuation and conjunctions to link complete and incomplete ideas, verbs, pronouns, apostrophes, and transitions. Can't identify what the question is testing? Apply the 4 C's.

In this book, we teach you how to crack two topics students find the trickiest: commas and apostrophes. We also teach you how to crack strategy questions, another heavily tested category.

But first, you need to know how crack the test and apply our 5-step Basic Approach.

HOW TO CRACK THE ENGLISH TEST

The Passages

As always on the ACT, time is your enemy. With only 45 minutes to review 5 passages and answer 75 questions, you can't read a passage in its entirety and then go back to do the questions. For each passage, work the questions as you make your way through the passage. Read from the beginning until you get to an underlined selection, work that question, and then resume reading until the next underlined portion and the next question.

The Questions

Not all questions are created equal. In fact, ACT divides the questions on the English test into two categories: Usage and Mechanics, and Rhetorical Skills. These designations will mean very little to you when you're taking the test. All questions are worth the same amount of points, after all, and you'll crack most of the questions the same way, regardless of what ACT calls them. Many of the Rhetorical Skills questions, however, are those on organization and style, and some take longer to answer than other questions do. Since there is no order of difficulty of the passages or of the questions, all that matters is that you identify your *Now, Later, Never* questions and make sure you finish.

The Basic Approach

While some of the Rhetorical Skills questions come with *actual* questions, the majority of the 75 questions provide only 4 answer choices and little direction of what to do. So allow us to tell you *exactly* what to do.

Step 1: Identify the Topic

For each underlined portion, finish the sentence and then look at the answers. The answers are your clues to identifying what the question is testing. Let's start off with this first question.

For the first episode of its new radio

series, CBS decided to adapt H.G. Wells' <u>*The*</u>

<u>*War of the Worlds'*</u>, the story of a Martian

invasion of Earth.

1. **A.**   NO CHANGE
    B.   Wells' *The War of the World's,*
    C.   Wells' *The War of the Worlds,*
    D.   Wells *The War of the Worlds,*

Do any of the words change? No. What is the only thing that does change? Apostrophes. So what must be the topic of the question? Apostrophes.

Always identify the topic of the question first. Pay attention to what changes versus what stays the same in the answers.

Step 2: Use POE

You may have chosen an answer for question 1 already. If you haven't, don't worry: We'll review all the rules of apostrophes later in the lesson. But let's use question 1 to learn the next step, POE. To go from good to great on the English test, you can't just fix a question in your head and then find an answer that matches. Instead, after you've identified what's wrong, eliminate all the choices that do not fix the error.

For question 1, no apostrophe is needed for *Worlds*. Cross off choices (A) and (B).

1. **A.**   NO CHANGE
    B.   Wells' *The War of the World's,*
    C.   Wells' *The War of the Worlds,*
    D.   Wells *The War of the Worlds,*

Now compare the two that remain, choices (C) and (D). Do you need the apostrophe for *Wells*? Yes, you do, so choice (C) is the correct answer. Here's where you could have messed up if you didn't use POE: If you fixed it in your head and looked for your answer, you could have missed the absence of the apostrophe in choice (D) and chosen incorrectly. POE on English isn't optional or a backup when you're stuck. You have to first eliminate wrong answers and then compare what's left.

Let's go onto the next step.

Step 3: Use the Context

Even though you may struggle with time on the English test, you can't skip the non-underlined text in between questions in order to save yourself a few minutes. Take a look at this next question.

In order to tell the story in traditional
<u>2</u>
radio play format, however, the young

director Orson Welles decided to present it

as an unfolding news story and hired actors

to portray radio reporters "stunned" by the

horrific events unfolding before their eyes.

2. **F.** NO CHANGE
   G. Rather than
   H. Therefore, to
   J. Thus, to

Don't forget to apply the first two steps. The transition word is changing in the answers. Transitions test the correct direction to match the flow of the sentence. How do you know which direction to use? Read the entire sentence for the full context. The information that follows indicates Welles' direction would be a departure; the word *however* also helps. Eliminate all answers that are not *consistent* with the clues in the non-underlined portion and only choice (G) remains.

Always finish the sentence before attacking the question, and don't skip from question to question. The non-underlined text provides context you need.

Let's move on to the next step.

Step 4: Trust Your Ear, But Verify

Your ear can be pretty reliable at raising the alarm for outright errors and clunky, awkward phrasing.

You should, however, always verify what your ear signals by confirming the actual error. Steps 1 and 2 will help with that: Use the answers to identify the topic, and use POE heavily.

But remember to be careful of errors your ear *won't* catch. Using the answers to identify the topic will save you there as well.

Let's try another question.

Any listener who tuned in after the
program's start believed that the United
States faced an alien invasion in their skies.
$_3$

3. **A.** NO CHANGE
   B. there skies.
   C. it's skies.
   D. its skies.

Need a Pronoun Refresher?
Check out the box
on page 220.

That sounded pretty good to us, how about you? But before we circle NO CHANGE and go on our merry way, look at the answers to identify the topic and confirm there is no error. Only the pronoun changes, so the question is testing pronouns. *Their* is a plural pronoun, but all countries take the singular verb and pronoun, including the *United States.* Cross off choices (A) and (B)—(B) isn't even the right type of pronoun, plural or not. Since we need a possessive pronoun, cross off choice (C) as well. Choice (D) is the correct answer.

Let's move on to our last step.

Step 5: Don't Fix What Isn't Broken
Read the next question.

In retrospect, it seems strange that so
many could have been fooled by what surely
could not have been all that convincing a
$_4$
radio play.
$_4$

4. **F.** NO CHANGE
   G. all that believable or credible a radio play.
   H. all convincing.
   J. considered convincing by most who listened to it.

Go to Step 1, and identify the topic. *Everything* seems to be changing in the answers for question 4: What the question is testing isn't obvious at all. You can't confirm what you can't identify, so leave "NO CHANGE," and apply the 4 C's.

Does one of the answers fix something you missed?

Does one of the answers make the sentence better by making it more concise?

If the answer to both questions is *No* for all three other answers, the correct answer choice is (F), NO CHANGE.

NO CHANGE *is* a legitimate answer choice. Don't make the mistake of assuming that all questions have an error that you just can't spot. If you use the five steps of our Basic Approach, you'll catch errors your ear would miss, and you'll confidently choose NO CHANGE when it's the correct answer.

THREE-TO-KNOW

We've chosen three types of questions to tackle in this book. Commas and apostrophes are heavily tested, and most students find them devilishly confusing. Strategy questions are among the most heavily tested Rhetorical Skills questions.

COMMAS

Find a reason to use a comma, not a reason to take it out. There are four reasons to use a comma on the ACT. If you can't justify a comma by one of these rules, it shouldn't be used. In other words, if a choice offers no commas, it's right unless you can name the reason to add a comma.

1. Stop Punctuation

ACT tests the correct way to link ideas in several ways. If two ideas are complete (that is, each could stand apart as a complete sentence), use Stop punctuation in between: a period, a semi-colon, a question mark, or an exclamation mark.

A comma on its own can never come in between two complete ideas. On their own, coordinating conjunctions (*for, and, nor, but, or, yet, so*)—or FANBOYS, as we like to call them—can never come in between two complete ideas. But a comma paired with one of the FANBOYS becomes Stop punctuation.

Consider the following incorrect sentence:

Orson Welles wanted listeners to know the upcoming broadcast was a work of fiction he made sure that the program began with a disclaimer.

If you break this sentence in between *fiction* and *he*, you'll see that the two ideas could each be a complete sentence. Two complete ideas have to be properly linked. Here are three correct options:

Orson Welles wanted listeners to know the upcoming broadcast was a work of fiction. He made sure that the program began with a disclaimer.

Orson Welles wanted listeners to know the upcoming broadcast was a work of fiction; he made sure that the program began with a disclaimer.

Orson Welles wanted listeners to know the upcoming broadcast was a work of fiction, and he made sure that the program began with a disclaimer.

On the ACT, any of these would be fine. In fact, ACT rarely makes you choose the nuanced difference among them. The particular FANBOYS word adds an element of direction that could affect the answer, but there is no structural difference among a period, a semi-colon, or a comma + FANBOYS. All are Stop punctuation, and all could work above.

2. Go Punctuation

An incomplete idea can't stand on its own. A comma is one way to link the incomplete idea to a complete idea to form one sentence.

Consider the following examples:

Once the broadcast began, listeners who tuned in late believed the Martian invasion to be real.

Many people reportedly tried to flee, desperate to escape certain destruction.

In the first example, *Once the broadcast began* is incomplete. In the second example, *desperate to escape certain destruction* is incomplete. In each case, a comma links the incomplete idea to the complete idea.

3. Lists

Use a comma to separate items on a list.

The chilling broadcast of The War of the Worlds was a long, tense hour for many listeners.

Long and *tense* are both describing *hour.* If you would say *long and tense,* then you can say *long, tense.*

Welles went on to direct such classics as Touch of Evil, The Magnificent Ambersons, and Citizen Kane.

Whenever you have three or more items on a list, always use a comma before the "and" preceding the final item. This is a rule that not everyone agrees on, but if you apply the 4 C's, the extra comma makes your meaning *Clear.* On the ACT, always use the comma before the "and."

4. Unnecessary Info

Use a pair of commas around unnecessary info.

It did not occur to Welles, however, that a great number of people would tune in after the broadcast had started.

If information is necessary to the sentence in either meaning or structure, don't use the commas. If the meaning would be exactly the same but less interesting, use a pair of commas—or a pair of dashes—around the information.

Try a few questions.

CBS hoped to draw on highbrow viewers

who were more interested in serious literary
$\overline{\qquad\qquad}$
5

material, than in the songs and jokes that
$\overline{\qquad\qquad}$
5

dominated most radio programs.

5. **A. NO CHANGE**
   B. serious, literary material, than
   C. serious literary, material than
   D. serious literary material than

Here's How to Crack It

Step 1 identifies commas as the topic. Run through the four reasons to use a comma and see if any is in play, and use Step 2, POE. Choice (D) offers no commas at all, so find a reason to *not* pick it. There are no FANBOYS included, so it's not Stop punctuation. The two commas in choice (B) would make the information in between them unnecessary; the information is necessary, so eliminate (B). Compare choices (A) and (C). Each has one comma but in a different placement. Is this a list? Is there a separate complete idea embedded in the sentence to link an incomplete idea to? No, and no. The correct choice is (D).

No other station reported the invasion,
$\overline{\qquad}$
6

but listeners still believed the program to be
$\overline{\qquad}$
6

breaking news.

6. **F. NO CHANGE**
   G. invasion but listeners
   H. invasion, listeners
   J. invasion, but, listeners

Here's How to Crack It

Step 1 identifies commas as the topic. With the presence of *but*—one of our FANBOYS—decide first if the two ideas are complete on either side of *, but*. They are complete, so use Step 2, POE, to eliminate wrong answers. The correct choice is (F).

APOSTROPHES

Apostrophes make your writing more concise. They have two uses, possession and contraction.

Possession

To show possession with single nouns, add 's, and with plural nouns, add just the apostrophe. For tricky plurals that do not end in s, add 's.

Consider the following examples:

The career of Orson = *Orson's career*
The actions of the boys = *the boys' actions*
The voices of the men = *the men's voices*

To show possession with pronouns, never use apostrophes. Use the appropriate possessive pronoun.

His *direction*
Their *fear*
Its *legacy*

Quick and Dirty Pronoun Lesson

Pronouns vary by number, gender, and case, that is, the function they perform in the sentence.

	1st person	2nd person	3rd person
Subject	I, we	you	she, he, it, they
Object	me, us	you	her, him, it, them
Possessive	my, mine, our, ours	your	her, hers, his, its, their, theirs

Contractions

Whenever you see a pronoun with an apostrophe, it's (it is) a contraction, which means the apostrophe takes the place of at least one letter.

Consider the following examples.

It is a classic. = **It's** *a classic.*
They are fans of the production. = **They're** *fans of the production.*
Who is the star of the play? = **Who's** *the star of the play?*

Because these particular contractions sound the same as some possessive pronouns, these questions can be very tricky on the ACT. You can't use your ear: You have to know the above rules.

Try a question.

_____◯_____

While some suspect the reports were at best wildly overstated, the young directors notoriety soared.
   7
                                            7

7. **A.** NO CHANGE
   B. director's notoriety,
   C. directors' notoriety,
   D. director's notoriety

Here's How to Crack It

Step 1 identifies apostrophes and commas as the topic. Use Step 2, POE, to eliminate wrong answers. *Director* is singular, so eliminate choice (C). The *notoriety* does belong to the *director*, so you need an apostrophe and can therefore eliminate choice (A). Between choices (B) and (D), decide if there is a reason to use a comma. In fact, the added comma would make *the young director's notoriety* unnecessary, which makes no sense. The correct choice is (D).

_____◯_____

RHETORICAL SKILLS STRATEGY

Many Rhetorical Skills questions look just like the Usage and Mechanics questions, accompanied by four answer choices. But others feature a bona fide question. Of those, Strategy questions are among the most common and confusing.

Strategy questions come in many different forms, but they all revolve around the *purpose* of the text. Among the different types of Strategy questions, expect to see questions asking you to add and replace text, determine if text should be added or deleted, evaluate the impact on the passage if text is deleted, or judge the overall effect of the passage on the reader.

Try a question.

Many of them, assuming that what they were hearing was genuine on-the-scene coverage, panicked; they were very frightened.

8. If all of the choices below are true, which of them best uses specific detail to convey the panic that the broadcast of *The War of the Worlds* caused?

   F. NO CHANGE.

   G. the highways were clogged with cars full of people seeking escape, and train stations were crowded with mobs willing to buy tickets to anywhere far away.

   H. many felt that they had never encountered anything as terrifying in their lives and fully believed that what they were hearing was the absolute truth.

   J. they did not stop to think that what they were hearing might be fiction; instead they leaped to the unlikely conclusion that an interplanetary invasion was indeed occurring.

Here's How to Crack It

Identify the purpose of the proposed text. According to the question, one of these choices *uses specific detail to convey the panic that the broadcast of The War of the Worlds caused*. We don't even need to go back into the passage: Find an answer choice that fulfills the purpose. Answer choices (F), (H), and (J) all may be true, but they do not offer any *specific detail* conveying the panic. Only (G) does that, and it is our correct answer.

Try another.

In addition to directing the production, Orson Welles also acted as the narrator of *The War of the Worlds.* 9

9. At this point, the writer is considering adding the following true statement:

> In the 1970s, Orson Welles made television commercials for a winery.

Should the writer add this sentence here?

A. Yes, because it explains that Welles became famous outside of radio.
B. Yes, because it explains why many people forgot he directed and narrated *The War of the Worlds.*
C. No, because it doesn't explain why Welles stopped directing.
D. No, because it distracts the reader from the main point of this paragraph.

Here's How to Crack It

Whenever the strategy question asks if you should add or delete new text, evaluate the reasons in the answer choices carefully. The reason should correctly explain the purpose of the selected text. Here, (D) is correct because there is no reason to add text that is irrelevant to the topic.

Try another.

In the 1930s, most American households
₁₀
owned a radio. After all, it seems likely that
₁₀
most people would have questioned why all of the other radio stations continued to play their regular programs if such a disaster of global proportions were underway.

10. Given that all choices are true, which one provides the best opening to this paragraph?

F. NO CHANGE
G. Soon the reports of panic were dismissed as overblown if not outright false.
H. At the time of the broadcast, fears of a German invasion of Europe were growing.
J. Today, many Americans believe in life on other planets.

Here's How to Crack It

In many strategy questions, the purpose is to add a sentence to open or close a paragraph, or tie two paragraphs together. Use the context of the paragraph, and read through to the end before deciding. Since the author provides a reason why most listeners would have doubted the story, choice (G) provides the best introduction to the paragraph.

Three-to-Know Drill

Part 1A

In the following sentences, cross out the commas IF they are unnecessary or incorrectly placed. Some sentences have more than one comma error, and some sentences are correct as written.

1. The book, you're reading right now, looks really interesting.

2. I always meant to study more for the ACT, but I just couldn't find the time.

3. Jack loved to listen to music, and to play games on his new iPhone, which he had purchased the day before.

4. Every time, I go on Twitter, there's always something interesting next to something really annoying.

5. When I see an action movie, I love the explosions, but not the romantic subplot.

6. Every, single time I work out I feel like I'm going to puke.

7. The Flyers won the game in overtime, but they should have won it earlier.

8. My grandparents used to listen, to the radio, but now they just watch TV.

9. Of all the cities, I've visited, my favorites are probably Paris, France, and San Francisco, California.

10. Squash is not well known in the United States, yet it is one of the most popular sports, in Egypt.

11. Next time I go to the store, I'm going to get peanut butter, jelly, and, bread.

12. It seemed like the characters' treatment of their dog in the movie was exceedingly, inhumane, and hurtful.

13. On sunny summer days, history, museums don't seem so appealing.

14. Jazz, whether you like that style of music or not, was one of the most important cultural movements of the twentieth century.

15. Sometimes, when Americans, who love Chinese food, go to China, they find, ironically, that they don't like the food.

Part 1B

Add commas if necessary. If you add commas, state why you need them.

1. We'd like to hire you for the job and we hope you can start Monday.

   Why?

   _____

2. If you'd like to lose weight try eating better drinking more water and exercising regularly.

   Why?

   _____

3. The Philadelphia Phillies my favorite baseball team won the World Series in 2008.

   Why?

   _____

4. We took a scary drive on a dark stormy night.

   Why?

   _____

5. When used properly commas can really help to improve the clarity of a sentence.

   Why?

   _____

6. The lecturer's style was a little dull but so informative.

   Why?

   _____

7. I don't typically like Thai food yet I must admit I could drink Thai iced teas all day long.

   Why?

   _____

8. Some people still buy CDs but most have switched to digital music mainly for the convenience.

   Why?

   _____

9. I prefer a walk in the park to a walk around a city block.

Why?

_____

10. Around here you're out of luck if you won't buy your groceries at A&P Shop-Rite or Pathmark.

Why?

_____

11. The author Philip Roth wrote some of my favorite books.

Why?

_____

12. Sometimes I think plums the red ones especially are the best fruits in the world.

Why?

_____

13. Ice hockey is a fun challenging sport and it's great to watch.

Why?

_____

14. I don't think I could go five minutes without checking my e-mail or updating my Facebook status.

Why?

_____

15. When I was in college I had nothing but time but not anymore now that I'm working.

Why?

_____

Part 2A

In the following sentences, cross out any apostrophes that don't belong. If a word is spelled or used incorrectly because of an apostrophe error, write the correct word in the margin.

1. My arteries' seemed to get more and more clogged with every trip to the donut shop.

2. The pie was delicious when I first made it, but it's not so great anymore.

3. I absolutely did not expect them to be here on time, but they're they are.

4. If this device needs them, then why are there no battery's included?

5. I know the car seems out of her price range, but I'm pretty sure it's hers'.

6. It was time to go back to class, but the teacher didn't want to interrupt the children's game.

7. Do you have any idea who's letter this is?

8. Thank you so much for the cookies. Their delicious.

9. There's no dog in the world whose as much fun as ours'.

10. The politician ran on the idea that he was the people's candidate.

Part 2B

In the following sentences, add any apostrophes that are missing. If a word is spelled or used incorrectly because of an apostrophe error, write the correct word in the margin.

1. I need to start exercising more if I want to improve my arteries health.

2. St. Louis seems close to Chicago, but its actually five hours away by car.

3. I prefer red grapes, but there never available at the grocery store.

4. Because of all the corrosion, I cannot read the part where it lists this batteries charge.

5. There are two hamburgers here: one is his, and the other is hers.

6. The childrens treehouse was marked with a sign that said, "No Girls Allowed."

7. I cannot tell whose on the phone: I do not recognize the voice.

8. Were going to the concert later, so were trying to relearn some of the lyrics.

9. I think I see your car across the street, and ours is over there.

10. I thought the singer was terrible, and I had no idea why he was chosen as the peoples choice.

Part 2C
Choose the correct word from the parentheses.

1. My parents didn't give us permission, but (we're/were) going anyway.

2. I don't want to start a movie now: (it's/its) almost midnight!

3. My (adversary's/adversaries) favorite team was losing, and I was delighted.

4. (Who's/whose) child is this, and (who's/whose) responsible for him?

5. My wallet feels full right now, but most of the bills are (one's/ones).

6. The cat guarded (it's/its) toy, as if to suggest, "(It's/Its) mine."

7. These (dictionary's/dictionaries) seem identical to me, so I'm not sure which one to get.

8. I thought my essay was pretty good, but (her's/hers) was much better.

9. Were you the one looking for the lost sunglasses? (They're/There) over (they're/there).

10. You can say (it's/its) (society's/societies) fault all you want: I still insist (it's/its) (your's/yours).

Part 3A
Find the correct answer using only the information given in the question.

1. Which of the following choices would most effectively communicate the parents' skeptical attitude toward the narrator's plans?
   A. Enthusiastically,
   B. Distracted by other tasks,
   C. Because they were older,
   D. Despite their clear doubts,

2. Which of the following begins this paragraph and conveys the importance of this album?
   F. The Mars Volta's debut album was just like the debut albums of many other bands: underappreciated.
   G. It's hard to choose a single Mars Volta album to represent the band's huge range.
   H. The Mars Volta's debut album showed that a band could write complex, unique music but still sell records.
   J. There was a time when it seemed like progressive rock would never reach the major labels again.

3. Given that all the choices are true, which one best develops the paragraph's focus on the place of radio in Welles' career?
   A. Welles' voice performances over the airwaves well outnumber his appearances in film.
   B. Though he is best known for film, Welles was initially a famed director in the theater.
   C. Welles performed in thousands of radio broadcasts, but many of them are lost today.
   D. Many Americans considered radio their main news source during the Second World War, and Welles was no exception.

4. Given that all the choices are true, which one would most clearly suggest the songwriting collaboration between Lennon and McCartney?
   F. listened to the song.
   G. liked the song more than he thought he would.
   H. thought about the song a lot the next day.
   J. heard one part of the song, then added his own.

5. Given that all the choices are true, which one is most relevant to the writer's intention to help readers hear the sound produced by the car horn?
   A. almost like two trumpets playing dissonant notes.
   B. as if the driver were honking in a panic.
   C. like the horn on one of the other cars in the traffic jam.
   D. just like a horn I remembered hearing on the road in Italy.

Part 3B

Using only the information given in the question, cross off the answer choices that could NOT be the correct answer. Any of the remaining answers could be the correct answer, but without the essay, it's impossible to pick for certain.

15. Suppose the writer's goal had been to write a brief persuasive essay encouraging students to question what they are taught in school. Would this essay fulfill that goal?
    A. Yes, because the essay lists examples of Harleen questioning what her teachers taught her.
    B. Yes, because the essay focuses on scientific discoveries made by students outside the classroom.
    C. No, because the level of strictness varies depending on the type of school one attends.
    D. No, because the essay gives only one example of a student who disagreed with his teachers.

30. Suppose the writer's goal had been to write an essay that details how religious study influences the work of famous philosophers. Would this essay successfully fulfill that goal?

    F. Yes, because the essay makes clear that Walter Benjamin's study of Jewish tradition influenced his philosophical writings.

    G. Yes, because the essay suggests that Benjamin was very devout.

    H. No, because the essay outlines only a single philosopher's engagement with religious writings and tradition.

    J. No, because the essay demonstrates that Benjamin's study of Jewish texts had no influence on his philosophical writings.

45. Suppose the writer's goal was to draft an essay that would show the connection between economic conditions and voting patterns. Would this essay fulfill that goal?

    A. Yes, because it links Franklin Roosevelt's New Deal to the economic depression in the 1930s.

    B. Yes, because it details a historical event and focuses on one president's rise to power.

    C. No, because it is focused mainly on the rise of the Republican party in American politics.

    D. No, because it shows the economic conditions in the 1930s but does not show those conditions in later decades.

60. Suppose the author intended to write an essay that shows that athletes' skills often bear no relation to the environment in which those athletes are raised. Would this essay successfully fulfill that goal?

    F. Yes, because the essay describes Robyn Regehr's long, successful career in the NHL.

    G. Yes, because the essay shows that Robyn Regehr became a professional hockey player even though he was born in Brazil.

    H. No, because the author focuses on Robyn Regehr and his career rather than on athletes in general.

    J. No, because the essay reveals that Regehr's family returned to Canada when he was seven.

75. Suppose the author intended to write a sketch of a painter that would show that painter's contributions to the art world. Does this essay successfully accomplish that goal?

    A. Yes, because it outlines Kehinde Wiley's career as an artist and his unique position among twentieth-century artists.

    B. Yes, because it details how Kehinde Wiley became interested in art history and eventually chose to become an artist.

    C. No, because it does not succeed in showing that Kehinde Wiley has contributed in any substantial way to the art world.

    D. No, because it doesn't adequately list Kehinde Wiley's inspirations, models, and awards.

THREE-TO-KNOW DRILL ANSWERS AND EXPLANATIONS

Part 1A

1. The book/ you're reading right now/ looks really interesting.
2. I always meant to study more for the ACT, but I just couldn't find the time.
3. Jack loved to listen to music/ and to play games on his new iPhone, which he had purchased the day before.
4. Every time/ I go on Twitter, there's always something interesting next to something really annoying.
5. When I see an action movie, I love the explosions/ but not the romantic subplot.
6. Every/ single time I work out I feel like I'm going to puke.
7. The Flyers won the game in overtime, but they should have won it earlier.
8. My grandparents used to listen/ to the radio, but now they just watch TV.
9. Of all the cities/ I've visited, my favorites are probably Paris, France/ and San Francisco, California.
10. Squash is not well known in the United States, yet it is one of the most popular sports/ in Egypt.
11. Next time I go to the store, I'm going to get peanut butter, jelly, and/ bread.
12. It seemed like the characters' treatment of their dog in the movie was exceedingly/ inhumane/ and hurtful.
13. On sunny summer days, history/ museums don't seem so appealing.
14. Jazz, whether you like that style of music or not, was one of the most important cultural movements of the twentieth century.
15. Sometimes, when Americans/ who love Chinese food/ go to China, they find, ironically, that they don't like the food.

Part 1B

1. We'd like to hire you for the job↓, and we hope you can start Monday.

   Why? Stop.

2. If you'd like to lose weight↓, try eating better↓, drinking more water↓, and exercising regularly.

   Why? Go, List.

3. The Philadelphia Phillies↓, my favorite baseball team↓, won the World Series in 2008.

   Why? Unnecessary information

4. We took a scary drive on a dark, stormy night.

   Why? List.

5. When used properly, commas can really help to improve the clarity of a sentence.

   Why? Go.

6. The lecturer's style was a little dull but so informative.

   Why? No commas necessary.

7. I don't typically like Thai food, yet I must admit I could drink Thai iced teas all day long.

   Why? Stop.

8. Some people still buy CDs, but most have switched to digital music, mainly for the convenience.

   Why? Stop, Go.

9. I prefer a walk in the park to a walk around a city block.

   Why? No commas necessary.

10. Around here, you're out of luck if you won't buy your groceries at A&P, Shop-Rite, or Pathmark.

    Why? Go, List.

11. The author Philip Roth wrote some of my favorite books.

    Why? No commas necessary.

12. Sometimes I think plums, the red ones especially, are the best fruits in the world.

    Why? Unnecessary information

13. Ice hockey is a fun, challenging sport, and it's great to watch.

    Why? List, Stop.

14. I don't think I could go five minutes without checking my e-mail or updating my Facebook status.

   Why? No commas necessary

15. When I was in college, I had nothing but time but not anymore now that I'm working.

   Why? Go.

Part 2A

1. My arteries↑ seemed to get more and more clogged with every trip to the donut shop.
2. The pie was delicious when I first made it, but it's not so great anymore.
3. I absolutely did not expect them to be here on time, but ~~they're~~ there they are.
4. If this device needs them, then why are there no ~~battery's~~ batteries included?
5. I know the car seems out of her price range, but I'm pretty sure it's hers↑.
6. It was time to go back to class, but the teacher didn't want to interrupt the children's game.
7. Do you have any idea ~~who's~~ whose letter this is?
8. Thank you so much for the cookies. ~~Their~~ They're delicious.
9. There's no dog in the world who's as much fun as ours↑.
10. The politician ran on the idea that he was the people's candidate.

Part 2B

1. I need to start exercising more if I want to improve my **arteries'** health.
2. St. Louis seems close to Chicago, but **it's** actually five hours away by car.
3. I prefer red grapes, but **they're** never available at the grocery store.
4. Because of all the corrosion, I cannot read the part where it lists this **battery's** charge.
5. There are two hamburgers here: one is his, and the other is hers.
6. The **children's** treehouse was marked with a sign that said, "No Girls Allowed."
7. I cannot tell **who's** on the phone: I do not recognize the voice.
8. **We're** going to the concert later, so **we're** trying to relearn some of the lyrics.
9. I think I see your car across the street, and ours is over there.
10. I thought the singer was terrible, and I had no idea why he was chosen as the **people's** choice.

Part 2C

1. My parents didn't give us permission, but **we're** going anyway.
2. I don't want to start a movie now: **it's** almost midnight!
3. My **adversary's** favorite team was losing, and I was delighted at his agony.
4. **Whose** child is this, and **who's** responsible for him?
5. My wallet feels full right now, but most of the bills are **ones**.
6. The cat guarded **its** toy, as if to suggest, "**It's** mine."
7. These **dictionaries** seem identical to me, so I'm not sure which one to get.
8. I thought my essay was pretty good, but **hers** was much better.
9. Were you the one looking for the lost sunglasses? **They're** over **there**.
10. You can say **it's society's** fault all you want: I still insist **it's yours**.

Part 3A

1. D
2. H
3. A
4. J
5. A

Part 3B

15. B, C
30. G
45. A, B
60. F
75. B, D

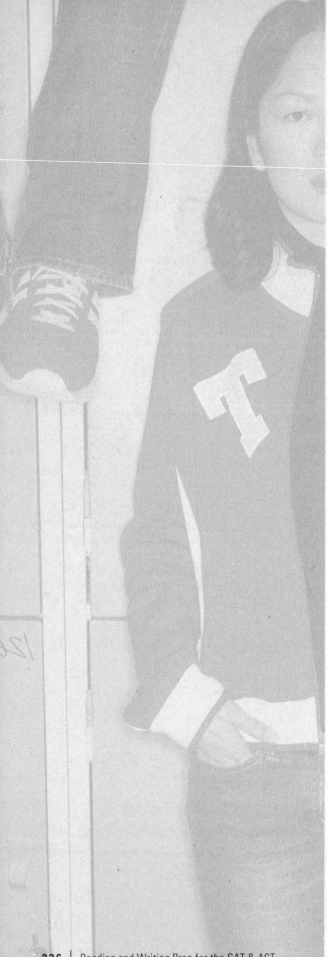

Summary

o   Identify what the question is testing by changes in the answer choices.

o   Use POE heavily.

o   Don't skip the non-underlined text: Use it for context.

o   Trust your ear, but verify by the rules.

o   NO CHANGE is a legitimate answer choice.

o   Good writing should be complete, consistent, clear, and concise.

o   There are only four reasons to use a comma. Name the reason to add a comma, and always be biased toward a choice with no commas.

o   Use an apostrophe with nouns to show possession. Use an apostrophe with pronouns to make a contraction. Be careful of your ear with contractions, since possessive pronouns will sound the same as a pronoun with a contraction.

o   Strategy questions always involve a purpose. Identify the purpose in the question, and pick an answer choice consistent with that purpose.

Chapter 12
English Drills

ID THE SUBJECT AND VERB DRILLS

Directions: Identify all the subjects and verbs in each sentence. Some sentences contain more than one subject and/or more than one verb.

Drill 1

1. Bruce played squash yesterday.

2. Alison likes the Yankees.

3. Who is having the cheeseburger and fries?

4. They are at the movies right now.

5. George writes 5 pages a day.

6. Where do I find Wrigley Field?

7. Students learn best by doing homework.

8. Junot Diaz won the Pulitzer Prize in 2008.

9. Ed called me the other day.

10. Amrita has been going to medical school for ten years.

Drill 2

1. Henry James is my favorite author.

2. Who even says "word up" anymore?

3. My dad's favorite team used to be the Indianapolis Colts.

4. Ten years is not such a long time.

5. Marc Maron's podcast should come out twice a week.

6. Super-Nintendo games are actually very rare these days.

7. Dashiell Hammett was one of the first detective writers.

8. How long has this band been popular?

9. Matt started his own wine company a few years ago.

10. The show has started tonight at 10 PM.

Drill 3

1. Are you ever going to be done with that book?

2. Now how did they make this ice cream taste so good?

3. No one's really sure what the secret to a good life is.

4. I wonder if there are any dogs at the park this late at night.

5. Buying a new iPad can be intimidating because it's so expensive.

6. Anna will know where she's moving as soon as she receives her acceptance letters.

7. I was really surprised how big the music library is on Spotify.

8. Nothing I've ever seen can compare to this new movie.

9. The stories on *The Daily Show* are funniest around election time.

10. We'll leave as soon as we're done packing all our things.

FIX THE STOP/GO PUNCTUATION DRILLS

Directions: For each question, choose the sentence that uses Stop/Go punctuation correctly.

Drill 1

1. A. I know I will be a successful warrior for I will never back down.

   B. I know I will be a successful warrior, for I will never back down.

2. F. This is a brand new suit, so you should wear it for a job interview or something.

   G. This is a brand new suit so you should wear it for a job interview or something.

3. A. He just goes to the mall and walks around.

   B. He just goes to the mall, and walks around.

4. F. I know it's childish, yet I can't fully let go of my rocking horse.

   G. I know it's childish yet I can't fully let go of my rocking horse.

5. A. Do you want to hang on to your old baseball cards or just throw them all away?

   B. Do you want to hang on to your old baseball cards, or just throw them all away?

6. F. I've never eaten at a Hardees, nor do I ever intend to.

   G. I've never eaten at a Hardees nor do I ever intend to.

7. A. James said he would come to my party but in the end said he couldn't.

   B. James said he would come to my part, but in the end said he couldn't.

8. F. Mario Lemieux stopped playing hockey for a reason few could understand at the time.

   G. Mario Lemieux stopped playing hockey, for a reason few could understand at he time.

9. A. He has neither rhyme nor reason for anything he does.

   B. He has neither rhyme, nor reason for anything he does.

10. F. Your love letter contains too many grammatical mistakes, so I think we should break up.

    G. Your love letter contains too many grammatical mistakes so I think we should break up.

Drill 2

1. A. Please don't look at my iTunes playlist. It's so embarrassing.

   B. Please don't look at my iTunes playlist, it's so embarrassing.

2. F. It seems like I only care about politics when: there's some big election going on.

   G. It seems like I only care about politics when there's some big election going on.

3. A. The Flyers are going to win the Cup this year, the team's goalie is one of the best in the league!

   B. The Flyers are going to win the Cup this year; the team's goalie is one of the best in the league!

4. F. Although it's a huge honor to get an academic book published, the books often sell only 200 or 300 copies.

   G. Although it's a huge honor to get an academic book published. The books often sell only 200 or 300 copies.

5. A. I'm not sure why I love furniture shopping so much: maybe it's because I feel like Ikea is a playground!

   B. I'm not sure why I love furniture shopping so much maybe it's because I feel like Ikea is a playground.

6. F. Humanities departments all over the country changed in the 1970s; when French literary theory became popular.

   G. Humanities departments all over the country changed in the 1970s when French literary theory became popular.

7. A. Every time I go to a squash match, I make sure to bring my lucky bandana and an extra racquet.

   B. Every time I go to a squash match, I make sure to bring: my lucky bandana and an extra racquet.

8. F. My favorite app is probably Angry Birds.

   G. My favorite app is probably: Angry Birds.

9. A. Michael Vick is a talented athlete, his animal-rights abuses notwithstanding.

   B. Michael Vick is a talented athlete; his animal-rights abuses notwithstanding.

10. F. To never split an infinitive, this is one of those grammar rules that's a little outdated.

    G. To never split an infinitive: this is one of those grammar rules that's a little outdated.

Drill 3

1. A. If you see Ravneet, tell him I said hi.

   B. If you see Ravneet: tell him I said hi.

2. F. The doctor told me I should eat more kale. Whatever that is.

   G. The doctor told me I should eat more kale, whatever that is.

3. A. I've lost a lot of weight on the grapefruit diet although I'm pretty sick of grapefruit.

   B. I've lost a lot of weight on the grapefruit diet; although I'm pretty sick of grapefruit.

4. F. It seems like things just keep getting worse: there was more crime in the city this year than last year.

   G. It seems like things just keep getting worse, there was more crime in the city this year than last year.

5. A. My favorite Beatle is Paul; Nathaniel's favorite is John.

   B. My favorite Beatle is Paul, Nathaniel's favorite is John.

6. F. First, she published a poem in *The Atlantic*. Then, she published a whole book of poems.

   G. First, she published a poem in *The Atlantic*, then, she published a whole book of poems.

7. A. When I learned that flourless chocolate cake was gluten free, I didn't feel so bad about my gluten allergy.

   B. When I learned that flourless chocolate cake was gluten free. I didn't feel so bad about my gluten allergy.

8. F. Many adults suffer from a Vitamin-D deficiency because they don't drink enough milk.

   G. Many adults suffer from a Vitamin-D deficiency; because they don't drink enough milk.

9. A. The Senator from Pennsylvania, took the whole legislature by storm.

   B. The Senator from Pennsylvania took the whole legislature by storm.

10. F. I don't like protein bars either, but I much prefer them to raw eggs.

    G. I don't like protein bars either but I much prefer them to raw eggs.

SUPPLY THE PRONOUN DRILLS

Directions: Fill in the correct pronoun. Choose from the following list: *I, me, you, he, him, she, her, it, we, us, they, them, who, whom.*

Drill 1

1. Once he calls me, John and _____ will go eat.

2. It was Jake's birthday, so I got _____ an iTunes gift card.

3. Anne won the award, for _____ was the best violinist.

4. I have two tickets to the concert, but I can't get anyone to go with _____.

5. _____ among you let the dogs out?

6. She and _____ sister are going to open a shop.

7. It is said that we all have at least one novel within _____.

8. Scott would be a better squash player if _____ were only a little more patient.

9.   _____ told us it wasn't possible, but we proved them wrong.

10. The American Airlines Center in Dallas is a great arena: _____ has so many great food options!

Drill 2

1.   Beyonce's new song isn't great, but I can't stop listening to _____.

2.   The owners haven't listed the price on the "For Sale" sign, so you should ask _____.

3.   _____ didn't have any idea where to buy our new couch.

4.   If only _____ had bought Microsoft stock early on, Melissa and I would be rich now.

5.   Willa Cather won the Pulitzer Prize for *One of Ours*, but _____ didn't consider it one of her own best novels.

6.   Bob Dylan's songs are so powerful because they speak to all of _____.

7.   No, not that girl, the one to the left of _____.

8.   You bought a Snuggie? For _____?

9.   Jeff got the promotion even though _____ doesn't do much work.

10. I know Justin Bieber is very popular, but I don't much like _____.

Drill 3 (who/whom set)

1.   Not one of us _____ owns a dog has any problem with cats.

2.   I'm going to sue the guy _____ sold me this defective banana tree.

3.   _____ are you going to invite to your retirement party?

4.   _____ is your roommate this year?

5.   They say you can be whoever you want when you go to college, but I'm not sure _____ I am now.

6.   You wrote, "From me to you." From you to _____?

7.   _____ did you vote for in the last election?

8. _____ was your preferred candidate last year?

9. My grandmother, _____ is Swiss, makes incredible Christmas cookies.

10. I've always been curious _____ figured out that plantains are edible.

SUPPLY THE PARTICIPLE DRILLS

Drill 1

Directions: Select the correct participle for each sentence. Choose from the following verbs: *to bake, to become, to choose, to drink, to fall, to hide, to ride, to shake, to swim, to wear.*

1. It has now _____ very obvious that you can improve your score on the ACT with a little practice.

2. It isn't always necessary to stick with whatever you've _____ as a major.

3. Mary thought she had _____ in love ten times before she met "the one."

4. If I hadn't _____ the cake for so long, it would've thawed out by now, and we'd be eating it.

5. Your birthday present is here, but it's _____ in a place where you'll never find it.

6. Although I've seen motorcycle sidecars in movies, I've never actually _____ in one.

7. I've never had a conversation with a famous author, but I've _____ hands with a few of them.

8. Michael Phelps must have _____ like a million laps a day to become as good a swimmer as he is.

9. I've _____ some pretty hideous shirts in my day. I still wear some of them today.

10. She had _____ so much coffee that she had trouble geting to sleep.

Drill 2

Directions: Select the correct participle for each sentence. Choose from the following verbs: *to begin, to come, to fly, to forget, to know, to receive, to ring, to sing, to take, to write.*

1. Before the hockey game had even _____, some of the players were already fighting.

2. At last, the chickens have _____ home to roost.

3. A two-hour flight is common, but few people have _____ for the seventeen hours it takes to get from New York to India.

4. Although it's supposed to be the "average" grade, many students have never _____ a C.

5. If Josh had only _____ how easy the ACT was going to be, he wouldn't have lost so much sleep over it.

6. If you had _____ the doorbell, you wouldn't have had to wait out side for so long.

7. She didn't have a great singing voice, so it was hard to believe that she had once _____ in a choir at Carnegie Hall.

8. I've _____ about all I can stand, and I'm not going to take any more.

9. Once you've _____ your essay, your application is nearly complete.

10. I know I haven't checked your homework yet, but I haven't _____ about it.

Drill 3

Directions: Select the correct participle for each sentence. Choose from the following verbs: *to become, to blow, to drink, to forbid, to give, to lie, to rise, to speak, to teach, to wake.*

1. A cold wind had _____ across the plain, signifying that the next day was to be a cold one.

2. If you hadn't _____ so much soda at dinner, you wouldn't be running to the bathroom every five minutes now.

3. I've _____ the use of cell phones in class, but you continue to use them anyway.

4.   Bill Gates has _____ so much of his money to charity, it's a wonder he still has any at all.

5.   I had just _____ down to take a nap when my roommate came in and blasted his awful music.

6.   The building was beautiful and had _____ much higher than I expected it to.

7.   My computer problem still isn't fixed even though I've _____ with everyone in customer service.

8.   The class was _____ by one of the most eccentric professors on campus.

9.   She could hardly play at all a few years ago, but she has since _____ one of the best pianists I know.

10. If I hadn't _____ up at such a late hour, I would've made it to school on time.

FIX THE COMMA DRILLS

Directions: For each question, choose the option that uses commas correctly.

Drill 1

1. A. Going for broke, Scottie shot the ball from half court.

   B. Going for broke Scottie shot the ball from half court.

2 F. A class, on literary theory, can be really interesting for non-English majors.

   G. A class on literary theory can be really interesting for non-English majors.

3. A. I got an A in math, English, and physics.

   B. I got an A in math, English and physics.

4. F. The most populous cities in New Jersey are Newark, Jersey City, Paterson and Elizabeth.

   G. The most populous cities in New Jersey are Newark, Jersey City, Paterson, and Elizabeth.

5. A. Either the Flyers, the Penguins or the Rangers will win the Atlantic Division this year.

   B. Either the Flyers, the Penguins, or the Rangers will win the Atlantic Division this year.

6. F. A filmmaker, particularly one who has gone to film school, should be well-versed in the editing process.

   G. A filmmaker particularly one who has gone to film school should be well-versed in the editing process.

7. A. Heeding the weather report Jonathan remembered to take his umbrella.

   B. Heeding the weather report, Jonathan remembered to take his umbrella.

8. F. It's hard to say who the greatest living American writer is, but I'd say it's a three-way tie among Philip Roth, Toni Morrison, and Thomas Pynchon.

   G. It's hard to say who the greatest living American writer is, but I'd say it's a three-way tie among Philip Roth, Toni Morrison and Thomas Pynchon.

9. A. Instant Messenger, an earlier version of Facebook chat, isn't as popular as it once was.

B. Instant Messenger an earlier version of Facebook chat isn't as popular as it once was.

10. F. I couldn't afford to go to the furniture store, so I checked Craigslist a yard sale, and a garage sale.

G. I couldn't afford to go to the furniture store, so I checked Craigslist, a yard sale, and a garage sale.

Drill 2

1. A. There are three ways to tell time in my room: my wristwatch, my pocketwatch, and my old grandfather clock.

B. There are three ways to tell time in my room: my wristwatch my pocketwatch, and my old grandfather clock.

2. F. The name Syd Barrett, Pink Floyd's original singer, is now known only to the band's superfans.

G. The name, Syd Barrett, Pink Floyd's original singer is now known only to the band's superfans.

3. A. I'm going to see a concert tonight at the Bowery Ballroom, one of New York's most notorious nightclubs.

B. I'm going to see a concert tonight at the Bowery Ballroom one of New York's most notorious nightclubs.

4. F. Turkish bread contains only four ingredients: water, flour, salt, and sesame.

G. Turkish bread contains only four ingredients: water, flour, salt and sesame.

5. A. Head to the nearest exit if you hear the fire alarm go off.

B. Head to the nearest exit, if you hear the fire alarm go off.

6. F. Eric Clapton, Jeff Beck and Jimmy Page were all members of the Yardbirds at one point.

G. Eric Clapton, Jeff Beck, and Jimmy Page were all members of the Yardbirds at one point.

7. A. Every time I go to the store, I have to buy a candy bar.

   B. Every time, I go to the store, I have to buy a candy bar.

8. F. Actually the new conditioner made her hair much shinier.

   G. Actually, the new conditioner made her hair much shinier.

9. A. The best time to see a hockey game is Saturday afternoon.

   B. The best time, to see a hockey game, is Saturday afternoon.

10. F. Whenever I'm at the airport, I'm always amazed that FedEx, UPS's main competitor, has such huge jets.

    G. Whenever I'm at the airport, I'm always amazed that FedEx UPS's main competitor has such huge jets.

Drill 3

1. A. *The Atlantic Monthly* does a fiction issue every summer.

   B. *The Atlantic Monthly* does a fiction issue, every summer.

2. F. Colleen's cuticles were especially dry, so the nail technician suggested lotion, ointment, or Vaseline.

   G. Colleen's cuticles were especially dry, so the nail technician suggested lotion, ointment or Vaseline.

3. A. No matter which song you like best you have to admit the Beatles have a lot of great songs.

   B. No matter which song you like best, you have to admit the Beatles have a lot of great songs.

4. F. Originally opened in 1871 Grand Central Station is one of the most impressive train stations in the world.

   G. Originally opened in 1871, Grand Central Station is one of the most impressive train stations in the world.

5. A. Uncertain why it mattered so much, Sally studied hard for the ACT.

   B. Uncertain why it mattered so much Sally studied for the ACT.

6. F. Named for the shape of its wings, the comma butterfly is mainly found in the temperate areas in Europe and Asia.

   G. Named for the shape of its wings the comma butterfly is mainly found in the temperate areas in Europe and Asia.

7. A. I need to take my dirty clothes to the laundromat the one on the corner.

   B. I need to take my dirty clothes to the laundromat, the one on the corner.

8. F. The south, of France, is beautiful this time of year.

   G. The south of France is beautiful this time of year.

9. A. I couldn't decide between Honey-Nut Cheerios, Raisin Bran, Golden Grahams and Apple Jacks, so I bought all four.

   B. I couldn't decide between Honey-Nut Cheerios, Raisin Bran, Golden Grahams, and Apple Jacks, so I bought all four.

10. F. In any case, brushing your teeth three times a day isn't such a bad thing.

    G. In any case brushing your teeth three times a day isn't such a bad thing.

FIX THE APOSTROPHE DRILLS

Directions: In each of the following sentences, one word is used incorrectly. Find the incorrect word and rewrite it correctly.

Drill 1

1. Butterflies' are known in France as *papillons*.

2. There are so many citation style's that I'm not sure which to use.

3. Most goalies save percentage is above 90 percent.

4. Let's go see whose inside.

5. A stories style is more important to me than its plot.

6. I usually don't like potatoes, but these potatoes preparation has made them really exceptional.

7. Because of all the young parents, there are so many baby's in Hoboken.

8. I'm not sure what it mean's, but there's a big envelope from Harvard at home.

9. My band's version of the song is pretty good, but theirs' is much better.

10. Whose ski's are these?

Drill 2

1. The first song from the album was the bands biggest hit.

2. The Harlem Globetrotters are fun to watch even if there not the best basketball players.

3. I forgot to take my contact's out last night, and now my eyes are burning.

4. F. Scott Fitzgerald was one of the best writers of the twenties'.

5. Cristiano Ronaldo is one of soccers biggest stars.

6. To write, one needs a little bit of money and a room of ones own.

7. In the proper season, there's nothing more delicious than raspberries'.

8. Because I've listened to so many, I can't remember all the sermons contents.

9. The restaurant serves everything, but their specialties Greek food.

10. I swear he has sent me a thousand texts' today.

Drill 3

1. Its' a real shame that people don't read more.

2. A religious communities presence does a lot to shape the character of a town.

3. In Latin, the meaning of a word depends a lot on that words declension.

4. Each of the questions' has its own particular slant on the concept.

5. They have a variety of purposes, but the drills main one is to test your knowledge of apostrophes.

6. I can't keep track of all the medicine's my grandmother takes.

7. Sushi would be much more popular if it's rawness weren't so weird to people.

8. If you like that place's pancakes, you should definitely try our's.

9. My English teachers love of grammar is a total mystery to me.

10. Someone must've left the door open and let all these fly's in.

WHAT'S IT TESTING? DRILLS

Directions: In each of the following questions, you are given only a list of answer choices. Compare the answer choices, and identify the ACT concept being tested. Choose from the following list and write your answer next to each question: *apostrophes, concise, pronouns, stop/go, verbs, transitions.*

Drill 1

1. A. shine
    B. shines
    C. shined
    D. is shining

2. F. critical reputation
    G. reputation among critics and writers
    H. being known as having repute among critics
    J. reputation among critical people

3. A. depth but a
    B. depth. A
    C. depth; a
    D. depth, a

4. F. uncles
    G. uncles'
    H. uncle's
    J. uncles's

5. A. frowned each
    B. frowned. Each
    C. frowned—each
    D. frowned; each

6. F. whose
    G. ours
    H. its
    J. who's

7. A. dog, but it's actually really smart.
    B. dog.
    C. dog, and it's sort of smart.
    D. dog—no bones about it.

8. F. but
   G. that
   H. because
   J. although

9. A. words, by
   B. words by
   C. words. By
   D. words if by

10. Which of the following alternatives to the underlined portion would NOT be acceptable?

    F. though
    G. because
    H. since
    J. for

Drill 2

1. A. will have gone
   B. would go
   C. have gone
   D. will be going

2. F. Montclair, where there is a theater called the Wellmont.
   G. Montclair, where the Wellmont is a popular theater.
   H. Montclair, a suburb of New York City.
   J. Montclair.

3. A. however,
   B. nevertheless,
   C. that is to say,
   D. therefore,

4. F. one's
   G. him
   H. one
   J. he

5. A. children's,
   B. childrens,
   C. children's,
   D. childrens',

6. F. needs
   G. needed
   H. is needing
   J. have been needing

7. Which of the following alternatives to the underlined portion would NOT be acceptable?

   A. fences. Before doing this, the builders
   B. fences, before which, they
   C. fences. The builders soon
   D. fences; next they

8. Which of the following alternatives to the underlined portion would NOT be acceptable?

   F. Because
   G. Although
   H. Even though
   J. While

9. F. variation,
   G. variation because,
   H. variation:
   J. variation

10. F. arisen
    G. arosen
    H. arised
    J. arise

English Drills Answers

ID THE SUBJECT AND VERB DRILLS

Drill 1

1. Bruce; played
2. Alison; likes
3. who; is
4. they; are
5. George; writes
6. I; do find
7. students; learn
8. Junot Diaz; won
9. Ed; called
10. Amrita; has been going

Drill 2

1. Henry James; is
2. who; says
3. my dad's favorite team; used to be
4. ten years; is
5. Marc Maron's podcast; should come out
6. Super-Nintendo games; are
7. Dashiell Hammett; was
8. this band; has been
9. Matt; started
10. the show; has started

Drill 3

1.	you	are going to be
2.	they	did make
3.	no one	is
	secret	is
4.	I	wonder
	dogs	are
5.	buying	can be
	it	is
6.	Anna	will know
	she	is moving
	she	receives
7.	I	was
	library	is
8.	nothing	can compare
	I	have seen
9.	stories	are
10.	we	will leave
	we	are done packing

STOP/GO DRILLS

Drill 1

1. B
2. F
3. A
4. F
5. A
6. F
7. A
8. F
9. A
10. F

Drill 2

1. A
2. G
3. B
4. F
5. A
6. G
7. A
8. F
9. A
10. F

Drill 3

1. A
2. G
3. A
4. F
5. A
6. F
7. A
8. F
9. B
10. F

SUPPLY THE PRONOUN DRILLS

Drill 1

1. I
2. him
3. she
4. me
5. who
6. her
7. us
8. he
9. they
10. it

Drill 2

1. it
2. them
3. we
4. we
5. she
6. us
7. her
8. whom
9. he
10. him

Drill 3

1. who
2. who
3. whom
4. who
5. who
6. whom
7. whom
8. who
9. who
10. who

SUPPLY THE PARTICIPLE DRILLS

Drill 1

1. become
2. chosen
3. been
4. frozen
5. hidden
6. ridden
7. shaken
8. swum
9. worn
10. drunk

Drill 2

1. begun
2. come
3. flown
4. gotten
5. known
6. rung
7. sung
8. had
9. written
10. forgotten

Drill 3

1. blown
2. drunk
3. forbidden
4. given
5. lain
6. risen
7. spoken
8. taught
9. become
10. woken

FIX THE COMMA DRILLS

Drill 1

1. A
2. G
3. A
4. G
5. B
6. F
7. B
8. F
9. A
10. G

Drill 2

1. A
2. F
3. A
4. F
5. A
6. G
7. A
8. G
9. A
10. F

Drill 3

1. B
2. F
3. B
4. G
5. A
6. F
7. B
8. G
9. B
10. F

FIX THE APOSTROPHE DRILLS

Drill 1

1. butterflies
2. styles
3. goalies'
4. who's
5. story's
6. potatoes'
7. babies
8. means
9. theirs
10. skis

Drill 2

1. band's
2. they're
3. contacts
4. twenties
5. soccer's
6. one's
7. raspberries
8. sermons'
9. specialty's
10. texts

Drill 3

1. It's
2. community's
3. word's
4. question's
5. drill's
6. medicine
7. its
8. ours
9. teacher's
10. flies

WHAT'S IT TESTING? DRILLS

Drill 1

1. verbs
2. concise
3. stop/go
4. apostrophes
5. stop/go
6. pronouns
7. concise
8. transitions
9. stop/go
10. transitions

Drill 2

1. verbs
2. concise
3. transitions
4. pronouns
5. apostrophes
6. verbs
7. stop/go
8. transitions
9. stop/go
10. verbs

Chapter 13
English Practice
Test 1

ACT ENGLISH TEST

45 Minutes—75 Questions

DIRECTIONS: In the five passages that follow, certain words and phrases are underlined and numbered. In the right-hand column, you will find alternatives for each underlined part. In most cases, you are to choose the one that best expresses the idea, makes the statement appropriate for standard written English, or is worded most consistently with the style and tone of the passage as a whole. If you think the original version is best, choose "NO CHANGE." In some cases, you will find in the right-hand column a question about the underlined part. You are to choose the best answer to the question.

You will also find questions about a section of the passage or the passage as a whole. These questions do not refer to an underlined portion of the passage but rather are identified by a number or numbers in a box.

For each question, choose the alternative you consider best and blacken the corresponding oval on your answer document. Read each passage through once before you begin to answer the questions that accompany it. For many of the questions, you must read several sentences beyond the question to determine the answer. Be sure that you have read far enough ahead each time you choose an alternative.

PASSAGE I

What You See Isn't What You Get

Two freshmen stand, looking uncertainly at what appears to be a pleasant seating area just ahead. There are two tables: one is occupied by a young woman but the other is empty. <u>Nevertheless,</u> no one else seems to be considering walking in.
₁

That's because the seating area is actually a life-size <u>painting</u>
₂
<u>on the wall</u> of one of the campus buildings.
₂

A life-size seating area that's only a painting? That's John Pugh's specialty: <u>large-scale public art that is available for</u>
₃
<u>anyone to see.</u> He employs the trompe l'oeil, or "trick of the
₃
eye," style. His paintings are strikingly realistic, <u>having carefully included</u> shadows and reflections, making his
₄
paintings appear to be three-dimensional, as well as numerous

details. The cafe scene includes not only the young woman <u>and</u>
₅
<u>also</u> a statute, a framed piece of art, and a small cat, peering

1. Which of the following alternatives to the underlined portion would NOT be acceptable?

   A. However,
   B. Therefore,
   C. Still,
   D. And yet,

2. F. NO CHANGE
   G. painting, on the wall,
   H. painting, on the wall
   J. painting; on the wall

3. A. NO CHANGE
   B. large-scale public art
   C. public art for everyone
   D. art that is public and freely available

4. F. NO CHANGE
   G. always including a variety of
   H. due to Pugh's inclusion of
   J. being careful to include

5. A. NO CHANGE
   B. nor
   C. or
   D. but

GO ON TO THE NEXT PAGE.

around a corner. ▢6

In another of his paintings, a wave looms across the entire front of a building. The painting is immense, the wave looks like it's about to crash, and three children appears to stand ___7___ directly in its path. Being life-size and incredibly life-like, a ___8___ group of firefighters ran over to save the "children" shortly before the piece was completed. When the men got close enough to realize it was only a painting, they had a good laugh. No one seems to mind being fooled by Pugh's paintings. Most people, like the firefighters, are just impressed by Pugh's skill. ▢9

Pugh believes that by creating public art, he can ___10___ communicate with a larger audience than if his art were in a ___10___ gallery. Many of his pieces, including the café scene described ___10___ above, use the existing architecture. One of his other pieces

created the illusion that part of a building's wall has collapsed, ___11___ revealing an ancient Egyptian storeroom in the middle of Los Gatos, California. Like the café scene, the Egyptian scene includes a human figure. [A] In this case, however, the woman is not part of the scene. [B] Instead, she appears to be a passer-by, peering in to the revealed room. [C] Cities around the world have commissioned works from Pugh. [D] It is Pugh's

6. If the writer were to delete the question "A life-size painting that's only a painting?" from this paragraph, the essay would primarily lose:

F. an acknowledgement that Pugh's work might seem unusual to some.

G. a statement of the writer's central thesis for the remainder of the essay.

H. an argumentative and persuasive tone.

J. nothing, because the question simply confuses the main idea.

7. A. NO CHANGE
B. appeared
C. appear
D. was appearing

8. F. NO CHANGE
G. Stopping their truck in the middle of traffic,
H. Appearing young enough to be swept away,
J. Like so many of Pugh's other works,

9. If the writer were to remove the quotation marks around the word "children," the paragraph would primarily lose:

A. an explanation of why the firemen were so concerned about the wave.

B. a rhetorical device that lessens the reader's fear.

C. a way to distinguish between the painted wave and the real children.

D. emphasis on the fact that the children were painted, not real.

10. Given that all the choices are true, which one best conveys the theory behind Pugh's method as discussed in the remainder of the paragraph?

F. NO CHANGE

G. Pugh prefers incorporating his work into the pre-existing environment to simply adding his art without regard for its surroundings.

H. Drawing his inspiration from many different cultures, Pugh enjoys startling the viewer by placing objects in an unexpected context.

J. The firefighters may not have been upset at Pugh's trick but they were certainly startled, just like so many other people who see Pugh's work.

11. A. NO CHANGE
B. is creating
C. creates
D. creating

GO ON TO THE NEXT PAGE.

ability to create an apparent mystery in the middle of everyday life that makes his work speak to so <u>much</u> people. After all, who doesn't appreciate being tricked once in a while? [13]
₁₂

12. F. NO CHANGE
G. more
H. most
J. many

13. If the writer were to divide this paragraph into two, the most logical place to begin the new paragraph would be at Point:

A. A.
B. B.
C. C.
D. D.

Question 14 asks about the preceding passage as a whole.

---

14. Suppose the writer's goal had been to write a passage exploring some of the current trends in the art community. Would this essay accomplish that goal?

F. Yes, because it looks at a variety of styles popular among muralists throughout the Los Angeles area.
G. Yes, because is considers some of the reasons for Pugh's preference for large-scale public art.
H. No, because it only explores Pugh's artistic vision without considering the broader context of the art world.
J. No, because it details a number of incidents in which people have been confused by Pugh's artwork.

PASSAGE II

Leaving the Nest

My mother flew out with me and stayed for a few days, to make the transition easier for me. We went shopping and bought odds and ends for my dorm room—pillows, small decorative items, even a few pots and <u>pans—to make it feel</u> more like home. It felt more like a vacation than anything else.
₁₅

15. A. NO CHANGE
B. pans; to make
C. pans: to make
D. pans. To make

Then suddenly her brief stay was over. Her plane was leaving for San Juan, and I realized I wasn't going with her. She was going home, but I already was home. This strange new city was my home now. <u>Sitting on my bed in the dorm room that remained half-empty, it hit me.</u> I had just turned
₁₆
eighteen. I was about to start college in a new place, with a new language, a new culture. I had just said my first real farewell

16. F. NO CHANGE
G. As I sat on the bed in my half-empty dorm room,
H. Nervously looking around the half-empty dorm room,
J. Looking around the half-empty dorm room from my bed,

GO ON TO THE NEXT PAGE.

to a mother whom I had never before been away from for more
than a weekend. I had to learn how to live on my own, with mi
17

familia so many miles away and me all by myself.
18

During high school, I had fantasized about moving to the
United States someday. I was born in a sleepy, rural village in
southern Puerto Rico. My high school class had fifty people
in it, and the small town where I grow up was a very close-knit
19
community. I had spent hours imagining what it would be like
to be surrounded not by a few dozen people but by a few million.

Living in such a small town, I was used to knowing
20
everyone and having everyone know me. The very first
20

17. Which of the following choices is most logically supported
by the first part of the sentence?

A. NO CHANGE
B. who had always done my laundry, prepared my meals,
and kissed me goodnight.
C. whom I hoped was having a pleasant flight back to San
Juan and then on to our village.
D. who had herself spent some years living in the United
States in her twenties, before I was born.

18. F. NO CHANGE
G. and no one with me.
H. not with me any more.
J. DELETE the underlined portion and end the sentence
with a period.

19. A. NO CHANGE
B. grew
C. grown
D. growth

20. Given that all the choices are true, which provides the best
transition to the topic discussed in the rest of the paragraph?

F. NO CHANGE
G. The idea of being surrounded by so many people, and
being able to meet and talk with any of them seemed like
a dream come true.
H. When the time came to apply to colleges, I picked several,
all in major metropolitan areas in the continental United
States.
J. I had considered applying to colleges in San Juan but
decided that it was still too close to home, too familiar,
too easy.

GO ON TO THE NEXT PAGE.

acceptance received by me was from this school, located in the
_____
21
middle of a city with millions of inhabitants. My parents

were so proud that I get this opportunity to see the world
                    ___
                     22
outside of our village. They had spent enough time outside

of Puerto Rico in the United States to know that the English
             _____
                      23
language was not the only thing that was different. We

celebrated the weekend before I left, inviting all the neighbors

over to my parents home. We played music and ate and danced
         _____
          24

past midnight. 25

As the memory faded; I looked around my new room
                _____
                    26
again. Sure, it was small and a little bit dingy. True, I didn't

know anyone yet. None of that mattered, though. I had finally

made it. My new roommate would be arriving the next day.

Hopefully she would be a new friend and even if she wasn't,

my classes were starting in a few days. I had literally millions

of people to meet; surely a few of them would become my new

friends. I smiled, suddenly feeling nervous but excited, not
                                    _____
                                           27

21. **A.** NO CHANGE
    B. acceptance I received
    C. acceptance, I received,
    D. acceptance, receiving by me

22. **F.** NO CHANGE
    G. will get
    H. was getting
    J. had to get

23. The best placement for the underlined portion would be:
    A. where it is now.
    B. after the word time.
    C. after the word language.
    D. after the word different (and before the period).

24. **F.** NO CHANGE
    G. parents's
    H. parent's
    J. parents'

25. At this point, the writer is considering adding the following true statement:

    My favorite dance has always been la bomba.

    Should the writer make this addition here?

    A. Yes, because it adds a detail that helps explain the personality of the narrator.
    B. Yes, because it provides a smooth transition to the following paragraph.
    C. No, because it gives the false impression that the narrator will study dance in college.
    D. No, because it would be an unnecessary digression from the main point of the paragraph.

26. **F.** NO CHANGE
    G. faded, and I looked
    H. faded, I looked
    J. faded. I looked

27. Which of the following alternatives to the underlined portion would NOT be acceptable?

    A. excitement nervous
    B. nervously excited
    C. nervous excitement
    D. excitedly nervous

GO ON TO THE NEXT PAGE.

lonely any more. I was eighteen, in the city, and <u>had to face</u>
₂₈

the world. 29

28. Which choice most effectively expresses the narrator's confidence about her new life?

   F. NO CHANGE
   G. ready to take on
   H. all alone in
   J. about to enter

29. The writer is considering adding a concluding sentence here. Which of the following would be most logical and best express one of the main ideas of the essay?

   A. Still, I knew I would miss Puerto Rico and my friends I had left behind.
   B. Little did I know that my new roommate would become a lifelong friend.
   C. My dreams of living in the big city were finally going to become a reality.
   D. I hoped that my classes would be as exciting as my move had been.

PASSAGE III

Dual Personalities

[1]

When Lois Lane finds herself in serious danger, she looks
to Superman for help. When <u>she needed</u> help with an article,
₃₀
on the other hand, she calls on Clark Kent. Of course, as the
reader knows, the two men are actually the same person.

30. F. NO CHANGE
     G. in need of
     H. she was needing
     J. needed

[2]

The tradition of giving superheroes alternate names and

characters, or "alter-egos" goes back as far as superhero stories

do. Today, <u>when</u> it's a commonplace writing technique.
₃₁
Batman fights crime by night, but he poses as millionaire Bruce

31. A. NO CHANGE
     B. where
     C. because
     D. DELETE the underlined portion.

GO ON TO THE NEXT PAGE.

Wayne at day. Spider-Man protects the streets of New York—
₃₂

when he's not busy going to school as Peter Parker. 33

[3]

Each of the superheroes have something in his (or her)
₃₄
back-story to explain the dual character. They all have a few

things in common too, though. Superheroes have a certain

image—the costume and the name, for example; that helps
₃₅

them maintain their authority. If Batman didn't fight crime,
₃₆
he would probably do something else to deal with his past. Peter
₃₆

32. **F.** NO CHANGE
    G. for
    H. by
    J. DELETE the underlined portion.

33. At this point, the writer is thinking about adding the following true statement:

    > Wonder Woman, on the other hand, is always herself, since she comes from a tribe of warrior women.

    Should the writer make this addition here?

    A. Yes, because it provides a balance for the previous examples of Batman and Spider-Man.
    B. Yes, because it emphasizes the author's earlier claim that the alter-ego is commonplace.
    C. No, because it strays from the primary focus of the passage by providing irrelevant information.
    D. No, because it poses the unnecessary hypothetical that no superhero really needs an alternate identity.

34. **F.** NO CHANGE
    G. has
    H. is having
    J. are having

35. **A.** NO CHANGE
    B. for example,
    C. for example.
    D. for example—

36. Given that all the choices are true, which one provides the best support for the statement in the preceding sentence?

    F. NO CHANGE
    G. Batman, who lost his parents when he was young, were younger, he might have a harder time.
    H. Batman were just a regular-looking man, it would be harder for him to strike fear into the heart of criminals.
    J. Batman needed to, he could probably fight criminals without his gadgets since he knows several martial arts.

GO ON TO THE NEXT PAGE.

Parker isn't a very awe-inspiring name, but Spider-Man is. At
the same time, the hero often has friends and family members
who are somehow completely unaware of their loved ones'
other identity. Providing the superheroes with everyday names
and jobs helps in their attempts to fit in with the people around
them.

[4]

Stan Lee, creator of Spider-Man, and dozens of other
superheroes, has often commented on what he believes makes
a true hero. His opinion is that in order for the reader to care
about the hero, the hero has to be flawed. Do you agree with
him? According to Lee, without some kind of flaw, the hero
wouldn't really seem human. Lee builds tension, in his stories,
by putting those human flaws and the hero's quest into conflict.
It is that tension, perhaps, that makes his storylines so gripping.
Even Superman, the least "normal" of all the heroes, has to
deal with the tension between his love for Lois Lane and her
love for Superman, not Clark Kent. 44

37. Which of the following alternatives to the underlined portion
would NOT be acceptable?

    A. name; on the other hand,
    B. name, because
    C. name, although
    D. name; however,

38. **F.** NO CHANGE
    G. one's
    H. individuals
    J. individuals'

39. **A.** NO CHANGE
    B. Assuming
    C. Offering
    D. Allowing for

40. **F.** NO CHANGE
    G. it's
    H. his
    J. one's

41. **A.** NO CHANGE
    B. Lee creator of Spider-Man,
    C. Lee creator of Spider-Man
    D. Lee, creator of Spider-Man

42. Which choice provides the most logical and effective transition to the rest of this paragraph?

    F. NO CHANGE
    G. Why would anyone want a hero to be less than perfect?
    H. Are you familiar with Lee's various characters?
    J. What kind of flaw could a superhero have?

43. **A.** NO CHANGE
    B. tension in his stories
    C. tension in his stories,
    D. tension, in his stories

44. The writer is considering deleting the preceding sentence.
Should this sentence be kept or deleted?

    F. Kept, because it provides a specific example of the theory
being discussed throughout the paragraph.
    G. Kept, because it demonstrates that the ultimate superhero
will not seem human under any circumstances.
    H. Deleted, because it takes away from the persuasiveness
of the point made in the previous sentences.
    J. Deleted, because it switches the focus from the more
"human" superheroes to the "least" human of them.

GO ON TO THE NEXT PAGE.

Question 45 asks about the preceding passage as a whole.

45. While reviewing this essay, the writer thinks of some additional information and writes the following sentence:

> Even though many readers feel that Lane's ignorance is hard to believe, the Clark Kent persona provides a valuable, and time-honored, element to the Superhero story: the alter-ego.

If the writer were to include this sentence in the essay, the most logical place to add it would be after the last sentence in Paragraph:

A. 1.
B. 2.
C. 3.
D. 4.

PASSAGE IV

Curly Hair: The Circular Trend

Is curly hair a blessing or a curse? Passing trends, which can last a day or a decade, typically influence hairstyles, which can vary <u>dramatically; every</u> bit as much as clothing. Some
₄₆
segment of the population will therefore always be fighting the natural tendency of their hair, unless the fashion becomes natural hair.

[47] In the 1950s, curls were in, and the average American woman spent countless hours pinning, rolling, and curling her hair every week. Without blowdryers or curling irons, women were left with few options, maintaining properly stylish

46. F. NO CHANGE
    G. dramatically, being every
    H. dramatically, every
    J. dramatically. Every

47. Given that all of the following statements are true, which one, if added here, would most clearly and effectively introduce the main subject of this paragraph?

A. Some people don't care for curly hair because it is considered more difficult to style than straight hair is.
B. As far back as the Renaissance, people have faked having curly hair by wearing wigs and using curlers.
C. Curly hair has bounced in and out of the American fashion scene for at least the last fifty years.
D. Clothing styles also change frequently, and sometimes influence hairstyles in a direct, easily visible way.

GO ON TO THE NEXT PAGE.

hair-dos to work hard and a great deal of time. By the mid-1960s, a lot of women started to wonder whether all that work was really necessary. Suddenly, natural hair was all the rage. Women began to grow they're hair out and allow it to remain in its natural state, whether curly or straight. For a brief moment, it looked like women would be able to embrace their natural hair, whether straight or curly, light or dark, or having length or being short.

The change was short-lived, however, and didn't last for long, perhaps unsurprisingly. The desire to have long, natural hair somehow turned into the desire to have long, straight hair. During the 1970s, the movie and television star Farrah Fawcett popularized a look that involved long hair that seemed naturally straight and feathered—cut into layers designed to frame the face—yet slightly messy. [53] Women who had

naturally curly hair were suddenly the ones to suffer now, as they painstakingly ironed their hair to achieve that "natural" look. The fashions of the 1980s, however, turned everything around yet again. Big was in, and that went for hair as well as clothes. Curly hair became incredibly popular, and the main fashion goal was to make one's hair as curly and as big as possible. Women who didn't have natural curls got "permanent

48. F. NO CHANGE
G. was hardly work
H. with hard work
J. by working hard

49. A. NO CHANGE
B. their
C. there
D. her

50. F. NO CHANGE
G. and regardless of length.
H. which can be long or short.
J. long or short.

51. A. NO CHANGE
B. wasn't fated to continue, though, so it
C. predictably enough failed to stick and
D. DELETE the underlined portion.

52. F. NO CHANGE
G. star, Farrah Fawcett
H. star, Farrah Fawcett,
J. star Farrah Fawcett,

53. The writer is considering deleting the phrase "cut into layers designed to frame the face" from the preceding sentence (adjusting the punctuation as needed). Should this sentence be kept or deleted?

A. Kept, because it contrasts the style popularized by Fawcett with earlier styles.
B. Kept, because it defines the word used immediately before the phrase.
C. Deleted, because it fails to adequately explain the term it is intended to modify.
D. Deleted, because it digresses from the main point of the paragraph.

54. F. NO CHANGE
G. suddenly we're
H. sudden were
J. sudden we're

55. A. NO CHANGE
B. the curlier, the better.
C. it.
D. it didn't seem possible to have hair that was too curly, or too big to be fashionable.

GO ON TO THE NEXT PAGE.

waves," or "perms" to create the rampant curls modeled by
their pop icons, such as Cyndi Lauper and Gloria Estefan.

[1] By the middle of the 1990s, however, the perm had
lost its appeal, and straight hair was back in fashion where it
remains today. [2] Some commentator's have recently claimed
that curly hair is making a comeback, but only time will
tell. [3] Instead of using an iron, women can have their hair
chemically straightened in a sort of "reverse perm." [4] While
it's hard to know what the trend of tomorrow will be, one thing
seems certain: no style lasts forever. 58

56. Which of the following alternatives to the underlined portion would NOT be acceptable?

   F. worn
   G. displayed
   H. imitated
   J. popularized

57. **A.** NO CHANGE
   B. commentators
   C. commentators'
   D. commentators's

58. For the sake of the logic and coherence of this paragraph, Sentence 3 should be placed:

   F. where it is now.
   G. before Sentence 1.
   H. after Sentence 1.
   J. after Sentence 4.

Question 59 asks about the preceding passage as a whole.

59. Suppose the writer had been instructed to write an essay discussing modern attitudes towards curly hair. Would this essay meet that requirement?

   A. Yes, because it explains why some women prefer to wear their hair straight, regardless of current fashions.
   B. Yes, because it analyzes the reasons behind changes in fashion that affect the popularity of curly hair.
   C. No, because it focuses more on the changeability of fashions than the attitudes towards them.
   D. No, because it focuses primarily on the popularity of straight hair and the effort of style maintenance.

GO ON TO THE NEXT PAGE.

PASSAGE V

Marie Curie: Physicist, Chemist, and Woman

Marie Curie is famous today for two main reasons: her scientific discoveries and her defiance of gender stereotypes. She, along with her husband, identified two new elements, polonium and radium. She then coined the term "radioactive"
 _____ 60

60. The writer is considering deleting the underlined phrase and adjusting the punctuation accordingly. If the phrase were removed, the paragraph would primarily lose:

   F. a specific detail that provides information about the result of some of Curie's research.

   G. an explanation of how Curie was able to make such a variety of important scientific discoveries.

   H. information that identifies the reason Curie was awarded two Nobel prizes.

   J. a definition of radioactivity included by the writer and necessary to the paragraph as a whole.

and developed a theory to explain the phenomenon. Curie first
 _____ 61
began to research radioactivity after noticing that the amount
 _____ 61
of radiation produced by a sample depended wholly on the
 _____ 61
quantity of uranium in the sample.
 _____ 61

61. Given that all of the choices are true, which provides the most effective transition from this paragraph into the rest of the essay?

   A. NO CHANGE

   B. Due to her discoveries, she was both the first woman to receive a Nobel Prize and the first person to receive two Nobel Prizes, though her road to success was paved with difficulties.

   C. Although physics and chemistry are treated as separate fields, like so many other branches of science, the two are so interconnected in some areas that it can be difficult to tell them apart.

   D. Curie's husband, Pierre, was also a noted scientist who wrote several famous pieces on magnetism, including one that detailed the relationship between temperature and paramagnetism.

Curie was proficient in the fields of physics and chemistry, though her education was somewhat unusual, which prevented
 _____ 62
her from attending university due to a lack of money, Curie
 _____ 62
initially studied in a laboratory run by her cousin. Determined to pursue her love of science, Curie eventually enrolled at the University of Paris, where she later became the first female
 _____ 63
professor.

62. **F.** NO CHANGE

   G. unusual, prevented

   H. unusual. Prevented

   J. unusual prevented her

63. **A.** NO CHANGE

   B. like

   C. when

   D. DELETE the underlined portion.

GO ON TO THE NEXT PAGE.

While Curie is widely given recognition and credit for
<u>   </u>
                                    64
discovering radioactivity, this is not entirely accurate. Henri
Becquerel, a French scientist, has that honor. When Curie
made her discovery, Becquerel <u>had already saw</u> that rays,
                                                    65
functioning much like X-rays but produced by uranium salt,
existed; however, he did not identify the underlying process.
<u>Becquerel of radioactivity</u> was performing
                      66

<u>experimental</u> involving photographic paper, and the discovery
        67
was accidental. He realized that something was exposing the
photographic paper to rays even before he placed the paper in
the sunlight. <u>Nevertheless, further</u> experiments revealed that
                              68
the substance emitting rays was the fluorescent substance,
potassium uranyl sulfate.

However, Becquerel didn't identify the underlying
scientific <u>principal, namely,</u> that the rays were produced not by
              69
a molecular interaction but by the atom itself. Curie was

the first to make this discovery; it was she that <u>isolated,</u> and
                                                      70
identified radium and polonium. The earliest scientist to
realize that there was an element in the fluorescent substance
more reactive than <u>uranium,</u> Curie dedicated the next twelve
                        71
years to developing a method for isolating that substance,

<u>which was not yet known but later came to be identified and is</u>
                                              72
<u>now called "radium."</u>
        72

64. **F.** NO CHANGE
    G. credited and acknowledged as the person responsible for
    H. generally credited with
    J. appreciated often as deserving credit and recognition for

65. **A.** NO CHANGE
    B. has already seen
    C. had already seen
    D. has already saw

66. The most logical placement of the underlined portion would be:
    F. where it is now.
    G. after the word *performing.*
    H. after the word *paper.*
    J. after the word *discovery.*

67. **A.** NO CHANGE
    B. an experimental
    C. experimentally
    D. an experiment

68. **F.** NO CHANGE
    G. Subsequently, further
    H. Further
    J. In contrast, further

69. **A.** NO CHANGE
    B. principle namely,
    C. principal namely,
    D. principle: namely,

70. **F.** NO CHANGE
    G. isolated
    H. isolated it
    J. isolated—

71. **A.** NO CHANGE
    B. uranium;
    C. uranium
    D. uranium:

72. **F.** NO CHANGE
    G. we now know as radium.
    H. scientists and laypeople alike are familiar with today under the name "radium."
    J. people in the present day refer to under the name of "radium."

GO ON TO THE NEXT PAGE.

Curie was progressive for a chemist; much less for a
                                          ——
                                          73

woman. Women in science would of often had a difficult
                            ——————
                              74

time, and Curie was no exception. She was refused a position

at Krakow University due to her gender, and was ultimately

denied membership in the French Academy of Sciences.

However, the general consensus is that Curie was not bitter

about these rejections. Instead, she worked as hard as she
                               ————————————————
                                        75

could even when she wondered whether she would ever be
——
                      75

recognized. She was a woman who knew her own worth, even
——————————
    75

when others did not: a trait as valuable today as during the

eighteenth century.

73. **A.** NO CHANGE
    B. chemist,
    C. chemist; moreover,
    D. chemist so

74. **F.** NO CHANGE
    G. might of
    H. have
    J. has

75. Given that all the choices are true, which one provides
    the most consistent description of Curie's personality as
    described in this paragraph?

    A. NO CHANGE
    B. became somewhat reclusive in her later years, preferring
        her work to society.
    C. spent many years in her eventually successful attempt to
        identify the source of Becquerel's mysterious rays.
    D. was generally described by those who knew her as per-
        sistent, friendly, and humble.

END OF TEST 1
STOP! DO NOT TURN THE PAGE UNTIL TOLD TO DO SO.

Chapter 14
English Practice
Test 1: Answers and
Explanations

ENGLISH PRACTICE TEST 1 ANSWERS

1.	B	39.	A
2.	F	40.	F
3.	B	41.	D
4.	H	42.	G
5.	D	43.	B
6.	F	44.	F
7.	C	45.	A
8.	G	46.	H
9.	D	47.	C
10.	G	48.	H
11.	C	49.	B
12.	J	50.	J
13.	C	51.	D
14.	H	52.	F
15.	A	53.	B
16.	G	54.	F
17.	A	55.	B
18.	J	56.	H
19.	B	57.	B
20.	H	58.	H
21.	B	59.	C
22.	H	60.	F
23.	D	61.	B
24.	J	62.	H
25.	D	63.	A
26.	H	64.	H
27.	A	65.	C
28.	G	66.	J
29.	C	67.	D
30.	G	68.	H
31.	D	69.	D
32.	H	70.	G
33.	C	71.	A
34.	G	72.	G
35.	D	73.	B
36.	H	74.	H
37.	B	75.	D
38.	G		

SCORE YOUR PRACTICE TEST

Step A
Count the number of correct answers: _____. This is your *raw score*.

Step B
Use the score conversion table below to look up your raw score. The number to the left is your *scale score*: _____.

English Scale Conversion Table

Scale Score	Raw Score	Scale Score	Raw Score	Scale Score	Raw Score
36	75	27	62	18	41–42
35	73–74	26	60–61	17	39–40
34	71–72	25	58–59	16	36–38
33	70	24	56–57	15	33–35
32	69	23	54–55	14	30–32
31	67–68	22	52–53	13	28–29
30	66	21	49–51	12	26–27
29	65	20	46–48	11	24–25
28	63–64	19	43–45	10	22–23

ENGLISH PRACTICE TEST 1 EXPLANATIONS

Passage I

1. **B**   The question asks you to find the answer choice that is NOT acceptable as a replacement for the underlined portion—remember, that means the passage is correct as written. Look at the answer choices—they are all transition words, so you need to find the one that can't be used to connect the two ideas. The original word, *Nevertheless*, is used to connect two different ideas. Choices (A), (C), and (D) are all used in the same way. Choice (B), *Therefore*, is used to connect two similar ideas, so it can't be used to replace *Nevertheless*.

2. **F**   When you see answer choices "stacked" like this, using all (or mostly all) the same words with Stop and Go punctuation changing in the same spot, check for Complete/Incomplete on either side of that spot. In this case, *That's because the seating area is actually a life-size painting* is a complete idea, and *painting on the wall of one of the campus buildings* is incomplete. Since Stop punctuation can only separate complete ideas, eliminate (J). There's not a good reason to insert a comma either after *painting* or *wall*, so the best answer is (F).

3. **B**   The answer choices here all say the same thing in slightly different ways, but none contains an obvious grammatical error. Remember your fourth "C," concise! *Public* denotes the same idea as *for anyone/everyone* and *freely available*, so there's no need to say both—eliminate (A), (C), and (D).

4. **H**   Here you have three answer choices with different "-ing" forms of verbs, and one without. Whenever you see a 3/1 split in the answer choices, take a look at the one that is different. We know ACT doesn't like the "-ing" form—it's not concise—and (H) has no grammatical errors; therefore, it's the best answer.

5. **D**   The answer choices are all transition words, but this time ACT is testing idioms—specifically the "*not only, ___ also*" construction. The proper word to use is *but*, (D).

6. **F**   To identify what the essay would lose by deleting the sentence, you must first determine the purpose of that sentence. In this case, the author asks, "A life-size painting that's just a painting?" rhetorically, anticipating the reader's possible surprise at such a notion. Choice (F) is the only answer choice that expresses that purpose.

7. **C**   You need to find the correct form of the verb here. Eliminate (A) and (D)—they are singular forms and don't agree with the plural subject, *children*. Choice (B) is the correct plural form but the wrong tense—the correct answer choice has to be consistent with the other present-tense verbs in the passage: *looms*, *is*, and *looks*—that is (C).

8. **G**   Here again you see a 3/1 split with three "-ing" verbs and one without, so check the one without. Unfortunately, (J) actually creates an error, because in this question, the answer choices are all modifying phrases, and ACT wants a modifying phrase to be right next to the thing that it describes. That means you need to find the phrase that describes a *group of firefighters*. Choice (F) describes the image of the wave, (H) describes the children, and (J) describes the painting itself, leaving (G) as the only possible choice.

9. **D**   The author is using the quotation marks to emphasize the fact that there weren't really any children there to rescue, so if you take out the quotation marks, you will lose that emphasis—(D). Choice (A) might seem tempting, but the firefighters' concern was for the "children," not the wave, and in any case, the quotations don't explain anything.

10. **G**   The remainder of the paragraph talks about how Pugh uses his art to transform the appearance of an existing building, which agrees with (G). There is no comparison with gallery displays as in (F), nor is there discussion of multi-cultural influence on his work, as in (H). Choice (J) refers to the preceding paragraph.

11. **C**   The correct form of the verb needs to be consistent with the preceding sentence: *use* is present-tense, so eliminate (A). Remember, ACT doesn't like "-ing" verbs, so you should only choose one if you have eliminated every other answer choice. In this case, even though (B) and (D) are both present-tense, (C) is as well, and it isn't an "-ing" verb, making it the best answer.

12. **J**   There is no comparison being made here, so eliminate (G) and (H). The author is trying to express a large number of people, so you have to use *many*—(J).

13. **C**   A good place to begin a new paragraph is a point where there is a shift in focus or topic. Prior to point C the author is describing one of Pugh's works; after point C the discussion turns to the high demand for his work and his worldwide popularity. Choices (A), (B), and (D) all separate sentences that belong together.

14. **H**   The question asks about "trends" in the plural, and only one artist and one style was discussed in the essay—eliminate (F) and (G). Choice (J) is incorrect because although the essay does talk about people being confused by Pugh's art, that's not the reason the essay doesn't accomplish the stated goal—it's a problem of scope, as outlined in (H).

Passage II

15. **A** On the ACT, a semicolon is used in exactly the same way as a period, so you can eliminate (B) and (D)—they can't both be correct! *Besides, to make it feel more like home* is an incomplete idea, and Stop punctuation can only be used to separate two complete ideas. The colon in (C) comes after a complete idea, which is correct, but saying *to make it feel more like home* after it is awkward. You'll need a dash to be consistent with the rest of the sentence and set off the unnecessary *pillows, … pots and pans* from the rest of the sentence—(A).

16. **G** The answer choices here all say the same thing in slightly different ways, but none contains an obvious grammatical error. Remember your fourth "C"—concise! Choice (G) is the only answer choice that doesn't use an "-ing" form of the verb (which ACT doesn't like), and has no grammatical errors, so it's the best choice.

17. **A** You need to find an answer choice that agrees with *I had just said my first real farewell to a mother.* The sentence as written accomplishes this by explaining that she had never been away from her mother *for more than a weekend.* Choices (B), (C), and (D) all introduce new and off-topic information.

18. **J** When you see DELETE or OMIT as an answer choice, do that first. If you can take out the underlined portion without creating an error, chances are you've found your answer. In this case, deleting *and me all by myself* doesn't create an error, and leaving it in would be redundant—the narrator has already described herself as *on my own*—so eliminate (F). Choices (G) and (H) are redundant for the same reason.

19. **B** The correct tense of the verb here needs to be consistent with the non-underlined portion of the passage. The narrator is talking about her life before coming to college, so you must use the past tense, *grew,* to be consistent with the other verbs in the sentence, *had* and *was.* Choice (A), *grow,* is present tense, and (D), *growth,* isn't a verb, so eliminate them. Choice (C), *grown,* could be past tense, but needs to be paired with a helping verb.

20. **H** The task here is to transition from a discussion of the narrator's life in high school to her acceptance at a major university in the United States. Choice (H) begins with her in high school—*when the time came to apply to colleges*—and ends with her applying to several in the United States. Choices (F) and (G) don't talk about applying to college at all, and (J) only talks about applying to college in Puerto Rico.

21. **B** There are a couple of things changing in the answer choices here—commas and pronouns—work with one first and then the other. Remember that unless you have a reason to use a comma, no punctuation is preferable. Here, we have no reason to use a comma after *acceptance,* so eliminate (C) and (D). Now it's a matter of comparing *acceptance received by me* or *acceptance I received.* They both say the same thing, but the latter is more concise—choose (B).

22. **H**   The answer choices are forms of the verb "to get." To choose the correct one, look at the non-underlined portion of the sentence. The narrator says her parents *were* proud, so you need a past-tense verb to agree with that—eliminate (F) and (G). Choice (J) changes the meaning of the sentence, so the only answer choice left is (H), even though it uses the "-ing" form of the verb.

23. **D**   The difference being talked about here is between Puerto Rico and the United States, so *in the United States* needs to be placed in the spot that will make that most clear. Choice (A) makes it sound like Puerto Rico is in the United States—eliminate it. Neither (B) nor (C) make it clear that the United States is where things are different—only (D) does.

24. **J**   Apostrophes are used to show either possession or contraction. The word after *parents* is *house*, so you want to show possession. The narrator is referring to the house that belongs to both of her parents, and with a plural noun that ends in "s," all you need to do is add an apostrophe—(J).

25. **D**   Remember that on the ACT, less is more, so you should have a really compelling reason to add something. In an essay discussing the narrator's feelings about being away from her home and family for the first time, it's not really important to know what is her favorite dance—eliminate (A) and (B). The reason it's not important isn't because of any false impression created, so (D) is the best answer choice.

26. **H**   Here you see nicely "stacked" answer choices with Stop and Go punctuation changing in the same spot. Check for Complete/Incomplete on either side: *As the memory faded* is Incomplete, so no matter what, you're not going to be able to use Stop punctuation—that can only connect two complete ideas. Eliminate (F), (G), and (J), and you're done.

27. **A**   You're looking for the answer choice that can NOT be used in place of the underlined portion—remember, that means the sentence is correct as written. Choices (B), (C), and (D) all express either how the narrator was feeling or what she was feeling; (A) is the only choice that makes no sense—you wouldn't feel "excitement nervous"—and is therefore the one to choose.

28. **G**   The assignment here is to *emphasize the narrator's confidence*, so the correct answer choice must do exactly that. Choice (G), *ready to take on*, does that much more effectively than *had to face*, *all alone in*, or *about to enter*.

29. **C**   Make sure to read the question carefully—the goal here is to not only pick a logical concluding sentence but also the one that *best expresses one of the main ideas of the essay*. A main idea is one that recurs throughout the essay, so you can eliminate (B) and (D). While Puerto Rico is certainly mentioned throughout the essay, it wouldn't be logical for the narrator to express her regret at leaving home—the preceding sentence has an upbeat and confident tone, which (C) continues while including another main idea—her dream of living in a large city.

Passage III

30. G Three of the answer choices offer a form of the verb "to need," and one offers no verb at all—that's a 3/1 split, and on the English test, you always want to check the "1" first. That makes the sentence read *When in need of help with an article, she calls on Clark Kent*, which is a present-tense sentence that is consistent with the first: *When Lois Lane finds herself in serious danger, she looks to Superman for help.* The verbs in (F), (H), and (J) are all past-tense, so (G) is the best answer.

31. D DELETE is an answer choice, so do that first—if you don't create an error by taking out the underlined portion, it's probably the correct choice. In this case, taking out the question word *when* leaves *Today it's a commonplace writing technique*—a perfectly good complete sentence. Leaving *when*, *where*, or *because* in there would make the sentence incomplete, so you shouldn't choose (A), (B), or (C).

32. H You've got DELETE as an option, so try it. This time, it creates an error: *...he poses as millionaire Bruce Wayne day* doesn't make sense, so eliminate (J). Now your choices are all prepositions, which means ACT is testing idioms. To express the notion that something occurs during the day, you need to say *by day*—(H).

33. C To decide whether to make the addition here, take a look at the main theme of the passage—Dual Personalities—and what's going on in the paragraph. The author is talking about the *tradition of giving superheroes alternate names and characters*, so adding a sentence about a superhero that doesn't need an alter-ego would be a bad idea—eliminate (A) and (B). Choice (D) is incorrect because the sentence poses no hypothetical situation.

34. G The correct verb here needs to agree in number with the subject, *Each*. Careful—*of the superheroes* is a prepositional phrase, so it's not the subject, but it can make the wrong verb sound correct. To avoid confusion, you should cross out prepositional phrases you find inserted between a verb and its subject, one of ACT's favorite tricks. Now you know the subject is *Each*, a singular noun, so it needs a singular verb—eliminate (F) and (J). Choices (G) and (H) are both singular and present-tense, but beware the "-ing" form! They both say the same thing, but (G) is more concise, making it the better answer choice.

35. D The phrase *the costume and the name, for example* is unnecessary. Unnecessary info can be offset by either a pair of commas or a pair of dashes, but you can't open with one and close with another. The dash used in the non-underlined text means a dash must be used here.

36. H You need to provide support for the preceding sentence, which states that impressive costumes and names help superheroes maintain their authority. Only (H) addresses anything to do with this theme by stating that it would be more difficult for Batman to fight crime if he lacked those things.

37. B You need to find the answer choice that can NOT be used to replace the underlined portion in the passage. A quick glance at the answer choices might give you the impression that Stop/Go punctuation is being tested here, but look closer; the words changing after the punctuation are all transition words, and that typically means ACT is testing direction. Remember, when NO CHANGE is not an answer choice, the sentence in the passage is correct as written, and that gives you an important clue: The transition word used is *but*, an opposite-direction transition—that means a suitable replacement will also have to use one. *On the other hand*, *although*, and *however* in (A), (C), and (D) are all opposite-direction transitions, but *because* in (B) is same-direction, and so can NOT be used—making (B) the correct answer.

38. **G** There are two things changing here: apostrophes showing possession and word choice between *one* and *individual*. In the sentence, the *loved one/individual* with the *other identity* refers back to *the hero*, so you know you need to choose a singular noun, and to show possession, you need to add an *'s*. Choice (G), *one's*, is the only one that offers that construction.

39. **A** The superheroes are given these alter-egos by their creators in order to help the characters fit into a societal context. *Providing* best communicates this meaning; there is no assumption being made, as in (B), and (C) and (D) make it seem as if the fictional characters had a choice in the matter.

40. **F** This is a pronoun question, so find the noun that's being replaced. In this case, it's the superheroes who are making the attempts, and *superheroes* is plural. That helps a lot, since, apostrophes or not, you can eliminate (G), (H), and (J)—they're all singular pronouns and can't be used to replace a plural noun.

41. **D** This is a comma question, so keep your comma rules in mind. There is unnecessary information in this sentence: *creator of Spider-Man and dozens of other superheroes*. This needs to be set off with commas—one after *Lee* (eliminate (B) and (C)) and one after *superheroes*. The only answer choice that offers this without adding additional, unnecessary commas is (D).

42. **G** The rest of the paragraph discusses the reasons Stan Lee gives his superheroes human flaws, so if you're going to introduce that sort of discussion with a rhetorical question, the natural choice for that question would be one that asks, "Why?" Choice (G) is the only one that asks that question.

43. **B** This question is testing comma usage, but none of the situational rules seem to apply—there's no introductory idea, list, or unnecessary information. Therefore, the issue is whether there is a definite need to pause at any point in *Lee builds tension in his stories by putting those human flaws and the hero's quest into conflict*. If it helps, you can take an exaggerated pause at the spots ACT suggests putting commas. If the pause creates a little tension, you probably need the comma; if the pause just seems irritating or awkward, you don't. This sentence is a little on the long side, but it doesn't need the commas—(B).

44. **F** The sentence should be kept, since it's giving an example of what the entire previous paragraph is talking about—eliminate (H) and (J). Choice (G) is the direct opposite of what's happening in the sentence: The ultimate superhero does in fact have human feelings.

45. **A** This sentence fits best with the discussion in the first paragraph about Lois Lane's misconception that Superman and Clark Kent are two different individuals. It also introduces the concept of the alter-ego, the subject of the second paragraph, so it functions nicely as a transition sentence as well.

Passage IV

46. **H** Here you have nicely "stacked" answer choices with Stop and Go punctuation changing in the same spot—check for Complete/Incomplete on either side. *Passing trends… vary dramatically* is Complete, and *every bit as much as clothing* is Incomplete. You'll need Go punctuation to connect these two—eliminate (F) and (J). Choice (G) uses the less-concise "-ing" form of the verb, making (H) the best answer.

47. **C** The assigned task is to introduce the main subject of the paragraph, which begins by talking about curly hair being the fashion in the 1950s and the progression towards "natural" hair by the mid-1960s. Choice (A) is addressed in the paragraph, but it's not a main subject. The Renaissance is never mentioned, so eliminate (B), and (D) introduces a new topic—clothing styles—so the best answer is (C).

48. **H** The answer choices here are all very similar and don't contain any obvious errors. You'll need to check the non-underlined portion on either side and make sure the answer is consistent with both. To the left you have *maintaining properly stylish hair-dos*, and to the right you have *and a great deal of time*. Choices (F) and (J) aren't consistent with both, and (G) is not only inconsistent, but it also contradicts the preceding sentence—these hairdos took a lot of work.

49. **B** There are pronouns changing in the answer choices, and an apostrophe in the sentence as written. If you're in doubt about whether you need the contraction or a pronoun, expand out the contraction: In this case, *they're* becomes "they are," which doesn't make sense—eliminate (A). The noun being replaced here is *Women*, which is plural, so you need a plural pronoun—eliminate (D). Choice (B) is the possessive, plural pronoun you're looking for, but watch out for its sound-alike, *there*, in (C).

50. **J** All the answer choices basically say the same thing, and none creates a grammatical error, so pick the one that says what they all do in the most concise way. That's (J)—*long or short*.

51. **D** DELETE is an answer choice, so try that first. Taking out the underlined portion leaves *The change didn't last long, perhaps unsurprisingly.* That is a complete sentence, and the meaning hasn't changed, so it's the best answer.

52. **F** This question is testing comma usage, so keep your comma rules in mind. It might be tempting to think of *Farrah Fawcett* as unnecessary information, but if you remove it from the sentence, it is no longer clear who *the movie and television star* is. Because it's necessary, no commas are needed, which corresponds with (F), NO CHANGE.

53. **B** Be careful—the question is asking whether the phrase inside the dashes *should* be deleted, not whether it *can* be. In this case, the author is using the phrase inside the dashes to define a term with which the reader may not be familiar, and you know ACT likes things to be clear. Therefore, the phrase should be kept—eliminate (C) and (D). Choice (A) is incorrect because there is no contrast made to an earlier style.

54. **F** There are two things changing here: apostrophes showing contraction and word choice between *sudden* and *suddenly*. You need the adverb *suddenly*, so eliminate (H) and (J). Choice (G) is incorrect because we're is a contraction of "we are," which wouldn't make sense in the sentence.

55. **B** Three of the answer choices say the same thing in slightly different ways, while one just says *it*. While you may be tempted to read *it* in the slang sense of "something really popular," remember there's no slang on the ACT—eliminate (C). Now you're left with the three answer choices that don't contain errors, but all say the same thing—pick the one that's most concise, (B).

56. **H** You need to find the answer choice that can NOT replace the underlined portion in the sentence, and since NO CHANGE isn't an option, you know the sentence in the passage is correct. The option here is to find an alternate word for *modeled*, so this is just a vocabulary question. Choices (F), (G), and (J) all work as replacements in the context of the sentence, so select (H), the one that does NOT. If this question tricked you, you may have picked *imitated*, since the sentence talks about women imitating the pop icons, but the pop icons are the ones doing the modeling.

57. **B** If you're unsure about whether an apostrophe is showing possession or expansion, expand it out. In this case, "commentator is" wouldn't make sense, so if you need an apostrophe at all, it would be to show possession. However, look at the word after the underlined portion: *have*. Only nouns can be possessed, and *have* is not a noun; therefore, you can't use an apostrophe here at all—eliminate (A), (C), and (D).

58. **H** Sentence 3 talks about how women can now have their hair chemically straightened. Both sentence 2 and sentence 4 talk about curly hair, so eliminate (F) and (J). Sentence 3 would naturally follow sentence 1, which transitions from the previous paragraph and introduces the idea of straight hair being the fashion now, so (H) is a better answer choice than (G).

59. **C** The essay mentions the "modern" preference for straight hair, but that's a long way from *discussing modern attitudes toward curly hair*—eliminate (A) and (B). Choice (D) is incorrect for the same reason: The primary focus is not on the popularity of straight hair.

Passage V

60. **F**   The phrase *polonium and radium* names the *two new elements* discovered by the Curies. It doesn't provide an explanation as (G) claims, nor does it offer the reason Marie Curie won the Nobel Prize, as in (H). Choice (J) is incorrect because the phrase does not define radioactivity—it simply lists two radioactive elements—leaving (F) as the best answer choice.

61. **B**   The assigned task is to *provide the most effective transition* to the rest of the essay. The next paragraph talks about some of the problems Curie encountered in her academic and professional career, so an *effective transition* will need to incorporate that theme, as (B) does. Choice (A) only provides a specific detail about Curie's research, (C) doesn't mention Curie at all, and (D) talks only about Curie's husband, Pierre.

62. **H**   Here you see nicely "stacked" answer choices with Stop and Go punctuation changing in the same spot, but before checking for Complete/Incomplete on either side to see which kind of punctuation you need, notice you have one answer choice with *which* in it, and three without. Whenever you see a 3/1 split like that on the English test, check the "1" first. In (F), the idea after the comma would be *which prevented her from attending university due to a lack of money, Curie initially studied in a laboratory run by her cousin*, which doesn't make sense—eliminate (F). The remaining three answer choices all have *prevented* as the first word in the second idea, but (J) has *prevented her*, which creates another error—eliminate (J). Now it's down to a choice between a period and a comma. The ideas on either side are both complete (make sure to read the entire sentence!), so you need Stop punctuation—(H).

63. **A**   You're given the option to DELETE the underlined portion, so try that first. Taking out *where* in this case leaves you with a comma joining two complete ideas, so eliminate (D). *Like* doesn't make sense, so eliminate (B). Both *when* and *where* might seem to work, but keep in mind that the two things happening in the sentence are Curie enrolling at the University of Paris and becoming the first woman professor there. Those two things didn't happen simultaneously, so you can't use *when* to connect them—choose (A).

64. **H**   All the answer choices here say basically the same thing, and none creates a grammatical error, so pick the one that says what they all do in the most concise way. That's (H)—*generally credited with*.

65. **C**   There are two things changing in the answer choices: We have *seen* vs. *saw* and *has* vs. *had*. Start with whichever seems easier, and eliminate answer choices that don't agree. The correct form of the verb (regardless of whether you use *has* or *have*) is *has/have seen*, so delete (A) and (D). To figure out which tense you need, check the non-underlined rest of the passage for context. In the same sentence, you have past-tense verbs: *made, existed, did*—(C) is past-tense and therefore consistent with the rest of the sentence.

66. **J**   Here it's really just a matter of inserting the underlined portion, *of radioactivity*, in each of the places in the answer choices; the only place it makes any sense at all is after *discovery*, (J).

67. **D**   This question is basically just testing word choice. If you happen to notice that there's a 3/1 split in the answers—one noun and three modifiers—then you could probably save a step or two, but from the context of the (now altered) passage, you know that *Bequerel was performing* [something] *involving photographic paper*, not *performing* [in some manner] involving photographic paper. If you need a thing, you need a noun, and the only choice you have is (D).

68. **H**   There are transition words changing in the answer choices, which can often be an indication that ACT is testing direction, but notice the 3/1 split—three answer choices with transitions and one without. If you try the one without, you're left with *Further experiments revealed… potassium uranyl sulfate*, which is a perfectly good sentence, and more concise than the other three. There's no real need for a transition at all here, so (H) is the best answer.

69. **D**   This is another word choice question with some punctuation thrown in to confuse the issue—start easy! *Principal* means something that is highest in rank or value; *principle* means a fundamental assumption. In the context of the sentence, you need to use *principle*—eliminate (A) and (C). Using a colon after *principle* might seem obviously preferable to the comma after *namely*, which seems awkward, but remember that ACT mandates that a colon must follow a complete idea, and must itself be followed by a list, definition, expansion, or explanation of that complete idea; make sure to check that. *However, Bequerel… principle* is a complete idea, and the idea after the colon is a definition (as evidenced by the introductory word *namely*)—pick (D).

70. **G**   You have a 3/1 split of sorts here: All the answer choices have *isolated* by itself with some kind of punctuation, and one that adds *it*—that's probably a good place to start. Adding the pronoun *it* here, though, creates an error: The pronoun is not replacing any noun—eliminate (H). The action in the idea after the semicolon is *she* (Curie) *isolated and identified* the two elements, so there's no need for any punctuation in between the two verbs—choose (G).

71. **A**   The answer choices have Stop and Go punctuation changing in the same spot and all use the same word, so check for Complete/Incomplete on either side: Before the punctuation you have *The earliest scientist to realize that there was an element in the fluorescent substance more reactive than uranium*—an incomplete idea, and afterward you have *Curie dedicated the next twelve years to developing a method for isolating that substance, which was not yet known but later came to be identified and is now called "radium,"* which is a complete idea, so you need Go punctuation to separate them—eliminate (B) and (D), which has a colon, which you know has to follow a complete idea. You definitely need to pause after the incomplete idea, so leave the comma where it is—(A).

72. **G**   You know ACT is testing concise when all the answer choices here say basically the same thing, and none creates a grammatical error. That's what's happening here, so pick the one that says what they all do in the most concise way. That's (G)—*we now know as radium*.

73. **B** Here you see Stop and Go punctuation changing in the same spot and nicely "stacked" answer choices, so check for Complete/Incomplete on either side: Before the punctuation you have *Curie was progressive for a chemist*—a complete idea, and afterward you have *much less for a woman*, which is an incomplete idea, so you need Go punctuation to separate them—eliminate (A) and (C). Choice (D) is awkward and doesn't really make sense—choose (B).

74. **H** There are two things changing in the answer choices here: word choice and helping verbs. It's incorrect to say *would of* or *might of*—it's "would have" and "might have." Eliminate (F) and (G). Helping verbs need to agree with the subject in number, just like regular verbs. In this case, the subject is *Women*, which is plural, so choose (H), *have*.

75. **D** The correct answer choice will provide *the most consistent description of Curie's personality as described in this paragraph*. There is no mention in the paragraph of her seeking recognition as in (A), and likewise in (B), no proof that she became reclusive. Choice (C) doesn't talk about her personality at all, leaving (D) as the best answer choice.

Chapter 15
English Practice
Test 2

ACT ENGLISH TEST

45 Minutes—75 Questions

DIRECTIONS: In the five passages that follow, certain words and phrases are underlined and numbered. In the right-hand column, you will find alternatives for each underlined part. In most cases, you are to choose the one that best expresses the idea, makes the statement appropriate for standard written English, or is worded most consistently with the style and tone of the passage as a whole. If you think the original version is best, choose "NO CHANGE." In some cases, you will find in the right-hand column a question about the underlined part. You are to choose the best answer to the question.

You will also find questions about a section of the passage or the passage as a whole. These questions do not refer to an underlined portion of the passage but rather are identified by a number or numbers in a box.

For each question, choose the alternative you consider best and blacken the corresponding oval on your answer document. Read each passage through once before you begin to answer the questions that accompany it. For many of the questions, you must read several sentences beyond the question to determine the answer. Be sure that you have read far enough ahead each time you choose an alternative.

PASSAGE I

A Day in the City

When I woke up this morning, I made myself a bowl of cereal and sat, listening to the traffic. Some of my friends ask me how I can stand living somewhere so noisy. It's true that

1. Which of the following alternatives to the underlined portion would NOT be acceptable?
- **A.** cereal and sat while listening
- **B.** cereal, sat listening
- **C.** cereal, sat, and listened
- **D.** cereal before sitting and listening

there's always some kind of noise in my neighborhood—taxi drivers honking their horns, kids playing their radios so loud that the bass makes my teeth vibrate, or people yelling in the street. I know that some people wouldn't like it, but to me, these are the sounds of life. ☐3

2. F. NO CHANGE
- **G.** neighborhood, taxi drivers honking
- **H.** neighborhood; taxi drivers honking
- **J.** neighborhood taxi drivers honking

3. If the writer were to delete the preceding sentence, the essay would primarily lose:
- **A.** a contrast to the positive tone of the essay.
- **B.** an explanation for the narrator's trip to the park.
- **C.** information that shows the author's attitude toward the place she lives.
- **D.** nothing at all; this information is not relevant to the essay.

It's Saturday, so this morning I decided to go to the park. The train is the fastest way to go but I took the bus instead.

4. F. NO CHANGE
- **G.** Since today it is finally
- **H.** Allowing for it being
- **J.** The day of the week is

When I ride the bus, you get to see so much more of the city. It can be kind of loud on the bus, with some people talking

5. A. NO CHANGE
- **B.** one is riding
- **C.** you ride
- **D.** they are riding

GO ON TO THE NEXT PAGE.

on their phones, others chatting sociable with their friends, and
others playing music. Just like the traffic's sounds, though, the

noise on the bus represents people working, relaxing, and living.

Once I get to the park, I pick a bench over near the play
area. The city added the bench so they could play while their

parents sit nearby, obviously I like to sit there because there's a
great big oak tree for shade. I can see and hear almost

everything from there. I sit there watching, and listening to the
people around me. People-watching is one of my favorite

things to do, I like listening even better. The park is the best
place because you get to see and hear everything. The only
problem is that there's so much to see and hear!

That's why people get so tired after a little while. That way,
I can pay more attention to the sounds and not get distracted by
what I see. With my eyes closed, I can pick out parts of

two old men's familiar conversation. One of them is telling the
other about something his grandson said. I can't hear the rest,
but whatever it was must have been hilarious because his

friends' laugh is so loud, it startles me.

Later that night, after I've ridden the bus back home, I think
about those old men. When I'm old, I hope that I too will have
a friend who will sit in the park with me, and who will enjoy
listening to the sounds of the city as much as I do.

6. **F.** NO CHANGE
   G. sociably, with
   H. sociable with,
   J. sociably with

7. **A.** NO CHANGE
   B. people, working;
   C. people; working
   D. people, working,

8. **F.** NO CHANGE
   G. kids
   H. because they
   J. that it

9. **A.** NO CHANGE
   B. nearby.
   C. nearby,
   D. nearby, because

10. **F.** NO CHANGE
    G. there, watching, and listening,
    H. there, watching and listening
    J. there watching and listening,

11. **A.** NO CHANGE
    B. do, nevertheless,
    C. do, but
    D. do, however

12. Which choice most effectively introduces the idea discussed in this rest of the paragraph?

    F. NO CHANGE
    G. I close my eyes
    H. the park is interesting
    J. some people like quiet

13. Which choice would emphasize the narrator's curiosity and interest in the old men's conversation in the most logical and effective way?

    A. NO CHANGE
    B. noisy chatter.
    C. animated discussion.
    D. entertaining stories.

14. **F.** NO CHANGE
    G. friends's
    H. friends
    J. friend's

GO ON TO THE NEXT PAGE.

Question 15 asks about the preceding passage as a whole.

15. Suppose the writer's assignment was to write an essay analyzing one reason people might choose to live in a large city. Would this essay fit that description?

   A. Yes, because it discusses the convenience of public transportation.
   B. Yes, because it explains the narrator's enjoyment of one of the city's parks.
   C. No, because it focuses on one detail of city living that most people dislike.
   D. No, because it only discusses why the narrator prefers listening to watching.

PASSAGE II

The Bridge They Said Couldn't Be Built

Visible in the fog as well as the sun, the Golden Gate Bridge is a symbol of San Francisco. The bridge was once famous for having the longest suspension span in the world; even today, its suspension span is the second longest in the United States. It is open to cars and pedestrians alike, and has only been shut down three times in that seventy-year history.
<u>The amount</u> of concrete needed to anchor the bridge was
16

enough to construct a <u>sidewalk five feet wide</u>, all the way
17
from San Francisco to New York City. Since the Golden Gate opened, almost two billion cars have crossed the bridge and it has been featured in countless movies.

The fame of the Golden Gate Bridge wasn't always assured. [A] When Joseph Strauss announced his intention of building the bridge, <u>people flocked to support him.</u> A combination of
18
factors made building a bridge in that location difficult: cold, stormy seas below, foggy and damp weather, and winds that regularly reach speeds of 60 miles per hour.

16. F. NO CHANGE
    G. their
    H. its
    J. DELETE the underlined portion.

17. A. NO CHANGE
    B. sidewalk five feet wide
    C. sidewalk—five feet wide
    D. sidewalk, five feet wide

18. Which choice provides the conclusion that relates to the rest of the paragraph in the most logical way?
    F. NO CHANGE
    G. many said it was impossible.
    H. some admired his vision.
    J. he had already built other bridges.

GO ON TO THE NEXT PAGE.

[B] After two years of discussion, the voters approved a

bond: that would raise $35 million, all dedicated to building the
—————
19

bridge. Even then, there were many skeptics whom believed
—————
20
that it couldn't be done.

Strauss, a veteran bridge builder, refused to give up.

Construction began in 1933 and ended in 1937, and lasted a
—————————————
21

little more than four years. On May 28, 1937. The bridge,
——————————————————————
22
arching grandly over the water, opened to pedestrians. More
———————
22
than 200,000 people walked across the bridge that day to

celebrate the grand achievement.
———————————————
23

[C] By the time it was completed, the bridge had exceeded

everyone's expectations. Not only was it built, it was also

ahead of schedule and under budget. To top it off,

it was beautiful. Nevertheless, the Golden Gate Bridge is
——————————
24
considered an artistic masterpiece, recognizable all around the

world. At its highest point, the bridge rises 746 feet into the

air—191 feet taller than the Washington Monument.
———
25

The name "Golden Gate" refers not to the color of the

bridge, which is actually orange, but to the stretch of water

below, where the San Francisco Bay connects to the Pacific

Ocean. [D] The color, called "International Orange," was

chosen partly because it matched the natural surroundings and
——————————————————
26

19. **A.** NO CHANGE
    B. bond, that
    C. bond; that
    D. bond that

20. **F.** NO CHANGE
    G. that
    H. who
    J. DELETE the underlined portion.

21. **A.** NO CHANGE
    B. being completed by 1937,
    C. ending four years later
    D. DELETE the underlined portion.

22. **F.** NO CHANGE
    G. On May 28, 1937; the bridge arching grandly
    H. On May 28, 1937, the bridge, arching grandly
    J. On May 28, 1937, the bridge, arching grandly,

23. **A.** NO CHANGE
    B. an achievement that was extremely impressive because it symbolized a significant victory over difficult circumstances.
    C. the successful completion of a project that was amazing both because of the obstacles that had been overcome and because of the magnitude of the product that was the result of the project.
    D. DELETE the underlined portion and end the sentence with a period.

24. **F.** NO CHANGE
    G. At the time,
    H. Regardless,
    J. Even today,

25. **A.** NO CHANGE
    B. air;
    C. air
    D. air, rising

26. **F.** NO CHANGE
    G. nature surrounding
    H. nature surrounded
    J. natural surrounds

GO ON TO THE NEXT PAGE.

partly because it would allow the bridge to remain visible on

foggy days. [27]

      Today, the bridge is divided into six lanes for cars,

and pedestrian lanes for people and bicycles. On sunny days,

crowds of people flock to the bridge to enjoy the view. Rising

out of the sea like a vision from a dream, the Golden Gate

Bridge captures the imagination today, just as it did when

Strauss first envisioned it. [28]

27. The writer is considering deleting the phrase "on foggy days" from the preceding sentence in order to make the paragraph more concise. If the writer were to make this deletion, the sentence would primarily lose information that:

A. explains why the color of the bridge is referred to as "International Orange."

B. demonstrates the ways in which the bridge's color matches the environment.

C. reveals the danger that the bridge can cause for some ships during bad weather, regardless of color.

D. adds a detail that provides a specific situation in which the bridge's visibility is particularly important.

28. The writer is considering adding a sentence that demonstrates the wide variety of the bridge's uses today. Given that all the following statements are true, which one, if added here, would most clearly and effectively accomplish the writer's goal?

F. On weekdays, during the busiest times of day, the direction of certain lanes changes to accommodate rush hour commuters.

G. The weather in San Francisco is often foggy, but when the sky is clear, the bright orange of the bridge stands out against its surroundings.

H. The bridge is 1.7 miles long, so some people walk across in one direction but hire a taxi or take the bus to return.

J. People use it to commute to work, to go on day trips to Marin or San Francisco, and even just to enjoy the beauty of the bridge itself.

> Question 29 asks about the preceding passage as a whole.

29. Upon reviewing the essay, the writer realizes that some information has been omitted. The writer wants to incorporate that information and composes the following sentence:

> The local community began to consider building a bridge to connect the San Francisco peninsula in 1928.

If the writer were to add this sentence to the essay, the most logical place to insert it would be at Point:

A. A

B. B

C. C

D. D

GO ON TO THE NEXT PAGE.

PASSAGE III

Father of a Language

The Italian language wasn't always the single, unified,
language that it is today. In fact, during the Middle Ages, Italy
wasn't a unified country. Even today, though Italy is politically
unified, each region speaks its own dialect. In some regions,
such as Tuscany, the dialect is virtually identical to the "official"
Italian language. In other regions, such as Venice, however, the
language is still distinct in many ways.

Dante Alighieri, more commonly known simply as Dante,
is sometimes called the "father of the Italian language." He
was born in Florence during the thirteenth century and was
a prolific writer. In approximately 1305, he published an
essay entitled "De Vulgari Eloquentia," or "In Defense of the
Vernacular." About three years later, Dante began work on his
masterpiece: *The Divine Comedy*. Today he is considered one

of the greatest writers of the Western world. ☐32 During his

life, however, his work was more controversial. Some of the
main reasons for this was his decision not to write in Latin, but
in "Italian."

30. **F.** NO CHANGE
    G. single yet unified,
    H. single, and unified,
    J. single, unified

31. The writer is considering removing the underlined phrase.
The primary effect of the deletion would be the loss of a
detail that:

    A. provides context that may be helpful in understanding
the passage.
    B. creates confusion regarding the writer's point in this
paragraph.
    C. interrupts the flow of the passage without adding any new
information.
    D. provides a grammatically necessary connection.

32. The writer is considering adding the following phrase to
the end of the preceding sentence (changing the period
after "world" to a comma)

       alongside other recognized greats such as Homer,
       Shakespeare, and Sophocles.

Should the writer make this addition?

    F. Yes, because it provides necessary context for the sen-
tence's previous statement.
    G. Yes, because it explains the important role the creation
of Italian played in Western literature.
    H. No, because it adds details that distract from the primary
point of the sentence.
    J. No, the list of important writers does not include all
important writers in the Western tradition.

33. **A.** NO CHANGE
    B. One
    C. Few
    D. Each

GO ON TO THE NEXT PAGE.

At that time, high literature was written not in the various local languages and in Latin. Dante believed that literature

should be available not only to the educated elite who had education but also to the common people. In order to make

this dream possible, Dante "created" a new language as he called "Italian." This new language wasn't really new at all; it consisted of bits and pieces from the different languages already spoken throughout Italy, and drew most heavily on Dante's native Tuscan dialect. Dante's creation laid the foundation for the unified language to be spoken in Italy today.

The Divine Comedy is, in some ways, the beginning of national Italian literature. By writing it in the language spoken by the Italian people; Dante made *The Divine Comedy*

available to the people. Dante for his opinion that literature to anyone should be accessible drew criticism. However, the

movement that Dante helped begin led to diminished literacy among the Italian people, which, in turn, eventually led to the Renaissance.

The title of *The Divine Comedy* confusing some people. At one time, the label of "comedy" was attached to any work not written in Latin. *The Divine Comedy* wasn't written in

Latin, but it was considered a comedy; however, today it is widely considered a masterpiece of serious literature. Dante's

34. F. NO CHANGE
G. for
H. as
J. but

35. A. NO CHANGE
B. who had been taught
C. with a school background
D. DELETE the underlined portion.

36. F. NO CHANGE
G. and called
H. that he called
J. calling

37. A. NO CHANGE
B. spoken
C. if spoken
D. to speak

38. F. NO CHANGE
G. people, Dante
H. people. Dante
J. people: Dante

39. A. NO CHANGE
B. Dante should be accessible for his opinion that literature to anyone drew criticism.
C. Dante drew criticism for his opinion that literature should be accessible to anyone.
D. Dante drew criticism to anyone for his opinion that literature should be accessible.

40. The writer wants to imply that prior to Dante's development of "Italian," illiteracy was common. Which choice best accomplishes that goal?

F. NO CHANGE
G. an increase in
H. a passion for
J. compulsory

41. A. NO CHANGE
B. confusing
C. confuses some
D. that confuses

42. F. NO CHANGE
G. since
H. because
J. so

GO ON TO THE NEXT PAGE.

brave decision, while, in defiance of the common beliefs of
his time, demonstrated that it was not necessary for a literary
masterpiece to be written in Latin, paved the way for future
writers and readers alike. Nevertheless, *The Divine Comedy*
remains a symbol of both literature and innovation today.

43. A. NO CHANGE
    B. and
    C. which,
    D. so that,

44. F. NO CHANGE
    G. In contrast,
    H. However,
    J. DELETE the underlined portion.

PASSAGE IV

Baking Lessons

[1]

Both of my parents worked full-time when I was a little
girl, so my grandmother would stay at our house during the day.
We would sit in the living room on the couch at my family's
house and watch game shows. Our favorite was

The Price is Right. We would call out their answers along with
the contestants. When our answers were right, we would

scream with excitement, and when the contestants were wrong,
we would moan with disappointment.

[2]

[1] When I got older and started going to school, we
couldn't watch our game shows regular. [2] That was okay
with me, though, because the one thing I liked better than
watching game shows with my grandmother was helping her
bake. [49] [3] Watching her in the kitchen was magical: she
never seemed to need the recipes but everything she made
tasted like heaven.

45. A. NO CHANGE
    B. on the couch in the living room at my family's house
    C. in the living room at my family's house on the couch
    D. at my family's house on the couch in the living room

46. F. NO CHANGE
    G. my
    H. our
    J. her

47. Which of the following alternatives to the underlined por-
    tion would NOT be acceptable?

    A. excitement, when
    B. excitement; when
    C. excitement. When
    D. excitement, or when

48. F. NO CHANGE
    G. as regular.
    H. but regularly.
    J. as regularly.

49. The writer is considering deleting the preceding sentence.
    If the sentence were removed, the essay would primarily
    lose:

    A. a transition from the narrator's discussion of watching
       game shows to the subject focused on in the remainder
       of the essay.
    B. unnecessary information that serves only to detract from
       the primary subject being discussed in the paragraph.
    C. details that are critical to understanding why the narra-
       tor took such pleasure in watching game shows with her
       grandmother.
    D. an insight into why the narrator would choose to spend
       her afternoons watching television with her grandmother.

GO ON TO THE NEXT PAGE.

[3]

[1] As I got older, she let me help with the easy parts, such
     ‾‾50
as sifting the flour and measuring the sugar. [2] At first I would

just sit on the kitchen stool and watch, even though I didn't
                                    ‾‾‾‾‾‾‾‾‾‾‾‾‾‾‾‾‾
                                          51
understand what she was doing. [3] The day she let me separate
‾‾‾‾‾‾‾‾‾‾‾‾‾‾‾‾‾‾‾‾‾‾‾‾‾‾‾‾‾‾
       51

the eggs, I felt like I had reached the pinnacle of success. 52

[4]

Eventually, my parents decided that I could take care of
myself, and my grandmother stopped coming over every day
because I didn't need someone to keep an eye on me anymore.
‾‾‾
                                      53
The love of baking that she had inspired, however, stayed with
me. I started baking by myself, and even if the cookies ended

up burned
‾‾‾‾‾‾‾
   54

sometimes, more often they turned out pretty well. I dropped
                                                   ‾‾‾‾‾‾‾
                                                      55
in new recipes, and whenever I got to a tricky part, I would call
‾‾
55
my grandmother for advice. Sometimes I would call her just to

talk, too. I felt like I could talk to her about anything.

---

50. Which of the following alternatives to the underlined portion would NOT be acceptable?

    F. during
    G. her with
    H. out with
    J. along

51. Which of the following would best express the narrator's respect for her grandmother's abilities in the kitchen, and the enjoyment the narrator feels at watching her grandmother bake?

    A. NO CHANGE
    B. or work on whatever homework I had for the next day.
    C. awed by her skills and eager to taste whatever she was creating.
    D. confused by all the different steps that went into each dish.

52. Which of the following is the most logical ordering of the sentence in Paragraph 3?

    F. NO CHANGE
    G. 3, 1, 2
    H. 2, 3, 1
    J. 2, 1, 3

53. A. NO CHANGE
    B. since I was considered old enough to stay home by myself.
    C. due to my parents' decision that I didn't need a babysitter.
    D. DELETE the underlined portion and end the sentence with a period.

54. Which of the following alternatives to the underlined portion would NOT be acceptable?

    F. spoiled
    G. burnted
    H. ruined
    J. burnt

55. A. NO CHANGE
    B. auditioned for
    C. tried out
    D. fell into

GO ON TO THE NEXT PAGE.

[5]

Last week, I found a recipe book she made for me. It included her recipes for brownies, cookies, and my favorite, lemon meringue pie. As I flipped through the pages, I thought
<u>56</u>

for a moment I could hear her voice, although she's gone, I
<u>57</u>
know that in the way that matters most, she'll never really be

gone at all. She was the one which taught me not just about
<u>58</u>
baking,

but about life. I imagine that I will enjoy baking for the rest of
<u>59</u>
my life.
<u>59</u>

56. Which of the following alternatives to the underlined portion would NOT be acceptable?

   F. leafed through
   G. looked through
   H. tossed out
   J. read over

57. **A.** NO CHANGE
   B. voice; but
   C. voice. Although
   D. voice although

58. **F.** NO CHANGE
   G. whom
   H. who
   J. whose

59. Given that all the choices are true, which one would provide a concluding sentence that best captures the main idea of the essay?

   A. NO CHANGE
   B. To this day, I love watching game shows and baking delicious food for my family.
   C. Baking is a great way to relax, and it's often less expensive than buying cakes and pastries from a bakery.
   D. Every day, when I enter the kitchen, I remember my grandmother and everything she taught me.

Question 60 asks about the passage as a whole.

---

60. After completing the essay, the writer realizes that she forgot to include some information and composes the following sentence:

> My grandmother passed away ten years ago, but I still think of her every day.

This sentence would most logically be placed:

   F. at the end of Paragraph 1.
   G. after Sentence 1 in Paragraph 2.
   H. at the beginning of Paragraph 5.
   J. at the end of Paragraph 5.

GO ON TO THE NEXT PAGE.

PASSAGE V

Global Rat-titudes

The relationship between humans and animals have always
₆₁
been complicated. Some cultures have developed entire

belief systems around favored animals. For example, cows

are treated with reverence in Hindu societies, in part because

some followers of the Hindu religion believe that any cow

could carry the spirits of one of their ancestors. Certain Native

American tribes believe that they're favored animal, the buffalo,
₆₂
had a connection to the divine. The tribes still hunted the

buffalo, but carefully, according to such strict rules that the
₆₃
hunt seemed more like a religious ritual. Even in cultures

with less formalized belief systems, regular interactions
₆₄
between people and animals still lead to common opinions.
₆₄

These stories usually develop around the animals that
₆₅
interact with humans most frequently. Therefore, it should not

be surprising that so many stories surround the most common

of animals: rats. Rats live side-by-side with humans all over

the world, regularly interact with people. Human-rat
₆₆

coexistence may be common all around the world, with
₆₇
different cultures respond to that closeness in different ways.

In the United States and Europe, one typical attitude is that

the rat is a pest. This could be due to the common belief that
₆₈

61. A. NO CHANGE
   B. should of
   C. had
   D. has

62. F. NO CHANGE
   G. their
   H. theirs
   J. there

63. A. NO CHANGE
   B. so that
   C. as to mean
   D. because

64. Given that all of the choices are true, which of the following concludes this paragraph with the clearest allusion to the story of "The Pied Piper of Hamlin," which is discussed later in the essay?

   F. NO CHANGE
   G. it is well-known that other cultures hold religious beliefs about some animals.
   H. people still tend to have beliefs, either individual or cultural, relating to animals.
   J. folklore and stories relating to humans' relationship with animals abound.

65. Which of the following alternatives to the underlined portion would NOT be acceptable?

   A. tales
   B. legends
   C. narrators
   D. fables

66. F. NO CHANGE
   G. world and regularly
   H. world, regular
   J. world, regularly,

67. A. NO CHANGE
   B. world,
   C. world, but with
   D. world, but

68. F. NO CHANGE
   G. pest, which is a common opinion.
   H. pest, a belief many people share.
   J. pest, moreover.

GO ON TO THE NEXT PAGE.

rats spread disease. They don't, at least not directly; but many
people don't know that. "The Pied Piper of Hamlin," a well-
known children's story, is one example of how rats have been
portrayed in a different way in Western literature: in that story,
rats cause such a problem that a town has to hire a piper to call
them all away.

What's really wild is that in many Latin American countries,
and some European countries as well, the rat is portrayed in
a very different light. The tooth fairy legend is common all
over the world, but in Latin America, the "fairy" is a rat! Rats
do have very strong teeth, which could explain the association.
Clearly, this shows another attitude toward rats that is much
more positive.

[1] Yet another attitude toward the rat can be seen in the

Chinese *Zodiac*. [2] The Rat is one of the animals, of the
zodiac along with the Sheep, the Rooster, the Boar, and eight
others. [3] Like the other zodiac animals, the Rat is neither
entirely good nor entirely bad. [4] It's described as clever and
friendly, but also tricky and not entirely honest. [5] That may
be the most accurate description of the rat so far. [6] Whether
you like rats or not, it's hard to deny their reputation for
cleverness. [7] As many people are discovering these days, rats
can even make excellent pets, so long as you remember to latch
the cage carefully! [75]

69. **A.** NO CHANGE
    B. don't, at least not directly,
    C. don't: at least not directly,
    D. don't, at least not directly

70. Given that all the choices are true, which one states a
    detail that most clearly relates to the information conveyed
    at the end of this sentence?
    F. NO CHANGE
    G. mystical
    H. negative
    J. juvenile

71. **A.** NO CHANGE
    B. In
    C. Dig this: in the minds of those born and raised in
    D. You'll be shocked to discover that in

72. Given that all the choices are true, which one provides a
    physical detail about rats that relates most clearly to the
    preceding sentence?
    F. NO CHANGE
    G. particularly curious natures,
    H. a reputation for excessive chewing,
    J. long and somewhat unusual tails,

73. **A.** NO CHANGE
    B. China's
    C. Chinese mysticism's
    D. Their

74. **F.** NO CHANGE
    G. is one of the animals, of the zodiac,
    H. is one of the animals of the zodiac,
    J. is one, of the animals of the zodiac

75. The writer wants to create a concluding paragraph that
    focuses on one characteristic of rats outside of any specific
    cultural frame of reference by dividing the preceding para-
    graph in two. The best place to begin the new paragraph
    would be at the beginning of Sentence:
    A. 4.
    B. 5.
    C. 6.
    D. 7.

END OF TEST 2
STOP! DO NOT TURN THE PAGE UNTIL TOLD TO DO SO.

Chapter 16
English Practice
Test 2: Answers and
Explanations

ENGLISH PRACTICE TEST 2 ANSWERS

1.	B	39.	C
2.	F	40.	G
3.	C	41.	C
4.	F	42.	J
5.	C	43.	C
6.	J	44.	J
7.	A	45.	B
8.	G	46.	H
9.	B	47.	A
10.	H	48.	J
11.	C	49.	A
12.	G	50.	J
13.	D	51.	C
14.	J	52.	J
15.	B	53.	D
16.	H	54.	G
17.	B	55.	C
18.	G	56.	H
19.	D	57.	C
20.	H	58.	H
21.	D	59.	D
22.	H	60.	H
23.	A	61.	D
24.	J	62.	G
25.	A	63.	A
26.	F	64.	J
27.	D	65.	C
28.	J	66.	G
29.	A	67.	D
30.	J	68.	F
31.	A	69.	B
32.	H	70.	H
33.	B	71.	B
34.	J	72.	F
35.	D	73.	A
36.	H	74.	H
37.	B	75.	C
38.	G		

SCORE YOUR PRACTICE TEST

Step A

Count the number of correct answers: _____. This is your *raw score*.

Step B

Use the score conversion table below to look up your raw score. The number to the left is your *scale score*: _____.

English Scale Conversion Table

Scale Score	Raw Score	Scale Score	Raw Score	Scale Score	Raw Score
36	75	27	62	18	41–42
35	73–74	26	60–61	17	39–40
34	71–72	25	58–59	16	36–38
33	70	24	56–57	15	33–35
32	69	23	54–55	14	30–32
31	67–68	22	52–53	13	28–29
30	66	21	49–51	12	26–27
29	65	20	46–48	11	24–25
28	63–64	19	43–45	10	22–23

ENGLISH PRACTICE TEST 2 EXPLANATIONS

Passage I

1. **B**   The question asks you to find the answer choice that is NOT acceptable as a replacement for the underlined portion—remember, that means the passage is correct as written. Look at the answer choices—some change words, some change punctuation. In a case like this, you'll need to check each answer choice. Choices (A), (C), and (D) can all be inserted in place of the underlined portion without creating an error, but (B) makes the sentence *When I woke up this morning, I made myself a bowl of cereal, sat listening to the traffic*, which isn't an appropriate way to join two complete ideas and therefore can NOT be used.

2. **F**   When you see answer choices "stacked" like this, using all the same words with Stop and Go punctuation changing in the same spot, check for Complete/Incomplete on either side of that spot. In this case, *It's true that there's always some kind of noise in my neighborhood* is complete, and *taxi drivers honking their horns, kids playing their radios so loud that the bass makes my teeth vibrate, or people yelling in the street* is incomplete. Since Stop punctuation can only separate two complete ideas, eliminate (H). You definitely need some kind of pause after *neighborhood*, so (J) can be eliminated. Now you must choose between a comma and a dash. Using a comma would make it seem like the sentence is giving a list of things that are true, when the intention is to list the kinds of noises in the neighborhood. Remember a single dash is the same thing as a colon—it must follow a complete idea and must itself be followed by a list, definition, or explanation of the first complete idea. That's what the sentence has as written, so choose (F).

3. **C**   The preceding sentence is *I know that some people wouldn't like it, but to me, these are the sounds of life.* This is almost the exact opposite of what (A) says—the narrator is putting a positive spin on what many would find an annoyance. There is no trip to the park mentioned as in (B), and (D) is incorrect because this sentence is very much relevant to the essay—choose (C).

4. **F**   None of the answer choices contains a grammatical error, and they all say roughly the same thing, so pick the one that says it with the fewest words—*It's*.

5. **C**   Careful—all of these answer choices may seem fit to use, but on the ACT, there is always a reason to choose the best answer choice. In this case the entire sentence reads *When I ride the bus, you get to see so much more of the city.* The underlined portion you select must have a pronoun that is consistent with the non-underlined *you get*, which is (C), *you ride*.

6. **J**   Here you need to choose between *sociable* and *sociably*, but there's punctuation changing as well—start easy! You need the adverb *sociably* because it's describing how the people are chatting—eliminate (F) and (H). Choice (G) is incorrect because there's no need for a pause after *sociably*, so no comma is needed.

7. **A**   The answer choices have "stacked" words with Stop and Go punctuation changing in one spot, so check for Complete/Incomplete on either side of that spot. *Just like the traffic's sounds, though, the noise on the bus represents people* is complete (but awkward), and *working, relaxing, and living* is incomplete, so you need Go punctuation—eliminate (B) and (C). Choice (D) is incorrect because you don't need a comma after *people*—you only need commas to separate the items in the list of things the people are doing.

8. **G**   Here you have a 3/1 split with three answer choices using pronouns and one that uses the noun *kids*, so check that one first. *Kids* makes sense in the context of the sentence and is consistent with the non-underlined *their parents*.

9. **B**   In the answer choices, you see Stop and Go punctuation changing after the word *nearby*, so check for Complete/Incomplete on either side of the punctuation. *The city added the bench so kids could play while their parents sit nearby* is complete, and, regardless of whether it begins with *obviously*, or not, *I like to sit there because there's a great big oak tree for shade* is also complete. Two complete ideas must be connected with Stop punctuation—eliminate (A) and (C). While adding the word *because* in (D) makes the second idea incomplete and might make you think it's okay to use a comma, it's still incorrect: To use the word *because*, you need a causal relationship between the ideas, and there is none in this case.

10. **H**   This question is testing proper comma placement. You don't need a comma after either *watching* or *listening*, since the idea being expressed is *watching and listening to the people around me*—eliminate (F), (G), and (J).

11. **C**   In the answer choices, you see Stop and Go punctuation changing after the word *do*, so check for Complete/Incomplete on either side of the punctuation. *People-watching is one of my favorite things to do* is complete, and *I like listening even better* is complete as well. Two complete ideas must be connected with Stop punctuation—eliminate (A). You can also eliminate (B) and (D), because even though they respectively add *nevertheless* and *however* after the punctuation change, both of those are transition words that only indicate direction—they don't make a complete idea incomplete. Choice (C), which uses a comma + FANBOYS (but), is the only choice that gives you the Stop punctuation you're looking for.

12. **G**   The following sentence says *That way, I can pay more attention to the sounds and not get distracted by what I see,* so the most logical introduction would be one that has the narrator closing her eyes—(G).

13. **D**   You need to emphasize the narrator's curiosity and interest in the old men's conversation, so the correct answer choice needs to incorporate the narrator's point of view. Choices (A), (B), and (C) are all objective descriptions of the conversation itself or the old men. Choice (D) characterizes the stories as entertaining, meaning *entertaining* to the narrator, and so is the best answer.

14. **J**   Here apostrophes are being used to show possession. You know there are two old men having the conversation, so the laugh that comes in response to the story one of them is telling must come from his *friend*, not his *friends*. To show possession for a singular noun, all you have to do is add *'s*—(J).

15. **B** This essay is definitely pro-city living, and really only explores one aspect of what the narrator likes about the city, so you can eliminate (C) and (D). Choice (A) is incorrect, because although public transportation is mentioned, it isn't the convenience the narrator enjoys—it's the sounds and sights of the city.

Passage II

16. **H** When you see DELETE as an answer choice, try that first. In this case, taking out *that* causes a syntax error—you wouldn't say *…three times in seventy-year history*. You need to find the correct pronoun, so the first step is to identify the noun that the pronoun replaces—it's *bridge*. Since *bridge* is a singular noun, eliminate (G); you can't replace a singular noun with a plural pronoun. The pronoun *that* in the sentence as written is incorrect; you can't use it because there is no prior reference to the seventy-year history.

17. **B** The sentence is saying the amount of concrete was *enough to construct a sidewalk five feet wide all the way from San Francisco to New York City*. There isn't a reason to use commas here, so eliminate (A) and (D). Choice (C) has a dash (which is the same as a colon) after *sidewalk*, which creates an awkward and unclear construction afterwards.

18. **G** The sentence immediately following details the various reasons San Francisco Bay is a bad spot for bridge-building, so a logical introduction will introduce this theme. Neither (F), (H), nor (J) do this as well as (G).

19. **D** Here you see Stop and Go Punctuation changing after the word *bond* in each answer choice, so check for Complete/Incomplete on either side of the punctuation. *After two years of discussion, the voters approved a bond* is complete, and *that would raise $35 million, all dedicated to building the bridge* is incomplete, so eliminate (C). Choice (A) has a colon after a complete idea, but the incomplete idea after it is awkward and unclear. Choice (B) is incorrect because the phrase *that would raise $35 million* is necessary, and thus there is no need for a comma here, much less two.

20. **H** You have the option to DELETE the underlined portion, so try that first. That leaves *Even then, there were many skeptics believed that it couldn't be done*, which is a bad sentence—eliminate (J). Now you have to choose the correct pronoun, so identify the noun that's being replaced—it's *skeptics*. You can't use *that* to replace skeptics: It's singular and *that* can't be used to refer to people, so eliminate (G). If you have trouble deciding between *who* and *whom*, try substituting a different pronoun: There are multiple skeptics, so you can use "they" and "them." You would use the subject-case "they believed it couldn't be done," not the object-case "them believed it couldn't be done." That means you need to use the subject-case *who*—(H).

21. **D** When DELETE is an option, you should always check that first—you know ACT likes things concise. Taking out the underlined portion leaves *Construction began in 1933 and lasted a little more than four years*. That's a perfectly good sentence, and you're not adding any new information with (A), (B), or (C)—(D) is the best (most concise) answer.

22. **H**   The answer choices have "stacked" words with Stop and Go punctuation changing after *1937*, so check for Complete/Incomplete on either side of that spot. *On May 28, 1937* is an incomplete idea, so you know you can't use Stop punctuation—that's only for connecting two complete ideas—eliminate (F) and (G). Choices (H) and (J) both give you the comma you need after *1937*, but (J) goes a little too far by adding another that you don't need after *grandly*.

23. **A**   DELETE the underlined portion first, since that's an option. That leaves *More than 200,000 people walked across the bridge that day to celebrate*, which is a complete idea, but is not as clear as it could be (celebrate what?) The better option is (A)—it's a little less concise, but much more clear. Choices (B) and (C) are much too wordy; neither says anything that (A) doesn't.

24. **J**   The answer choices are all transition words, which is usually a sign that the question is testing direction. The two sentences on either side are *To top it off, it was beautiful* and *the Golden Gate Bridge is considered an artistic masterpiece*—two similar ideas (although note the shift in tense between the two from past to present.) You can eliminate the two opposite-direction transitions, (F) and (H), and eliminate (G) because it's still past-tense; you want a transition that will make the change to present tense, as *Even today* does.

25. **A**   The answer choices all have Stop and Go punctuation (and a dash) changing after the word *air*, so check for Complete/Incomplete before and after the punctuation. Before the punctuation is *At its highest point, the bridge rises 746 feet into the air*, which is complete, and afterward is *191 feet taller than the Washington Monument*, an incomplete idea. Eliminate (B)—you can't use Stop punctuation here. We can do without the extra *rising*, so eliminate (D). We do, however, need some kind of pause after *air*, so eliminate (C).

26. **F**   The answer choices are all different word combinations—you just have to pick the correct one. The idiomatic expression for "environment" is *natural surroundings*—(F). If you're not sure here, you can try substituting each answer choice into the sentence; you should at least be able to eliminate one or two answer choices. Always keep in mind that NO CHANGE is going to be correct about 25 percent of the time it appears, so don't be afraid to pick it—especially if you can't identify an error in the sentence as it's written.

27. **D**   The whole sentence says *The color, called "International Orange," was chosen partly because it matched the natural surroundings and partly because it would allow the bridge to remain visible on foggy days*. Saying *on foggy days* provides a detail about when the bridge might be hard to see, so if you take out that portion, you would lose that detail. That most closely matches (D).

28. **J**   You need to emphasize the *wide variety of the bridge's uses* here, so the correct answer choice must do that. Choice (F) only talks about commuter traffic, (G) describes the bridge itself, not how it is used, and (H) talks about how some people cross the bridge—none of which describe *a wide variety of uses*. Choice (J) talks about the bridge's multiple uses for commuters and travelers and as a tourist destination in its own right, so it is the best answer choice.

29. **A**   The added sentence talks about the original idea for building the bridge, so it belongs somewhere very early in the discussion of its construction—eliminate (C) and (D). Between (A) and (B), the more logical choice for the placement of the original idea for the bridge would be (A), just before the decision to actually build it.

Passage III

30. **J**   Here you have nicely "stacked" answer choices with Stop (comma + FANBOYS) and Go punctuation changing after *single*—check for Complete/Incomplete on either side. *The Italian language wasn't always the single* is incomplete, as is *unified, language that it is today.* You'll need Go punctuation to connect these two—eliminate (H). Remember your comma rules; there's no reason to use a comma after *unified*—eliminate (F) and (G), leaving (J) as the best answer choice.

31. **A**   The phrase *during the thirteenth century* introduces the time period the passage will be talking about, so that's what you lose if you take it out—there's no confusion created as in (B), no interruption as in (C), and it's not grammatically necessary as (D) claims; (A) is the best answer.

32. **H**   Remember that less is more on the ACT; any time you have the option to add anything, make sure you have a compelling reason to do so. In this case, the sentence (not to mention the passage as a whole) is talking about Dante Alighieri, so adding a list of other writers doesn't add anything necessary to the essay. If you're still unsure, you can check the reasons given in the answer choices and eliminate those that don't agree with the passage: You can eliminate (F) as previously stated, there's no discussion of the creation of Italian as (G) states, and the reason you aren't adding the list isn't because it's not exhaustive, as (J) claims—it's because it's unnecessary.

33. **B**   The underlined portion acts as the subject of the singular verb *was* in the non-underlined portion. Choices (A) and (C) are plural. Choice (D) doesn't fit the context of the sentence.

34. **J**   The meaning of the sentence is not to say that literature was not written in the local languages and also not in Latin; the idea is that high literature was written in Latin instead of the local languages. To express that, you need to say *literature was written not in the various local languages but in Latin*—(J).

35. **D**   DELETE is an answer choice, so try that first. Taking out the underlined portion leaves *Dante believed that literature should be available not only to the educated elite but also to the common people.* That is a complete sentence, and the meaning hasn't changed, so (D) is the best answer.

36. **H**   Three of the answer choices use *called* and one uses *calling*, so you should check that one first, but remember that ACT doesn't really like the "-ing" form of verbs, and you should only pick it when all the other answer choices have an actual error. In this case, however, it doesn't make sense in the sentence—Dante was not literally calling out the word "Italian"—you can eliminate (J), and also (F) and (G), which make the sentence read the same way.

37. **B** Three of the answer choices use *spoken* and one uses *speak*, so you should check that one first. However, *to speak* doesn't make sense in the context of the sentence, so eliminate (D). There's no need to include *to be* or *if* as in (A) and (C); (B) makes the most sense—and it's the most concise—so it's the best answer choice.

38. **G** The answer choices all have Stop and Go punctuation (plus a colon) changing after the word *people*, so check for Complete/Incomplete on either side to see which you need. In this case, *By writing it in the language spoken by the Italian people* is incomplete, and since Stop punctuation can only connect two complete ideas, you can now eliminate (F) and (H). You can also eliminate (J), since a colon can only follow a complete idea. That leaves (G) as the only possible choice.

39. **C** All of the answer choices use the exact same words, just in different orders—you'll need to select the one that is most clear. Dante thought literature should be available to everyone, and was criticized for that opinion. The answer choice that expresses that idea in the most clear fashion is (C).

40. **G** Remember when ACT gives you a task to accomplish with an answer choice, you must read very literally—an answer choice that does the thing you want is a better choice than one that "could" do the thing you want. In this case, we need an answer choice that will imply that illiteracy changed from more common to less common. Be careful! If you just look at the words in the answer choices, *diminished* might seem the perfect candidate, but the passage is talking about *literacy*, not illiteracy. Therefore, you want the answer choice that says that literacy became more common, which would *imply* that illiteracy became less common—(G). Both (H) and (J) might conceivably accompany an increase in literacy, neither state that as clearly as (G) does.

41. **C** A good place to start here is to decide which verb form you need—always keeping in mind ACT's opinion of the "-ing" form. *Confuses* agrees with the subject, *title*, so eliminate (A) and (B). The use of *that* in (D) makes the sentence an incomplete idea, so the best answer is (C).

42. **J** There are transition words changing in the answer choices, but not punctuation, which will typically mean ACT is testing direction. Make sure you read enough to get the proper context! The two ideas we have to connect are *The Divine Comedy wasn't written in Latin* and *it was considered a comedy*. The sentence prior to this says *the label of "comedy" was attached to any work not written in Latin*, so you're going to need a same-direction transition—eliminate (F). Choices (G), (H), and (J) are all same-direction transitions, but (G) and (H) have the relationship wrong—*The Divine Comedy* wasn't written in Latin as a result of being considered a comedy; it was the other way around. Note that in this case, (G) and (H) are "same" answer choices: *since* and *because* mean the exact same thing in this context, which means one cannot be more correct than the other; therefore, you cannot select either one.

43. **C**   The answer choices all feature different transition words, but there's some punctuation changing as well. In fact, three of the answer choices use a comma and one doesn't—start there. In this instance, *and* causes an error, so eliminate (B). All the other answer choices end in a comma, which means the phrase *in defiance of the common beliefs of his time* is unnecessary since it's set off by a pair of commas—it may help to cross it out or simply ignore it to help answer the question. Without the unnecessary phrase (and its commas), the sentence now reads *Dante's brave decision, while demonstrated that it was not necessary for a literary masterpiece to be written in Latin, paved the way for future writers and readers alike.* That's not correct, so eliminate (A), and substituting *so that* for *while* doesn't help either—eliminate (D). That leaves (C), *which,* as the correct answer.

44. **J**   You have the option to DELETE the underlined portion, so try that first. You're left with a complete sentence, so it's at least possible to take out that word without creating an error. However, notice that the other choices are all transition words, so it may be a good idea to assess whether a transition is needed here. The prior sentence (now) reads *Dante's brave decision, which, in defiance of the common beliefs of his time, demonstrated that it was not necessary for a literary masterpiece to be written in Latin, paved the way for future writers and readers alike,* and then you have *The Divine Comedy remains a symbol of both literature and innovation today.* No transition is really needed here, and even if one were, it wouldn't be an opposite-direction one, as are (F), (G), and (H).

Passage IV

45. **B**   The answer choices are all different arrangements of the same three modifying phrases. On the ACT, (and in good writing in general), a modifying phrase must be placed next to the thing it's modifying. In this case, the words right before the underlined portion are *We would sit,* and the phrase that most directly modifies that is *on the couch,* so the correct answer choice must start with that phrase. Only (B) matches that description.

46. **H**   You have possessive pronouns changing in the answer choices, so to choose the correct one, you'll need to find the context in the non-underlined part of the passage. The answers being called out belong to the narrator and her grandmother, and since the passage is written in the first person, you need to use *our,* (H). If you're still unsure, notice that using *our* is consistent with the following sentence: *When our answers were right....*

47. **A**   You need to find the answer choice that is NOT a suitable replacement for the correctly-written underlined portion in the passage. The answer choices all have Stop and Go punctuation changing after the word *excitement,* so you should check for Complete/Incomplete on either side. Notice the sentence as written uses Stop punctuation (comma + FANBOYS), so you know the two ideas are complete. Choices (B) and (C) both use different forms of Stop punctuation, and so can be used as replacements, and (D), even though it uses Go punctuation, inserts the word *or* into the second idea, making it incomplete, and so is also correct. What can NOT be used as a replacement is (A), which uses a comma to separate two complete ideas.

48. **J** The first decision to make here is whether you need *regular* or *regularly*. The verb *watch* is being modified, so you need the adverb *regularly*—eliminate (F) and (G). Choice (H) is incorrect because it uses the correct adverb but the wrong conjunction—the narrator and her grandmother don't watch the shows *as regularly* as they did prior to school starting.

49. **A** The sentence *That was okay with me, though, because the one thing I liked better than watching game shows with my grandmother was helping her bake* introduces the main idea of the essay, and so serves as a transition between the discussion of the two activities the narrator enjoys with her grandmother. That's not unnecessary or detracting information as in (B), and (C) and (D) can be eliminated because they only talk about watching television.

50. **J** You need to find the answer choice that is NOT a suitable replacement for the correctly-written underlined portion in the passage. Choices (F), (G), and (H) all keep the original meaning of the sentence, but *help along* has a different meaning, and *help along the easy parts* doesn't really make sense; therefore, (J) is NOT a suitable replacement.

51. **C** (C) describes the narrator as *awed* and *eager to taste*, which accomplishes both tasks: expressing both respect and enjoyment. Choices (A) and (D) express lack of understanding and confusion, and (B) talks about homework.

52. **J** The three sentences describe a progression in the amount of help the narrator was allowed to give her grandmother in the kitchen: *At first* she only sat and watched (sentence 2). As [she] *got older*, she helped with the easier tasks (sentence 1). Finally, she reaches *the pinnacle of success* when she gets to separate the eggs (sentence 3).

53. **D** Whenever DELETE is an option, you should try that first. In this case, taking out *because I didn't need someone to keep an eye on me anymore* does not create an error or change the meaning; in fact, it gets rid of redundancy because the narrator has already said *my parents decided that I could take care of myself*. Choices (B) and (C) are both redundant and wordy as well—pick (D).

54. **G** You need to find the answer choice that is NOT a suitable replacement for the correctly-written underlined portion in the passage. Choices (F), (H), and (J) can all be used in place of *burned* in this context, but (G), *burnted*, far from being a replacement, can NOT be used—it's not even a word.

55. **C** The answer choices all have different pairs of words; notice the second word in each is a preposition. When you see prepositions changing, that's a good sign that ACT may be testing idioms. In this case, in order to express the idea of "attempted something for the first time," you need to use *tried out*, (C).

56. **H** You need to find the answer choice that is NOT a suitable replacement for the correctly-written underlined portion in the passage. Notice the answer choices all have different pairs of words, and the second word in each is a preposition: That's a good sign that ACT is testing idioms. In the context of the sentence, *flipped through* means, "quickly read the contents of a book." Choices (F), (G), and (J) all convey that same meaning, but *tossed out* in (H) would imply she threw the book away, and so can NOT be used as a replacement.

57. **C** The answer choices all have Stop and Go punctuation changing after the same word: *voice*. Check for Complete/Incomplete on both sides. *As I flipped through the pages, I thought for a moment I could hear her voice* is complete, as is *although she's gone, I know that in the way that matters most, she'll never really be gone at all*. You need to use Stop punctuation to separate two complete ideas—eliminate (A) and (D). Choice (B) is incorrect because the transition word *but* makes the second idea incomplete, so you can't use it with a semicolon.

58. **H** When you see pronouns changing in the answer choice, find the noun that's being replaced: *She* (referring to the narrator's grandmother). Eliminate (F) because you can't use *which* to refer a person. Choice (J) is the possessive pronoun *whose*, so look at the word that follows it; only nouns can be possessed. You can't possess *taught*, so eliminate (J). In this case, the pronoun is the subject of the verb *taught*, so you need *who*—(H).

59. **D** The main focus of the passage isn't baking; it's the relationship between the narrator and her grandmother—eliminate (A). Choices (B) and (C) have the same problem. Choice (D) is the only answer choice that mentions the narrator's grandmother.

60. **H** This sentence doesn't fit in the narrative of either paragraph 1 or 2, so eliminate (F) and (G). It should also come before the narrator says *Although she's gone* so that it's clear to the reader that her grandmother has passed away—(H) is the better answer choice for that reason.

Passage V

61. **D** You have helping verbs changing in the answer choices, and recall the helping verbs need to agree with the subject, just like regular verbs. In this case, the subject of the sentence is *relationship*, which is singular, so eliminate (A), which is plural. Choice (B) is an incorrect construction: It's "should have," not "should of." Choice (C) makes the sentence seem to imply that the relationship was only complicated in the past, and isn't anymore, but there's no support for the latter in the passage. Choice (D) is the best answer choice: The relationship *has always been complicated*.

62. **G** The answer choices are all similar-sounding, so your ear isn't going to help much on this question. Expand out (F)—it means "they are," which doesn't make sense here. You need a word that shows the buffalo was the favored animal of the tribes, and in this context, that's the possessive pronoun *their*, (G).

63. **A** The passage says the hunts were carried out *according to such strict rules… the hunt seemed more like a religious ritual*. When you use the word *such* in this context, you have to pair it with *that*, (A). If you chose (D), you may have misunderstood the relationship; the rules weren't strict as a result of the hunts seeming like a religious ritual—it's the other way around.

64. **J** You need to choose an answer choice that makes a *clear allusion* to a story later in the essay. The only answer choice that even mentions a story is (J): *folklore and stories relating to humans' relationship with animals*.

65. **C**   You need to find the answer choice that is NOT a suitable replacement for the correctly-written underlined portion in the passage. Choices (A), (B), and (D) all mean the same thing as the underlined word, *stories*. *Narrator* does NOT mean the same thing—it refers to someone who tells stories—so (C) is the correct choice.

66. **G**   You have three answer choices with *regularly* and one with *regular*, so check that one first. You need an adverb to modify the verb *interact*, so eliminate (H). In both (F) and (J), the verb *interact* has no subject, so eliminate them—(G), which joins the two verbs *live* and *interact* with *and*, giving them both a subject, is correct.

67. **D**   The answer choices all have Stop (comma + FANBOYS) and Go punctuation changing after the same word: *world*, so check for Complete/Incomplete on either side. *Human-rat coexistence may be common all around the world* is complete, and so is the part after the underlined portion: *different cultures respond to that closeness in different ways*. Choice (A) has Go punctuation and adds *with*, which makes the second idea incomplete, but also doesn't make sense. Choice (B) joins two complete ideas with a comma—eliminate it. Choice (C) has the FANBOYS conjunction you're looking for, but like (A), adds *with*, which makes no sense. Choice (D) is the best answer choice—it uses Stop punctuation to separate the two complete ideas.

68. **F**   All four answer choices say the same thing in slightly different ways, and none contains a grammatical error. Therefore, pick the one that is the most concise: (F), NO CHANGE.

69. **B**   The answer choices mostly have commas changing around, but one uses a colon, so start there. The colon follows a complete idea, *They don't*, which is proper, but what follows the colon is not a list, definition, or expansion of that idea (not to mention it's an extremely awkward construction), so eliminate (B). To choose the correct comma placement, remember your comma rules: *at least not directly* is unnecessary information, so you need to set it off with commas—the only answer choice that does that is (B).

70. **H**   In the end of the sentence, you have the statement *rats cause such a problem that a town has to hire a piper to call them all away* and you need to find the word to describe how rats have been portrayed that agrees with that most closely. Choice (H), *negative*, agrees with the notion of the rats being a *problem* better than *different, mystical*, or *juvenile*.

71. **B**   Aside from being the most concise, (B) avoids the problems found in the other choices. Remember, there's no slang on the ACT! Choices (A) and (C) are too informal, besides being far too wordy. Choice (D) might be tempting, but it's not concise as well as being a bit too strong; remember the author has already told you different cultures respond to that [human-rat] closeness in different ways, so an example of one of those ways shouldn't really shock you.

72. **F**   The correct answer choice has to provide a physical detail about rats, so (G) and (H) can be eliminated—neither of those is a physical detail. Choice (J) certainly is a physical characteristic, but probably has less to do with the rat's association with teeth than a description of the rat's *very strong* teeth.

73. **A**   The underlined portion introduces a new paragraph and the sentence *attitude toward the rat can be seen in the Chinese zodiac*. Choices (B) and (C) cause redundancy in the sentence: The phrase *Chinese zodiac* already tells you you're talking about mysticism in China. Choice (D) is temptingly concise, but the pronoun *their* has no noun to refer to, so you can't use it. Choice (A) is the best answer since it both makes sense in the sentence and acts as an effective transition to the new paragraph after the discussion of a different example of people's attitude toward rats in the previous paragraph.

74. **H**   Remember your comma rules here: This isn't a list, introductory idea, or unnecessary information, so there's really no reason to use a comma between any of the underlined words—eliminate (F), (G), and (J); the only choice you have is (H).

75. **C**   If you want to divide the last paragraph into two based on a non-cultural frame of reference, you'll need to begin after the rat's description based on the Chinese zodiac—eliminate (A) and (B). The most logical place to begin the new paragraph, then, is (C), which begins talking about the rat's *cleverness*.

Chapter 17
English
Practice Test 3

ACT ENGLISH TEST

45 Minutes—75 Questions

DIRECTIONS: In the five passages that follow, certain words and phrases are underlined and numbered. In the right-hand column, you will find alternatives for each underlined part. In most cases, you are to choose the one that best expresses the idea, makes the statement appropriate for standard written English, or is worded most consistently with the style and tone of the passage as a whole. If you think the original version is best, choose "NO CHANGE." In some cases, you will find in the right-hand column a question about the underlined part. You are to choose the best answer to the question.

You will also find questions about a section of the passage or the passage as a whole. These questions do not refer to an underlined portion of the passage but rather are identified by a number or numbers in a box.

For each question, choose the alternative you consider best and blacken the corresponding oval on your answer document. Read each passage through once before you begin to answer the questions that accompany it. For many of the questions, you must read several sentences beyond the question to determine the answer. Be sure that you have read far enough ahead each time you choose an alternative.

PASSAGE I

Cheeseburgers and Cats That Can Make You "lol"

Everyone knows that cats love to chase mice, <u>but who knew</u> <u>they also love to eat cheeseburgers?</u> [A] It's a very special kind of cat that does: a *lolcat*. The concept is simple: take a funny

photograph of a cat and <u>written</u> a humorous caption over it. [B] The name is a compound word combining *cat* and *lol*, the slangy Internet abbreviation for "laughing out loud." [C] In some ways, the phenomenon of the lolcat is nothing new. [D] In the 1870s, Brighton-based <u>photographer, Henry Pointer</u> took a series of images of his pet cats. The images were intended to form the backgrounds for *cartes de visite*,

<u>having at times been called</u> "visiting cards." To enhance a photo's appeal, Henry Pointer would often add a humorous caption.

<u>Pointer's first photographs, those without captions, did</u> <u>not sell well initially, though they have recently been better</u> <u>appreciated.</u> Pointer made a good deal of money from his photos because photography equipment was still

1. If the writer were to delete the underlined portion (changing the comma after *mice* to a period), the sentence would primarily lose:
   A. a description of one of the things that make lolcats unique.
   B. a scientific fact describing a well-known species.
   C. a concise statement of the essay's main idea.
   D. nothing at all, because it strays from the topic unnecessarily.

2. F. NO CHANGE
   G. is writing
   H. wrote
   J. write

3. A. NO CHANGE
   B. photographer Henry Pointer
   C. photographer, Henry Pointer,
   D. photographer; Henry Pointer

4. F. NO CHANGE
   G. a French term meaning
   H. being things called
   J. and naming them

5. Given that all the choices are true, which one best conveys the idea that captions contributed to the humor of Pointer's photographs?
   A. NO CHANGE
   B. Pointer would occasionally reuse captions when the picture could communicate most of what he wanted it to.
   C. In fact, he soon understood that the humorous caption could make even the most mundane cat pictures charming or funny.
   D. Pointer took so many pictures and wrote so many captions that neither required much effort of him.

GO ON TO THE NEXT PAGE.

relatively rare and expensive for his day. He likely never knew,
_____
                                   6
however, that his pictures would be the basis for a hugely

popular movement over a century later. [7]

Today, though, anyone with a camera and a computer can
_____
       8
create a lolcat image. The only requirement is a basic fluency

in the language of *lolspeak*, a grammatically-incorrect, often

misspelled form of English. The most famous

phrase known widely in all of lolspeak is "I can has
_____
         9
cheezburger?", or "Can I have a cheeseburger?"

Additional phrases and the language are fairly easy to
                                        ___
                                        10
learn, and lolcats have become some of the trendiest images on

the Internet.

    As a result of their popularity, lolcats have attracted all
    _____
                  11
kinds of new press in recent years. *Time* magazine covered

lolcats in a July 2007 issue. Even the American Dialect Society

has named "lolcat" one of the mainly creative coinages of the
                               _____
                                 12
decade. There have been financial gains as well: in 2007, the

"I Can Has Cheezburger?" website was purchased by a group

of investors for $2 million and has spawned many spinoffs.

It would seem, then, that the lolcat is here to stay, and that

6. **F.** NO CHANGE
   G. with
   H. in
   J. of

7. If the writer were to divide this paragraph into two, the most logical place to begin the new paragraph would be at Point:

   A. A.
   B. B.
   C. C.
   D. D.

8. Which of the following alternatives to the underlined portion would NOT be acceptable?

   F. in fact,
   G. however,
   H. by contrast,
   J. on the other hand,

9. **A.** NO CHANGE
   B. phrase
   C. phrase that many people know
   D. phrase that is pretty popular

10. **F.** NO CHANGE
    G. is being
    H. is
    J. were

11. **A.** NO CHANGE
    B. Now earning lots of money,
    C. With their cameras in hand,
    D. Promoting them on the Internet,

12. **F.** NO CHANGE
    G. more
    H. most
    J. a lot

GO ON TO THE NEXT PAGE.

cheeseburger-flavored cat food can't be far off. [13]

13. If the writer were to delete the phrase "cheeseburger-flavored" in the preceding sentence and replace it with "another line of," the paragraph would primarily lose:

  A. a particular detail that ends the essay on a humorous note.
  B. a more detailed discussion of the different types of cats discussed in the essay.
  C. a resolution to a difficult problem posed earlier in the essay.
  D. an open question that is left to the reader to decide.

Question 14 asks about the preceding passage as a whole.

---

14. Suppose the writer's goal had been to write a brief essay describing a new generation's interest in animal photography. Would this essay accomplish that goal?

  F. Yes, because it shows how important lolcats have been to a broader interest in photography.
  G. Yes, because it narrates the simultaneous rise of digital photography and Internet usage.
  H. No, because it details the different types of animal photography popular on the Internet.
  J. No, because it focuses on lolcats and their history, not on photography more generally.

PASSAGE II

My Summer as a Teacher . . . or as a Student?

I was there only for a summer, but the memories I have of teaching English in Mexico have stayed with me. The experience didn't start well. I was assigned to a small village—located a few hours west of Monterrey; in the central north part of the country, in the state of Durango. The most direct route was to fly into the large city of Monterrey and then take a seven-hour bus ride. Once we got out of the city, the ride was bumpy, and the bus's air conditioning was no match for the heat of the desert sun burning overhead.

15. **A.** NO CHANGE
  B. Monterrey. In
  C. Monterrey in
  D. Monterrey—in

16. **F.** NO CHANGE
  G. burning.
  H. scorching.
  J. DELETE the underlined portion and end the sentence with a period.

GO ON TO THE NEXT PAGE.

Mexico's climate is warmer than that of the United States
<u>because Mexico is closer to the equator.</u> The adults in the
                    17
village, many of whom did not even know I was coming,

welcomed me <u>when they got around to it.</u> More than that, my
                        18
host family had reserved a room in their house exclusively
for me, so I could have some privacy when I needed it. Even
though I was in a new place, I already felt like I was at home.

The language situation was more difficult than I expected. I
learned very quickly that the good grades I had received in my
Spanish classes would not necessarily translate to success here

where people spoke the <u>Spanish language and no other.</u> Still,
                                        19
my host family and others in the village were very patient
with me. Before long, we <u>had held</u> all of our conversations in
                                20
Spanish.

The <u>family I was hosting</u> in Mexico asked me about my family
            21
and encouraged my school interests. They told me about their

lives and some of their <u>childrens'</u> previous English teachers. In
                                22
particular, my host father became a very close friend, and I still
correspond with him today.

I had been sent to this town to teach English to some of
the children and their parents, but I soon realized that I was
learning <u>all about Mexican food and culture.</u> I was learning
                23

---

17. Given that all the choices are true, which provides material most relevant to what follows in this paragraph?

    A. NO CHANGE
    B. I had only been to Mexico one time before, when I went with my parents to the beach.
    C. Once I got there, though, I didn't have any of the problems that I had worried about in advance.
    D. The heat from the sun was nothing compared to the heat of the spicy food my family liked to cook.

18. Which choice most effectively expresses that the narrator's host family was extremely welcoming?

    F. NO CHANGE
    G. as if I had lived there my whole life.
    H. and asked how long I would be staying.
    J. to their town.

19. Which of the following alternatives to the underlined portion would NOT be acceptable?

    A. no language other than Spanish.
    B. Spanish language others or no.
    C. Spanish and no other language.
    D. no other language.

20. F. NO CHANGE
    G. hold
    H. have held
    J. held

21. A. NO CHANGE
    B. family that hosted me
    C. family I hosted
    D. family, which hosted me,

22. F. NO CHANGE
    G. childrens's
    H. childrens
    J. children's

23. Which choice most logically contrasts with the first part of this sentence?

    A. NO CHANGE
    B. my way around the town.
    C. more than I could ever teach.
    D. about the lives of those in my host family.

GO ON TO THE NEXT PAGE.

in circumstances not only how to speak everyday Spanish, but
<u>24</u>

also how to coexist with people who lived unlike my own. [25]

On my last day of class. I noticed a map of North America
<u>26</u>
on the wall. I realized then what I had sensed all along.

In one sense, I was farther away from home than I'd ever was.
<u>27</u>
However, in another sense, I had simply found a new place that

I could call home. <u>Remembering the details of my trip,</u> I'm
<u>28</u>
more and more convinced that the river that separates

Mexico and the United States is actually very small next to all

of the wonderful things that bring us together. [29]

24. The best placement for the underlined portion would be:

    F. where it is now.
    G. after the word *speak.*
    H. after the word *Spanish.*
    J. after the word *lived.*

25. At this point, the writer is considering adding the following true statement:

> In Spanish, the word for "coexistence" sounds just like ours: *coexistencia.*

    Should the writer make this addition here?

    A. Yes, because it clarifies the narrator's earlier discussion of how welcome he felt with his host family.
    B. Yes, because it supports the paragraph's main idea by translating a word into Spanish.
    C. No, because it digresses from the main topic of the paragraph.
    D. No, because it shows that the narrator's Spanish was not as proficient as he claimed.

26. **F.** NO CHANGE
    G. class, I
    H. class but I
    J. class; I

27. **A.** NO CHANGE
    B. had been.
    C. been.
    D. being.

28. **F.** NO CHANGE
    G. Identified as one of the borderlands,
    H. Showing all the mountains and rivers,
    J. Becoming a new place for me,

29. Which of the following sentences, if added here, would most effectively express one of the main ideas of the essay?

    A. To be honest, though, I was really glad to get home when it was all over.
    B. The main thing I miss about the trip is the opportunity to practice my Spanish.
    C. Ever since that time, I've often thought how alike my two homes really are.
    D. That was my initial reaction, but I don't think I really want to go back.

GO ON TO THE NEXT PAGE.

PASSAGE III

"Haunted" Authors

[1]

In 1915, Maurice E. McLoughlin, a well-known tennis player
published an instructional autobiography called *Tennis as
I Play It*. Two years earlier, McLoughlin had become the first
American finalist at the Wimbledon tournament in England,
and tennis fans were excited to uncover the tricks of his
success. Anticipation for McLoughlin's story grew even more

in 1914. He was winning a number of major tournaments that
year, he was declared the Number 1 tennis player in the world.
When *Tennis as I Play It* finally did come out in 1915, no
one had any reason to suspect that it might have been written
by someone else. However, the author of *Tennis as I Play It*
was not McLoughlin at all, but the as-yet unknown novelist
Sinclair Lewis, his ghostwriter. Why, then, is *Tennis as I Play It*
considered the tennis player's book?

[2]

A ghostwriter is an author who writes a text that is officially
credited to another author, and the history of such practices
are lasting

longer than we might expect. [36]

30. **F.** NO CHANGE
    G. McLoughlin a well-known tennis player
    H. McLoughlin, a well-known tennis player,
    J. McLoughlin a well-known tennis player,

31. **A.** NO CHANGE
    B. skills
    C. secrets
    D. abilities

32. **F.** NO CHANGE
    G. Won
    H. He won
    J. Winning

33. **A.** NO CHANGE
    B. for
    C. about
    D. DELETE the underlined portion.

34. **F.** NO CHANGE
    G. the athletes'
    H. the tennis players
    J. the athletes

35. **A.** NO CHANGE
    B. were
    C. are
    D. is

36. At this point, the writer is thinking about adding the following true statement:

    > Some suggest that ghostwriting is as old as authorship itself.

    Should the writer make this addition here?

    F. Yes, because it provides a transition from the previous paragraph to this one.
    G. Yes, because it expands upon a point made in the preceding sentence.
    H. No, because it does not apply to the main subject discussed in this paragraph.
    J. No, because it suggests that most historical texts are ghostwritten.

In other words, *Tennis as I Play It* was not, the first famous ghostwritten book, and it won't be the last. Ghostwriting can

happen for a number of reasons, and although it's merits are debatable, it remains an acceptable practice in the publishing world.

[3]

Today, ghostwriting can take a number of different forms. It is perhaps most prominent in the autobiographies and memoirs of celebrities. How does a celebrity decide to ask a ghostwriter to write his or her book? No, ghostwriting is equally prominent in lesser-known spheres as well. Political speeches, for example, are often credited to the politician who

delivers them, and then that politician just reads the speech from a teleprompter. In addition, many popular songs claim a

popular singer or performer as songwriter, although they have been shaped more by a producer than by any of the credited songwriters.

[4]

Ghostwriting—whether we approve of it or not—is here to stay. Sometimes, as in the case of Sinclair Lewis,

37. **A.** NO CHANGE
    B. was not the first,
    C. was not the first
    D. was, not the first,

38. **F.** NO CHANGE
    G. its
    H. her
    J. their

39. Which choice provides the most logical and effective transition to the rest of the paragraph?

    A. NO CHANGE
    B. Is the practice restricted to celebrity autobiographies and memoirs?
    C. Why would celebrities want other people to tell their stories?
    D. What makes celebrities think ghostwriters know all the details of their lives?

40. Given that all the choices are true, which one provides the best support for the statement in an earlier part of this sentence?

    F. NO CHANGE
    G. but the speeches are usually written by a team of speech-writers.
    H. but very few politicians have the oratorical skills of politicians from the last century.
    J. although many politicians like to speak from notes rather than fully written speeches.

41. Which of the following alternatives to the underlined portion would NOT be acceptable?

    A. songwriter, yet
    B. songwriter; therefore,
    C. songwriter, but
    D. songwriter; however,

42. **F.** NO CHANGE
    G. not
    H. not,
    J. not;

GO ON TO THE NEXT PAGE.

the ghostwriters will eventually become famous authors in their own right. [43] Much more often, though,

since we are moved by the writing of authors whose names we
<u>44</u>
will never learn.

43. The writer is thinking about deleting the preceding sentence. Should this sentence be kept or deleted?

   A. Kept, because it shows the importance of ghostwriting to Sinclair Lewis's career.

   B. Kept, because it provides a contrast to the fact stated in the next sentence.

   C. Deleted, because it discusses a famous novelist in a paragraph about ghostwriters.

   D. Deleted, because Sinclair Lewis is already mentioned in the first paragraph.

44. **F.** NO CHANGE
   G. because
   H. yet
   J. DELETE the underlined portion.

Question 45 asks about the preceding passage as a whole.

---

45. While reviewing his research for this essay, the writer discovers a statistic and composes the following sentence:

> Some in the industry suggest that as many as half of non-fiction books are written with help from ghostwriters.

If the writer were to include this sentence in the essay, the most logical place would be after the last sentence in Paragraph:

   A. 1.
   B. 2.
   C. 3.
   D. 4.

PASSAGE IV

From Broadcasts to Podcasts

In the first half of the twentieth century, Americans couldn't spend their evenings in front of the TV. The television didn't become a regular feature of the American home until well into the 1960s. Instead, the major form of mass entertainment in this period was provided by the radio. The radio had begun its rise to prominence in the 1930s. It was especially popular in the 1940s, when most American households, as many as 91%, had a radio. [46] The residents of many small towns and rural

46. The writer is considering deleting the phrase "as many as 91%" from the preceding sentence (adjusting the punctuation accordingly). Should this phrase be kept or deleted?

   F. Kept, because it supports the idea that radio was on the decline after the 1930s.

   G. Kept, because it gives specific evidence of radio's popularity in the 1940s.

   H. Deleted, because it discusses American households in a passage about radio listening.

   J. Deleted, because it doesn't describe the households that had radios.

GO ON TO THE NEXT PAGE.

areas in non-urban parts of the country didn't have access
to the newest movies or books, but those residents did have
radios.

[1] Throughout the 1930s and 1940s, Americans turned to
radio for all that. [2] During World War II, listeners could get
more frequent information from their radios than they could from

the newspapers. [3] In 1932, U.S. President Franklin Roosevelt,
began his series of "fireside chats" over the radio. [4] For those

looking for lighter fare, the radio had plenty of mystery
programs, comedy and variety shows, westerns, and quiz
programs. [5] These chats were intended to be as informal
as a chat between friends and family members by the fireside,
but they tackled some of the most complex political issues
of the day:

war, depression, and international affairs. [52]

By the 1950s, however, radio was losing its dominant
position. The main reason for radio's decline was the advent
of television. As television's continuing success has shown,
Americans would rather *see* their favorite stars mere than *hear*

them. Listening (to anything other than music) to appear with
a thing of the past.

47. **A.** NO CHANGE
    B. in parts of the country outside cities
    C. despite their possession of radios
    D. DELETE the underlined portion

48. **F.** NO CHANGE
    G. their wants and other things that might be perceived as
    needs, but were more likely wants.
    H. the things they needed to listen to, such as comedy, news,
    sports, and drama, or other kinds of programs sometimes.
    J. their listening needs.

49. **A.** NO CHANGE
    B. U.S. President Franklin Roosevelt
    C. U.S. President, Franklin Roosevelt
    D. U.S. President, Franklin Roosevelt,

50. Which of the following alternatives to the underlined portion
    would NOT be acceptable?
    F. scouring
    G. desiring
    H. wanting
    J. seeking

51. **A.** NO CHANGE
    B. day, these included
    C. day,
    D. day having been

52. For the sake of the logic and coherence of this paragraph,
    Sentence 5 should be placed:
    F. where it is now.
    G. before Sentence 1.
    H. after Sentence 2.
    J. after Sentence 3.

53. **A.** NO CHANGE
    B. merely then
    C. mere then
    D. than merely

54. **F.** NO CHANGE
    G. was apparently
    H. to appearance was
    J. appeared as

GO ON TO THE NEXT PAGE.

[55] This portable device could hold more music than any record, tape, or CD ever could before. The iPod also brought back forms other than music. New *podcasts* hearkened back to

old-time radio programs called *broadcasts*. Whether funny or
_____
56

serious, whether they're mainstream or they're underground,
_____
57
these podcasts might never reach the heights of old-time radio

broadcasts, but there basically bringing non-musical listening
_____
58
to a whole new generation. These days, when it can seem like everyone wants *more* visual culture—IMAX screens, 3D movies—along comes the podcast to provide a welcome but not altogether unfamiliar alternative.

55. Given that all the following statements are true, which one, if added here, would most clearly and effectively introduce the main subject of this paragraph?

   A. Radio's most popular programs, such as *Gunsmoke*, became popular television hits.

   B. At least it seemed like a thing of the past until the iPod came along in 2001.

   C. One of the last popular programs, *The Zero Hour*, was on in the early 1970s.

   D. The presidential radio address has become a custom ever since Roosevelt's early broadcasts.

56. **F.** NO CHANGE
   G. radio broadcasts.
   H. radio broadcasts'.
   J. radio broadcast's.

57. **A.** NO CHANGE
   B. being mainstream in the underground,
   C. mainstream or underground,
   D. if they're so underground they're actually mainstream,

58. **F.** NO CHANGE
   G. they're
   H. it's essentially
   J. their

Question 59 asks about the preceding passage as a whole

---

59. Suppose the writer's goal had been to write a brief essay focusing on how contemporary broadcasters have been influenced by earlier broadcasters. Would this essay fulfill that goal?

   A. Yes, because it makes clear that the podcast would not be likely to exist without old-time radio.

   B. Yes, because it implies that the podcast has encouraged listeners to go back to earlier recordings.

   C. No, because it does not offer a contemporary equivalent for Roosevelt's fireside chats.

   D. No, because it is more focused on sketching the rise in popularity of the podcast.

GO ON TO THE NEXT PAGE.

PASSAGE V

Vladimir Nabokov, Books, and Butterflies

Vladimir Nabokov (1899-1977) is best known as a novelist. His first novels <u>were written</u> in Russia in the 1920s.
₆₀
However, his <u>novels and books that people seem to like the most</u> were published in the United States and England in the
₆₁
1940s and 1950s. The most notorious of all was *Lolita* (1955), a novel praised for its skillful construction and beautiful style but often banned for its lurid descriptions and shocking plot. [62]

<u>Nabokov left Russia to escape persecution from the newly</u>
₆₃
<u>formed Soviet government.</u>
₆₃

In fact, he made significant contributions to <u>entomology;</u>
₆₄
the study of insects. Nabokov's work in charting the <u>structure,</u>
₆₅
and migration patterns of butterflies was a major contribution to science.

Moreover, at what might have seemed a high point in his literary <u>career</u> Nabokov accepted a research fellowship from Harvard
₆₆
University's Museum of Comparative Zoology.

60. **F.** NO CHANGE
    G. was written
    H. were wrote
    J. was wrote

61. **A.** NO CHANGE
    B. most famous works
    C. works that are the most popular among readers
    D. books that are very popular among critics and general readers alike

62. The writer is considering deleting the parenthetical information (and the parentheses) from the preceding sentence. If the writer were to make this deletion, the paragraph would primarily lose:
    F. a detail that helps to place *Lolita* chronologically in Nabokov's literary career.
    G. the time during which Nabokov stopped writing to conduct his entomological research.
    H. a detail needed to understand the historical and literary significance of *Lolita*.
    J. the number of years that Nabokov spent writing *Lolita*.

63. Given that all the choices are true, which one most effectively leads the reader from this paragraph into the remainder of the essay?
    A. NO CHANGE
    B. Nabokov's other novels include *Pnin*, *Pale Fire*, and the highly experimental *Ada*.
    C. However, Nabokov was not exclusively a novelist and a man of letters.
    D. *Lolita* is now considered an American classic, despite its original reception.

64. **F.** NO CHANGE
    G. entomology being
    H. entomology of
    J. entomology,

65. **A.** NO CHANGE
    B. structure of
    C. structure
    D. structure;

66. **F.** NO CHANGE
    G. career;
    H. career.
    J. career,

GO ON TO THE NEXT PAGE.

Then, he used this fellowship to conduct his fieldwork and to
curate the museum's butterfly collection at a time when
<u>67</u>

he could just as well, of been earning a fellowship to work
<u>68</u>
exclusively on writing.

Although Nabokov's work <u>by the scientific community</u>
<u>69</u>
was occasionally dismissed as the ideas of an amateur, recent
findings have supported some of his hypotheses. For example,

Nabokov was <u>the primary one in a long list of scientists</u> to
<u>70</u>
suggest that the *Polyammatus blue* species of butterfly came to
North America from Asia in five waves over the Bering Strait.

Moreover, Nabokov was <u>mainly interested in the study of</u>
<u>71</u>
<u>moths and butterflies, but studied some plants.</u> In belated
<u>71</u>
recognition of his contributions, a genus of butterfly was

renamed. *Nabokovia* in his honor.
<u>72</u>
We can't know whether Nabokov's fiction or his scientific

work was more important, <u>than</u> which pursuit Nabokov found
<u>73</u>

more enriching. Nabokov the famous novelist <u>could of been</u>
<u>74</u>
Nabokov the famous entomologist. Who can say? What we
can say is that Nabokov's story is a reminder of the vastness of
human potential. One might say that Nabokov was just

<u>an exceptional</u> person, but isn't it equally possible that these
<u>75</u>
alternate personalities exist inside of all of us?

67. **A.** NO CHANGE
    B. He
    C. Finally, he
    D. Consequently, he

68. **F.** NO CHANGE
    G. could just as well, have
    H. could, just as well of
    J. could just as well have

69. The best placement for the underlined portion would be:

    A. where it is now.
    B. after the word *dismissed*.
    C. after the word *ideas*.
    D. after the word *supported*.

70. **F.** NO CHANGE
    G. the first
    H. the one before anyone else
    J. the scientist that was before others in the field

71. Given that all the choices are true, which one most effec-
    tively concludes the sentence by giving a specific example of
    Nabokov's contribution to the study of moths and butterflies?

    A. NO CHANGE
    B. aided in his scientific researches by his wife, Vera, who
        drove Vladimir to his research sites.
    C. the first to describe some species of moth and butterfly,
        including the Karner blue.
    D. working on his novels at the same time that he made his
        scientific discoveries.

72. **F.** NO CHANGE
    G. renamed, *Nabokovia*
    H. renamed *Nabokovia*
    J. renamed; *Nabokovia*

73. **A.** NO CHANGE
    B. for example
    C. nor
    D. DELETE the underlined portion.

74. **F.** NO CHANGE
    G. could have
    H. has
    J. have

75. **A.** NO CHANGE
    B. an exception to
    C. exceptionally a
    D. an exceptionally

END OF TEST 3
STOP! DO NOT TURN THE PAGE UNTIL TOLD TO DO SO.

Chapter 18
English Practice
Test 3: Answers and
Explanations

ENGLISH PRACTICE TEST 3 ANSWERS

1.	A		39.	B
2.	J		40.	G
3.	B		41.	B
4.	G		42.	F
5.	C		43.	B
6.	H		44.	J
7.	C		45.	B
8.	F		46.	G
9.	B		47.	D
10.	F		48.	J
11.	A		49.	B
12.	H		50.	F
13.	A		51.	A
14.	J		52.	J
15.	D		53.	D
16.	J		54.	G
17.	C		55.	B
18.	G		56.	G
19.	B		57.	C
20.	J		58.	G
21.	B		59.	D
22.	J		60.	F
23.	C		61.	B
24.	J		62.	F
25.	C		63.	C
26.	G		64.	J
27.	C		65.	C
28.	F		66.	J
29.	C		67.	B
30.	H		68.	J
31.	C		69.	B
32.	J		70.	G
33.	A		71.	C
34.	F		72.	H
35.	D		73.	C
36.	G		74.	G
37.	C		75.	A
38.	G			

SCORE YOUR PRACTICE TEST

Step A
Count the number of correct answers: _____. This is your **raw score**.

Step B
Use the score conversion table below to look up your raw score. The number to the left is your **scale score**: _____ .

English Scale Conversion Table

Scale Score	Raw Score	Scale Score	Raw Score	Scale Score	Raw Score
36	75	27	62	18	41–42
35	73–74	26	60–61	17	39–40
34	71–72	25	58–59	16	36–38
33	70	24	56–57	15	33–35
32	69	23	54–55	14	30–32
31	67–68	22	52–53	13	28–29
30	66	21	49–51	12	26–27
29	65	20	46–48	11	24–25
28	63–64	19	43–45	10	22–23

ENGLISH PRACTICE TEST 3 EXPLANATIONS

Passage I

1. **A** The question *but who knew they also love to eat cheeseburgers?* introduces a unique feature of the cats described in this passage. *Lolcats* are not an actual species, eliminating (B). The essay deals with *lolcats* themselves, not their love of cheeseburgers, eliminating (C). However, their love of cheeseburgers *is* unique, which means that this detail is important, eliminating (D). Only (A) remains.

2. **J** The verb in this sentence will need to agree with the other verb in the sentence, *take*, which is in the present tense. Of the choices, only (G) and (J) are in the present tense, eliminating (F) and (H). Of choices (G) and (J), (J) is better because (G) introduces a participle unnecessarily. Note: Be careful of verbs ending in "-ing." They can often make sentences unnecessarily wordy!

3. **B** This sentence would be incomplete if the photographer's name were removed. In other words, *In the 1870s, Brighton-based photographer took a series. . .* would be incomplete. Therefore, the photographer's name should not be set off by commas as it is in (A) and (C), nor should it be set off by a semi-colon as in (D). Only (B) correctly indicates that *Henry Pointer* is essential to the meaning of the sentence.

4. **G** Only (G) contains specific information that is not redundant. Choice (J) cannot work because it does not indicate who is doing the *naming*, and (F) and (H) do not make sense in the given context.

5. **C** The question asks for an option that shows that *the caption was an essential part of the humor of Pointer's photographs*. Therefore, we will need a choice that suggests the importance of captions. Choices (B) and (D) suggest that captions were not important, so they can be eliminated. Choice (A) does not address the importance of captions, so it, too, can be eliminated. Only (C) remains, and it works because it shows that captions could often be used to enliven otherwise dull pictures.

6. **H** The idiom *in his day* must be kept intact here, making (H) the best choice. Choices (F) and (J) create a meaning different from the intended one, and (G) creates the phrase *with his day*, which is not used, thus eliminating these choices.

7. **C** Sentences A and B offer a general description of the *lolcat*. Sentence C changes the focus of the paragraph to the *lolcat*'s historical roots. Therefore, because it changes the focus of the paragraph, Sentence C offers a good place to start a new paragraph. Sentence D continues the historical discussion and should therefore be in the same paragraph with Sentence C.

8. **F** Each answer choice offers a word or phrase of transition. Choices (G), (H), and (J) offer transitions that suggest a contrast, matching the contrasting word *though* in the passage. Choice (F) offers a transition that suggests a continuation. Therefore, (F) is the answer that does NOT work in the given context, meaning that it is the correct answer.

9. **B**   The non-underlined portion of this sentence contains the words *most famous*. These make the words in the following redundant: *known widely* in (A), *that many people know* in (C), and *that is pretty popular* in (D). Only (B) contains no redundant phrasing, and (B) is therefore the correct answer.

10. **F**   The subjects of the underlined verb are *phrases* and *language*. Therefore, the verb will need to agree with a plural subject, eliminating (G) and (H). The passage is talking about phrases and language in the present tense, eliminating (J). Only (F) offers a verb that agrees in number and tense.

11. **A**   The noun being modified by the underlined portion is *lolcats*. Choice (B) cannot work because the *lolcats* are not *earning lots of money*. Choice (C) cannot work because *lolcats* do not have *cameras in hand*, nor can (D) work because *lolcats* are not *promoting*. Only (A) provides an appropriate modifier for the word *lolcats*.

12. **H**   Of all the *creative coinages* of the decade, the *lolcat* has been called one of the *most creative*. Choice (G) cannot work because more than two coinages are being compared. Choices (F) and (J) cannot work because they do not offer comparative words in a sentence that requires them. Only (H) can work in the given context.

13. **A**   Choice (B) cannot work because the *cheeseburger* refers only to one type of cat. Choice (C) cannot work because *cheeseburger-flavored* does not solve any problem posed in the essay. Choice (D) cannot work because no question is being posed. Only (A) can work, suggesting that *cheeseburger-flavored* is more detailed than *another line*, and that it is intended for humorous effect.

14. **J**   The passage as a whole discusses the past, present, and future of the *lolcat*. Though it touches on photography, Internet usage, and types of animals, none of these can be described as the passage's main idea. Only (J) reflects the passage's main idea accurately, while suggesting that the writer has *not* succeeded in writing a passage that discusses *animal photography* more generally.

Passage II

15. **D**   Note the dash in the non-underlined part of the sentence. The answer will need to contain another dash to keep this notation consistent and to set off the unnecessary phrase *located a few hours west of Monterrey*. Only (D) contains a dash. Choice (A) contains a semi-colon, which can only be used when separating two complete ideas.

16. **J**   The words *burning* and *scorching* mean similar things, and when they are paired with the word *heat* in the non-underlined portion, they become redundant. Therefore, in order to remove this redundant construction, it is best to remove these words—eliminating (F), (G), and (H)—and to delete the underlined portion. Note: Always give "DELETE" or "OMIT" special consideration. They are often correct!

17. **C**   The first paragraph discusses the author's difficult trip to the small town in Mexico, but the second paragraph switches to the pleasant time he had there with his host family. The discussion of the weather does not continue, which eliminates (A). The paragraph does not discuss Mexican cuisine, which eliminates (D). The paragraph does not discuss the author's earlier trip with his parents, which eliminates (B). Only (C) offers the appropriate transition into the new paragraph.

18. **G**   Read the question carefully. It asks for an option that shows that the narrator's host family was *extremely welcoming*. Choices (F), (H), and (J) do not contain any indication that the family was welcoming. Choice (G), however, suggests that the family was as welcoming as they would have been if the narrator had *lived there* [his] *whole life*. Choice (G) is therefore the best answer.

19. **B**   This question asks for the alternative that would NOT be acceptable. Choices (A), (C), and (D) rearrange the words, but they are not grammatically or idiomatically incorrect. Choice (B) is unclear, though, in that it makes *Spanish language* modify the word *others*, whereas the sentence requires that *Spanish language* and *others* be separate nouns. Choice (B), therefore, would NOT be acceptable and is the correct answer.

20. **J**   Note the other verbs in this paragraph: *were, asked, told, became*. The verb in this sentence must be consistent with these verbs. Therefore, only (J), *held*, is consistent with the simple past tense. Choices (F) and (H) change the type of past tense and the meaning of the sentence, and (G) switches to the present.

21. **B**   The sentence as written cannot work, because the narrator does not host the family; rather, the family hosts the narrator. Choice (C) makes the same mistake. Then, the words *that/which hosted me* are necessary to the meaning of the sentence: They clarify which *family* the narrator is referring to. Therefore, because this information is necessary, the information should not be set off by commas and should contain the word *that*, as in (B).

22. **J**   The sentence describes the *previous English teachers* of the *children* and therefore requires that *children* be made possessive. Choice (H) contains no apostrophe and can therefore be eliminated. Choice (F) and (G) make the word *children* possessive in incorrect ways. Only (J) offers the correct possessive form of *children*. Note: What comes before the apostrophe must be a word. In other words, *childrens'*, as in (F), is incorrect because *childrens* is not a word. The same is true for (G).

23. **C**   The first part of the sentence discusses the narrator teaching English. Therefore, in order to contrast with the first part of the sentence, we will need some indication that he is *not* teaching English, or that he is not exclusively teaching English. Choices (A), (B), and (D) are not related to English, nor do they contrast with the idea that the narrator is a teacher. Only (C) offers the appropriate contrast: While the narrator is a teacher, he is also *learning more than [he] could ever teach*.

24. **J**   The current placement of the underlined portion cannot work because it does not clarify what the *circumstances* are, eliminating (F). The same is true for (G) and (H). Only (J) clarifies: *circumstances unlike my own*; therefore, (J) is the best answer.

25. **C** When you are asked whether to add a sentence to the given passage, make sure you have a very good reason to do so. In this particular case, the proposed sentence does not contribute meaningfully to the main idea or development of the paragraph or passage, so it should not be added, eliminating (A) and (B). Choice (D) can be eliminated because the passage does not give adequate grounds to assess the narrator's proficiency in Spanish. Only (C) works.

26. **G** The sentence as written cannot work because the phrase *On my last day of class* does not offer a complete idea, meaning that (F) and (J) can be eliminated. Then, the word *but* suggests a contrast where none is present, eliminating (H). Only (G) works, setting *On my last day of class* off as an introductory idea.

27. **C** Separate the contraction *I'd* into its component parts: *I had*. This makes (B) clearly redundant. This also eliminates (A) and (D), which use *had* again incorrectly. Only (C) works in the context created by the non-underlined portion.

28. **F** The word after the underlined portion is *I'm*; therefore, the underlined portion must modify the word *I*. The sentence works as written because *Remembering the details of my trip* refers appropriately to the *I* it is modifying. Choice (G) can be eliminated because *Identified as one of the borderlands* refers to some part of Mexico or the United States. *Showing all the mountains and rivers* refers to the *map*, eliminating (H). Choice (H) can also be eliminated because *Becoming a new place for me* refers to the village.

29. **C** The essay details the author's trip to Mexico, where he goes to teach English and also learns a good deal about the people and himself. The first paragraph suggests that the start was difficult but that the narrator quickly feels at home. There is no indication that (A) and (D) will work in the context because both suggest that the narrator did not enjoy his trip. Choice (B) foregrounds the importance of Spanish, but it does so too much. Only (C) can work in the context of the paragraph and the essay as a whole.

Passage III

30. **H** This sentence conveys the information that McLoughlin published a book. The phrase *a well-known tennis player* is not essential to conveying this meaning, and therefore that information is not essential to the meaning of the sentence. Because the information is not essential, it must be set off by commas, as in (H). Note: On questions that test restrictive and non-restrictive information, the correct answer will typically have two commas or none, so if you're unsure, eliminate answers with only one comma.

31. **C** Pay close attention to the non-underlined portion of the sentence. The word *uncover* indicates which word will be needed in the underlined portion. One does not uncover *tricks*, *skills*, or *abilities*, eliminating (A), (B), and (D). One does, however, uncover *secrets*, as in (C).

32. **J** The sentence as written creates a comma splice because *He was winning a number of major tennis tournaments that year* and *he was declared the Number 1 tennis player in the world* are both complete ideas. We can't change the comma, so this eliminates (F) and (H). Choice (G) does not make sense in the given context. Only (J) correctly makes the first part of the sentence incomplete by turning it into the modifying phrase *Winning a number of major tournaments that year*.

33. **A** A variety of prepositions can come after the word *written*, but each has a different meaning. *Written for* suggests that the book was written as a gift for someone, or that it was dedicated to that person. This can't work with the *someone else* in this sentence because there is no indication that the book was written *for* anyone in particular. Eliminate (B). The book is *about* McLoughlin, but there is no indication that the book was written *about* someone else, eliminating (C). We cannot delete the underlined portion because *written someone else* does not make sense. Only (A) remains: The book was not written *by* McLoughlin but *by* a ghostwriter.

34. **F** This sentence refers to the *book* belonging to *the tennis player*; therefore, there should be an apostrophe to indicate possession. This eliminates (H) and (J). Choice (G) makes the word *athletes* into a plural possessive when there is only one athlete involved, eliminating (G). Choice (F) gives the correct singular punctuation of *the tennis player*. Note: If you were not sure whether to choose *the tennis player* or *the athlete*, you could still have solved this question by looking at apostrophes and using Process of Elimination.

35. **D** The subject of the underlined verb is *history*, not the prepositional object *practices*. Therefore, the verb in the underlined portion should be singular, eliminating (A), (B), and (C). Only (D) offers a present-tense verb that agrees with a singular subject and has no redundant information.

36. **G** The previous sentence concludes with the idea that *the history of such practices is longer than we might expect*. This suggests the following sentence should make some historical claim or give some historical detail. The proposed addition does this, so it should be added, eliminating (H) and (J). It cannot, however, provide a transition from the previous paragraph because it is not the first sentence of this paragraph, eliminating (F). Only (G) correctly states that this sentence should be added and that it expands upon a point made in the preceding sentence.

37. **C** The answer choices offer different opportunities to insert pauses in the phrase *was not the first*. In the given sentence, though, no pause is necessary, so no commas are necessary, eliminating (A), (B), and (D). Choice (C) gives the best option because it contains no unnecessary commas.

38. **G** The sentence describes the *merits* of *ghostwriting*: in other words, *ghostwriting's merits* or *its* merits. Choice (F), *it's*, is the contraction of *it is*, not a possessive pronoun. Ghostwriting is not a person, so (H) can be eliminated, nor is it a plural, so (J) can be eliminated. Only (G) offers the correct possessive pronoun.

39. **B**   The sentence that follows reads, *No, ghostwriting is equally prominent in lesser-known spheres as well*. Therefore, the sentence in this problem should offer some question to which the next sentence could answer *No*, particularly one that deals with ghostwriting in *well-known spheres*. The preceding sentence says that ghostwriting is *most prominent in the autobiographies and memoirs of celebrities*. Only (B) expands upon this idea and sets up the appropriate contrast with the following sentence. Choices (A), (C), and (D) deal exclusively with the details of celebrity ghostwriting.

40. **G**   The passage as a whole discusses ghostwriting, and the sentence preceding this one reads *No, ghostwriting is equally prominent in lesser-known spheres as well*. Therefore, the sentence in the underlined portion should address ghostwriting somehow. The sentence will not be concerned with styles of reading, *oratorical skills*, or speech notes, eliminating (F), (H), and (J). Only (G) sets up the contrast that speeches *are often credited to the politician who delivers them* but actually are *written by a team of speechwriters*.

41. **B**   The question asks for the punctuation and transition that would NOT be acceptable. The ideas surrounding this punctuation-transition combination are as follows: *In addition, many popular songs claim a popular singer or performer as songwriter* and *they have been shaped more by a producer than by any of the credited songwriters*. As the original sentence shows with the word *although*, these ideas should contrast. Therefore, (A), (C), and (D) WOULD be acceptable and can be eliminated. Only (B) removes this contrast and therefore would NOT be acceptable.

42. **F**   Note the dash in the first part of this sentence, which sets off the non-essential phrase *whether we approve of it or not*. The answer will need to include another dash in order to keep this punctuation consistent. The sentence must be correct as written because only (F) contains that dash.

43. **B**   The sentence following this one begins with the words *Much more often, though*. If we remove this sentence, we are left with the question *Much more often* than what? Therefore, the sentence should be kept, offering as it does a description of what happens *sometimes*. Eliminate (C) and (D). Then, eliminate (A) because it does not show the importance of ghostwriting to Sinclair Lewis's career: In fact, the sentence suggests that Lewis became a well-known novelist *even though* he was initially a ghostwriter. Only (B) addresses the fact that this sentence gives the first part of a contrast completed in the next sentence.

44. **J**   As written, this sentence is actually a sentence fragment. The subordinating conjunction *since* makes the sentence incomplete, so eliminate (F). Eliminate (G) for the same reason. The word *yet* in (H) is a coordinating conjunction, but it does not fix the problem. The only viable solution to the problem is to remove the conjunction entirely, as in (J). Note: Give serious consideration to "DELETE" and "OMIT" when you see them. They are often correct!

45. **B** The proposed sentence addresses the prevalence of ghostwriting, suggesting as it does that ghostwriting is a much more common practice than we might suspect. This sentence does not belong in Paragraph 1, which discusses a particular example of ghostwriting. The sentence does not belong in Paragraph 3, which gives some of the places where ghostwriting is used. The sentence does not belong in Paragraph 4, which offers some concluding ideas on ghostwriting. The only possible place for the sentence would be in Paragraph 2, which discusses ghostwriting and its historical importance and prevalence.

Passage IV

46. **G** The phrase in question appears in the sentence *It was especially popular in the 1940s when most American households, as many as 91%, had a radio.* In this instance, the *91%* statistic gives a specific number of how many *American households* had radios. Therefore, because the information serves a specific purpose in the sentence, it should be kept. Eliminate (H) and (J). Then, eliminate (F) because the statistic does not indicate that radio was on the decline.

47. **D** The sentence as written is redundant because the non-underlined portion already contains the words *of many small towns and rural areas.* This eliminates (A), and (B) can be eliminated for the same reason. Choice (C) is redundant with a later part of the sentence, *those residents did have radios.* The only viable alternative is to delete the underlined portion entirely, as in (D). Note: Give serious consideration to "DELETE" and "OMIT" when you see them. They are often correct!

48. **J** The sentence as written does not contain adequate information because it is unclear what *that* refers to. Eliminate (F). Choices (G) and (H), however, go to the opposite extreme by giving way too much information, so eliminate them as well. Choice (J) strikes a happy medium: It is not too long and not too ambiguous.

49. **B** In order to determine whether the name *Franklin Roosevelt* is essential to the meaning of the sentence, see if the sentence works without it. Without the name, the sentence would read *In 1932, U.S. President began his series of "fireside chats" over the radio.* There's something missing from this sentence, which means that the name *Franklin Roosevelt* is essential to the sentence's meaning. Therefore, the information should not be set off by any commas, and only (B) can work.

50. **F** The sentence as written is correct: One can be *looking for lighter fare.* This question is asking for an alternative that would NOT be acceptable. One can be *desiring lighter fare, wanting lighter fare,* or *seeking lighter fare,* eliminating (G), (H), and (J). One cannot be *scouring lighter fare,* however, which means that (F) would NOT be an acceptable alternative to the underlined portion.

51. **A** *War, depression, and international affairs* are some examples of the *complex political issues* mentioned in the first part of the sentence. The word *day* is not part of this list, eliminating (C). Choice (D) creates an awkward construction, and (B) creates a comma splice by making the second half of the sentence into a complete idea. Only (A) can work: A complete idea comes before the colon, and a list comes after it.

52. **J** The first words of Sentence 5 are *These chats*, which suggest that the sentence that precedes Sentence 5 will clarify what the *chats* are. Only Sentence 3 has any mention of *chats*, in its discussion of Roosevelt's *fireside chats*. Therefore, Sentence 5 must come directly after Sentence 3, as in (J).

53. **D** There are two main parts to this answer. First, the sentence offers a comparison between *seeing* and *hearing*, suggesting that the sentence will need the comparative word *than*, not the time word *then*. Eliminate (B) and (C). Second, the remaining word will modify the verb *hear*. Because the word will modify a verb, the word must be the adverb *merely*, making (D) the best choice.

54. **G** The sentence does not make sense as written, because one cannot *appear with a thing of the past*. Eliminate (F). The same can be said of (H). Choice (J) creates a different meaning from the intended meaning, so it can be eliminated. Only (G) offers an alternative that turns the sentence into the clear expression of an idea.

55. **B** This paragraph discusses the rise to prominence of the iPod, and the attendant rise of podcasting. It does not continue the discussion of specific radio programs, eliminating (A) and (C), nor does it address political speechmaking on the radio, eliminating (D). Only (B) can work because it is the only choice that addresses either podcasting or the iPod.

56. **G** The *broadcasts* mentioned in the sentence are not in possession of anything; therefore, an apostrophe is unnecessary, eliminating (H) and (J). The two remaining choices have essentially the same meaning, but (G) is more concise, which means it is the better answer.

57. **C** The underlined portion is part of a list that includes *funny or serious*. All items in a list must be parallel, and only (C) gives a parallel construction. The other choices break this parallelism and add unnecessary words, so eliminate (A), (B), and (D).

58. **G** The sentence may *sound* correct, but this could be said for a number of the choices. Moreover, the adverb *there* does not apply here because no place or location is being indicated. Eliminate (F). Choice (H) cannot work because the singular *it's* does not agree with its plural antecedent, *podcasts*. We don't need a possessive pronoun in this portion of the sentence, which eliminates (J). Only (G), *they're*, the contraction of the words *they are*, makes this sentence clear and complete.

59. **D** The main idea of the passage is that new *podcasts* are similar to old-time radio *broadcasts*. It does not create a direct line of influence between *contemporary broadcasters* and *earlier broadcasters*. If it had been the writer's goal to discuss this line of influence, then this essay would not fulfill that goal, eliminating (A) and (B). It is true that the essay does not offer a contemporary equivalent for Roosevelt's fireside chats, but the essay is not primarily concerned with these chats. Instead, (D) offers the best reason that the essay has not fulfilled the writer's goal. The essay is more concerned with *podcasts* than with *contemporary broadcasting* generally.

Passage V

60. **F** This answer will have two main parts. First, the verb must agree with the plural subject *novels*, which only (F) and (H) do. Then, we will need the form of the verb that goes with the helping verb *were*. Because *wrote* needs no helping verb, it can't work as *were wrote*, eliminating (H). Only (F) remains.

61. **B** Since all the options have essentially the same meaning and are grammatically correct, choose the option that is the most concise. This is clearly (B), which is much shorter than the other choices and does not contain any excessive words.

62. **F** Most sentences of this first paragraph contain a year or some piece of the chronology of Nabokov's career. Therefore, the parenthetical portion of this sentence, containing the year of publication of the novel *Lolita*, continues to situate Nabokov's life and work historically. The mere mention of a year cannot give *historical and literary significance*, eliminating (H). It would be unreasonable for Nabokov to have spent 1,955 years writing this novel, eliminating (J). Also, because this is the date of publication of a novel, we can't assume that Nabokov stopped writing at this point, eliminating (G). Only (F) makes the appropriately modest claim that the year gives historical context.

63. **C** The first paragraph discusses Nabokov's fame as a novelist, but the remainder of the essay discusses his significant contributions to entomology. Therefore, a transitional sentence should somehow signify that the remainder of the essay will be about something other than Nabokov's career as a novelist. This eliminates (B) and (D). The essay does not turn to Nabokov's political beliefs, eliminating (A). Only (C) indicates that the remainder of the essay will be about something other than Nabokov's career as a novelist.

64. **J** Choice (F) can be eliminated because semi-colons separate only complete ideas, and *the study of insects* is not a complete idea. Choice (G) introduces the awkward construction of the participle *being*, so it can also be eliminated. *Entomology* is the *study of insects*; therefore, it would not make sense to do the *entomology of entomology*, eliminating (H). Choice (J) indicates appropriately that *the study of insects* is meant as an appositive defining the word *entomology*.

65. **C** This sentence describes the way that Nabokov charts the *structure and migration patterns of butterflies*. There is no reason to set the word *structure* off from the rest of this phrase, eliminating (A) and (D). The word *of* in (B) is redundant because the word *of* is already contained in the non-underlined portion of the sentence. Therefore, the best answer is (C) because it includes no unnecessary pauses.

66. **J** The words *In fact, at what might have seemed a high point in his literary career* do not create a complete idea or a sentence that can stand on its own. Therefore, these words should not end with a period or a semi-colon, eliminating (G) and (H). However, they do offer an introductory idea that will lead into the rest of the sentence, so the words should be set off with a comma, eliminating (F) and making (J) the best answer.

67. **B** Choices (A), (C), and (D) all introduce transition words where no transition word is necessary. Choice (B) is the best choice because it is the most concise while preserving the meaning of the sentence.

68. **J**   Although the two forms may sound identical, the correct verb form is *could have*, not *could of*, eliminating (F) and (H). Then, because the words *could have* are part of a single verb, they should not be separated by a comma, as in (G). Therefore, the correct verb form with the correct lack of unnecessary pauses is shown in (J).

69. **B**   The sentence as written is idiomatically incorrect. If the underlined portion were to go where it is now, it would need to read *in, with,* or *for the scientific community*. Eliminate (A). Choices (C) and (D) insert the underlined phrase awkwardly. Only (B) provides a viable placement for the underlined portion, suggesting that Nabokov's work was *dismissed by the scientific community*.

70. **G**   All four answer choices have the same basic meaning, and all are grammatically correct. When this is the case, choose the most concise of the answer choices. In this case, the most concise choice is (G).

71. **C**   Read the question carefully. The correct answer must contain a *specific example of Nabokov's contribution to the study of moths and butterflies*. Choice (A) speaks of his work too generally. Choice (B) discusses Nabokov's wife. Choice (D) returns to a discussion of his novels. None of these gives a *specific example of Nabokov's contribution*. Only (C) does that in giving the name of one of the butterfly species he discovered.

72. **H**   The phrase Nabokovia *in his honor* cannot stand on its own, so it cannot be punctuated with either a semi-colon or a period, eliminating (F) and (J). Then, (G) adds an unnecessary pause before the word *Nabokovia*, so it can be eliminated. Only (H) remains, and it correctly omits unnecessary punctuation.

73. **C**   The sentence begins *We can't know*, and the second part of the sentence should continue in this vein, as if to suggest *nor can we know*, making (C) the best answer. The word *than* suggests a comparison where none is present, eliminating (A). The words *for example* are not followed by an example, eliminating (B). Then, deleting the underlined portion suggests that the phrase *which pursuit Nabokov found more enriching* modifies *more important*, which it does not, eliminating (D).

74. **G**   The first paragraph of the passage suggests that Nabokov is most famous as a novelist, but the rest of the passage suggests that he *could have* been a famous entomologist instead. It would not make sense to say that Nabokov *has* an entomologist, eliminating (H) and (J), which offers an incorrect verb in any case. Only (G) works because the similar-sounding words *could of* are not used.

75. **A**   Nabokov was a person, but to say that he was *exceptionally a person* doesn't make sense, eliminating (C) and (D). The same is true of calling Nabokov *an exception to a person*, eliminating (B). Only (A) gives the correct form: The noun *person* is modified by the adjective *exceptional*.

Chapter 19
The ACT
Reading Test

Even students with superior reading skills find this test to be tough. To crack the Reading test, you have to learn a strategic approach of *how* to work the passages in an order that makes sense for you. In this chapter, you'll learn how to order the passages and apply a basic approach.

FUN FACTS ABOUT THE READING TEST

The Reading test consists of 4 passages, 10 questions each, for a total of 40 questions that you must answer in 35 minutes. There are many factors about the structure of this test that make it difficult. For one thing, the particular passages will obviously vary from test to test, so you can't predict whether you'll like the topic or find the passage more readable than not. Moreover, the questions are in neither order of difficulty nor chronological order. And while line references in the questions can make finding answers easier, it's not unusual to have passages with few line reference questions.

There are, however, several consistent factors on each test. The passages are all roughly the same length, and they always come in the same order: Prose Fiction, Social Science, Humanities, and Natural Science. But just because that's ACT's order doesn't mean it has to be yours.

Proven Techniques

PERSONAL ORDER OF DIFFICULTY (POOD)

To get your best score on the Reading test, you have to pick your own order of the passages, and on each passage, your own order of the questions. When time is your enemy, as it is on the ACT, find and work up front what's easier for you. Leave for last, or never, what's difficult for you.

The Passages

You can't risk doing the passages in the order ACT provides *just* because they're in that order. What if the Natural Science passage turned out to be the easiest and you ran out of time before you could get to it?

Every time you take the ACT, for practice and for real, pick the order of the passages that makes sense for you. There are four issues to consider when picking your order. In practice, you may build up a track record to determine a typical order. But pay attention to the particulars of each test and be willing to adapt your order.

1. Your POOD

Use your own POOD to identify the genres and topics you like best. For example, do you rarely read fiction outside of school? Then the Prose Fiction is unlikely to be a smart choice to do first. The topics, however, may change your mind. Read the blurbs to see if that day's Social Science, for example, is a topic you know more about than, say the topic of the Humanities.

2. Paragraphs

The passages are all roughly the same length, but how they're arranged in paragraphs will differ. It's much easier to find answers on a passage with more, smaller paragraphs than on a passage with just a few huge paragraphs. Look for passages with six to eight decent-sized paragraphs.

3. Questions

ACT can be pretty cheap with line references, so the more questions with line references the better. Glance at the questions: Do you see many with numbers? That's a great sign.

4. Answers

Difficult questions tend to need longer answers. So look for many questions with short answers. Just like with line references, the more the better.

Be Flexible and Ruthless

Picking your order isn't a long, deliberative process. Use the practice tests in Chapters 10, 12, 14, and 16 to determine a typical order, but always be prepared to adapt. Take 10 seconds at the start of every ACT to look at the topics, paragraphs, questions, and answers to confirm or adapt your order.

Need More Practice?
1,296 ACT Practice Questions provides 6 tests' worth of Reading passages. That's 24 passages and 240 questions.

The Questions

Same song, different verse. You can't do the questions in the order ACT provides. They're not in order of difficulty, and they're not in chronological order. Instead, think of *Now, Later, Never*. Do Now any question that is either easy to answer OR for which the answer is easy to *find*. Do Later, or perhaps Never, questions that are both difficult to answer AND for which the answers are difficult to find.

1. Easy to Answer

ACT describes the questions in two categories: those that ask you to *refer* to what is directly stated, and those that require you to *reason* an implied meaning. In other words, reference questions ask what does the author *say*, while the reasoning questions ask what does the author *mean*. It's easier to answer "what does the author say?" than to answer "what is the author *really* saying?"

2. Easy to Find the Answer

A question easy to answer may do you no good if you can't find the answer in the passage. On the other hand, a reasoning question with a line reference tells you exactly where you can find the answer. Even if it's a tougher question to answer, do it Now if you know where to find the answer.

In a perfect world, we'd give you an exact order to follow every time. The ACT is not a perfect world. Instead, you have to consider the particulars of each test and know how to make an order that works on that test.

PACING

With just 35 minutes to do 4 passages and 40 questions, you don't have even 9 minutes for every passage. But should you do all 4 passages? Think about the pacing chart we discussed in Chapter 1. You may hit your scoring goals if you take more time and if you do fewer passages. On the other hand, you may decide that you can't get all of the questions right no matter how much time you spend. In that case, you're better off getting to as many Now questions as you can.

35 ÷ 4 ≠ 36

Whichever pacing strategy works for you, don't treat all the passages you work equally. That is, even if you work all 4, you shouldn't spend 8.75 minutes on each. Spend more time on your best passages and spend less on your worst. For example, spend 12 minutes on your first passage, 10 minutes on your second, 8 minutes on your third, and 5 minutes on your last. This is just an example: practice, practice, and practice to figure out a pacing strategy that will reach your target score.

POE

Many students destroy their pacing with one particular bad habit on the Reading test: They keep rereading and rereading part of the passage, trying to understand the answer to a tough question. But you're ignoring the one advantage of a multiple-choice test: The correct answer is right on the page. Use POE to eliminate three wrong answers to find the correct answer. It's not always easy to answer these questions, but you will likely be able to spot at least one wrong answer. In fact, using POE is a crucial step of our 4-step Basic Approach.

Now that you know how to pick your order of the passages, it's time to learn the Basic Approach.

THE BASIC APPROACH

The Reading test is an open-book test. You wouldn't read a whole book and answer all the questions from memory, so you shouldn't do that on the ACT. Instead, you need a smart, effective strategy.

Step 1: Preview

This step involves two parts.

First, check the blurb to see if there is additional information other than the title, author, and copyright. There usually isn't, but occasionally there is. You have to check each time to see if this one time is the exception.

> **HUMANITIES:** This passage is taken from *The Century* by Peter Jennings (© 1998 by ABC Television Network Group).

Second, map the questions. Put a star next to each line or paragraph reference, and underline the lead words. By lead words we mean words you'll actually find in the passage. Don't underline generic words like "main idea" or "how the author would characterize."

Here are ten mapped questions.

21. One of the main points the author formulates is that:

☆ **22.** The author mentions a "photographic motion study" (line 36) in order to emphasize what quality of <u>Duchamp's *Nude*</u>?

☆ **23.** The first paragraph states that certain early <u>critics of modern art</u>:

☆ **24.** It can be inferred from the author's reference to "an explosion" and "an earthquake" (lines 38–40) that <u>Duchamp's *Nude*</u>:

☆ **25.** As it is used in line 42, the word *abhorrent* most nearly means:

26. It can be reasonably concluded from the passage that the most important characteristic of <u>"modern" art</u> was that it was:

27. Which of the following best describes <u>Roosevelt's reaction to modern art</u>?

☆ **28.** It can reasonably be inferred that the use of the words "Ellis Island" (line 17) indicated that:

☆ **29.** It can be inferred from the last paragraph that the <u>organizers of the Armory Show</u>:

30. Which of the following is NOT answered by the passage?

Spend no more than 30 seconds mapping the questions. Do not read the questions thoroughly for comprehension at this stage. Just spot the line and paragraph references to star and the lead words to underline.

Do look at the lead words you've underlined, however. They telegraph the main idea before you've read one word of the passage: This passage is about modern art.

Step 2: Work the Passage

In this next step, spend no more than 3 minutes on the passage. Look for and underline your lead words. If you struggle with time, read only the first sentence of each paragraph. You'll read what you need to answer specific questions.

Here are the first sentences of each paragraph to our passage, with the lead words from some questions found and underlined.

> The show was grandly titled "The International Exhibition of <u>Modern Art</u>," but the dynamite, as *The New Yorker* later commented, was in the word <u>"modern."</u>

> The star image of the exhibition was most certainly <u>Duchamp's *Nude Descending a Staircase*</u> (or, as <u>Roosevelt</u> called it, "a naked man going downstairs"), a painting so abstract it defied its own title, which, of course, was the point.

> <u>Roosevelt said Duchamp's *Nude*</u> reminded him of a Navaho rug he stood upon while shaving each morning in his bathroom.

> Anticipating a reluctant audience, the <u>organizers of the Armory Show</u> had included an editorial in the exhibition catalog urging viewers to greet the new art with an open mind.

Between the stars and the lead words you found in the first sentences of the paragraphs, you have a lot of questions whose answers are easy to find, and you're ready to move on to the next step.

Step 3: Work the Questions

Work the questions in an order that makes sense: Do Now the questions that are easy to answer or whose answers are easy to find. Look at all the stars on questions 22, 23, 24, 25, 28, and 29. You know where to read to find those answers. But when you worked the passage, you found the locations for questions 26 and 27.

Do Later, or Never, questions that are both difficult to answer and whose answers are difficult to find. Questions 21 and 30 are both good Later/Never questions.

As you make your way through the Now questions, read a window of five to ten lines to find the answer.

Here's an example.

---

22. The author mentions a "photographic motion study" (line 36) in order to emphasize what quality of Duchamp's *Nude*?

Now read lines 27–37 to find the answer.

> The star image of the exhibition was most certainly
> Duchamp's *Nude Descending a Staircase* (or, as Roosevelt
> called it, "a naked man going downstairs"), a painting so
> 30 abstract it defied its own title, which, of course, was the point.
> As critic Robert Hughes has pointed out, the nude had a long
> and distinguished history with painting, where she (and, more
> rarely, he) was usually portrayed in a blissful state of recline;
> by contrast, Duchamp's *Nude*, to the degree that it looked at
> 35 all like what it was supposed to be, was a nude on the move
> (indeed, the painting had the quality of a photographic motion
> study), a metaphor for the change that it heralded.

You may feel you've spotted the exact line with the answer, but don't worry if you haven't. Move to the last step, and Work the Answers with POE.

Step 4: Work the Answers

If you can answer the question in your own words, go through the answers and look for a match. If you can't answer it, don't worry. Review each answer, and eliminate the ones you're confident are wrong.

F. The different interpretations of the painting
G. The painting's photographic realism
H. The painting's inappropriate subject matter
J. The movement implied in the painting

Here's How to Crack It

Lines 35–37 describe the painting as *a nude on the move*, which choice (J) paraphrases well. Alternatively, use POE to get rid of choice (F), because there is only one interpretation of the painting, and choice (H), because there is no proof that the author disapproves of the subject matter. Choice (G) may tempt you because of *to the degree that it looked at all like what it was supposed to be* in lines 34–35, but those lines actually argue against photographic realism.

Repeat

Steps 3 and 4 repeat: Make your way through the rest of the questions, reading what you need for each. Use POE to find the answers. Continue to make smart choices about the order of your questions, doing Now every question that is easy to answer or whose answer is easy to find.

Save for Last

The toughest reasoning questions should be done last (if at all—your pacing strategy may mark them as Never). After you've worked all the specific questions on the passage, you understand the main theme better. Questions 21 and 30 for this passage are both smart choices to do last.

Now move to Chapter 11 to practice picking your order and applying the Basic Approach.

Summary

o   Pick your order of the passages.

o   Use your POOD to identify the genres and topics you like best.

o   Pay attention to your track record in practice.

o   Examine the particulars of each test and be prepared to confirm or change your order each time.

o   Look for passages with many, small paragraphs.

o   Look for passages with many line reference questions.

o   Look for passages with many short answers.

o   Use the 4-step Basic Approach.
    1.   Preview
    2.   Work the Passage
    3.   Work the Questions
    4.   Work the Answers

Chapter 20
Reading Practice
Test 1

READING TEST

35 Minutes—40 Questions

DIRECTIONS: There are four passages in this test. Each passage is followed by several questions. After reading each passage, choose the best answer to each question and blacken the corresponding oval on your answer document. You may refer to the passages as often as necessary.

Passage I

PROSE FICTION: The following passage is adapted from the short story "Between Two Homes" by Herbert Malloy (© 1993 by Herbert Malloy).

The fact that air travel allows me to fall asleep on the west coast and wake up on the east coast is bittersweet magic. On a red-eye flight, the continent passes stealthily underneath like an ugly secret we prefer not to acknowledge. Passengers drift
5 in and out of an unsteady slumber, reluctantly awakening to the realization that they are still stuck on an airplane. Sometimes I open my eyes wide enough to gaze out the window at the twinkling lights of the towns and cities below.

I try to decipher which city glimmers below from the size
10 of its grid of light, as well as my perception of how long I have been flying. Could that be Denver? Have I already napped a third of the flight? I look around the cabin to see how many other people are having trouble sleeping and become instantly jealous of the families and couples who have the luxury of
15 leaning on each other.

The aura of cool sunlight begins to infiltrate the cabin as we near Dulles, Virginia. We see flocks of birds sharing the sky with us. By the time we arrive, we will have flown through three time zones, compressing a normal night by removing three of
20 its sacred hours. We are not only cheating space by crossing a continent in the course of a long nap, but also cheating time by turning back our watches and rushing prematurely toward the sunrise.

My hometown is still a car ride away, but the vicinity of
25 the airport is close enough to be a tonic to my nostalgic yearnings. As soon as I see the dense stands of oak and hickory blanketing the hills, I know I am back home. There's no trace of palm trees, no unrelenting flat stretches of compacted and perpendicular city streets. Left behind in our plane's exhaust,
30 Southern California is still fast asleep.

*   *   *   *   *   *

My dad has driven to the airport to pick me up, but I very nearly miss him—I'd forgotten he now drives a different car. I'm sure I've heard him speak of his new blue Toyota, but I always expect him to be driving the brown Lexus he owned
35 when I moved away. Happily, the smell inside the car remains the same: stretched leather, cologne, and the faint hint of a cigarette that was meant to go undetected. I covertly scan the

side of his face while he drives, hoping to see the same face I remember. Instead I see new wrinkles, new spots on his face,
40 new folds of skin on his neck.

We pass by familiar landmarks as we near our house, as well as some not-so-familiar ones. The performance stage in the town center that was merely a proposal when I left is now up-and-running, according to the marquee listing its upcom-
45 ing shows. The Olde Towne Tavern is apparently now called Summit Station. The old dance studio above the apartment buildings on West Deer Park seems to have finally closed — I always wondered how it stayed in business. The cluster of shops that famously burned to the ground near the high school
50 has open doors and cars gliding in and out of the parking lot.

We've arrived at the house, and as soon as I walk through the door, I am flooded with further reminders of my absence — trinkets on the wall I don't recognize, rearranged furniture in the kitchen and living room, sugary cereals and snacks strangely
55 absent from the top of the fridge. What was once my home has become someone else's house — my parents' house.

I suddenly see the mundane routines of my parents cast in a tragic light: my mother's agitation at the grackles that scare the goldfinches away from the bird-feeders, my father's habit
60 of pretending to read the newspaper on the porch (just an opportunity to keep an eye on the neighborhood), the uninspired television they watch at night, often in separate rooms, and, most depressingly, the way they often fall asleep in front of the television, mouths gaping.

*   *   *   *   *   *

65 The in-flight movie on the way back to California portrays the story of a physicist who awakens after spending ten years in a coma. His initial joy gradually subsides and ultimately leads to confusion and sadness as he attempts to reintegrate into a world that has moved on without him. Even science, that rock
70 of immutable truths, has changed in his absence. He finds the entire body of research he had been working on prior to his coma now obsolete—years of advances in his field had furnished the answers he was pursuing.

As a physicist, he knew that time is a relative phenomenon,
75 a concept that only has meaning in relation to an individual's succession of experiences and ordering of memories. Clearly, though, his world, like mine, had continued to age, changing despite his lack of participation in it. Years are passing whether you're there to observe them or not.

1. It can reasonably be inferred from the passage that the narrator thinks air travel is:

   A. the most enjoyable way to travel.
   B. an ordinary part of the world.
   C. more uncomfortable than convenient.
   D. somewhat unnatural in what it makes possible.

2. The first three paragraphs (lines 1–23) establish all of the following about the narrator EXCEPT that he is:

   F. onboard an airplane
   G. traveling east.
   H. departing from Denver.
   J. noticing sights below.

3. The point of view from which the passage is told is best described as that of:

   A. a young adult returning from a vacation to Southern California.
   B. an adult relating his reactions to visiting to his hometown.
   C. a young adult awakening from a long coma.
   D. an adult who prefers Southern California to his new home.

4. According to the narrator, which of the following things is relatively new to his parents' house?

   F. Certain trinkets on the wall
   G. The fridge
   H. His father's brown Lexus
   J. The bird-feeders

5. The passage contains recurring references to all of the following EXCEPT:

   A. difficulty sleeping.
   B. birds.
   C. grids of light.
   D. dancing.

6. The narrator indicates that the most upsetting habit of his parents is:

   F. buying new cars.
   G. how and where they fall asleep.
   H. what they watch on television.
   J. how many trinkets they buy.

7. According to the passage, the coma victim has a sense of time as a relative phenomenon because:

   A. ten years had gone by quickly.
   B. he was a physicist.
   C. it was a side effect of his medical treatments.
   D. it was the focus of his research before his coma.

8. Based on the narrator's account, all of the following are part of the present, rather than the past, in his hometown EXCEPT:

   F. the closed dance studio.
   G. the upcoming show marquee.
   H. Summit Station.
   J. the burnt remains of a shopping center.

9. Details in the passage most strongly suggest that one characteristic of the narrator's hometown is:

   A. flat stretches.
   B. palm trees.
   C. oak trees.
   D. perpendicular streets.

10. When the narrator refers to science as "that rock of immutable truths" (lines 69–70), he is most likely directly referring to:

   F. the unchanging nature believed to be characteristic of scientific knowledge.
   G. the physicist's inability to understand the recent advances in science.
   H. the body of research conducted in the physicist's field during his coma.
   J. the ten years' worth of scientific advances that the narrator had missed.

Passage II

SOCIAL SCIENCE: The following passage is adapted from the 2002 article "Indigenous Goes Global" by Sally Mayfield.

MayaWorks is a nonprofit organization that attempts to promote fair trade practices with Mayan artisans who would otherwise have little commercial outlet for their talents. In a broader sense, the organization aims to help traditionally
5 marginalized Guatemalan women attain the literacy, advanced skills, business acumen, and confidence they need to contribute to the economic well-being of their families.

"Buried deep in the Guatemalan mountains are these amazing pockets of Mayan communities," begins Dennis Ho-
10 gan, a chief program administrator for Berhorst Partners for Development. Communities such as Agua Caliente, Xetonox, and Tzanjuyu are often as small as 50–100 people. They speak their own ancient Mayan dialects and rarely interact with the Spanish-speaking majority of Guatemala. "They have a rich
15 lineage of religious, linguistic, and artistic traditions that get passed down from generation to generation. However, they are deeply threatened by extreme poverty and lack of potable water. We want to find a way for these women to grow with the times, despite rigidly-defined gender roles that relegate women to food
20 preparation and child care, but also to help them utilize and preserve the cultural traditions that make them so irreplaceable."

When representatives from MayaWorks first reached out to women in Agua Caliente in 1994, the men of the village were deeply suspicious. The women were extremely shy, avoiding
25 almost all eye contact with the strangers. Ultimately, though, the women of the village agreed to the idea of forming a weaving cooperative and came up with an initial product order they felt they could fill. Each of eight women was to weave a dozen brightly colored wall hangings that spelled the word "peace"
30 in a number of languages. Weeks later, with great pride, the women delivered their order, using local material for the hanging rods and the finest yarn they could find, dyed and then washed to prevent staining.

"When we returned to pick up the finished products and
35 pay them, there was a remarkable change in the way we were received by the villagers," Hogan reflects with deep satisfaction. "The women were beaming with self-confidence, and the children even thanked us in their native tongue for helping give their mothers work."

40 The variety of wares created by MayaWorks artisans has greatly expanded over time. Corn husks are used to make decorative angels. Yarn is woven into brightly-colored placemats, napkins, pouches, Beanies, and footbags. Some groups even make religious items, such as stoles for Christian priests
45 and yarmulkes, or kippahs, for Jewish observers. Making the kippahs was initially an engineering challenge for the villagers, as the small head-coverings frequently came out either too flat or too round. Given a mannequin, however, the villagers were soon able to master the correct shape. Once told that the kippah

50 was a symbol for the wearer's reverence to God, the villagers became even more devoted and loving in their craft.

The capacity of these artisans for learning, adapting, and innovating has delighted the founders of MayaWorks. As relationships develop between MayaWorks and individual groups of
55 artisans, new equipment and training is introduced to broaden their design capacity. 36-inch treadle-foot looms now allow members of Xetonox to create fabrics that can be sold by the yard side-by-side with mass-manufactured textiles.

In addition to broadening the range of products these vil-
60 lagers can create, MayaWorks hopes to expand the knowledge base of the women and help provide infrastructure to enable a better life for them and future generations. Leslie Buchanan heads up the Literacy Initiative for MayaWorks and explains, "Part of the challenge these communities face is their cultural
65 isolation from other Guatemalans. They avoid going to marketplaces in nearby cities because they don't speak Spanish. That makes it difficult for them to navigate the buses and other transportation. And it makes it hard to negotiate with Spanish-speaking merchants. In an economy where the first price you
70 hear is never supposed to be the final price, the inability to haggle makes you unfit to make purchases."

Although literacy programs provided by outsiders are typically met with resistance by Mayan communities, MayaWorks has achieved considerable success in motivating Mayan villag-
75 ers to learn Spanish. This success where others have failed has more to do with the economic initiatives of MayaWorks than its literacy campaigns: once the villagers have the opportunity and means to expand their economic base, the desire to learn Spanish comes naturally, from within, as a tool to help them
80 achieve even greater success. Rather than appearing as a threat to their traditions, the Spanish language now appears as a means of preserving the well-being of their traditional communities.

Another component of MayaWorks is coordinating and encouraging the financing of microcredit loans, small loans
85 offered to impoverished people who have no collateral or credit history (and thus could never qualify for a traditional banking loan). By providing these Mayan villagers with much-needed capital, MayaWorks helps them to upgrade their weaving equipment, install water pumps (which greatly reduces the
90 health problems associated with meager and contaminated water sources), and buy crops such as blackberries, potatoes, and strawberries. These measures both increase the sustainability of the community and encourage entrepreneurship. So far, MayaWorks reports, 100% of their microcredit loans have
95 been paid back in full and on time.

11. In the context of the passage, the statement "the men of the village were deeply suspicious" (lines 23–24) most nearly suggests that Mayan men:

A. felt uneasy about the potential interest in employing their village's women.
B. didn't believe that MayaWorks representatives were who they said they were.
C. rarely were visited by people who could speak Spanish.
D. were skeptical that the women of the village had artistic talents.

12. The main purpose of the second paragraph (lines 8–21) is to:

F. lend support to the notion that women in Guatemala deserve stronger legal rights.
G. point out the small number of people who live in Amazon villages.
H. establish the value that programs such as MayaWorks could provide.
J. explain how Berhorst Partners for Development became based in Guatemala.

13. The passage indicates all of the following as problems initially faced by the fledgling Mayan artisans EXCEPT that:

A. they lacked a mannequin to facilitate designing head-wear.
B. they could not communicate well in Spanish-speaking marketplaces.
C. they did not have looms capable of making yard-width fabrics.
D. they were unable to find material for the hanging rods in their wall hangings.

14. It can most reasonably be inferred from the passage that regarding MayaWorks, the author feels:

F. appreciative of the organization's methods and intentions.
G. convinced that mountain villagers in other countries will join MayaWorks.
H. doubtful about the quality of the artisans' wares.
J. confused by the organization's conflicting priorities.

15. Which of the following assumptions would be most critical for a reader to accept in order to agree with the author's claims in the passage?

A. Mayan communities should fully assimilate into their surrounding Spanish-speaking communities.
B. One's self-esteem can be improved by performing productive work in exchange for money.
C. Mayan artisans have much difficulty in adapting to design specifications of items that are not traditionally Mayan.
D. Most major banks would consider the Mayan artist co-operatives to be appealing candidates for loans.

16. The passage indicates that approximately how many wall hangings were part of the initial order filled by the Agua Caliente village?

F. Eight
G. A dozen
H. One hundred
J. One thousand

17. According to the passage, when villagers were told of the religious function of a kippah, they became even more:

A. confused about its shape.
B. appreciative of their mannequin.
C. intrigued about Judaism.
D. dedicated to their work.

18. The passage states that each of the following is among the products made by MayaWorks artists EXCEPT:

F. yarmulkes.
G. wall hangings.
H. mass-manufactured textiles.
J. placemats.

19. The main function of the last paragraph (lines 83–95) is to:

A. discuss the specific terms and requirements of several types of loans.
B. describe some important ways that outside investment has helped strengthen Mayan communities.
C. itemize some of the ways Mayan artisans have reinvested their earnings.
D. demonstrate that Mayan villagers are as trustworthy in business as they are skilled in art.

20. The passage indicates that the efforts of MayaWorks to increase the Spanish literacy of the Mayan community may succeed because they:

F. have instilled in the Mayan women an economic incentive to learn Spanish.
G. have familiarized Mayan women with the bartering rules of Guatemalan marketplaces.
H. convinced Mayan women that their traditions will be better preserved in Spanish.
J. designed a more innovative and thoughtful literacy campaign than had previous initiatives.

Passage III

HUMANITIES: This passage is adapted from the article "Life in the Pits" by Bob Gullberg (© 2003 by Hennen Press).

Mozart and Handel refer to Wolfgang Amadeus Mozart (1756-91), Classical-era composer, and George Frideric Handel (1685-1759), Baroque-era composer.

Looking back over a twenty-year career of playing, composing, and now conducting orchestra music, I often feel a sense of wonder—not at what I have accomplished, but how someone with my agrarian, rather workaday upbringing should
5 have chosen such a path at all. It would have been easy for me to stay on the family farm, eventually to become part-owner, as my brother did quite successfully. However, rewarding as this existence was, it was somehow unfulfilling; my youthful imagination, much to my parents' dismay, often cast about for
10 other, greater pursuits to occupy it. Still, growing up as I did in a household where the radio dispensed milk prices instead of Mozart and hog futures instead of Handel, the thought of embarking on a career in classical music went beyond even my wildest imagination.

15 Perhaps what started me down this unforeseen path was my fascination with other languages. At church services I would hear snippets of Latin and Greek; I was learning Spanish at school; I was instantly drawn to the German, Italian, and Yiddish words and phrases I heard in movies and on TV.
20 Surrounded as I was by the fairly common language of farm and field, these "glamorous" expressions seemed to fill a void in me, and I collected them with the energy of a lepidopterist netting butterflies. As my interest in other languages grew, so did my awareness that music is itself a language, just as capable
25 of expressing and inspiring emotion or thought as the spoken word—sometimes even more so. Take The Tempest, the piece I'm currently rehearsing with my orchestra. It begins in a major key, with just the stringed instruments playing lightly, evoking a sense of peace and contentment—a calm, sunny summer's
30 day. In the second movement, the key diminishes; the mood darkens—clouds and apprehension are building. As the piece progresses, wind instruments, as if blown by the storm, begin to howl, horns blare and shout, overwhelming the senses, thrilling and frightening at once. As the "storm" reaches its height,
35 timpani-roll thunder echoes, and cymbal-clash lightning bolts crash relentlessly, until, when it becomes almost unbearable, the music eases, hope and reason are restored, and soothing notes help the listener forget the chaos and fear he or she felt only moments ago. I've read many accounts of severe weather,
40 even seen them in movies and on TV, but few of them, if any, have been able to replicate not only the sensory experience of a thunderstorm, but also the emotional one the way this piece of music can.

I believe it was music's emotive influence—particularly
45 powerful in my impressionable youth—that ultimately led me to pursue a career in music. Once I began to experience music on an emotional level, I remember having the feeling that others just didn't "get it" like I did, as if somehow music were meant just for musicians. It was only later that I became
50 aware of music's true value—it is a universal language, able to speak to all people, regardless of the linguistic differences that may exist between them. Eventually, of course, music began to eclipse the numerous other "passions" I had throughout my adolescence. Years before I began to pursue music in earnest,
55 I had developed quite an interest in all things motorized. I've always had a mechanical bent (which has served me well in later life, allowing me to turn my hand to almost any musical instrument), and being around farm equipment from an early age certainly gave me an outlet to exercise my abilities. How-
60 ever, my real focus was on cars—I virtually never set down *Automobile Monthly*, a magazine for auto enthusiasts, and I eagerly devoured articles describing which models had the highest horsepower or quickest times in the quarter-mile, and effortlessly committing that information to memory. Eventu-
65 ally, though, like my previous infatuations with archery, and before that dinosaurs, my fixation on cars was to take a "back seat" to a new, greater, and this time lasting, passion for music.

So what made the difference? What made my passion for music continue to burn where other passions had fizzled out?
70 Maturity, perhaps—I know I'd like to think that's the case—or maybe it was just a process of compare-and-contrast; trying different things until I found the one that "fit." If I'm honest with myself, however, I'm forced to admit the answer isn't a "what" or "when," but a "who." For me, like many who find
75 themselves adrift on a sea of uncertainty, it took a mentor to help me find my way to dry land. In my case, that mentor was the conductor of my high-school orchestra, Ms. Fenchurch. A woman of boundless energy and enthusiasm, and with an all-consuming love for music, it was she who first taught me the
80 joy of composition and creation, and helped me to realize that making music is more than just playing notes in a particular order, no matter how well it's done—it's about expression, and perhaps more important, communication. Just like a language.

21. The author mentions *Automobile Monthly* and his mechanical bent primarily to suggest that his:

A. infatuation with cars was at one time as intense as his passion for music.

B. interest in and love of all things motorized has remained unchanged throughout his life.

C. experience with motorized things accounts for his mechanical style of playing music.

D. obsession with automotive knowledge distracted him from focusing on music.

22. In the first paragraph, the author most nearly characterizes his upbringing as:

  F. easy and usually spent working with his brother.
  G. frustrating yet able to translate easily into music.
  G. somewhat satisfying yet ultimately unable to captivate.
  J. unfulfilling and invariably resulting in his parents' approval.

23. Based on the passage, which of the following was most likely the first to engage the author's passionate interest?

  A. Automobiles
  B. Archery
  C. Dinosaurs
  D. Music

24. Viewed in the context of the passage, the statement in lines 39–43 is most likely intended to suggest that:

  F. music more vividly conveys some experiences than do visual or written accounts.
  G. movies can provide a misleading experience of what a thunderstorm is like.
  H. news reports should more accurately reflect emotional experiences.
  J. thunderstorms are among the hardest experiences to accurately replicate.

25. The passage suggests that the lepidopterist netting butterflies represents:

  A. the author as a child, relishing learning foreign expressions.
  B. the author presently, enjoying his most recent passion.
  C. Ms. Fenchurch, with her boundless energy.
  D. the opening movement of The Tempest.

26. In the context of the passage, lines 34–39 are best described as presenting images of:

  F. jealously, mercy, and resentment.
  G. hate, fear, and disbelief.
  H. conflict, optimism, and love.
  J. chaos, resolution, and relaxation.

27. The author discusses "playing notes in a particular order" (lines 81–82) as part of Ms. Fenchurch's argument that:

  A. the order of notes matters less than the speed at which they are played.
  B. all music consists of the same parts but rearranged in creative ways.
  C. while one aims to be skilled at performing notes, one should also aim to convey their meaning.
  D. although communication is important, there is more joy to be found in composition itself.

28. Which of the following does NOT reasonably describe a transition presented by the author in lines 27–34?

  F. Lightness to darkness
  G. Calm to thrilling
  H. Apprehension to fright
  J. Overwhelmed to peaceful

29. The main purpose of the last paragraph is to:

  A. describe the lasting influence of Ms. Fenchurch's encouragement.
  B. present an anecdote that conveys Ms. Fenchurch's unique conducting style.
  C. provide detailed background information about Ms. Fenchurch.
  D. illustrate the effect music has on teachers such as Ms. Fenchurch.

30. The passage is best described as being told from the point of view of a musician who is:

  F. telling a linear story that connects momentous events from the beginning of his career to some from the end.
  G. describing how modern works of music such as The Tempest have advanced the vision of classical composers such as Mozart and Handel.
  H. suggesting that people who have an interest in universal languages would be well served in studying music.
  J. marveling at his eventual choice of career and considering the people and interests that contributed to it.

Passage IV

NATURAL SCIENCE: This passage is adapted from the article "Debunking the Seahorse" by Clark Millingham (© 2002 by Halcyon Press).

Scientists and laymen alike have long been fascinated by fish known colloquially as seahorses, due to the species' remarkable appearance, unusual mating habits, and incredibly rare reversal of male and female parental roles. The scientific
5 name for the genus is Hippocampus, which combines the Greek word for "horse," *hippos*, with the Greek word for "sea monster," *kampos*. Its distinctive equine head and tapered body shape are a great disadvantage when it comes to the seahorse's swimming ability. It manages to maneuver about by fluttering
10 its dorsal fin up to 35 times a second, but it lacks the caudal, or "tail" fin, which provides the powerful forward thrust for most fish. Instead of swimming to find food, the seahorse coils its signature prehensile tail around stationary objects while using its long snout like a straw to suck in vast numbers of
15 tiny larvae, plankton, and algae. Because the seahorse lacks teeth and a stomach, food passes quickly through its digestive tract, resulting in the need for nearly incessant consumption of food (a typical seahorse can ingest more than 3,000 brine shrimp per day).

20 The peculiar physical features of the seahorse are intriguing, but its mating and reproductive habits are most often the subject of scientists' fascination and debate. Seahorses' courtship rituals often involve a male and a female coordinating their movements, swimming side by side with tails intertwined or coiling around
25 the same strand of sea grass and spinning around it together. They even "dress up" for these rituals, turning a whole array of vivid colors—a sharp contrast to the dull browns and grays with which they typically camouflage themselves among the sea grasses. Courtship typically lasts about two weeks, during
30 which the female and her potential mate will meet once a day, while other males continue to compete for the female's attention, snapping their heads at each other and tail-wrestling.

By the end of the courtship, the female has become engorged with a clutch of around 1,000 eggs, equivalent in mass to one-
35 third her body weight. It is the male, however, who possesses the incubating organ for the eggs, a brood pouch located on his ventral (front) side. The male forces sea water through the pouch to open it up, signifying his readiness to receive the eggs. Uncoiling their tail-grips, the two attach to each other and begin
40 a spiraling ascent towards the surface. The female inserts her ovipositor, a specialized biological apparatus for conducting the eggs into the male's pouch, and the eggs are transferred over the course of eight or nine hours. After that, the male stays put while the female ventures off, only to check in briefly once a
45 day for the next few weeks.

Inside the male's brood pouch, the eggs are fertilized and receive prolactin, the same hormone mammals use for milk production. The pouch delivers oxygen to the eggs via a network of capillaries and regulates a low-salinity environment. As the
50 gestation continues, the eggs hatch and the pouch becomes increasingly saline to help acclimate the young seahorses to the salt water that is waiting outside. The male typically gives birth at night, expelling anywhere from 100 to 1,500 live fry from its pouch. By morning, he once again has an empty pouch
55 to offer his partner if she is ready to mate again.

Because male parenting is such a rarity in the animal kingdom, and male gestation almost unheard-of, scientists often speculate on why male seahorses assume birthing duties. Since giving birth is so energy-intensive and physically limiting,
60 it greatly increases one's risk of death and therefore needs an explanation in terms of evolutionary cost. Bateman's principle holds that whichever sex expends less energy in the reproductive process should be the sex that spends more energy competing for a mate. Only with seahorses do we see the males both
65 compete for mates and give birth. A study conducted by Pierre Robinson at the University of Tallahassee argued that, contrary to appearances, the total energy investment of the mother in growing the clutch of eggs inside of her still outweighed the energy investment of the male in the incubation and birthing
70 process. Male oxygen intake rates go up by 33% during their parental involvement, while the female spends twice as much energy when generating eggs.

In addition to male pregnancy, seahorses also have the distinction of being one of a very small number of monoga-
75 mous species. Scientists believe this is due to the tremendous investment of time and energy that goes into each clutch of eggs a female produces. If her eggs are ready to be incubated and the female does not have a trustworthy male partner ready to receive them, they will be expelled into the ocean and months
80 will have been lost. Additionally, by transferring incubation and birthing duties to the male, a stable monogamous couple can develop an efficient birthing cycle in which he incubates one clutch of eggs while the female begins generating the next.

31. The passage notes that the courtship rituals of seahorses include:

   A. males snapping their heads at females.
   B. camouflaging their body coloring.
   C. allowing sea water to open the brood pouch.
   D. daily meetings for two weeks.

32. The passage states that the seahorse's swimming ability is hindered by its:

   F. tapered body shape.
   G. weak caudal fin.
   H. fluttering dorsal fin.
   J. lack of teeth.

33. Which of the following pieces of information does the most to resolve scientists' confusion as to why male seahorses both compete for mates and give birth?

   A. The fact that the female seahorse possesses an ovipositor
   B. Pierre Robinson's research on the total energy investment of each sex
   C. The habit of seahorses to mate with only one partner
   D. The length of time male seahorses devote to courtship rituals

34. One of the main ideas established by the passage is that:

   F. seahorses are actually quite capable swimmers, despite their unusual appearance.
   G. scientists cannot come up with any coherent explanation for why male seahorses have the evolutionary burden of gestation.
   H. the brood pouch of the male is located on its ventral side.
   J. it is not customary in the animal kingdom for animals to keep the same mating partner for life.

35. As it is used in line 13, the word *signature* most nearly means:

   A. distinctive-looking.
   B. very useful.
   C. autograph.
   D. legally obligated.

36. The main purpose of the fourth paragraph (lines 46–55) is to describe the:

   F. process linking fertilization to hatching.
   G. intricacies of the seahorse's capillary network.
   H. quantity of fry to which males give birth.
   J. amount of salinity seahorse eggs can tolerate.

37. The passage most strongly emphasizes that the monogamy of seahorse mates is most advantageous for the transition from:

   A. low-salinity to high-salinity.
   B. one birthing cycle to the next.
   C. fertilization to incubation.
   D. courtship to mating.

38. As it is used in line 80, the word *lost* most nearly means:

   F. mislaid.
   G. disoriented.
   H. squandered.
   J. defeated.

39. According to the passage, which of the following aspects of a male seahorse's pregnancy provides the best evidence that the seahorse species conforms to the idea behind Bateman's Principle?

   A. Brood pouch
   B. Ovipositor
   C. Prolactin
   D. Oxygen intake

40. The passage indicates that the brood pouch becomes increasingly saline because seahorse eggs:

   F. would otherwise run the risk of prematurely hatching.
   G. begin gestation in a low salinity environment but ultimately get released into the surrounding water.
   H. have salt extracted from them by the capillary network that delivers oxygen to the brood pouch.
   J. receive the hormone prolactin but do not have the exposure to salt that other mammals do.

END OF TEST 3
STOP! DO NOT TURN THE PAGE UNTIL TOLD TO DO SO.
DO NOT RETURN TO A PREVIOUS TEST.

Chapter 21
Reading Practice
Test 1: Answers and
Explanations

READING PRACTICE TEST 1 ANSWERS

1.	D	21.	A
2.	H	22.	H
3.	B	23.	C
4.	F	24.	F
5.	D	25.	A
6.	G	26.	J
7.	B	27.	C
8.	J	28.	J
9.	C	29.	A
10.	F	30.	J
11.	A	31.	D
12.	H	32.	F
13.	D	33.	B
14.	F	34.	J
15.	B	35.	A
16.	H	36.	F
17.	D	37.	B
18.	H	38.	H
19.	B	39.	D
20.	F	40.	G

SCORE YOUR PRACTICE TEST

Step A
Count the number of correct answers: _____. This is your *raw score*.

Step B
Use the score conversion table below to look up your raw score. The number to the left is your *scale score*: _____.

Reading Scale Conversion Table

Scale Score	Raw Score	Scale Score	Raw Score	Scale Score	Raw Score
36	40	27	30	18	18
35	39	26	29	17	16–17
34	38	25	27–28	16	15
33	37	24	26	15	14
32	36	23	24–25	14	12–13
31	35	22	23	13	11
30	34	21	22	12	9–10
29	32–33	20	20–21	11	8
28	31	19	19	10	6–7

READING PRACTICE TEST 1 EXPLANATIONS

Passage I

1. **D**   By saying that air travel is *bittersweet magic* (line 2) and that it is *cheating time*, the author is describing it as unnatural. Choice (A) is incorrect because no comparison is being made, and the author mentions some uncomfortable aspects of his flight. Choice (B) is incorrect since the author describes air travel as *magic*. Choice (C) is incorrect because, while the author does mention uncomfortable aspects of flying, he is still taking the flight for the convenience of getting from the west coast to the east coast in the course of a *long nap*.

2. **H**   The narrator is looking for Denver when he thinks the flight is a third of the way through, which means he did not depart from Denver. Choices (F) and (G) are revealed in the very first sentence. Choice (J) is supported by numerous references to estimating city size by the grid of light seen from above.

3. **B**   The passage involves the experiences of someone who has moved out of his parents' house, returns to visit them, and becomes a bit depressed by the changes that have taken place. Choice (A) is incorrect since the passage never mentions a vacation and suggests the narrator has been absent for some time (he doesn't remember what car his father drives). Choice (C) is incorrect because the coma was only involved in an in-flight movie the narrator watches. Choice (D) is incorrect—the narrator's new home is in Southern California.

4. **F**   In line 53 the author states he doesn't recognize the trinkets on the wall—they have been added during his absence. Choices (G), (H), and (J) can all be eliminated: Although the *fridge* (line 55), the *brown Lexus* (line 34), and the *bird-feeders* (line 59), are all mentioned, they are not described as "new."

5. **D**   Although a dance studio is mentioned, there is no mention of dancing. Choices (A) and (C) are both mentioned once in the first and once in the second paragraph. Choice (B) is mentioned in the third and eighth paragraph.

6. **G**   The narrator uses the phrase *most depressingly* to describe the way his parents *often fall asleep in front of the television, mouths gaping* (lines 63–64). Choice (F) is incorrect because, though a new car is mentioned, no habit of buying new cars is ever described. Choice (H) is incorrect because it is not described as the *most* depressing habit. Choice (J) is never discussed as a habit that upsets the narrator.

7. **B**   The passage states that *as a physicist*, the coma victim *knew that time is a relative phenomenon* (line 74), implying a connection between the two ideas. Choices (A), (C), and (D) are not supported by any details in the passage.

8. **J**   The narrator explains that a *cluster of shops famously burned to the ground* (lines 48–49), in the past, but that presently it is back up and running with customers filtering in and out. Choices (F), (G), and (H) are all mentioned in the sixth paragraph as present-day changes to his hometown that the narrator notices.

9. **C** The narrator says that as soon as he sees *dense stands of oak*, he knows he's home. Choices (A), (B), and (D) are details which describe Southern California, which is not the author's hometown.

10. **F** The narrator refers to science as *that rock of immutable truths* as a way to emphasize the physicist's sense of bewilderment—before his coma he had believed scientific truth to be unchanging, but awoke to find his life's work obsolete. Choice (G) is incorrect because there is no support for the physicist's inability to comprehend the scientific advances. Choices (H) and (J) can be eliminated since both refer to the time he spent in a coma, not before.

Passage II

11. **A** The men felt suspicious because, as stated in the previous paragraph, the traditional roles for women in these villages were food preparation and child care. Choice (B) is incorrect because no mention is made of how the representatives introduced themselves or why the men would doubt such an introduction. Choice (C) is incorrect because the passage does not suggest that the strangeness of the MayaWorks representatives was due to their language, but more that it was due to their intention of partnering with the village women. Choice (D) is unsupported by anything in the passage relating to men's estimation of the women's artistic abilities.

12. **H** The content of the second paragraph depicts the problems facing Mayan villagers as well as the *irreplaceable* nature of their heritage, foreshadowing the way in which MayaWorks hopes to modernize and sustain these communities. Choice (F) is unsupported since *legal rights* are never mentioned in the passage. Choice (G) is incorrect because, although the size of Mayan villages is mentioned in this paragraph, it is too narrow a fact to be considered the purpose of the paragraph in relation to the rest of the passage. Choice (J) is incorrect because the passage does not indicate that Berhorst is based in Guatemala, nor is Berhorst an important part of the paragraph in relation to how it functions in the passage.

13. **D** In the third paragraph, it says that the artisans used local materials for the hanging rods. Choice (A) is supported by information in the fifth paragraph, as the artisans worked on kippahs. Choice (B) is supported by information in the seventh paragraph about the complications of not speaking Spanish in a Spanish-speaking marketplace. Choice (C) is supported by information in the sixth paragraph about a 36-inch treadle loom that allowed the artisans to now sell fabric by the yard.

14. **F** While the author writes in a relatively neutral voice, she provides nothing but positive affirmations of what MayaWorks intends to do and what its partnerships have accomplished. Choice (G) is unsupported because the author doesn't discuss whether people in other countries will join MayaWorks. Choice (H) is unsupported because the author never questions the quality of the Mayan commodities. In fact, she mentions at one point that the artisans use the finest yarn they can find. Choice (J) is incorrect because, although MayaWorks has several objectives in mind, they are never indicated to be in conflict with each other.

15. **B**   The fourth paragraph describes the more confident demeanor shown by the Mayan artisans when they were through with their work and getting paid for it. More generally, the author discusses the positive effects these art partnerships have had on the morale and self-sufficiency of the Mayan communities. Choice (A) is incorrect because, although the author points out the advantages of having some Spanish literacy, the author portrays the efforts of MayaWorks as being directed at helping the women grow with the times while retaining their invaluable heritage. She would not want *full* assimilation. Choice (C) is incorrect because the author mentions the success of the Mayan women learning to make Jewish kippahs. Choice (D) is incorrect because the final paragraph indicates that Mayan villagers would be typically excluded from *traditional banks*, hence the need for innovative micro-loans.

16. **H**   The passage states that *each of eight women was to weave a dozen* (line 28). Eight times twelve is 96, leaving (H) as the only possible answer choice—the others are far too big or small.

17. **D**   The last sentence of the fifth paragraph says the effect of being told of the kippah's symbolic meaning was becoming *even more devoted and loving in their craft* (line 51). Choice (A) is incorrect because the confusion regarding the shape had no relation to the kippah's religious significance. Choices (B) and (C) are unsupported by anything in the passage.

18. **H**   Although the passage indicates that MayaWorks artists make fabrics that are sold side-by-side with mass-manufactured textiles, it does not imply that the Mayan artists are mass-manufacturing textiles. Choices (F) and (J) are supported in the fifth paragraph. Choice (G) is supported by the third paragraph.

19. **B**   The paragraph relates another way that MayaWorks seeks to improve these communities, via coordinating loans that allow Mayans to improve their quality of living and sustainability. Choice (A) is incorrect because the terms of the loans are not explicitly discussed or focused upon. Choice (C) is incorrect because the money in the final paragraph comes from loans, not from money the artisans have earned selling their wares. Choice (D) is incorrect because the function of this paragraph is not to convince the reader that Mayans are trustworthy, but rather inform the reader of another way in which MayaWorks provides a benefit to these communities.

20. **F**   The passage states that the success of MayaWorks *has more to do with the economic initiatives...than its literacy campaigns* (lines 75–77); eliminate (J). While the rules of the marketplace are certainly mentioned, there is no indication that the Guatemalan women had to learn them from the people at MayaWorks—eliminate (G). Choice (H) is unsupported and goes against the goal of helping the Mayans preserve their culture.

Passage III

21. **A** The discussion of the author's infatuation with cars is prefaced by the explanation that it came before his interest in music. The end of the discussion (lines 64–67) of cars states that *Eventually...my fixation on cars was to take a "back seat" to a new, greater, and this time lasting, passion*, (music). Choice (B) is incorrect because the author indicates that his infatuation with cars was ultimately overtaken by his interest in music. Choice (C) is incorrect because the passage never describes the author's playing style, so there is no support for calling it "mechanical." Choice (D) is incorrect because the author explains his love of cars came before his love of music; this answer makes it seem as though they were in competition and his love of cars was winning.

22. **H** The author says *rewarding as this existence was* (lines 7–8) it did not fulfill him; he needed *greater pursuits to occupy* (line 10) his imagination. Choice (F) is wrong because the passage does not support that the author usually worked with his brother. Choice (G) is incorrect because the passage makes it seem like the author's upbringing made *the thought of embarking on a music career* beyond his *wildest imagination*. Choice (J) is incorrect because the passage does not support invariably resulting in parental approval. It even contains the phrase *much to my parents' dismay* (line 9).

23. **C** The third paragraph (lines 44–67) explains the author's previous obsession (*years before I began to pursue music*) with cars. The end of that paragraph refers to his *previous infatuations* (before cars) of *archery, and before that dinosaurs*. This means that dinosaurs is the earliest. Choices (A), (B), and (D) are incorrect because the passage clearly indicates that some other passion predated each of them.

24. **F** The context of the statement is the author summarizing his impressed delight with how effectively the music replicates the sensory and emotional experience of a thunderstorm. Choice (G) is incorrect because the passage does not suggest movies mislead the audience, only that they often do not replicate the experience of the thunderstorm as well as this music does. Choice (H) is incorrect because the author is not concerned with changing the character of news reports. He is only pointing out how well music can communicate. Choice (J) is incorrect because the author does not comment on whether thunderstorms are "among the hardest." Though it is suggested that it is not easy to replicate a thunderstorm, since *few, if any*, movies or television programs can do it, the context of this statement is not trying to make a point about thunderstorms but rather a point about music's ability to convey a rich experience.

25. **A** In the second paragraph, the author is recounting the early experiences in his youth that led him to have an interest in music. He describes the thrill he took in learning Latin, Greek, Yiddish, German, Spanish, and Italian and compares the eagerness with which he learned them to *the energy of a lepidopterist netting butterflies* (lines 22–23). Eliminate both (B) and (D) because the comparison being made is between collecting butterflies and learning foreign phrases, not anything music-related. Choice (C) is incorrect because Ms. Fenchurch does not have anything to do with this paragraph or what it is describing.

26. **J** There is chaos described in the thunder and lightning stage, resolution when *the music eases, hope and reason are restored* (line 37), and relaxation in *soothing notes*. Choice (F) is incorrect because jealousy and resentment do not match up with anything. Although there is a violent thunderstorm described, violence is different from jealousy and resentment. Choice (G) is incorrect because "hate" and "disbelief" do not match up very well with the storm being described. Although storms are sometimes described as "angry," they are not described as "hateful." Also, *disbelief* is not a strong match for anything in the sentence. Choice (H) is incorrect because love is not a strong match for anything described in the sentence.

27. **C** The lesson Ms. Fenchurch imparts to the author is that music is more than just the notes on the page, *it's about expression, and perhaps more important, communication* (lines 82–83). Since language involves conveying meaning, (C) is supportable. Choice (A) is incorrect because the speed of notes is not discussed. Choice (B) is incorrect because it does not provide an accurate summary of the "argument" being made by Ms. Fenchurch in the last paragraph. Choice (D) is incorrect because Ms. Fenchurch places greater emphasis on communication.

28. **J** These two lines portray a calm lightness darkening into a cloudy apprehension and ultimately becoming a howling, thrilling, and frightening sensory overload. Choice (J) describes the transition in reverse. Choices (F), (G), and (H) all match up with something in these two sentences and are in correct chronological order.

29. **A** The last paragraph begins with the author's rhetorical question *So what made the difference?* The author reveals that what made his love for music *continue to burn where other passions had fizzled* (line 69) was a "who," Ms. Fenchurch. Choice (B) is incorrect because an anecdote means a specific story, which the author does not provide, and there are no details relating to Ms. Fenchurch's "conducting style." Choice (C) is incorrect because, although there are some character traits mentioned about Ms. Fenchurch, there is little "detailed background information," and even if there were, the purpose of the paragraph is to explain how influential Ms. Fenchurch was on the author's musical development. Choice (D) is incorrect because the paragraph does not mention the effect music has on Ms. Fenchurch. Rather, the paragraph mentions the influence Ms. Fenchurch had on the author's love of music.

30. **J** Phrases such as *sense of wonder* and *unforeseen path*, support that the author is surprised by his career choice, and several paragraphs deal with people, events, and subject matter that influenced the author's interest in music. Choice (F) is incorrect because the passage is not linear. It moves back and forth in time. Also, the passage does not list momentous events in the author's career, but more momentous influences on why the author has such a career. Choice (G) is incorrect because the passage does not delve into any specifics regarding Mozart and Handel, and the description of *The Tempest* is presented without comparison to any other piece of music. Choice (H) is incorrect because the passage as a whole is not persuasive in nature. The author is relating personal reflections, not advocating a certain course of action.

Passage IV

31. **D**   The end of the second paragraph (lines 29–30) indicates that *courtship typically lasts about two weeks, during which the female and her potential mate will meet once a day*. Choice (A) is incorrect because the males snap their heads at other males to try gain the attention of females. Choice (B) is incorrect because during courtship, the seahorses *dress up* their body coloring, whereas it is normally camouflaged. Choice (C) is incorrect because it relates to mating/birth, not courtship.

32. **F**   The third sentence of the first paragraph (lines 7–9) states that the seahorse's *tapered body shape is a great disadvantage* when it comes to *swimming ability*. Choice (G) is incorrect because the seahorse *lacks* a caudal fin. Choice (H) is incorrect because the dorsal fin is what gives the seahorse what little swimming ability it has. Choice (J) is incorrect because the passage does not link the seahorse's lack of teeth to swimming ability.

33. **B**   The confusion relates to Bateman's principle, which holds that whichever sex expends less energy in the reproductive process should be the sex that spends more energy competing for a mate. It may then seem confusing to scientists that males both compete for mates and give birth. However, Robinson's research shows that females do in fact expend more energy in the reproductive process than do males, which means that males should be the ones competing for mates after all. Choice (A) is incorrect because, although it is a detail involved in the mechanics of males giving birth, it does not resolve the confusion surrounding why the males also compete for mates. Choice (C) is incorrect because it provides no illumination as to why males give birth yet compete for mates. The monogamy of seahorses is explained by efficient birthing cycles, but it does not itself explain anything. Choice (D) is incorrect because the length of time spent competing for mates still does not explain why males, who give birth, are the ones who compete for mates.

34. **J**   The very first sentence of the passage foreshadows that the seahorse's *unusual mating habits* will be addressed. The last paragraph also begins by explaining that seahorses *have the distinction of being one of a very small number of monogamous species* (lines 73–75). Choice (F) is contradicted by information in the first paragraph. Although the passage explains that the seahorse manages some mobility, it still portrays the seahorse as a poor swimmer. Choice (G) is contradicted by information provided in the second to last paragraph. Pierre Robinson's research would potentially provide a coherent explanation for why male seahorses are responsible for birth. Choice (H) is incorrect because, although true, it can hardly be said to be a main idea of the passage.

35. **A**   The first paragraph mentions the seahorse's *remarkable appearance* and *distinctive equine head*. This mention of its *signature* prehensile tail is another indication that this feature is associated primarily with seahorses. Choice (B) is incorrect because, although the tail is useful, that is not what *signature* conveys. Choice (C) is a trap answer based on the equivalent meanings of "autograph" and "signature." Choice (D) is incorrect because it makes no sense to call a seahorse's tail legally obligated. This choice is also tempting because of the association to one's signature.

36. **F** Because the paragraph begins with fertilization, ends with hatching, and contains sequential details in between those two events, (F) is well supported. Choices (G) and (H) may be eliminated since both capillaries and the number of fry are only mentioned in passing. Choice (J) is incorrect since the amount of tolerable salinity is never specified. Also, salinity does not relate to the whole paragraph, which means this could not be the main purpose of the paragraph.

37. **B** The last paragraph explains that *a stable monogamous couple can develop an efficient birthing cycle in which* (lines 81–82) the male is incubating eggs at the same time that the female is generating eggs. Therefore, when the males give birth to one clutch of eggs, the females are almost ready with the next clutch. Choices (A) and (C) are incorrect because the transition from low to high salinity and the transition from fertilization to incubation both take place in and only relate to the gestation stage within the male's brood pouch. Choice (D) is incorrect because the initial transition from courtship to mating is when a female would actually select her mate. Monogamy only has meaning once a mate has been selected.

38. **H** If the female can't find a male to receive her eggs, she expels them into the ocean, which is essentially throwing them away. The months she spent growing the eggs are wasted, or *squandered*. Choices (F), (G), and (J) are synonyms for *lost*, but none make sense in the context of the passage.

39. **D** The second to last paragraph (lines 56–72) explains the paradox scientists see in the seahorse species, which is that males both give birth and compete for mates. According to Bateman's Principle, the sex that expends more energy in the reproductive process should NOT be the sex that competes for mates. Pierre Robinson found that male seahorses' increased oxygen intake during pregnancy does not qualify males as the sex that expends more energy in the reproductive process. Hence, seahorses conform to Bateman's Principle. Choices (A), (B), and (C) are incorrect because, although they refer to aspects of the seahorse's reproductive process, they do not relate to Bateman's Principle, which focuses on energy expenditure.

40. **G** The fourth paragraph (lines 46–55) states that the brood pouch regulates a low-salinity environment initially, but the salinity increases *to help acclimate* the eggs to the salt water of the ocean that awaits them. Choice (F) is incorrect because nothing suggests or supports the idea of premature hatching. Choice (H) is incorrect because nothing suggests that the capillary network extracts salt. Choice (J) is incorrect because the passage does not suggest other mammals have exposure to salt.

Chapter 22
Reading Practice
Test 2

READING TEST
35 Minutes—40 Questions

DIRECTIONS: There are four passages in this test. Each passage is followed by several questions. After reading each passage, choose the best answer to each question and blacken the corresponding oval on your answer document. You may refer to the passages as often as necessary.

Passage I

PROSE FICTION: This passage is adapted from the novel *The Smell of Fresh Muffins* by Woody Jessup (©1985 by Woody Jessup).

The narrator is going to help his grandfather paint a room in the narrator's house. Garth is a friend of the narrator's grandfather.

Garth should be here any minute. I'm kind of glad, actually, that Grandpa sent his buddy to pick us up. Daddy always runs late because he tries to squeeze in one extra thing at the last minute, and Grandpa tends to misjudge how slowly he drives
5 nowadays. Garth has only picked us up a couple times before, but each time he was here at 2:17 on the nose.

Garth seems to see his schedule as various-sized blocks of activities that must be inserted into the correct-sized slot of time. Grandpa says that since Garth's wife died, Garth has
10 married his schedule. He says people use a routine to distract themselves from their life. Grandpa seems to know human nature pretty well, so I believe him.

We see Garth's tan Oldsmobile pull slowly into the parking lot. His car is a good match for his personality: boring but reli-
15 able. Garth doesn't joke too much with people besides Grandpa. He was in the Marines for many years in the fifties. His posture and his way of speaking to people are both perfectly upright.

"Hey, kids. How was school?" Garth asks as we start piling into the back seat. "You know, one of you can sit up front."

20 Sis and I exchange a look with each other, hiding our feelings of reluctance. I remind her, with my eyes, that last time I rode up front, and she silently accepts her fate.

We start to drive off towards our house, where my Grandpa is currently re-painting our living room.

25 "You two ever done any painting?" Garth asks. We shake our heads. "It's like icing a cupcake. Does your mom ever let you do that? I mean, did she?"

"Sometimes." Clara chimes in. "She normally gave us one or two to play with, but she knew we couldn't make 'em as
30 pretty as she could, with that little swirl thing on top."

"Ah, of course." Garth grins. "Well, that swirl is what painting is all about. If you start with too little icing, you smear it

out thin to cover the whole top of the cupcake, but you can still see the cake peeking through, right?"

35 We nod. He continues, "But if you start with a good dollop, more than you really need, you can swoosh it around with one clever twist of your wrist. The extra stuff just comes off onto your knife ... or your paintbrush if you're painting."

"Maybe I need smarter wrists," Clara sighs skeptically.

40 We park a block down from our house so that Daddy won't see Garth's car when he gets home from work. Grandpa wanted the painted room to be a surprise.

As soon as we step in our kitchen door, we can smell the paint from the living room. Grandpa is wearing paint-covered
45 overalls, but the paint stains are dry, and none of them are the bright sky color that Clara picked for the living room.

"Hey, Sam. Hey, Clara. Grab yourself a brush and a smock before I steal all the good spots for myself!" Grandpa chuckles. We assume he will not let us up on a ladder, so he must be
50 counting on us to work on the bottom three feet of the wall.

Sis and I grab two new brushes that Grandpa must have just bought at the store. It seems a crime to dip them into the paint the first time and forever ruin their purity.

"Don't be afraid to give it some elbow grease, now." Grandpa
55 encourages, letting us watch him as he applies thick strokes of paint to the wall.

We begin working in our own areas, creating splotchy islands of blue.

Grandpa pauses from his work to watch our technique. He
60 grins. "Fun, isn't it?"

"What if Daddy's disappointed he didn't get to do this himself?" I ask.

"Disappointed I did him a favor? If I know Arthur, he'll be happy to have avoided the manual labor. He'll just be dis-
65 appointed he didn't get to see his kids finally covering up the awful beige wall that camc with the house."

Grandpa resumes painting and adds, "Maybe when we're done, we can cover up the awful beige on Garth's car." He starts laughing.

70   Garth seems not to mind or notice. He is concentrating on painting the corner without getting any stray streaks on the ceiling.

Grandpa notices Garth's serious expression and says, "He even paints like a Marine." Another chuckle. Garth does not
75 look away from his corner but adds, "and your Grandpa likes talking more than working—just like a civilian." Sis and I are accustomed to their jovial back-and-forth.

I feel sad to hear Grandpa say we will cover up the wall that came with the house. That is the color we grew up with.
80 That is the color of the living room with Mom still in it. I don't want to cover up our memories, even though they make us sad now. But covering up is different from removing. We will put a layer of sky blue on the surface so that we feel invigorated, but we will know that Mom's layer is always protected underneath.

1. Which of the following statements regarding the idea for painting the room is best supported by the passage?

A. While Clara was reluctant to do it, Grandpa ultimately convinced her it was okay.
B. Garth suggested the idea to Grandpa, who then told the narrator and her sister.
C. Clara envisioned the idea, and Garth helped provide some of the supplies.
D. Although Grandpa planned the activity, Clara was involved in the decision making.

2. As presented in the passage, the exchange between the narrator and his sister when Garth comes to pick them up can best be described as:

F. an expression of frustration due to the curiosity the narrator and his sister felt regarding Garth's unusual tardiness.
G. a situation that is initially confusing to the narrator until his sister reminds him about the project to repaint the living room.
H. a favorite game that the narrator plays with his sister to determine which person gets the honor of sitting in front.
J. a nonverbal conversation that allows the narrator and his sister to determine which of them receives an unfavorable consequence.

3. Based on the passage, Garth and Grandpa can be reasonably said to share all of the following characteristics EXCEPT:

A. painting experience.
B. good posture.
C. the ability to drive.
D. willingness to poke fun.

4. Clara's reference to having smarter wrists (line 39) primarily serves to suggest her:

F. remaining doubt about equaling her mother's skills.
G. growing excitement regarding learning how to paint.
H. deepening confusion about how painting relates to cupcakes.
J. increasing concern that people see her as intelligent.

5. Viewed in the context of the passage, Grandpa's grin (lines 59–60) most nearly reflects a feeling of:

A. irony.
B. intense relaxation.
C. mild satisfaction.
D. harsh disapproval.

6. The narrator's statement "His car is a good match for his personality" (line 14), most nearly means that in the narrator's opinion, Garth is:

F. too conservative in his choice of cars.
G. highly dependable, but not very flashy.
H. more upright than many Oldsmobile drivers.
J. too concerned with how others see him.

7. Garth clearly recommends that the children apply both paint and icing in which of the following ways?

A. Gently
B. Respectfully
C. Conservatively
D. Confidently

8. In the second paragraph, the main conclusion the narrator reaches is that:

F. Garth considers tardiness a character flaw.
G. Garth is extremely talented at organizing his schedule.
H. people can use a routine to avoid focusing on something painful.
J. Grandpa is a very keen observer of human behavior.

9. In terms of the development of the narrator as a character, the last paragraph primarily serves to:

A. add to the reader's understanding of his guilt.
B. explain his relationship to his mother.
C. describe his underlying emotional conflict.
D. portray the strained relationship he has with Grandpa.

10. It can most reasonably be inferred that Arthur is the name of:

F. Garth and Grandpa's friend.
G. the narrator.
H. the narrator's father.
J. the neighbor who lent them the ladder.

Passage II

SOCIAL SCIENCE: The following is an excerpt from the article "Electric Cars Face Power Outage" by Justin Sabo (© 2010 by Justin Sabo).

Many people look forward to the day when an American automobile company will mass-produce an emissions-free vehicle. Those people may be surprised to learn that day actually came to pass almost fifteen years ago.

5   So why are there hardly any purely electric vehicles on the road today? In 1996, General Motors released the EV1, the first fully electric vehicle designed and released by a major auto manufacturer. GM entered this unfamiliar territory bravely but reluctantly, motivated by emissions-control legislation enacted 10 by the California Air Resources Board (CARB). CARB felt automakers were dragging their feet in developing lower emissions vehicles, so it mandated that American car companies make a certain percentage of their cars available for sale in California to be electric vehicles.

15   This could not possibly have been good news for American automakers. Many believed that electric vehicles were not commercially viable. It would be very expensive to research, develop, and market a new type of car, and with consumer demand for such cars a big unknown, the companies feared stiff 20 economic losses would result from the new regulations. GM was pessimistic its EV1 could be a viable commodity, but it felt that the best way to force CARB to undo the mandate was to play ball: they would bring an electric car to the market and let everyone watch it fail.

25   Previous electric vehicle prototypes from major automakers had consisted of converting existing gasoline models, a process neither elegant nor inexpensive. The EV1, however, was designed from the start as an electric car, and lightness and efficiency were incorporated throughout the design. Engineers 30 selected aluminum for the EV's body, which, unlike the steel typically used in car frames, is a relatively light metal. The wheels were made with a magnesium alloy, which was another lightweight but sturdy replacement. The EV1's unusual, futuristic body shape is a consequence of aiming for a low drag 35 coefficient and reference area.

Early versions of the EV1 used a lead-acid based battery, replaced by nickel metal hydride in second generation models. Owners could charge their cars in their garages overnight or at power stations situated around the cities where they were 40 leased. A full charge would last 70 to 100 miles. The cars were only available to be leased, because GM wanted to be able to reclaim them if necessary. This also allowed GM to avoid having to comply with a law that requires car companies to maintain service and repair infrastructure for fifteen years fol- 45 lowing the sale of any model of car (something GM thought would surely become a moot point since they didn't expect production of EV1's to get past the initial trial stage).

The public reaction to the EV1 is a source of ongoing debate to this day. The initial fleet of 288 EV1's that GM released was 50 not enough to meet consumer demand, as waiting lists began growing with customers who wanted their chance to lease an EV1. At a suggested retail price of $34,000, the cars were leased at a rate between $400–550/month. This high monthly payment skewed demand toward a more affluent customer 55 base, which included many famous and wealthy celebrities, politicians, and executives. However, the auto industry used the lessees' fame to portray the car as something beyond the limits of the average consumer (despite the fact that GM had hand-picked the lessees).

60   Ultimately, GM reclaimed all the EV1's it had leased, intending to destroy them. EV1 owners were livid that their prized possessions were going to become scrap metal. They offered GM "no-risk" purchasing terms, essentially begging GM to let them buy the car while exempting GM from being accountable 65 for any future maintenance or repair issues. They were denied.

Why? Skepticism brewed regarding GM's deeper motives for canceling the EV1 program. Alleged pressure from the oil industry helped coax CARB into repealing their electric-car mandate. Others pointed to the fiscal losses GM would suffer 70 if electric cars became popular: GM was currently making billions per year in the spare parts market, selling the types of mufflers, brake pads, air filters, and the like that would no longer be required with electric car technology.

While the passion and protest surrounding the recall of 75 the EV1 suggest a burning desire for electric vehicles, other researchers portrayed a different story. Dr. Kenneth Train of UC Berkeley presented a study which claimed Americans would only be interested in buying an electric car if it were priced at least $28,000 less than a comparable gasoline-fueled car. 80 This study was frequently touted by automakers who hoped to prove that the electric car was not a financially viable product. Meanwhile, similar studies conducted by the California Electric Transportation Coalition (CETC) disagreed, finding that consumer demand for electric vehicles would represent 85 12–18% of the market for light-duty new cars.

Whether the electric car can transcend consumers' distrust of the unfamiliar and the auto and oil industries' reluctance to change is unknown. What is certain is the fact that a new technology poses challenges that go well beyond mechanical 90 engineering. Technological hurdles can often come in the form of political, economic, and social obstacles.

11. The author implies that for an electric car to be more appealing to most car buyers, the most important factor would be changing which of the following?

    A. Body shape
    B. Distance per charge
    C. Aluminum frame
    D. Price

12. The statement in lines 16–17 most likely represents the view of all of the following groups EXCEPT:

    F. the executives at GM who commissioned the design of the EV1.
    G. the members of the California Air Resources Board who issued the mandate.
    H. the other American automakers at the time the CARB mandate was issued.
    J. Dr. Kenneth Train and his research team at UC Berkeley.

13. According to the passage, the number of drivers who first leased an EV1 was around:

    A. 70–100.
    B. 288.
    C. 400–550.
    D. 12–18% of the light duty market.

14. The author most nearly portrays the efforts of GM to design an electric car as:

    F. resulting from overconfidence in estimating consumer enthusiasm for electric vehicles.
    G. directed more at perfecting the marketing than at perfecting the science.
    H. intended to showcase GM's superiority over its competitors.
    J. motivated in part by a desire to fail.

15. According to information presented in the fourth paragraph (lines 25–35), which of the following comparisons between previous electric vehicle prototypes and the EV1 would the author make?

    A. The EV1s were more deliberately and insightfully designed.
    B. The EV1s were just converted from previous gasoline prototypes.
    C. The previous electric prototypes were basically the same as the EV1.
    D. The previous electric prototypes were made out of cheaper, lighter materials.

16. Based on information presented in the sixth paragraph (lines 48–59), it can reasonably be inferred that which of the following determinations would have the biggest effect on the potential marketability of electric vehicles?

    F. The strength of affiliation that most car buyers have for environmental organizations
    G. Whether most car buyers would consider buying an automobile that costs more than one powered by gasoline
    H. How many other states might enact regulations similar to that of CARB's in California
    J. The extent to which most car buyers identify with wealthy politicians and celebrities

17. According to the passage, aluminum's role in the EV1 was:

    A. a lightweight wheel.
    B. to lower drag coefficient.
    C. an alternative to steel.
    D. magnesium alloy substitute.

18. The author most likely intends his answer to the question posed in line 66 to be:

    F. definitive; he believes the real reasons are plain to see.
    G. incomplete; he is convinced that CARB had some unknown involvement.
    H. genuine; he is unsure about GM's motives for the denial.
    J. speculative; he thinks that plausible explanations have been put forth.

19. The author indicates that one cause behind GM reclaiming EV1's from their owners may have been:

    A. the unwillingness of owners to renew their leases.
    B. CARB's decision to change the terms of its original low-emissions mandate.
    C. a financial disincentive GM would face should the EV1 become popular.
    D. customers' sticker shock at the $28,000 price tag.

20. It can reasonably be inferred from the last paragraph that the author thinks that any forthcoming electric vehicle will:

    F. have to solve non-technological problems.
    G. be embraced by most automakers.
    H. overcome the skepticism of consumers.
    J. succeed if sold at a lower price.

Passage III

HUMANITIES: The following passage is adapted from the essay "The Torres Revolution" by Greg Spearman (©2001 by Greg Spearman).

The question of who invented the guitar may forever remain a mystery. However, the father of the modern classical guitar is generally regarded as Antonio Torres Jurado, a carpenter from Sevilla, Spain, who began making guitars as a hobby in
5 the 1850's and ultimately created the design that practically all classical guitar makers use to the present day. By refining the craft of guitar-making, Torres expanded the dynamic and tonal range of the instrument, allowing the guitar to go beyond its traditional, supporting role and into the spotlight as a featured
10 concert solo instrument.

Early guitars had four pairs of strings—the word "guitar" itself being a translation from a Persian word meaning "four strings." During the Renaissance, instruments resembling the modern guitar had begun to appear throughout Europe. One
15 of these, the lute, became the standard stringed instrument across most of Europe, but in Spain there was more variation in developing forms of the guitar. A plucked version called the *vihuela* was popular in aristocratic society, while a strummed instrument referred to as the *guitarra latina* was used by com-
20 moners. Once a fifth string was ultimately added to the latter, the *guitarra latina* became the national preference and rendered the *vihuela* obsolete.

As the 17th century progressed, Spanish guitars, widely adored by monarchs, noblemen, and common folk alike, spread
25 throughout the rest of Europe and began to displace the once-popular lute. Along the way a sixth string was added to the design. The 18th century saw the more "prestigious" music of harpsichords, pianos, and violins come to the fore, while the guitar was relegated back to the informal gatherings of com-
30 mon folk. Eventually, however, the virtuosity of such Spanish guitarists as Ferdinand Sor rekindled the public's respect and admiration for guitar music. Esteemed composers such as Haydn and Schubert began writing guitar music, but while the performances of the Spanish guitar masters were wildly popular,
35 the acoustic and structural limitations of the guitar continued to present a problem when playing in large concert halls—a problem that Andres Torres meant to solve.

One of the guitar's chief limitations that Andres Torres tackled was its feeble sound output. Torres enlarged the body
40 of the guitar, particularly the "bouts" (rounded parts) in the soundbox, significantly increasing its volume and giving the guitar its familiar hourglass shape. Because the guitar also had to compete with the impressive polyphony (the number of notes that can be played at one time) of the piano, Torres also
45 reduced the width of the fretboard, making it easier for guitarists to reach many notes at once and allowing them to perform music with a complexity comparable to that of pieces played on keyboard instruments.

The genius of Torres's design, however, was the way he
50 re-engineered the internal structure of the instrument. Because the strings on a guitar must be wound tightly to produce enough tension to vibrate at the correct pitch, they constantly pull on the neck of the guitar, essentially trying to snap it in two. The arch of the neck counters some of this force, but the majority
55 is absorbed by wooden braces inside the instrument. Torres did not invent the idea of fan-bracing, which refers to pieces of wood laid out diagonally inside the body to distribute both tension and sound waves, but he did perfect it. He increased the number of braces from three to seven, and organized them
60 in a symmetric pattern allowing the vibrations of the guitar to be evenly distributed within the soundbox.

The effectiveness and elegance of Torres's design was immediately apparent in the improved tone and volume of the instrument, and ultimately revealed by the fact that his design
65 has remained virtually unchanged in over 150 years. Torres guitars were extremely rare and highly-sought by musicians in the 19th century. One aspiring guitarist of the time, Francisco Tarrega, traveled to Sevilla in the hopes of buying one of Torres's famous guitars. Although Torres initially intended to sell Tarrega
70 one of the stock guitars he had available, he reconsidered once he heard Tarrega play. Deeply impressed, Torres instead gave Tarrega a guitar he had made for himself several years before.

Just as Torres revolutionized the design of classical guitars, so would Tarrega eventually become recognized as the singular
75 authority on classical guitar playing techniques. Tarrega had grown up playing both guitar and piano, the latter being recognized as the more useful compositional tool, while the guitar was regarded as merely a functional accompaniment to a singer or a larger ensemble. Once Tarrega beheld the beauty and range
80 of expression of the Torres guitar, he committed himself fully to exploring its compositional palette.

Tarrega, who studied at the Madrid Conservatory, rose to great prominence, not only playing original pieces but also translating the great piano works of such composers as Beethoven
85 and Chopin for guitar. He became a global ambassador for the guitar, introducing and refining many of the techniques that classical guitarists worldwide now consider essential, including how to position the guitar on one's knee and optimal fingering and plucking techniques for the left and right hand.

21. Based on the passage, the author would most likely agree that both Torres and Tarrega were:

    A. not fully appreciated for their musical genius until after their deaths.

    B. local sensations whose reputation never reached the global fame of other composers.

    C. extremely influential contributors to the evolution of classical guitar playing.

    D. very talented instrument makers who gained much fame for their talents.

22. As it is used in line 49, the phrase *the genius of Torres's design* most nearly refers to the:

    F. innovative idea that classical guitars could be the centerpiece of a performance, rather than merely an accompaniment.

    G. improved tonal quality and volume resulting from the number and positioning of wooden braces within the soundbox.

    H. invention of an arched neck, which counters the effects of the tension caused by the tightly wound strings.

    J. expansion of the width of the guitar, in order to accommodate a sixth string and allow for more polyphony.

23. Which of the following statements best describes how the second paragraph (lines 11–22) relates to the first paragraph?

    A. It provides supporting details concerning Torres's innovative idea to use a fifth string.

    B. It compares the modern guitar to its earlier relatives, such as the lute and *vihuela*.

    C. It moves the discussion to a period that predates the innovator described in the first paragraph.

    D. It counterbalances the argument in the first paragraph by providing details that suggest early guitars were superior in many ways to later guitars.

24. As it is used in line 81, the phrase *compositional palette* most nearly means:

    F. artistic potential.

    G. colorful components.

    H. volume output.

    J. physical features.

25. For purposes of the passage, the significance of Spanish guitarists such as Ferdinand Sor is that they:

    A. were reluctant to accept modifications to the traditional design of the guitar.

    B. gave Torres suggestions about his design.

    C. were among the most talented lute players in Europe at the time.

    D. helped develop and sustain interest in the guitar as a reputable instrument.

26. Which of the following questions is NOT answered by the passage?

    F. What is the meaning of an instrument's polyphony?

    G. When was the beginning and the ending of the Renaissance?

    H. Who is the father of the modern guitar?

    J. What were some of the earlier forms of the guitar?

27. According to the passage, the *vihuela* was a Renaissance version of the guitar that:

    A. was ultimately overtaken in national popularity by another type of guitar.

    B. became the Spanish aristocrats' version of the lute.

    C. initially came to fame through the notoriety of Ferdinand Sor.

    D. one of Torres's earlier models before he perfected his fan-bracing design.

28. According to the passage, the Torres guitar was better suited than previous versions of the guitar to:

    F. Beethoven's works.

    G. being a featured instrument.

    H. five strings.

    J. folk music.

29. According to the passage, the popularity of Spanish-style guitars during the 18th century was:

    A. increasing due to the simultaneous decline in popularity of the lute.

    B. aided by the growing popularity of other instruments that complemented the guitar's sound.

    C. hindered by common folk's inability to master fingering and plucking techniques.

    D. diminished by the perception that it was not as refined as other contemporary instruments.

30. It can most reasonably be inferred that which of the following was a direct expression of respect for Tarrega's playing abilities?

    F. The manner in which Torres determined which guitar he would sell to Tarrega

    G. The translation of Beethoven's and Chopin's works from piano to guitar

    H. The eventual end to the popularity of the *guitarra latina*

    J. The way Haydn and Schubert began composing music specifically for guitar

Passage IV

NATURAL SCIENCE: The following passage is adapted from the article "Heavyweights of the Sea" by Carmen Grandola (©2001 by Carmen Grandola).

The earth's oceans possess an incredible variety of life, ranging from nearly microscopic plankton to the blue whale, the largest animal on the planet. In the world of fish, the mola sunfish and the whale shark are the two biggest varieties. The
5 mola is the biggest bony fish, whereas the whale shark, which is a cartilaginous fish, is simply the biggest fish there is. While most ocean-dwellers spend their days balancing their position on the food chain as both predators and prey, these titanic swimmers have little to worry about from predators. Instead, they must
10 focus on finding enough food to sustain the massive amounts of nutrients needed to support their bulky bodies.

Truly one of the most unusual-looking products of evolution's creative hand, the mola sunfish resembles a giant fish head with a tail. Most fish have long bodies, with fins in the
15 middle roughly dividing their length in two. Rather than having a caudal (tail) fin, like most fish, the mola looks like a fish that has been chopped just past the halfway point, with a rounded clavus joining its dorsal (top) and anal (bottom) fins. The mola uses its clavus to steer its rather awkwardly-shaped body
20 through the water. Its body has a very narrow cross-section—it is basically a flattened oval with a head at the front, and very high dorsal and anal fins at the back. In fact, the mola's height is often equal to its length, which is unusual in fish, which are typically elongated. Mola means "millstone" in Latin, and these
25 fish live up to their name, growing to 10–20 ft. in length and height and weighing in at an average of 2,000 lbs.

The mola's diet is extremely varied but nutrient-poor, consisting mainly of jellyfish, but also comb jellies, squid, and eel grasses. In order to consume enough daily nutrients, the mola
30 must be a voracious eater and be willing to travel through a wide range of oceanic depths—from surface to floor in some areas—in search of their food. After ascending from cooler waters, the mola will float on its side at the ocean's surface in order to warm itself through solar energy. Molas have a beaked
35 mouth that does not totally close, so they chew their food in several stages, breaking down each mouthful into smaller chunks before spitting them out and then going to work on the more bite-sized pieces.

The whale shark, another giant of the sea, grows to sizes
40 that dwarf the maximum size of a bony fish. Some have been measured at over 40 ft. in length and over 75,000 lbs. in weight. This leviathan, like the mola, mostly frequents tropical and warm-temperate waters. The whale shark possesses over 300 rows of teeth, but it does not use them in the same manner as
45 most other sharks. The whale shark is one of only a handful of filter-feeding sharks. This means rather than using powerful teeth and jaws to rip apart large prey, the whale shark eats tiny, nearly microscopic food such as zooplankton, krill, and macro-algae. The whale shark "hunts" by opening its mouth

50 and sucking in a huge mouthful of ocean water. It then closes its mouth and expels the water through its gills, at which point gill rakers act as sieves, separating the tiny, sometimes millimeter-wide, life forms from the water. Once all the water is expelled, the food is swallowed.

55 When you're one of the biggest species in your neighborhood, you probably don't have to worry about getting picked on much. This is certainly true of the whale shark, which has no natural predators and can easily live 70–100 years in the ocean. Its biggest health risk comes through exposure to
60 humans. The whale shark does much of its feeding near the surface of the water, where it has been known to accidentally bump into boats. Both animal and vessel can end up severely damaged in these exchanges. The other hazard humans create for whale sharks is pollution in the water. As the whale
65 shark filter feeds, it sometimes takes in garbage and nautical debris such as oars.

The mola, on the other hand, has a few challenges. Its thick skin is covered in a dense layer of mucus, which is host to a vast array of parasites. To try and rid itself of these uninvited
70 guests, the mola will often float on its side near the surface of the water, inviting gulls and other birds to feast on the parasites. Similarly, the mola will sometimes launch its considerable bulk up to ten feet out of the water before crashing back down in an effort to dislodge some of the parasites. With its habit of
75 floating near the surface, the mola, like the whale shark, often runs the risk of being hit by boats. Finally, smaller molas are sometimes subject to attack by sea lions.

31. The author's attitude regarding molas and whale sharks can best be described as one of:

A. conviction that human interference will ultimately jeopardize each species.

B. resentment towards their need to eat so much other marine life on a daily basis.

C. impartiality in considering the perils of their environment compared to other fish.

D. interest in how their grandiose size affects their habits and survival.

32. It can reasonably be concluded from the passage that the mola temporarily expels its food when eating due to the fact that it:

F. is a bony fish rather than a cartilaginous one.

G. possesses a mouth that cannot completely close.

H. hunts on the ocean floor but eats at the surface.

J. is normally floating on its side near the surface.

33. According to the passage, the most significant difference between the predatory threats facing the whale shark and the mola is that the whale shark:

    A. does not compete for the same food as its predators do, while the mola competes for the same food its predators do.

    B. is unaffected by its proximity to humans, while the mola is sometimes endangered by humans.

    C. faces few genuine environmental threats but must contend with the nuisance of parasites.

    D. is less likely to be attacked by another ocean-dwelling species than is the mola.

34. It can most reasonably be inferred from the passage that nautical vessels pose a threat to both the mola and the whale shark primarily because these vessels:

    F. can sometimes unsuspectingly collide with fish.

    G. stir up a violent wake that disrupts the ocean currents.

    H. jettison large debris overboard which can land on fish.

    J. deplete the fish's supply of prey through over-fishing.

35. The passage indicates that the quantity of food a fish must eat is primarily determined by the:

    A. mass of the fish's body.

    B. depth at which the fish hunts.

    C. type of gill rakers it has.

    D. number of its teeth and size of its mouth.

36. The passage supports the idea that all of the following are included in the diet of the mola EXCEPT:

    F. comb jellies.

    G. zooplankton.

    H. eel grasses.

    J. squid.

37. The main purpose of the last two paragraphs is to:

    A. provide additional support for the earlier claim that the mola and the whale shark are two of the biggest creatures inhabiting the ocean.

    B. convey to the reader to the ironic fact that such large species of fish can be vulnerable to miniature threats such as parasites.

    C. summarize the types of threats, or lack thereof, present in the environments of the mola and whale shark.

    D. demonstrate the fact that even the biggest fish in the sea have to worry about being preyed upon by something.

38. According to the passage, the gill rakers a whale shark has are primarily intended to:

    F. spit out partially chewed food.

    G. rip apart the whale shark's large prey.

    H. bridge together its 300 rows of teeth.

    J. filter out food from a mouthful of water.

39. According to the passage, the Latin-derived name for the mola refers to the:

    A. atypical rounded clavus of the mola.

    B. mola's distinctive half-fish shape.

    C. voracious eating the mola's diet requires.

    D. mola's enormous size and weight.

40. The main purpose of the passage is to:

    F. offer support for the notion that the mola is pound-for-pound a better hunter than is the whale shark.

    G. provide a general overview of the habitats, eating habits, and survival challenges relating to two of the biggest species of fish.

    H. increase awareness for the fragile status of mola and whale shark populations and encourage conservationists to intervene.

    J. suggest that the unlikely traits possessed by the mola and the whale shark do not have clear evolutionary answers.

END OF TEST 3
STOP! DO NOT TURN THE PAGE UNTIL TOLD TO DO SO.
DO NOT RETURN TO A PREVIOUS TEST.

Chapter 23
Reading Practice
Test 2: Answers and
Explanations

READING PRACTICE TEST 2 ANSWERS

1. D
2. J
3. B
4. F
5. C
6. G
7. D
8. H
9. C
10. H
11. D
12. G
13. B
14. J
15. A
16. G
17. C
18. J
19. C
20. F

21. C
22. G
23. C
24. F
25. D
26. G
27. A
28. G
29. D
30. F
31. D
32. G
33. D
34. F
35. A
36. G
37. C
38. J
39. D
40. G

SCORE YOUR PRACTICE TEST

Step A

Count the number of correct answers: _____. This is your *raw score*.

Step B

Use the score conversion table below to look up your raw score. The number to the left is your *scale score*: _____.

Reading Scale Conversion Table

Scale Score	Raw Score	Scale Score	Raw Score	Scale Score	Raw Score
36	40	27	30	18	18
35	39	26	29	17	16–17
34	38	25	27–28	16	15
33	37	24	26	15	14
32	36	23	24–25	14	12–13
31	35	22	23	13	11
30	34	21	22	12	9–10
29	32–33	20	20–21	11	8
28	31	19	19	10	6–7

READING PRACTICE TEST 2 EXPLANATIONS

Passage I

1. **D** The passage states that the bright sky color was something *Clara picked*, and it suggests that Grandpa *wanted to do* the narrator's father *a favor* and *wanted the painted room to be a surprise*. There is no support for Clara's reluctance, which eliminates (A). There is no support for Garth coming up with the idea, which eliminates (B). There is no support for Garth providing any of the supplies, which eliminates (C).

2. **J** The passage explains that the narrator and his sister feel *reluctance* about sitting up front. The narrator reminds her with his *eyes* that it is her turn to accept that *fate*. Choice (F) is unsupported by the passage because nothing ever suggests that Garth shows up late. Choice (G) is unsupported because the narrator does not suggest confusion, and their exchange is purely about who is riding in front. Choice (H) is off the mark because the context does not portray the front seat as an *honor*, nor is their taking turns much of a *game*.

3. **B** Posture is only mentioned while describing Garth. Since Garth offers painting advice (lines 31–38), and Grandpa wears *paint-covered overalls* (lines 44–45), (A) is supported. Because they have both picked up the narrator and his sister before, (C) is supported. Because the passage mentions their *jovial back-and-forth*, (D) is supported.

4. **F** The context leading up to this quote involves Clara mentioning a talent her mother had for swirling icing that Clara does not possess. Once Garth explains how to achieve that effect, Clara remains skeptical about her own ability to perform the feat. Choice (G) lacks support because Clara's sigh and her skepticism do not indicate *excitement*. Choice (H) is incorrect because there is no context to indicate Clara's confusion. Choice (J) is incorrect because Clara is not self-conscious of her intelligence. Her use of the adjective *smarter* applies only to her wrists and is in response to Garth's phrase *clever twist*.

5. **C** Since the context is Grandpa watching the kids getting started painting, and his following comment is making sure they're having fun, we can infer that he is feeling good about the situation. There is nothing in the context to support *intense* relaxation, as (B) implies. There is also nothing in the context to support *irony* or *disapproval*, as (A) and (D) imply.

6. **G** The narrator describes both the car and Garth's personality as *boring but reliable* (lines 14–15). This agrees with (G). The narrator is not critiquing Garth's choice in cars, as (F) indicates, rather the narrator says Garth's car is a very fitting choice. There is no comparison between Garth and other Oldsmobile drivers in the passage to support (H). There is also no support for (J), that Garth is concerned about how he is seen by others.

7. **D** Garth's painting and icing advice consists of starting with a large dollop and then *cleverly* swooshing it on. Because the context emphasizes applying a healthy quantity of paint in a single motion, (D) is supported. Choices (A), (B), and (C) seem to go against the idea of large dollop of paint and one swift but effective motion. They all suggest a more tentative process.

8. **H** The paragraph describes Garth's habitual planning and Grandpa's assessment of the motivation for Garth's behavior. When he says *I believe him* (line 12), the narrator concludes that Grandpa is correct about the idea that Garth uses his routine to distract himself from his wife's death. Choices (F) and (G) mention traits resembling the paragraph's description of Garth, but neither are the main conclusion the narrator reaches. Similarly, (J) says something that the narrator believes seems to be true about Grandpa, but it is not the main conclusion he reaches in the paragraph. He only mentions Grandpa's ability to judge human nature as part of his analysis of Garth's behavior, which is the real point of the paragraph.

9. **C** In the last paragraph (lines 78–84), the passage implies that the narrator's mom has died and reveals the reluctance the narrator feels to move on without her. Although the narrator's sadness about painting over the old color of wall may imply some degree of guilt, (A) is incorrect because the paragraph is not focused solely on that one negative emotion and the answer implies that the last paragraph *adds* to the portrayal of the narrator's guilt, when such an emotion is never discussed before this paragraph. Choice (B) is close, but the paragraph does not provide any details explaining their relationship. It provides details about the narrator's reaction to covering up a memory of his mother. Choice (D) is unsupported because there is no context in the passage that portrays a strained relationship between the narrator and Grandpa.

10. **H** Since in lines 61–62 the narrator asks about his father, it makes sense to think that Grandpa's response is referring to the narrator's father by name. There is no context to suggest it's Grandpa's friend, as (F) states. Grandpa is responding to the narrator about a third person, so there is no context for (G). And there is no discussion of the ladder belonging to a neighbor to support (J).

Passage II

11. **D** In the sixth paragraph, the author states that the monthly lease payment *skewed demand towards a more affluent customer base* (lines 54–55). Choice (A) is incorrect because, though unusual, the body shape is not mentioned as undesirable. Choices (B) and (C) are mentioned in the passage, but there is no indication of consumers' negative reactions to them.

12. **G** CARB would not have required automakers to offer electric vehicles if it thought that they would lose money in doing so. Choice (F) is incorrect because the passage indicates that the EV1 was designed with the expectation that it would fail. Choice (H) is incorrect because the passage suggests that automakers considered the CARB mandate to be bad news that would potentially be very costly. Choice (J) is incorrect because Dr. Train's study suggested that consumers would only buy electric vehicles if they cost much less than gas-powered cars.

13. **B**   The sixth paragraph states the *initial fleet* (line 49) was 288 EV1s. Choice (A) refers to the distance in miles an EV1 got on one battery charge. Choice (C) refers to the average monthly payment of lease holders. Choice (D) refers to the CETC's estimate.

14. **J**   At the end of the third paragraph, the author says that GM planned to show CARB an electric car was not viable by bringing one to the market and letting everyone *watch it fail*. Choice (F) is incorrect because GM was pessimistic about the market for electric cars. Choice (G) is incorrect because, if anything, GM was more concerned about building a working car and less concerned about helping it succeed in the marketplace. Choice (H) is incorrect because the passage never mentions a competitive motivation. Rather, it suggests the motivation was to demonstrate that CARB's mandate was ill-advised.

15. **A**   The author states that the EV1 was *designed from the start as electric*, while the previous prototypes were just converted from gasoline models. He also mentions that *lightness and efficiency were incorporated into the design* (lines 28–29). Choice (B) is incorrect because the electric prototypes were converted, not the EV1. Choice (C) is incorrect because the author points out a distinct difference in the design process of EV1s and lists several details that resulted. Choice (D) is incorrect because the prototypes were described as expensive conversions and the light materials were only mentioned in relation to the EV1.

16. **G**   The passage indicates that electric cars cost more than gasoline-powered cars, and the higher cost is cited in the passage as a potential concern for buyers. Choice (F) is incorrect because the study did not address environmental concerns of customers. Choice (H) is incorrect because the study did not address the motivation of car companies to comply with other states' regulations. Choice (J) is incorrect because the study did not address a psychological connection between car buyers and famous wealthy people.

17. **C**   The passage explains that aluminum was used for the car's body unlike the typical choice of steel. Choice (A) is incorrect because that describes the role of the magnesium alloy. Choice (B) is incorrect because that describes the role of the body shape. Choice (D) is incorrect because the aluminum replaced what would have otherwise been steel.

18. **J**   The author presents the two explanations offered in the eighth paragraph (lines 66–73) as *alleged* and something *others pointed to*. The author treats these theories with some degree of legitimacy but does not fully endorse either. Choice (F) is incorrect because the author does not use language supporting "definitive, real answers." Choice (G) is incorrect because the author does not mention an undiscovered influence from CARB. Choice (H) is incorrect because the author is not unsure about the motives— he goes on to talk about what they may have been.

19. **C** The passage states that *GM was currently making billions per year on the spare parts market* (lines 70–71) that would be threatened by an expanded electric vehicle market. Choice (A) is incorrect because the owners were willing to do anything to keep their vehicles, including renew their leases. Choice (B) is incorrect because the passage only mentions CARB repealing its mandate, not changing its terms. Choice (D) is incorrect because the suggested retail price of the car was $34,000, not $28,000.

20. **F** The last paragraph discusses the *political, economic, and social obstacles* new technologies face. None of these are technological problems. Choices (G) and (H) are incorrect because the author states that whether the electric car can transcend the obstacles of consumer skepticism and automaker reluctance is *unknown*. Choice (J) is incorrect because, even though the passage discusses the price of electric cars as a disincentive for consumers, the author never says anything strong enough to justify (J)'s prediction.

Passage III

21. **C** The author credits Torres as *the father of the modern classical guitar* (line 2) and Tarrega as the *singular authority on classical guitar playing techniques* (lines 74–75). Choice (A) is unsupported because there is nothing in the passage that relates to being appreciated more after death. Choice (B) is unsupported because there is nothing in the passage that restricts the influence of either man to a certain geographical area. Choice (D) is incorrect because Tarrega was famous for playing guitar, not making guitars.

22. **G** The fifth paragraph (lines 49–61) describes the genius of Torres's design is the way he re-engineered the *internal structure* of the guitar. Choice (G) refers to the fan-bracing layout that Torres *perfected* (line 58). Choice (F) is incorrect because nothing in this paragraph relates to the idea of the guitar as a showcased instrument. That guitars became a more featured instrument is an effect of Torres's ingenious restructuring, but it isn't referring to Torres's design. The passage does not say that Torres invented the arched neck, nor does it say that he widened it to fit a sixth string—eliminate (H) and (J).

23. **C** Although the first paragraph establishes that the passage will focus on how Torres paved the way for the modern guitar, the second paragraph (lines 11–22) begins providing background info on the emergence of early guitar forms. Choice (A) is unsupported because there is no mention that Torres was involved in adding a fifth string. Choice (B) is incorrect because the second paragraph does not mention the modern guitar and, thus, did not compare it to anything. Choice (D) is incorrect because there is nothing in the second paragraph that mentions or compares advantages of early guitars versus later ones.

24. **F** Since Tarrega went from composing music on a piano, as did most people, to composing on guitar, he would be searching for the songwriting possibilities on the guitar. This agrees with (F). Choice (G) is too literal, and it is a trap answer based on similarity between colors and palettes. Volume output and structural limitations are mentioned as a consideration for performing music (lines 35–36 and 38–39), not composing it—eliminate (H) and (J).

25. **D** The passage states that Spanish guitarists *rekindled the public's respect and admiration for guitar music* (lines 31–32). There is nothing supporting their reluctance to consider new designs as (A) says; in fact, the passage explains the limitations of the traditional design that frustrated them. There is no support for (B), that they had contact with Torres during his design process. They are guitar players, not lute players, as (C) suggests.

26. **G** Specific dates for the Renaissance are never given. Choice (F) is answered in the fourth paragraph. Choice (H) is answered in the first paragraph. Choice (J) is answered in the second paragraph.

27. **A** The passage states that the *guitarra latina became the national preference and rendered the vihuela obsolete* (lines 21–22). Choice (B) is incorrect because the passage does not indicate that the *vihuela* was intended to be a substitute for the lute. Choice (C) is incorrect because there is no mention that Ferdinand Sor played or popularized the *vihuela*. Choice (D) is incorrect because the passage never mentions Torres as having any involvement with the *vihuela*.

28. **G** The first paragraph explains that Torres's innovations allowed the guitar to go from being a *supporting* instrument to a *featured solo* instrument. Choice (F) is unsupported because the passage never discusses the demands placed on a guitarist in playing Beethoven's works. Choice (H) is incorrect because Torres did not work with five string guitars. Choice (J) is incorrect because it is the opposite of what Torres guitars accomplished: They brought the guitar out of its folk context and into the spotlight of formal concerts.

29. **D** The passage states that as more *"prestigious"* (line 27) instruments rose in popularity, the guitar was *relegated* (line 29) back to being a folk instrument. Choice (A) is incorrect because it describes what happened in the 17th century. Choice (B) is incorrect because the passage states that the growing popularity of other instruments hurt the guitar's popularity. Choice (C) is unsupported, as the passage never discusses whether common folk could master playing techniques.

30. **F** The passage indicates that Torres originally planned to sell Tarrega a stock guitar until Torres heard him play. *Deeply impressed* (line 71), Torres instead sold him a more sentimentally valuable guitar. Choice (G) is incorrect because this is something Tarrega did himself, not something someone did for Tarrega out of respect. Choice (H) is incorrect because the passage attributes this to the fifth string added to the *guitarra latina*. Choice (J) is incorrect because the passage attributes this to the popularity of Spanish guitarists such as Ferdinand Sor.

Passage IV

31. **D** From the outset, the author introduces the fish as the two biggest of their kind, explains that their size puts them near the top of their local food chain, and goes on to describe their behaviors. Choice (A) is incorrect because, although the author mentions each species potentially being harmed by proximity to humans, these dangers are not described as species-threatening. Choice (B) is incorrect because nowhere is the author's tone or language resentful. Choice (C) is incorrect because the author suggests in the first paragraph that the mola and whale shark have much less to worry about in terms of predators than do other fish.

32. **G** The passage states that *molas have a beaked mouth that does not totally close, so they chew their food in several stages* (lines 34–36). Choice (F) is unsupported, since the passage does not discuss eating habits as a function of being bony or cartilaginous. Choice (H) is unsupported since the passage does not indicate that the mola eats only at the surface. Choice (J) is unsupported since the passage indicates the mola floats on its side to warm up, not to eat.

33. **D** The passage indicates that the whale shark has *no natural predators* (line 58), while smaller molas are *sometimes subject to attack by sea lions* (line 77). Choice (A) is unsupported since neither species is subject to consistent predation, and there is no discussion of a predator's food source. Choice (B) is incorrect because the passage indicates that both species are sometimes adversely affected by contact with humans. Choice (C) is incorrect because the passage only speaks of molas being bothered by parasites.

34. **F** The passage states that the *mola, like the whale shark, often runs the risk of being hit by boats* (lines 74–76). Choices (G) and (J) are unsupported by any details in the passage. Choice (H) is incorrect because, although nautical debris is said to be a hazard for the whale shark's filter feeding, it is not identified as a threat to both species, and the threat is not from debris landing on the fish.

35. **A** The first paragraph states that molas and whale sharks *must focus on finding enough food to sustain the massive amounts of nutrients needed to support their bulky bodies* (lines 9–11). Choice (B) is incorrect because the passage never connects ocean depth and food requirements. Choice (C) is incorrect because this only relates to how the whale shark eats, not the quantity that any fish eats. Choice (D) is incorrect because the passage doesn't connect teeth or mouth size with dietary needs.

36. **G** Choices (F), (H), and (J) are all mentioned as part of the mola's diet in the third paragraph (lines 27–38). Zooplankton are specifically described as part of the whale shark's diet (lines 47–49).

37. **C** The transition into the last two paragraphs begins with a mention of how these big fish are rarely picked on (lines 55–57). The paragraphs then go on to detail the types of dangers each fish faces, which are not very numerous or threatening in nature. Choice (A) is incorrect because, although some details in these paragraphs reinforce the large size of the two species, the purpose of the paragraphs is to discuss potential threats. Choice (B) is incorrect because it would only relate to the mola and conveying irony is not the main purpose of these paragraphs. Choice (D) is incorrect because the whale shark *has no natural predators*, so this answer couldn't apply to the second to last paragraph.

38. **J** The passage indicates that the gill rakers function by *separating the tiny* (line 52) bits of food from the mouthful of water. Choice (F) is incorrect because the mola, not the whale shark, spits out partially chewed food. Choice (G) is incorrect because the whale shark does not rip apart prey. Choice (H) is incorrect because the gill rakers are not mentioned in connection with the whale shark's teeth.

39. **D** The passage explains that *these fish live up to their name* (lines 24–25) and proceeds to discuss the mola's impressive size. Choices (A), (B), and (C) are details mentioned about the mola but not connected to the explanation of the Latin name presented in the passage.

40. **G** The tone of the passage is mostly objective and informative. Choice (F) is incorrect because the two fish are rarely compared and never on the level of their hunting abilities. Choice (H) is incorrect because, though he does discuss what threats are present in their environment, the author does not specifically mention that either species is threatened. Choice (J) is incorrect because although the author refers to evolution in one passing remark, his discussion of the two fish is not based on how they evolved.

Chapter 24
Reading Practice
Test 3

READING TEST

35 Minutes—40 Questions

DIRECTIONS: There are four passages in this test. Each passage is followed by several questions. After reading each passage, choose the best answer to each question and blacken the corresponding oval on your answer document. You may refer to the passages as often as necessary.

Passage I

PROSE FICTION: This passage is an excerpt from the short story "Whimpering Wanderlust" by Gretchen Mueller (© 1955 by Gretchen Mueller).

Jacob Mathinson accepted, almost too early in his life, that he would never be a world-famous architect. His grandmother had instilled an indelible streak of humility in Jacob as a boy, telling him that he was special to her, but that the rest of the world
5 was under no obligation to feel the same way. He attended Mount St. Mary's College, not because it had a renowned architectural program, but because he was able to get a partial scholarship by playing on the school's tennis team. Jacob did not want to admit it, especially years later, but his decision may have also
10 been swayed by his desire to follow Erin Crawford, his high school crush, wherever she decided to go. Architecture was not his first calling, and, hence, his ambition towards ascending in the field extended only so far as his desire to walk through the streets of, say, Prague one day, a fetching girl on his arm,
15 commenting on the array of Baroque, Renaissance, and even Cubist masterpieces along the Old Town Square.

Growing up in Gettysburg, Pennsylvania, Jacob, an average though not exceptional student, was not exactly exposed to a climate of forward thinking. The local economy was a traditional,
20 if unimaginative, one. Most of the infrastructure had been built during the Reconstruction to support the railroad industry. In the summer of 1919, when Jacob was born, the town seemed frozen in the late 19th century, with bootblack, locksmith, and apothecary shops that seemed more at home in pre-industrial
25 times. This lack of innovation deepened Jacob's disinterest in personal or academic enterprise. His impression was that there was little of interest to be discovered outside of Gettysburg, save a patchwork of towns as predictable as the repeating pattern of black and white tiles on a checkerboard.

30 During his junior year in high school, Jacob worked as a tour guide on one of the double-decker buses that shuttled tourists, Civil War enthusiasts mostly, around the perimeter of Gettysburg. Fancying himself as cutting quite a figure in his clean, pressed uniform, it was his great hope that one day Erin
35 Crawford might take the tour and see him in action. He even went so far as to give her a voucher for a free ride, but as each tour began, he would heave a lonesome sigh, crestfallen that she with her sweet lilac fragrance had not whisked past him as the customers loaded on to the bus.

40 Nonetheless, Jacob enjoyed the job, partly because it was easy—it consisted of reading a script of noteworthy details about the Gettysburg Battlefield—but mostly because it allowed for personal embellishment, since the tour included some of the area's historic buildings as well. Jacob spent months explain-
45 ing to his customers that the sloping roof on the Dobbin House Tavern is a pristine example of Celtic style architecture, and that the Shriver House Museum is one of the oldest standing pre-colonial buildings in America. Although for months he described these buildings of architectural interest, it wasn't
50 until he left that job that he actually began to think about them, notice them, and allow the buildings to "speak" to him in an aesthetic conversation.

The following summer, Jacob worked with his uncle, a residential plumber. Jacob enjoyed seeing homes in the in-
55 termediate stages of construction, half-naked, their internal structure exposed. Jacob found great satisfaction in the task of finding the most efficient and cohesive way to intertwine the circulatory system of plumbing into the skeletal structure of each house's wooden framework. Again, he found a way to
60 incorporate visions of Erin into his work, imagining that Erin's parents would get a flooded basement, and he and his uncle would arrive heroically, save the day, and leave her parents thinking, "that Jacob is a great boy." (Jacob's fascination with the science and art of building blossomed in his freshman
65 year at Mount St. Mary's, as did his fascination with the many young women also attending the school. Perhaps their attentions provided much-needed distraction from the difficulties he was having in his pursuit of Erin.)

He had not accounted for Mount St. Mary's size relative
70 to his high school and the difficulty of "accidentally" running into someone in the halls. Throughout the first semester, Erin might as well have been a ghost to Jacob, who tried his very best to make her acquaintance, but to no avail. Many years later, already married to Martha, a seamstress from Gettysburg, Jacob
75 would daydream about the single time he and Erin had something resembling a date. With a resigned sigh, he remembered his hands trembling, even while jammed into the pockets of his pressed Ogilvy's slacks; and the curious nature of her fragrance that seemed floral from a distance but minty up close; and the
80 musical sound her shoes made on the cobblestone road leading to the assembly hall; and the way she seemed to be fearlessly striding toward an unknown future while he was just trying to acclimate to the present.

1. The passage supports all of the following statements about Jacob's job as a tour guide EXCEPT that:

   A. he observed many buildings with their skeletal structure exposed.
   B. there were some prepared remarks that Jacob was to read.
   C. the tour catered to certain people with a common interest.
   D. he wore what he considered to be a flattering uniform.

2. One of the main ideas of the second paragraph (lines 17–29) is that:

   F. due to the nature of Gettysburg, Jacob did not have much desire to travel elsewhere.
   G. Jacob imagined a better architectural plan for the town's older buildings.
   H. it was hard for Jacob to find a job with mainly pre-industrial types of merchants.
   J. Jacob lacked motivation for his studies because he planned to work for the railroad.

3. The events in the passage are described primarily from the point of view of a narrator who presents the:

   A. actions and thoughts of both Jacob and Erin.
   B. the inner emotions and thoughts of only Jacob.
   C. actions and thoughts of all the characters discussed.
   D. dialogue of all the characters, which suggests their thoughts.

4. According to the passage, all of the following were aspects of Jacob's job with his uncle EXCEPT:

   F. seeing unfinished construction.
   G. impressing Erin's parents.
   H. daydreaming while he worked.
   J. finding efficient paths for plumbing.

5. According to the passage, Jacob's ambition toward becoming an architect included a desire to:

   A. point out interesting architecture to a girl.
   B. find a new way to utilize plumbing.
   C. redesign the Dobbin House roof.
   D. enroll at a renowned architectural school.

6. Which of the following questions is NOT answered by the passage?

   F. What factors influenced Jacob's choice to go to Mount St. Mary's College?
   G. Did Erin ever use her voucher for a free tour with Jacob?
   H. How many people went to Jacob's high school?
   J. What effect did the old infrastructure of Gettysburg have on Jacob?

7. The passage indicates that compared to when Jacob worked as a tour guide, after he stopped working there he found the buildings of Gettysburg:

   A. less fascinating.
   B. more fascinating.
   C. less historically noteworthy.
   D. more historically noteworthy.

8. The passage indicates that Jacob's primary response to the events described in the last paragraph is:

   F. remorse that he and Erin were largely disconnected.
   G. anger concerning the excessive size of Mount St. Mary's.
   H. gratitude for ultimately meeting and marrying Martha.
   J. contentment regarding the fact that he got to date Erin.

9. That Jacob had an indelible streak of humility was:

   A. a quality shared by most people who grew up in a working class community like that of Gettysburg.
   B. a consequence of accepting that he would probably never be a world-famous architect.
   C. an effect of Jacob's grandmother's words of caution regarding the unbiased impressions of the rest of the world.
   D. a character trait that evolved through years of pursuing but never obtaining Erin's affection.

10. In the passage, the statement that Erin was fearlessly striding toward an unknown future (lines 81–82) is best described as the opinion of:

    F. the author of the passage, but not the opinion of Jacob.
    G. Jacob as he struggled to "accidentally" run in to Erin at Mount St. Mary's.
    H. Erin, who has little interest in Jacob because he has no urge to leave Gettysburg.
    J. Jacob as he reflects on the one date he had with Erin.

Passage II

SOCIAL SCIENCE: This passage is excerpted from the article "The Irresistible Force" by Angela Suspak. (© 2008 by Luminary)

The author is reviewing the biographical book *The Long Walk Home* by Grace Jergensen.

During the summer of 1892, a reputable black store owner was lynched in Memphis, Tennessee. This outraged many local citizens, but Ida B. Wells felt compelled to take action and write a letter decrying the horrific act in the local press. However, as a
5　black woman, her race and identity posed formidable obstacles. The volatility of her message, combined with the pervasive chauvinism of the times, made her "a hushed voice in the race debate," according to Grace Jergensen, who writes a biography of Wells, entitled *The Long Walk Home*. Wells, taking matters
10　into her own hands, joined a fledgling black newspaper called *The Free Speech and Headlight* as co-owner and editor.

Writing under the pseudonym of "Iola," Wells lashed out against the intolerance and brutality of racially-motivated lynchings. She vilified the perpetrators of the crime, while also
15　chastising the white community at large for virtually condoning these actions by its inaction. With her incendiary rhetoric, Wells became a hero in the civil rights community and a potential target for violence. Jergensen details the difficulties Wells underwent shortly after her article was published. While at an
20　editing convention in New York, Wells learned that she had become a despised figure in Memphis, and the target of death threats. Considering the imminent danger she would face if she returned home, "Wells had to decide whether she would rather be a nomad or a martyr."

25　Wells was not used to backing down from a challenge, though. She was born just months before the Emancipation Proclamation declared an end to slavery. She grew up with the mindset of equal rights for all, despite being exposed to the deeply ingrained and intractable racial divisions in the South.
30　Her parents perished when she was only 18 during a bout of yellow fever that plagued her hometown of Holly Springs, Mississippi. Wells, the oldest of eight siblings, was thrust into the role of caretaker. Wells's Aunt Georgine recalls that "Ida saw herself now as the grown-up and wanted to be strong. She
35　did all her crying in private so the little ones wouldn't see her." Jergensen reflects that Wells learned early on "that she was in charge of protecting her brothers and sisters, and that feeling extended later in life to her figurative brothers and sisters in the struggle for racial and gender equality."

40　Wells went to Rust College to become a teacher, and her ability to mold the thought processes of others made her a persuasive orator and writer. Jergensen compares Wells's debating style to that of Socrates, who used shrewdly-worded questions and statements to lead his opponent from his original
45　sense of certainty into a state of doubt about the correctness of his convictions. Similarly, Wells frequently started her essays and speeches with general questions about morality, fairness,

and human rights, baiting her opposition into admitting certain core principles before challenging them to reconcile these
50　fundamental rights with the unfair and discriminatory laws and practices they endorsed.

After a public speaking tour of England, Wells made a home for herself in Chicago, where she met the man who would eventually become her husband, Ferdinand Barnett. Together, they
55　raised two sons and two daughters, though later in life, Wells would bemoan the fact that she felt as though the responsibility of raising and supporting the four children became her primary concern, while her husband became engrossed in a political bid to become a Circuit Court judge.

60　Domestic life didn't spell the end of Wells's struggle against inequality, however—during her time in Chicago, she founded the nation's first civic organization for black women. It was initially called the Women's Era Club, though it would later be renamed the Ida B. Wells Club. In 1895, her book
65　*A Red Record* was published, documenting the history of racially-motivated lynchings in America. Although the book succeeded in motivating an audience of progressive thinkers, race-related riots and violence continued virtually unabated into the early 20th century.

70　Jergensen conveys a clear appreciation for the deep reserves of patience on which Wells was repeatedly forced to draw in order to maintain her devotion to both family and society, despite often being castigated or ignored by both. By retracing Wells's "long walk home" from the grueling aftermath of her
75　parents' death, through her exile from Memphis, to her eventual involvement in creating the NAACP (National Association for the Advancement of Colored People), Jergensen leaves the reader feeling exhausted, expending such vast amounts of sympathy for the injustices Wells faces. As portrayed by Jergensen, Wells is a
80　protagonist who nobly walks a self-chosen path of monumental toil, with rewards few and far between. One such reward must have been the passage of women's suffrage in 1920 with the 19th Amendment which Wells, then a grandmother, was finally able to see first-hand.

11. In the statement in lines 36–39 Jergensen most strongly stresses:

A. a consistent propensity Wells had to take care of those in need of help.

B. the way Wells's family persuaded her to take part in the civil rights struggle.

C. the lessons of equality that Wells learned by acting like a parent to her siblings.

D. a powerful metaphor Wells would later use in many of her incendiary speeches.

12. As portrayed in the passage, the reaction of Wells to her parents dying from a bout of yellow fever is best described as:

    F. sad and frightened.
    G. mournful but resilient.
    H. relieved and emboldened.
    J. brave but hopeless.

13. The passage's author most strongly implies that Wells's relationship with her husband:

    A. began a decline in her activism as she turned her focus to starting a family.
    B. was the most lasting consequence of her public speaking tour in England.
    C. did not halt her efforts in the struggle for equality.
    D. was the main reason behind her starting the Ida B. Wells Club.

14. Lines 6–9 most nearly mean that Wells:

    F. faced the problem of audiences reluctant to hear what she had to say.
    G. spoke too softly for many people to take her ideas seriously.
    H. did not believe that people would discredit her because of her race or gender.
    J. had to create a pen name in order to have her newspaper articles be read by the mainstream.

15. According to the passage, who disapproved of the ideas described in lines 12–16?

    A. Wells herself
    B. Jergensen
    C. Some people in Memphis
    D. The civil rights community

16. Another reviewer of Jergensen's book sums up Wells in this way:

> A tireless and outspoken advocate of equality, Ida B. Wells did not shy away from making controversial demands of her audience ... sometimes jeopardizing her own safety, always reminding her listeners that equality was in accord with their fundamental sense of fairness.

How does this account of Wells compare to that of the passage's author?

    F. This account portrays Wells's demands as fair, whereas the passage's author remains less convinced.
    G. This account emphasizes the danger Wells put herself in, whereas the passage's author does not mention this.
    H. Both provide a comparably unflattering portrayal of Wells's goals and tactics.
    J. Both provide a comparably flattering portrayal of Wells's goals and tactics.

17. For the passage's author, lines 81–84 mainly support her earlier point that:

    A. Wells did manage to see some of her goals realized in her lifetime.
    B. family was an essential factor in motivating Wells's struggle.
    C. significant changes happen in society with each new generation.
    D. Wells became much wiser and more thankful in her old age.

18. According to the passage, Jergensen believes that Wells' had a style of debating similar to that of Socrates because Wells:

    F. had a strong sense of certainty about her philosophical convictions.
    G. did not advance her own agenda but only wanted to understand her opponent.
    H. understood that clever oration can only do so much to further a cause.
    J. used points of agreement to show her opponents problems with their points of view.

19. The passage's author characterizes the book *A Red Record* most nearly as:

    A. a good effort that was troubled by philosophical inconsistencies.
    B. unusually radical compared to other books from the same era.
    C. impressively broad in the scope of social issues it tackled.
    D. mainly effective at inspiring its like-minded readers.

20. The passage most strongly suggests that Wells approached her life as a:

    F. bleak marathon.
    G. determined struggle.
    H. confusing journey.
    J. constant triumph.

Passage III

HUMANITIES: This passage is adapted from the novel *Southern Charmed Life* by Robert Anderson (© 1978 by Robert Anderson).

B.B. King has been a popular singer and blues guitarist since the 1950s.

In the summer of 1953, Uncle Randy was particularly excited for our visit. Sis and I got to spend a couple weeks with him each summer, to escape the heat of our home in Thibadeux, Louisiana. He was choir director at St. Peter's church in Des
5 Moines, Iowa. Sometimes we went with him to visit the homes of the older parishioners, helping him clean up their yards, grocery shopping for them, or cleaning their gutters.

Uncle Randy told us his friend from Mississippi was coming through town, a man named Riley King, although people
10 called him 'B.B'. He spoke in hushed awe of his friend B.B., who was "King of the Blues." "I don't much like the Blues," Sis would say. "You can't dance to it."

Before we left for B.B.'s hotel, to take him over to Sunday mass, Uncle Randy cleaned his Chevrolet Deluxe like an infantry
15 man would his rifle. It was a humble man's car, but we got it shining like the President's limousine.

As we pulled into the parking lot of the Majestic Hotel, I saw a man waiting near the front doors, looking off into the distance. His guitar case stood vertically, parallel with his up-
20 right posture, his hands folded serenely on the top of the case, slightly rocking back and forth on his heels.

"Hey! Somebody! I need the world's best guitarist! It's an emergency!" yelled my Uncle, to get B.B.'s attention. B.B. recognized his voice immediately, but paused a half second to
25 finish his thought before smiling and turning to see us driving up.

"Well, then, let me get in the car and help you look for T-Bone Walker," B.B. said, leaning in through the passenger-side window. Seeing us, he added with a mischievous smile, "So these are the troublemakers?"

30 "Yup. Kathie Mae and Bobby. Kids, this is Mr. King." my uncle warmly, yet formally, announced.

"Aw, they don't gotta call me 'Mister'. I'm B.B." He offered each of us a handshake, which we timidly accepted. His hands were large and calloused, and he wore several gold rings
35 on his fingers.

Sis and I sat silently in the back, peering nervously at this strange new arrival who was filling the car with his large frame, his guitar, and his Sunday-best cologne. His pockmarked face was worn but jubilant. He seemed like a man who had seen
40 all the hardships of the road, but whose youthful, joyous spirit still remained.

My uncle was chatting with B.B., asking him about his recent performances, and about all the money he must be making, but B.B. seemed reluctant to boast. "Ah, you know. We just
45 make enough money to get to the next town and get a meal in us. Maybe sometimes a little extra to bring home."

My sister burst out, inquisitively, "Where's home?" B.B. was seated in front of Sis, but wanting to acknowledge her, he turned his head halfway and said, "Itta Bena." She asked back,
50 "Itta Whatta?" The adults laughed. Uncle Randy clarified that it was a town in Mississippi, near Indianola, where we had come to visit him before he moved to Iowa. Feeling particularly fearless for a ten year old, Sis asked B.B. why he likes playing sad music. B.B. gave a rich chuckle and decided he had to look
55 Kathy Mae in the eyes for this one. He shifted his guitar to the side and turned his husky frame as far as he could, until his marbled, twinkling brown eyes could look straight into hers.

"Honey, the music isn't sad. Life is sad ... sometimes. And the Blues is just how you get through it. It's hard for a young
60 'un to hear the Blues right because you haven't been through enough pain of livin' yet." My Uncle was smiling, looking in the rear-view mirror at Sis, trying to judge her reaction. She seemed to be partly insulted by the implication that she would not be able to "get" the Blues.

65 "Have you ever cried yourself to sleep?" B.B. asked. Sis tightened her lips in resentment. "Don't be shy. We all have. Didn't you feel better when you woke up?" Sis tentatively agreed.

B.B. explained, "it's because the pain is distant when you wake up. The Blues is how I cry myself to sleep. It puts a dream
70 in between me and the pain, just like a thick frosted window pane that muffles it and makes it fuzzy to see." Sis and I turned to each other, finding this pearl of wisdom difficult to digest and resigning to the fact that some things were not meant for kids.

75 Years later, I would find a deep appreciation for B.B.'s music. Whenever I hear him play, I can't help but to imagine a waterfall—the pressure of the falling water was the weight of the pain. The mournful verses he sung made me think of the space behind the waterfall, a calm place of imprisonment,
80 where a thundering curtain of water is all you see in front of you. And when he started his guitar solo, it was like I turned into a bird that flew out through the waterfall. The heavy water pounded my light, buoyant frame down as I passed through it, but, once through, I was able to feel the freedom of lift, the
85 droplets of water rolling off my wings as I soared up towards the clouds, and the waterfall was only something beautiful to behold in the distance.

21. According to the passage, which of the following events occurred last chronologically?

    A. The narrator meets B.B. in the hotel parking lot.
    B. The narrator develops a strong fondness for B.B.'s music.
    C. The narrator helps his uncle perform chores for parishioners.
    D. The narrator helps clean his uncle's car.

22. Based on the passage, how old was the narrator's sister when she met King?

    F. Six
    G. Ten
    H. Twelve
    J. Fifteen

23. As it is used in line 72, the word *digest* most nearly means:

    A. understand.
    B. stomach.
    C. memorize.
    D. study.

24. The point of view from which the passage is told is best described as that of someone:

    F. trying to learn more about Mississippi culture.
    G. vacationing with his sister and his Uncle Randy.
    H. recounting how he learned to play blues guitar.
    J. remembering fondly an encounter with B.B. King.

25. Through his description of his meeting with B.B. King, the narrator portrays King most nearly as:

    A. flashy.
    B. morose.
    C. undignified.
    D. modest.

26. King uses the simile in lines 70–71 to convey the ability of the Blues to:

    F. get the most emotion out of a musical instrument.
    G. dull the sharpness of suffering.
    H. transform complex feelings into simple ones.
    J. help people relax and get to sleep.

27. Based on the passage, the narrator's and his sister's initial reaction to meeting King is one of:

    A. warmth and informality.
    B. caution and anxiety.
    C. amazement and confusion.
    D. skepticism and disappointment.

28. The narrator compares the feeling created by King's guitar solos to the feeling of:

    F. "a thick frosted window pane" (lines 70–71).
    G. "the space behind the waterfall" (line 79).
    H. "a thundering curtain of water" (line 80).
    J. "a bird that flew out through the waterfall" (line 82).

29. It is most reasonable to infer from the passage that King believes a true appreciation of the Blues comes primarily from:

    A. an upbringing similar to King's in Mississippi.
    B. watching it performed live by musicians.
    C. recognizing the struggles of life.
    D. having deeply held religious beliefs.

30. It is reasonable to infer that, following King's explanation of the Blues to Kathy Mae, the narrator and his sister:

    F. resolved to listen to Blues music more in order to understand the meaning behind King's words.
    G. decided they would ask Uncle Randy more about the Blues once King was no longer in their company.
    H. accepted that the point King was attempting to communicate was beyond their level of comprehension.
    J. gained the newfound impression that Blues music is a response to, not a cause of, sadness.

Passage IV

NATURAL SCIENCE: The following is adapted from the article "Seeking an Intelligent Definition of Intelligence" by Clark Matthews (© 2010 by Clark Matthews).

Cognitive psychologists who study humans and other animals are perpetually attempting to understand the type and extent of intelligence possessed by their subjects. Hindering their efforts is the ongoing debate about how we should define
5　such a nebulous concept as 'intelligence' in the first place. A scatter-hoarder species of squirrel would probably define intelligence as the ability to remember and re-locate the thousands of caches of food it has burrowed in hiding places throughout its environment. A dog, on the other hand, may emphasize its
10　ability to trace the source of objects in its environment based on the direction of the air current containing that smell.

There is a risk of bias in how we define intelligence because each species has evolved very specialized abilities based on its unique environmental niche and the techniques and strategies
15　that niche requires for survival. If we use our concepts of human capacities to define intelligence, we may be creating a standard that other animals couldn't hope to meet. Conversely, if we only mean by intelligence "the most highly refined capacities of that species" we make intelligence something that can only
20　be compared within a species, not across species.

One definition of intelligence holds that it is "a wide range of abilities relating to learning from one's environment and experience, and combining that learning with abstract reasoning to solve problems." Scientists frequently begin assessing
25　an animal's intelligence based on its susceptibility to classical or operant conditioning. Both methods involve pairing either a stimuli or a behavior with certain consequences, and waiting to see if a subject learns to associate the two and act accordingly. The faster the animal appears to absorb and act on the
30　association, the faster we believe it has 'learned' it. This gives us one supposedly objective means of comparing intelligent behavior across species.

The other primary evidence of an animal's intelligence is its ability to solve novel and/or complex problems. A spider
35　that spins a web to solve the problem of trapping insects for food is not considered to be displaying intelligence because the problem (food gathering) and behavior (spinning webs) are both embedded in the evolutionary history of a spider's habitat. An elephant that picks a lock at the zoo is thought to be acting
40　intelligently, since elephants do not pick locks in their native habitat and hence have no instinctive knowledge of how do undo them. The veined octopus is seen as a tool-user, scouring the ocean for coconut shells, which it proceeds to bring back to its homestead for the sake of building shelter. Although many
45　other animals, such as crabs and ants will take shelter using nearby objects, animal psychologists consider the long-term planning involved in the veined octopus's behavior as better evidence that it can conceptualize a goal and then act on it.

As if defining intelligence weren't tricky enough, measur-
50　ing intelligence is also a tenuous task. Ultimately, scientists can only observe an animal's behavior. So how can they ascertain if the animal is just behaving instinctively or if it is actually conceptualizing, thinking abstractly, and aware of its problem solving process? Because understanding is a private experience,
55　observing an animal's external behavior and hoping to infer its level of understanding is always a guessing game.

Both "intelligent" behavior and "unintelligent" behavior can be deceiving. Irene Pepperberg's famous subject, the parrot Alex, showcased a variety of impressive problem solving and
60　communication abilities that suggested an internal awareness and capacity for intelligence was present. For instance, Alex correctly called a "key" a "key," no matter what size, color, or orientation a certain key was. This suggests Alex had grouped the individual keys used to train him into a general category that
65　could be applied to novel stimuli. However, sometimes Alex gave wrong answers to a task he had completed successfully many times before. This was interpreted as Alex's boredom and frustration at repeating a task he had already mastered. Although the behavior looked unintelligent, experimenters
70　believed it was not due to a lack of understanding. Conversely, there is also the perpetual concern of the Clever Hans Effect, in which seemingly intelligent behavior is not believed to be the result of genuine understanding. The name comes from a horse named Clever Hans who was paraded around Europe in
75　the early 20th century, supposedly a marvel of animal intelligence. Hans could indicate the correct solution to arithmetic problems by tapping his hoof the appropriate number of times. Ultimately, though, scientists realized that Hans was getting the answer by reading nonverbal clues from his trainer. The trainer
80　would unknowingly tense up as the correct number of taps was getting nearer, which signaled to Hans when it was time to stop tapping. So although Hans exhibited behavior that seemed indicative of underlying intelligence, scientists do not believe he was actually solving the problems conceptually in his mind.

31. The main function of the second paragraph (lines 12–20) in relation to the passage as a whole is to:

   A. explain the human bias that is the focus of the rest of the passage.
   B. advance the argument that intelligence should be defined in human terms.
   C. show how certain types of definitions have undesirable consequences.
   D. provide background information about the evolutionary niches of species.

32. According to the passage, what is the primary problem with defining intelligence as "the most highly refined capacities" of a given species?

   F. It would be a standard that no species could hope to meet.
   G. It would not take into account each species' unique environmental niche.
   H. It would too closely mimic our concepts of human intelligence.
   J. It would not be a standard we could use to compare one species to another.

33. According to the passage, all of the following behaviors seem to be intelligent EXCEPT:

   A. a spider solving the problem of trapping insects by spinning a web.
   B. an elephant picking a lock at the zoo.
   C. a veined octopus finding coconut shells for its shelter.
   D. a parrot identifying keys of various shapes and sizes.

34. According to the passage, scientists often start their assessment of animal's intelligence by:

   F. analyzing its ability to solve new and complex problems.
   G. identifying the most highly refined capacities of that species.
   H. stimulating the animal and observing its behavior.
   J. seeing how much information the animal can absorb.

35. Suppose beavers typically gather sticks from the forest floor and bring them to a stream to construct a dam. One beaver that cannot find enough sticks on the ground begins to strip bark from dying trees. Based on the passage, the author would most likely describe the behavior of this gopher as:

   A. intelligent if the lack of sticks is a novel problem.
   B. unintelligent if there was long-term planning.
   C. impressive and the result of operant conditioning.
   D. deceptive and illustrating the Clever Hans effect.

36. The passage indicates that the shelters of the veined octopus differ from those of crabs and ants in that the octopus shelters:

   F. are more likely to be constructed from nearby objects.
   G. are made of much sturdier materials than are crab and ant shelters.
   H. have more architectural interest than those of the crabs and ants.
   J. seem more to be the result of a long-term plan.

37. The primary purpose of the passage is to:

   A. define intelligence as it applies to non-human species.
   B. explore some of the challenges, both conceptual and practical, involved in assessing intelligence.
   C. identify the criteria used to discriminate between intelligent and unintelligent behavior.
   D. compare and contrast how intelligence appears within human species versus how it appears in non-human species.

38. The author mentions the behavior of the parrot Alex in the last paragraph primarily to:

   F. demonstrate that poor performance does not necessarily indicate poor comprehension.
   G. illustrate the meaning of intelligent behavior as applied to parrots.
   H. highlight an animal believed to be unintelligent which nonetheless acted intelligently.
   J. supply proof that animals can indeed learn the meaning of a concept.

39. As it is used in line 54, the word *private* most nearly means:

   A. internal.
   B. secretive.
   C. subtle.
   D. shy.

40. In the context of the passage, the phrase "can be deceiving" (line 58) most nearly suggests that an animal's behavior:

   F. often is intended to trick other animals in its environment.
   G. is the hardest thing about an animal to measure in a scientific way.
   H. will fool observers who are not trained to know better.
   J. does not always serve as a reliable indicator of that animal's mental activities.

**END OF TEST 3
STOP! DO NOT TURN THE PAGE UNTIL TOLD TO DO SO.
DO NOT RETURN TO A PREVIOUS TEST.**

Chapter 25
Reading Practice
Test 3: Answers and
Explanations

READING PRACTICE TEST 3 ANSWERS

1.	A		21.	B
2.	F		22.	G
3.	B		23.	A
4.	G		24.	J
5.	A		25.	D
6.	H		26.	G
7.	B		27.	B
8.	F		28.	J
9.	C		29.	C
10.	J		30.	H
11.	A		31.	C
12.	G		32.	J
13.	C		33.	A
14.	F		34.	H
15.	C		35.	A
16.	J		36.	J
17.	A		37.	B
18.	J		38.	F
19.	D		39.	A
20.	G		40.	J

SCORE YOUR PRACTICE TEST

Step A
Count the number of correct answers: _____. This is your *raw score*.

Step B
Use the score conversion table below to look up your raw score. The number to the left is your *scale score*: _____.

Reading Scale Conversion Table

Scale Score	Raw Score	Scale Score	Raw Score	Scale Score	Raw Score
36	40	27	30	18	18
35	39	26	29	17	16–17
34	38	25	27–28	16	15
33	37	24	26	15	14
32	36	23	24–25	14	12–13
31	35	22	23	13	11
30	34	21	22	12	9–10
29	32–33	20	20–21	11	8
28	31	19	19	10	6–7

READING PRACTICE TEST 3 EXPLANATIONS

Passage I

1. **A** Choice (A) refers to a detail that comes from the description of Jacob's job working for his uncle. During the tour guide job, Jacob pointed out completed buildings, not works in progress. Choice (B) is supported by the script the tour guide had him read. Choice (C) is supported by the fact that the tour mostly attracted *Civil War enthusiasts*. Choice (D) is supported by the phrase *fancying himself as cutting quite a figure in his clean, pressed uniform* (lines 33–34).

2. **F** The first few sentences of the second paragraph establish that Gettysburg is a town that is stuck in the past, or at least doing very little to modernize. *This lack of innovation* affects Jacob and gives him the impression that *there was little of interest to be discovered outside Gettysburg* (lines 26–27). Choice (G) is incorrect because the passage never offers Jacob's ideas for improving old buildings. Choice (H) is incorrect because the passage never discusses Jacob having difficulty finding a job. Choice (J) is incorrect because the passage does not suggest Jacob planned to work for the railroad.

3. **B** The passage is essentially narrating Jacob's thoughts the majority of the time, and otherwise providing exposition on Jacob's life. Choices (A) and (C) are incorrect because there is nothing in the passage that provides an inner thought from Erin. Choice (D) is incorrect because there is no dialogue in the passage.

4. **G** The passage refers to a fantasy Jacob had about being called to Erin's house and impressing her parents, but the passage never indicates that it happened. Choice (F) is supported in the second sentence of the fifth paragraph. Choice (H) is supported in the last sentence of the fifth paragraph. Choice (J) is supported in the second to last sentence of the fifth paragraph.

5. **A** The last sentence of the first paragraph says that Jacob's *ambition towards ascending in the field* (lines 12–13) was basically to be able to impress a *fetching girl on his arm* (line 14) by describing architectural features of their environment. Choice (B) is incorrect because the passage never mentions Jacob devising a new approach to plumbing. Choice (C) is incorrect because the passage never mentions a desire to redesign the Dobbin House. Choice (D) is contradicted by details in the first paragraph which state that Jacob went to Mount St. Mary's, *not because it had a renowned architectural program* (lines 6–7).

6. **H** Although Jacob's high school is mentioned as being small in comparison to Mount St. Mary's College, the number of students is never provided. Choice (F) is answered in the first paragraph—Jacob's tennis scholarship and yearning for Erin are the main factors. Choice (G) is answered in the third paragraph. *As each tour began*, Jacob was disappointed to not see Erin, so she never came to his tour. Choice (J) is answered in the second paragraph—*this lack of innovation deepened Jacob's disinterest in personal or academic enterprise* (lines 25–26).

7. **B**   The last sentence of the fourth paragraph (lines 48–52) indicates that it wasn't *until he left the job* that Jacob started thinking more about the buildings. Choice (A) is incorrect because it is the opposite of what the passage indicates. Choices (C) and (D) are incorrect because the passage provides no comparison between how historically noteworthy Jacob thought the buildings were during and after his job as a tour guide.

8. **F**   The paragraph begins with Jacob's frustration regarding his inability to run into Erin at college. It ends with Jacob, *With a resigned sigh* (line 76), recounting a memory of his one date with Erin. His final thought is that they were on two different tracks, hers a fearless stride toward the future and his an attempt to get used to the present. These sad details support (F)'s notion that he and Erin had grown apart. Choice (G) is incorrect because, although Jacob was frustrated by the campus size in his efforts to run into Erin, there is not support for something so strong as anger. Also, this would only relate to the beginning of the paragraph and not address the rest of it. Choice (H) is incorrect because there is no attitude mentioned or suggested towards Jacob's marriage to Martha. Also, this answer would not address the majority of the paragraph. Choice (J) is incorrect because, although you would assume Jacob was happy to get the date, the details in the paragraph are largely relating to why a relationship with Erin failed. There is no wording in the passage that indicates Jacob's contentment.

9. **C**   The wording *an indelible streak of humility* is used in the second sentence of the first paragraph (lines 2–5), attributed to Jacob's grandmother telling him that the rest of the world was under no obligation to think he was special. Choice (A) is incorrect because humility is never suggested by the passage to be a trait of working class communities. Choice (B) is incorrect because Jacob's humility is more the cause of his feeling that he won't be famous than it is a consequence. Choice (D) is incorrect because the passage never links humility to Jacob's pursuit of Erin.

10. **J**   This statement is from the last sentence of the passage, which begins *With a resigned sigh, he remembered....* Hence, all the details in the sentence are things Jacob remembers about his first date with Erin. Choice (F) is incorrect because this is Jacob's impression, not the author's. Choice (G) is incorrect because this detail is presented as part of Jacob's memory of his date with Erin, not as part of his struggle to find her at college. Choice (H) is incorrect because this is part of Jacob's reminiscence, not Erin's.

Passage II

11. **A**   The statement from Jergensen compares the way in which Wells looked out for her siblings to the way in which she looked out for the rights of any humans suffering from racial inequality. Choice (B) is incorrect because the passage does not suggest that any of her family members *persuaded* her to be an activist. Choice (C) is incorrect because the passage does not suggest she learned any *lessons of equality* via taking care of her siblings. Choice (D) is incorrect because the passage doesn't suggest any family metaphor used by Wells in her speeches.

12. **G** The passage relays Aunt Georgine's comment that Ida wanted to be the grown up she knew her brothers and sisters needed. Ida mourned privately in order to keep a strong appearance. Choice (F) is incorrect because *frightened* goes against the portrayal of Ida stepping into the caretaking role. Choice (H) is incorrect because *relieved* goes against the sadness Ida felt over her parents' passing. Choice (J) is incorrect because *hopeless* is too strong to be supported by anything in the passage.

13. **C** The passage states that *domestic life didn't spell the end of Wells's struggle against inequality* (lines 60–61), and the passage proceeds to describe Wells's activism after she was married. While care for the family did become primarily her concern rather than her husband's, the passage does not say her efforts in the struggle for racial equality were diminished, so cross off (A). Choice (B) is incorrect because Wells met her husband in Chicago, not England. Choice (D) is incorrect because there is no implied connection between her husband and the book club; additionally, she didn't start the club with that name.

14. **F** The passage calls Wells a *hushed voice in the race debate* (lines 7–8) since she was saying things people didn't want to hear. People were unaccustomed in those times to hearing such things from a woman and often sought to deny her her voice. Choice (G) is incorrect because the word *hushed* is not referring to softer volume, but rather, metaphorically, to being told to "hush!" Choice (H) is the opposite of the impression given by the passage, which is that Wells *did* recognize her gender and race as an obstacle to getting her message across. Choice (J) is incorrect because although the passage mentions her writing under a pseudonym (line 12), it was to protect her identity and it certainly wasn't for a "mainstream" newspaper.

15. **C** The passage indicates that following the publishing of Wells's article, she became *a despised figure in Memphis* (line 21). Choices (A), (B), and (D) are all incorrect because the passage states and/or implies that these parties would be sympathetic to Wells's public outcry.

16. **J** The passage provides a positive treatment of Wells, discussing her bold outrage in the first few paragraphs and her techniques of persuasion in the fifth paragraph. All these details correspond well with this account. Choice (F) is incorrect because the passage never calls into question the *fairness* of Wells's objectives. Choice (G) is incorrect because the passage *does* mention, in the first few paragraphs, the danger Wells put herself in. Choice (H) is incorrect because there is nothing to support the author's *unflattering* portrayal of Wells.

17. **A** Two sentences prior to this one, the author mentions Wells's long toil with only occasional rewards, and then mentions women's suffrage in 1920 as one of these "rewards." The sense of change on a societal level that the sentence in question refers to is women achieving suffrage in 1920, so it supports (A). Choice (B) is unsupported by the passage, which never says that family motivated Wells's struggle. Choice (C) is unsupported by the passage, which does not ever suggest each generation brings significant changes to society.

18. **J** The passage states that Wells baited *her opposition into admitting certain core principles before challenging them* (lines 48–49) to apply those principles to racial inequality. Choice (F) is incorrect because, though Wells certainly must have had strong philosophical convictions and Socrates sought to weaken the strong convictions of his opponents, a shared sense of certainty is not part of the comparison Jergensen makes to Socrates. Choice (G) goes against the passage since Wells definitely has an agenda to promote racial and gender equality. Choice (H) is incorrect because the passage never discusses Wells's thoughts on the limits of what oration can accomplish.

19. **D** The passage states in the last sentence of the sixth paragraph (lines 66–69) that the book motivated an audience of *progressive thinkers*, while the practical and statistical measures of the problem it addressed did not improve. Choice (A) is incorrect because *philosophical inconsistencies* are not mentioned or suggested. There is no support for calling the book *unusually* radical, as (B) does. The author does not praise the *scope* of the book, mentioning only its purpose of documenting racially influenced lynchings; eliminate (C).

20. **G** The last paragraph states that Wells *nobly walks a self-chosen path of monumental toil, with rewards few and far between* (lines 80–81). This agrees best with (G). Choice (F) is too pessimistic for the passage's overall heroic portrayal of Wells. Choice (H) is incorrect since the idea that Wells's steadfast struggle to attain equality was *confusing* is not justified. Choice (J) is incorrect because it goes against the passage's portrayal of Wells's life as being filled with challenge and strife.

Passage III

21. **B** The last paragraph begins *years later*, indicating that the narrator's explanation of his love for B.B.'s music developed years after the summer of 1953 trip. Choices (A) and (D) took place during the summer of 1953 trip. Choice (C) is suggested to have taken place before the summer of 1953 trip.

22. **G** In the eleventh paragraph (lines 47–57), the passage says *feeling particularly fearless for a ten year old, Sis asked* .... Choices (F), (H), and (J) are incorrect because they contradict the age given for the narrator's sister.

23. **A** Saying King's words are difficult to process is akin to saying they are difficult to understand. Choice (B) is a trap answer due to its similarity to the normal meaning of *digest*. Saying something is difficult to stomach means one is reluctant to accept its meaning, not that one does not understand its meaning. Choices (C) and (D) relate to the process of learning and understanding, but neither one itself is a good substitute for the concept of understanding.

24. **J** The narrator is retelling events from the summer of 1953 that involve him meeting B.B. King, and describes the effect B.B.'s music came to have on him. This best supports (J). Choice (F) is incorrect because, other than the fact that B.B. and Uncle Randy both lived in Mississippi, there is nothing in the passage about trying to learn that state's culture. Choice (G) is incorrect because, although some of the

passage's events take place during a vacation the narrator took with his sister to see his Uncle Randy, the narrator is describing those events in the past tense, not currently on vacation with them. Choice (H) is incorrect because it is never implied that the narrator plays guitar or learned to from B.B. King.

25. **D** B.B. is very polite with the narrator and his sister, having them address him informally by his first name. B.B. refuses to be acknowledged as *the world's best guitarist*, substituting instead the name of *T-Bone Walker*. And, in talking to the narrator's uncle about life on the road, he seemed *reluctant to boast* (line 44). These details all support (D). Choice (A) is not supported, other than by the fact that B.B. wore gold rings and his Sunday-best cologne. These are not necessarily *flashy* things, though, as any adult might wear such things. Choice (B) is not supported because, although B.B. plays the Blues and discusses times in his life where he is sad, the narrator describes him having a *youthful, joyous spirit* (line 40). Choice (C) is not supported by anything in the passage.

26. **G** King explains that the Blues helps him put some distance between himself and his pain, like a *frosted window* that *muffles it and makes it fuzzy* (lines 70–71). This supports the idea of dulling one's suffering in (G). Choice (F) is incorrect because King is not referring to any particular instrument. Choice (H) is close, but too broad—King is speaking about one particular feeling, not multiple ones. Choice (J) is too literal. Although sleep is mentioned in the extended metaphor/simile King describes, he is primarily discussing the way the Blues softens the feeling of pain.

27. **B** The passage states that the narrator and his sister *timidly accepted* (line 33) B.B.'s handshake. They *sat silently* (line 36) and peered *nervously*. These details support the adjectives used in (B). Choice (A) is incorrect because the kids were not warmly greeting him if they were timidly accepting his handshake. Choice (C) is incorrect because amazement and confusion both are more extreme than the general sense of curiosity and strangeness described in the passage. Choice (D) is incorrect because there is no support for either skepticism or disappointment in the passage.

28. **J** The author says when B.B. *started his guitar solo, it was like I turned into a bird that flew out through the waterfall* (lines 81–82). Choice (F) refers to how King compared the effect the Blues has on making pain feel more distant. Choice (G) refers to how the narrator compared the verses of King's music. Choice (H) refers to how the narrator compared the pain felt by the musician or listener.

29. **C** As King explains the Blues to Kathy Mae, he says she wouldn't *hear the Blues right* because she hasn't had enough *pain of livin' yet* (lines 60–61). Choices (A), (B), and (D) are incorrect because King never stresses his hometown, one's childhood upbringing, live versus recorded music, or one's degree of religious commitment.

30. **H** The passage indicates that the narrator and his sister had trouble digesting King's wisdom and resigned themselves to the idea that it was beyond a child's understanding. Choice (F) is incorrect because by resigning themselves to the fact that King's words were beyond them, they are giving up on understanding it, not resolving to expend more effort to understand it. Choice (G) is incorrect because the passage does not suggest any intent to speak with Uncle Randy about it. Choice (J) is incorrect because this answer sums up King's main message, which the children did not seem to absorb.

Passage IV

31. C The paragraph explains that if we define intelligence in human terms, other species might be hopeless to meet human criteria. However, if we define intelligence relative to a given species, we can't compare intelligence between animals of different species. These are suggested to be undesirable consequences. Choice (A) is incorrect because *human bias* is not the focus of the rest of the passage. Choice (B) is incorrect because the author does not endorse any specific definition of intelligence, and in this paragraph he explains a problem that would result from defining intelligence this way. Choice (D) is incorrect because the paragraph only mentions a general statement that every species has an evolutionary niche. This is not really background information, nor is that the focus of this paragraph.

32. J The last line of the second paragraph states that if we adopted this definition, we make intelligence something that cannot be compared *across species*. Choice (F) is incorrect because animals of the "given species" could definitely meet the standard as defined for their species. Choice (G) is incorrect because this definition, in being defined in terms of a given species, would take into account that species' unique traits. Choice (H) is incorrect because this definition would not use human intelligence as a measurement, but rather the unique capacities of each species.

33. A The passage specifically states that a spider that spins a web *is not considered to be displaying intelligence* (lines 35–36). Choices (B) and (C) are presented in the fourth paragraph as intelligent, and (D) is presented in the fifth paragraph as indicative of some intelligence.

34. H The passage states that *scientists frequently begin assessing an animal's intelligence* (lines 24–26) by analyzing the animal's *susceptibility to classical or operant conditioning*, which involves providing a stimulus and observing the animal's behavior. Choice (F) is incorrect because this is identified by the passage as the *other primary evidence* (line 33) of intelligence. Although this is an important form of evidence, it doesn't address the wording in the question stem, which specifically asks about where scientists *start* their assessments. Choice (G) is given (lines 18–19) as an example of something problematic in determining intelligence. Choice (J) is incorrect because the passage never mentions testing an animal's capacity to absorb information.

35. A The beginning of the fourth paragraph states that one of the primary sources of evidence for intelligence mentioned in the passage is the ability to solve novel problems. So if the lack of sticks is a new problem and the beaver devises a solution to address it, the author would call that intelligent behavior. Choice (B) is incorrect because *long-term planning* (lines 46–47) is described in the passage as evidence of intelligent behavior. Choice (C) is incorrect because there is no reason to think the beaver's behavior is the result of *operant conditioning*. Choice (D) is incorrect because there is no reason to assume the Clever Hans Effect is involved.

36. J The passage makes a contrast between crab and ant shelters and octopus shelters, saying the latter's *long-term planning* is better evidence of some intelligence. Choice (F) is incorrect because this would apply to crab and ant shelters. The veined octopus scours the ocean floor for coconut shells, which indicates a more extended search for materials. Choices (G) and (H) are incorrect because the passage mentions nothing about *sturdiness* and *architectural interest*, respectively.

37. **B** The passage spends the first four paragraphs (lines 1–48) discussing the conceptual difficulties involved in creating a definition of intelligence that would be applicable across a range of species. The rest of the passage describes the practical challenges involved in trying to measure intelligent behavior. Choice (A) is incorrect because the passage does not offer one clear definition for intelligence, but rather seeks a definition that would apply to human and non-human species alike. Choice (C) is incorrect because, although the passage describes some behavior as intelligent and other behavior as unintelligent, it does not identify specific criteria. Also, this answer is too narrow in terms of the passage's overall subject matter. Choice (D) is incorrect because the passage is not organized around a comparison between humans and non-humans. It is organized around the search for an understanding of intelligence that would relate to all animals.

38. **F** The author begins the paragraph by explaining that intelligent and unintelligent behavior aren't always what they seem. The example with Alex getting problems wrong is intended to demonstrate that *although the behavior looked unintelligent, experimenters believed it was not due to a lack of understanding* (lines 69–70). Choice (G) is incorrect because the author has no clear definition of intelligence, so he couldn't possibly be applying it to parrots. Choice (H) is incorrect because the parrot example mainly illustrated the opposite of this answer. Even though the parrot is described having seemingly intelligent behavior, the passage never says that parrots are believed to be unintelligent. Choice (J) is incorrect because the word *proof* is too strong. The author said that Alex's behavior *suggests* that it learned a concept, not that it *proves* it did.

39. **A** The sentence is making a contrast between the animal's private experience, which scientists can't observe, and the *external* behavior that scientists can observe. Choice (B) is incorrect because, although secrets are things that are hidden from some people, the adjective *secretive* implies an intention of hiding something, which is not present in the use of *private experience*. Choice (C) is incorrect because a private experience could be subtle or strong—either way it is something outsiders cannot perceive. Choice (D) is incorrect because *shy* implies being nervous or uncomfortable in the presence of others, and that is not what the passage implies about an animal's *private experience*.

40. **J** This topic sentence (lines 57–58) for the last paragraph foreshadows a discussion of a parrot who behaved unintelligently despite researchers believing it knew how to behave intelligently, and a horse who behaved intelligently but ultimately seemed to not have an intelligent grasp of its behavior. Choice (F) is incorrect because the examples provided do not suggest the animals intended to trick others; this is a trap answer based on the normal meaning of "deceive." Choice (G) is incorrect because the question asks about animal behavior, and that would not be the *hardest thing* to measure. The passage does not state what is the *hardest*, but it is suggested that the mental state of the animal is *harder* to measure than is the animal's behavior (lines 49–56). Choice (H) is incorrect because the passage maintains that even trained researchers still can only hazard a guess as to the thought processes that exist behind an animal's behavior. This answer implies that one can be trained enough to not be fooled.

Chapter 26
Reading Practice
Test 4

READING TEST

35 Minutes—40 Questions

DIRECTIONS: There are four passages in this test. Each passage is followed by several questions. After reading each passage, choose the best answer to each question and blacken the corresponding oval on your answer document. You may refer to the passages as often as necessary.

Passage I

PROSE FICTION: This passage is adapted from the novel *Birds of Paradise* by Minnie Foroozan (©2002 by Minnie Foroozan).

As a young woman, Ani Kealoha had never dreamt of someday owning a hotel on her native island of O'ahu, but—as she would happily tell any of the hotel guests and staff at her 120-room "home away from home"—her outgoing and car-
5 ing nature, along with a strong work ethic and natural ability for organization, had practically made it her destiny. Ani had grown up in a small but happy family of limited means. Most days, Ani would help her parents with their market stall on King Kekaulike Street, where they served increasing numbers
10 of tourists and military personnel. If she ever had aspirations of wealth, it was just to have enough money to visit the faraway places these visitors would talk about—Los Angeles, Sydney, or even New York. They captured her imagination and filled her with a desire for adventure.

15   In the years before statehood, once her sisters were old enough to assume some of her duties at the market, Ani Kealoha's desire to help her family and teenage sense of adventure led her to find other work as well. Hawaii's grow-ing and near year-round influx of tourists allowed ample
20 opportunity for someone of her character. She was a skillful musician and naturally graceful; she would play ukulele and dance to the *hapa-haole* music for the frequent tourist hula shows, eventually acting as "manager" for several groups of musicians and dancers. Ani "The Fearless" would walk from
25 hotel to hotel, asking to see the manager and, more often than not, convincing him that he should invite her group to perform. It was during these frequent visits that she became familiar with the already world-famous Moana Hotel. During one of her visits, she learned of, and was eventually offered,
30 an opening for a staff position at the hotel, and she accepted without hesitation.

Although she started there as a chambermaid, Kealoha recalled her time at the Moana with nostalgia. The endless parade of visitors, from the obscure to the famous, never grew
35 tiresome for her, and her enthusiasm for her work soon saw her managing the entire housekeeping staff. After again proving her capability and resourcefulness as a manager, she was even-tually to manage all guest services for the hotel.

With the arrival of statehood in 1959, everything changed.
40 Now a citizen of the United States, she, like her sisters and many of her friends, was eager to take advantage of the new opportunities citizenship offered. While her sisters chose to go to university on the mainland, Ani's experience qualified her to be employed as a civilian for the Quartermaster Corps,
45 helping to organize and distribute supplies to American units and troops still stationed throughout the Pacific.

Gazing out of her office window, listening to the sound of the surf and the ocean breeze in the palms, she often thought of her time as a clerk in the Quartermaster Corps, where she met
50 Lt. James Santos, to whose company she had been assigned, and with whom she would gradually fall in love and then marry a year later. In the days just after their marriage, they lived on the Army base in a small but neat bungalow-style home. When Santos, now "Jimmy," was later promoted to Lieutenant Colonel,
55 Kealoha left her clerking position and spent her time turning their little bungalow into a home—cooking meals in their tiny kitchen, adding a rug here, curtains there, and the big purchase, a brand-new radio. Then one day, Jimmy came home with a surprise: a tiny, half-starved, brown puppy, apparently orphaned.
60 They nursed him back to health, and gave him the grand name Pua Pua Lena Lena—after the beloved dog of Hawaiian myth—which was almost immediately shortened to "Pup."

Thinking about evenings at home with Jimmy, listening to programs like *Hawaii Calls* and with Pup sitting and staring
65 at the radio (looking for all the world like the dog on the RCA Victor label), Kealoha would smile and think about the first time she met Jimmy. Born in the Philippines and raised in Tacoma, Jimmy was young for his rank, being only 24 years old at the time, and newly-arrived in Hawaii. He was slightly-built and
70 fair-skinned, which made him look even younger than he was. As such, he made a special effort to maintain what he felt was the "proper" military bearing. At their first meeting, when she had reported to his office, he was terse, but not rude, and called her "Ms. Kealoha." She could tell that he was trying to make
75 his voice sound deeper than it actually was.

Lieutenant Santos was a tireless worker, and seemed to always find a reason to be at or near her desk, but at the same time, he would seldom speak to her or even make eye contact. Kealoha thought perhaps he felt that she, as a civilian, needed
80 extra supervision, and she made an extra effort to demonstrate just how capable she was.

1. The events in the passage are described primarily from the point of view of a narrator who presents the:

   A. thoughts of Kealoha, her customers, and her family as conveyed in dialogue.
   B. inner thoughts and sentiments of Kealoha only.
   C. inner thoughts of Kealoha and Santos only.
   D. inner thoughts and emotions of all the people in Kealoha's life.

2. The passage supports all of the following statements about the Moana Hotel EXCEPT that:

   F. it was one of the better-known hotels on the island of O'ahu.
   G. Kealoha worked there as a chambermaid.
   H. it had more rooms than the hotel Kealoha currently owns.
   J. its guests included celebrities as well as people who were not as well-known.

3. Which of the following questions is NOT answered by the passage?

   A. What kind of business did Kealoha's parents own?
   B. How long did Santos live in the Philippines before moving to Tacoma?
   C. How did Pup react when Kealoha and Santos listened to the radio?
   D. Under what circumstances did Kealoha first become aware of Santos?

4. One of the main ideas of the second paragraph (lines 15–31) is that:

   F. as a young woman, Kealoha often changed jobs because she quickly grew bored at each position.
   G. Kealoha's work as a musical group manager earned her the nickname Ani "The Fearless."
   H. working many jobs at once, Kealoha lost the opportunity to spend holidays with her family.
   J. because of her abilities and outgoing nature, Kealoha held a variety of jobs as a young woman.

5. According to the passage, all of the following were aspects of Kealoha's time at the Moana Hotel EXCEPT:

   A. cooking meals in the kitchen.
   B. working there as a chambermaid.
   C. receiving a promotion for her efforts.
   D. seeing celebrities.

6. In the passage, the statement that Santos appeared even younger than he was is best described as the opinion of:

   F. Kealoha that she expresses to him in an effort to compliment him.
   G. Santos that he states to the men in his command in hopes that Kealoha will overhear.
   H. Kealoha that she forms while working at Quartermaster Corps.
   J. Kealoha that replaced her earlier impression of him that he reminded her of someone she once knew.

7. The passage indicates that Kealoha's primary response to the events described in the fourth paragraph (lines 39–46) is:

   A. sadness due to her sisters' departure.
   B. concern about the loss of her heritage.
   C. optimism gained from new opportunities.
   D. dismay over the increased number of troops.

8. According to the passage, as a young woman, Kealoha made goals for herself that included:

   F. opening her own market.
   G. owning a farm on a different island.
   H. going to university on the mainland.
   J. traveling to different cities.

9. The passage indicates that compared to her work at her parents' market, Kealoha's job at the Moana offered:

   A. longer hours.
   B. shorter hours.
   C. fewer opportunities for advancement.
   D. more opportunities for advancement.

10. That Santos felt self-conscious about his age was:

   F. a confession he shared with the men in his platoon to put them at ease with him.
   G. an insight Kealoha made based on the manner in which he spoke to her.
   H. a question Kealoha posed to him in the first private conversation the two shared.
   J. an opinion he held because he had been promoted so early in his career.

Passage II

SOCIAL SCIENCE: This passage is adapted from the article "A Mann for All Seasons" by Tiptan Held (©2007 by Brookvale).

Held is reviewing the biography *Lasting Vision* by Thomas Younger.

In 1837 the state of Massachusetts formed the first-of-its-kind State Board of Education, and the search began for someone to fill the role of First Secretary. Horace Mann, a state senator from Massachusetts, accepted the position, despite a successful
5 and promising political career and the lack of any demonstrated interest in public education prior to his appointment. He was supposedly drawn to the role solely because it offered a dependable salary, a perk not offered to state legislators. Whatever his motivation may have been, as Thomas Younger writes
10 in his new biography, "Once the reins of the school system were placed in the sure hands of Horace Mann, the landscape of education in Massachusetts, and indeed the United States, was to change forever." And so it proved: after accepting the position, Mann turned to his duties with an unexpected, almost
15 unbelievable zeal, foregoing all other interests, both political and private, in their pursuit.

Thus began the legacy of the man who would eventually become known as the "Father of American Public Education," a surprising epitaph for a man whose own education, at least
20 during his formative years, was not particularly exceptional. Mann was born in 1796 in Franklin, Massachusetts and was raised by his parents on their family farm. From the time he was ten years old until he was twenty, he never attended more than six weeks of school in any given year. Some years, he didn't
25 attend at all. However, his Yankee upbringing had taught him the value of hard work and self-reliance. With the support of a tutor and using the resources of the town library, he studied on his own. He enrolled at Brown University at the age of twenty and graduated three years later as class valedictorian.

30 Younger's biography paints a picture of Mann as one of the most visionary and energetic reformers of his time, as well as one of the most prolific. He had already reached the relatively advanced age of forty-one when he was named First Secretary of the Board of Education, making the quality and quantity of
35 his accomplishments even more impressive. In what Younger calls "an unprecedented and daringly progressive campaign," Mann implemented the "common school" model, in which children from all social classes attended the same school. He argued that the common school model benefited all of society
40 and insisted that the single most important responsibility of a civilized state is the education of its citizens. In his description of Mann's reforms, Younger seems to invite a comparison to the similarly "radical" notions of abolition—a cause Mann would champion with equal fervor upon his election to the U.S. Senate
45 in 1848—and the Civil Rights movement almost a century later.

Mann's considerable dedication to reform was certainly impressive, all the more so considering the hardships he faced along the way, both public and private. Then, as now, education reform was a hotly-contested subject, and Mann encountered
50 resistance at nearly every turn, not only from the institutions he was trying to change but also from students, parents, and teachers. His stance on nonsectarian instruction angered many parents and various religious groups, just as his controversial proposal for the disuse of corporal punishment displeased a
55 group of schoolteachers in Boston. Mann also met with difficulty in his personal life; his grief over his first wife's death in 1832 never wholly left him. At about the same time, he inherited substantial debts left by his only brother. Despite these difficulties (or perhaps because of them), Mann's tireless
60 pursuit of his vision for change continued unabated, fueled by his singular passion and boundless energy.

Younger's well-structured narrative of Mann's life and works goes far beyond a simple recounting of his actions and achievements. By following him from his beginnings as a
65 self-educated young man, through his personal and professional travails and triumphs, to his eventually being named President of Antioch University, a larger story than that of a single individual emerges. Mann's crusade for public education becomes the story of reform itself, of drive and determination,
70 of struggle and sacrifice, and how the vision of one person, pursued relentlessly and with sufficient vigor, can spark change for an entire state, a nation, and indeed the world. Within a year of his appointment as Secretary of the Board of Education, Mann had visited every schoolhouse in the state to assess
75 personally the condition and quality of each. In 1838, Mann instituted the "normal" school system (a school whose primary purpose is to train high-school graduates to be teachers themselves, thereby establishing "norms") in Massachusetts and founded *The Common School Journal*, a publication in
80 which Mann, acting as sole editor, laid down his principles for public education. During his tenure, he also published a series of annual reports, which were circulated widely and influenced other school systems to adopt similar measures. It was this commitment not only to ideals but also to action,
85 Younger seems to tell us, that made Horace Mann an example for others who seek to effect social reform.

11. The passage's author most strongly implies that Mann's interest in public education:

A. was the result of a lifelong passion for education reform.
B. gradually lessened after his appointment as First Secretary of the Board of Education.
C. began in earnest after his appointment as First Secretary of the Board of Education.
D. ended abruptly after his wife's death in 1832.

12. According to the passage, who disapproved of the proposal described in lines 52–55?

F. A group of Boston schoolteachers
G. Younger
H. Mann's parents
J. Mann himself

13. As portrayed in the passage, Mann's reaction to the personal hardships he faced is best described as:

A. angry and afraid.
B. uncaring and selfish.
C. surprised but confident.
D. saddened but resolute.

14. In the statement in lines 10–13, Younger most strongly emphasizes:

F. the significance and impact of Mann's leadership as First Secretary of the Board of Education.
G. the folly of Mann's decision to give up a promising career in the legislature.
H. how Mann's upbringing had prepared him perfectly for his new position.
J. the contrast between the state education in Massachusetts and other places in the United States.

15. According to the passage, Younger believes Mann sets an example for others who seek social reform because Mann:

A. never sought the approval of others for his efforts to reform public education.
B. recognized that education reform can come about only through increased legislation.
C. was relentless in the pursuit of his own education.
D. was committed not only to his ideals but also to action.

16. The passage most strongly suggests that Mann felt the use of corporal punishment in education was:

F. necessary.
G. improper.
H. motivational.
J. justified.

17. Lines 35–38 most nearly mean that Mann:

A. patterned his model for a new school system on one that existed elsewhere.
B. cautiously instituted small reforms, one at a time, in order to achieve his goals.
C. fearlessly challenged the accepted social norms of the period in his efforts to reform education.
D. was more concerned with cost-saving measures than was his predecessor.

18. The passage's author characterizes Mann in the U.S. Senate most nearly as:

F. boldly engaged in other important reforms affecting the nation.
G. obsessively focused on the issue of education.
H. surprisingly inconsistent in his voting record on education issues.
J. amazingly articulate about the role of the state in educating its citizens.

19. For the passage's author, lines 72–75 mainly serve to support his earlier point that:

A. Mann had left the state legislature in order to be able to travel more.
B. there weren't enough schoolhouses in Massachusetts in the nineteenth century.
C. Mann tirelessly pursued his goal of improving and reforming education.
D. Mann was not effective at his job due to his extensive travel.

20. Another reviewer of Younger's book sums up Mann in this way:

Perhaps the single most important figure in American education reform, Horace Mann devoted himself entirely to the cause of public education. Despite facing widespread criticism, Mann never wavered in his commitment to universal education, and the effects of his reforms can still be seen today.

How does this account of Mann compare to that of the passage's author?

F. This account emphasizes Mann's commitment to reform, while the passage's author debunks it.
G. Both offer a similar and complimentary summary of Mann's work as a reformer.
H. Both offer a similar and critical summary of Mann's work as a reformer.
J. This account mentions Mann facing criticism, while the passage's author doesn't.

Passage III

HUMANITIES: This passage is adapted from the memoir *Sewing Circles* by Maria Erica Soreno (©2008 by Maria Erica Soreno).

Ingrid Bergman was a popular actress in Hollywood films of the 1940s and 50s.

In the autumn of 1945, my older sister Ines and I lived with Tìa Elena in her little house in Pasadena. There, working from her little shop on Paso Robles Street, Tìa Elena had made quite a name for herself as a skilled *costurera*, sewing beautiful
5 dresses for the women in the surrounding neighborhoods. In fact, her work was of such quality that sometimes she would get special orders from some of the nearby film studios, where she had worked years previously.

It was one such order she had received from RKO Radio
10 Pictures that seemed particularly important to her: a gorgeous, flowing, beige crepe evening gown, so intricate that I knew it must be for something or someone special.

"It's the most beautiful dress you've ever done, *tìa*," I told her.

Tìa Elena looked at me and smiled. "*Sì, hija*, and so it
15 should be—it's for the most beautiful woman in Hollywood. Would you and your sister like to meet her?"

Ines and I exchanged glances and said nothing, uncertain if our aunt was making a genuine offer.

The next day, however, with the just-finished gown pack-
20 aged carefully in a deceivingly plain white box, Tìa Elena called to Ines and me to join her on the trip to the studio to deliver the dress. Excited, but still a little doubtful, Ines and I climbed into the car, Ines in the front and I in the back, holding the box, with its delicate contents, on my lap.

25 We arrived at the studio lot, met by a guard at the gate who smiled at Tìa Elena and winked at my sister and me. "Welcome to RKO," he said and raised the gate to let us in. We parked the car and began walking towards one of the many buildings on the premises. Ines and I looked about in amazement at the
30 bustling studio lot—workers, costumed actors, cameramen, and hundreds of other people of every description were walking, running, standing, shouting, and laughing in a riot of noise and color. Tìa Elena took the package from me. "Hold your sister's hand, Maria," she said, "We need to stay together."

35 Despite the chaos and the fact that many of the large buildings looked nearly identical, Tìa Elena walked steadily onward, leading Ines and me up to one of the buildings, indistinguishable from the others apart from a large sign with the number 20 over the entrance. Inside was much the same
40 as outside—people everywhere, moving equipment, shouting

directions, and generally appearing rushed. Apparently unfazed by all the activity, Tìa Elena led us confidently through the maze of equipment and crowd of people until we arrived at a door with a star and the name "Ms. Bergman" on it.

45 After a quick, reassuring glance at my sister and me, Tìa Elena knocked on the door, which was answered almost immediately by a woman so strikingly tall and beautiful that I could barely think to say anything. Tìa Elena came to our rescue, however. "Ms. Bergman, these are my nieces, Ines and
50 Maria. I hope you don't mind visitors, but they were eager to hear your opinion about the dress."

Ms. Bergman smiled at us and crossed to where Tìa was unfolding the dress for her. She gasped and exclaimed, "Oh, Elena—it's the most wonderful gown I've ever seen; I'm
55 afraid I'll never do it justice!" Tìa Elena beamed with an artist's pride, but only replied modestly, "I'm so happy you like it, Ms. Bergman, but I could never have done it without help from Maria and Ines."

"Is that true, girls?" asked Ms. Bergman, and before we
60 could answer, said, "Well, your aunt is certainly lucky to have such helpful nieces. And please, enough of this 'Ms. Bergman' business; please call me Ingrid, and I'll call you Maria and Ines, just like friends should. Now, such expert work surely deserves a little reward." She took two photographs of herself
65 from a desk drawer and signed them. On mine she added, "For my friend, Maria," and then did likewise for Ines.

In my memory, our visit to the studio that day unfolds like a scene in my very own movie, full of spectacle and wonder and emotion. Ingrid was filming *Notorious* on the day of our
70 visit, and although I've seen all of her films, I still think of that particular film as "ours." Her masterful portrayal of the tragic character Alicia Huberman always makes me remember that day, if only because it stands in such stark contrast to the smiling, friendly, generous woman I met. She was to say, much
75 later, in an interview:

"I have no regrets. I wouldn't have lived my life the way I did if I was going to worry about what people were going to say."

I was only eleven when I met Ingrid Bergman and couldn't really understand the magnitude of her accomplishments, but as
80 I read those words now, spoken of a life lived on a stage, with successes and hardships alike in plain view for all to see, I can't help but recognize, and be inspired by, a truly independent spirit.

21. The point of view from which the passage is told is best described as that of someone:

   A. visiting a movie studio with her aunt and sister.
   B. wanting to become an actor like Bergman.
   C. trying to adjust to life in California.
   D. looking back warmly on meeting Bergman.

22. According to the passage, which of the following events occurred the last chronologically?

   F. The narrator feels inspired by Bergman.
   G. The narrator and her sister receive photographs from Bergman.
   H. The narrator visits a movie studio.
   J. Tía Elena finishes the beautiful gown.

23. Through her description of her meeting with Bergman, the narrator portrays Bergman most nearly as:

   A. snobbish.
   B. rushed.
   C. friendly.
   D. regretful.

24. Based on the passage, the narrator's reaction to being first addressed by Bergman is one of:

   F. fright and silence.
   G. envy and jealousy.
   H. awe and speechlessness.
   J. excitement and doubt.

25. It is reasonable to infer that, following their first meeting with Bergman, the narrator and her sister:

   A. instantly understood the impact that meeting Bergman would have on their lives.
   B. were too busy helping their aunt with her work to think much about it.
   C. continued to see Bergman's movies in order to recapture fond memories of meeting Bergman.
   D. sold the rare autographed photos to a collector so they could afford beautiful dresses.

26. The narrator describes the building they visit at RKO as:

   F. "a riot of noise and color" (lines 32–33)
   G. "full of spectacle and wonder" (line 68)
   H. "indistinguishable from the others" (line 38)
   J. "strikingly tall and beautiful" (line 47)

27. As it is used in line 68, the word *spectacle* most nearly means:

   A. marvel.
   B. performance.
   C. demonstration.
   D. extravaganza.

28. The narrator makes the comparison in lines 73–74 to describe Bergman's:

   F. ability to act in almost any kind of movie.
   G. portrayal of a character completely different from herself.
   H. appeal to fans of all ages.
   J. dramatic reaction to meeting the narrator.

29. Based on the passage, how old was the narrator when she met Bergman?

   A. Twenty
   B. Sixteen
   C. Thirteen
   D. Eleven

30. It is most reasonable to infer from the passage that the narrator gains an appreciation of Bergman's accomplishments primarily as a result of:

   F. the way Bergman treated her when they met.
   G. the influence of her aunt and sister.
   H. her perspective as an adult.
   J. finally seeing Bergman wearing the dress Tía Elena had made.

Passage IV

NATURAL SCIENCE: This passage is adapted from *What is Life?* by Harrison George. (©2002 by Melman University Press)

Few people have difficulty defining biology as "the study of life," which is a practical enough definition and certainly true. It may seem contradictory, then, that one of the most difficult and controversial issues biologists have to contend with
5   is defining what life really *is*. Since the time of Aristotle, there have been any number of definitions of life put forth, but as yet, there has been none that is accepted by all. Modern science, and particularly space exploration, has added a new twist to the old debate: we now have the ability to explore other planets
10 and search for, among other things, life—or at least evidence of it having once existed there. So, the question becomes, what exactly are we looking for?

The very essence of a definition is to describe the complex in terms of the simple, but with a concept as vastly complex as
15 life itself, the use of simple terms can be problematic. Some of the more frequently-used conditions put forth for "alive-ness" are complexity, autonomy, self-reproduction, evolution, and metabolism, all of which are assuredly qualities possessed by entities we would recognize as "alive." However, is a forest fire,
20 which self-reproduces and consumes fuel to produce energy (and therefore can be said to possess a "metabolism") alive? How about a computer virus that can evolve or mutate according to its "environment"? Are the individual cells of our bodies, which contain extremely complex internal machinery for the conversion
25 of nutrients into energy, to be considered separate, living entities? Our definition, it seems, requires terms general enough to include all living things but specific enough to exclude the non-living.

Another problem in finding specific terms for a definition is how far we carry their requirements. Terms like self-reproduction
30 and autonomy are useful but also problematic. Viruses self-reproduce, but they aren't autonomous because they depend on the metabolic functions of their host cells. Mules are autonomous living creatures, but they cannot reproduce—they are born sterile. And what of autonomy? Humans (and mules) depend on plants
35 for survival, so are they truly autonomous? Even plants, which don't require other organisms for food, depend on bacteria to break down atmospheric nitrogen, converting it from its inert form into one that allows photosynthesis to take place.

Regardless of the criteria we use for a definition, especially
40 for something as multiform and sublime as life itself, we must always be aware of the limitations we introduce in doing so. One such limitation is philosophical in nature—virtually all of our understanding of life comes from our observation of life on Earth. It was only recently, with the discovery of alternative
45 biochemistries, that it has become clear that a general definition of life will need to be flexible enough to also include life that is *not* necessarily dependent on oxygen and water.

This expansion of the notion of what it means to be alive has led to lively debate, to be sure, and it has also caused many
50 biologists to re-examine not only the terms used to define life but also the term "life" itself. The Gaia theory, for example, is a system of thought that treats the Earth as a whole as a single living organism. While it may not be surprising that such a radical departure from traditional systems of thought has
55 sparked heated opposition, the debate surrounding the issue has brought to light the difficulty of arguing that something is *not* alive without a widely-accepted definition for what *is* alive.

Perhaps the answer eventually to be found in the quest for a definition of life won't really be an answer at all, but
60 rather a whole series of new questions—questions that will open up new areas of study and help scientists gain a broader understanding of life and its place in the universe. Any good scientist knows that the importance of searching for knowledge far outweighs that of any single discovery, no matter how useful
65 or ground-breaking. Remember that it wasn't so very long ago that scientists considered there to be only four "elements" in the universe: fire, air, water, and earth. Each of these is easily enough described—fire, for example, is hot, needs fuel to burn, gives off light, etc. However, it was through efforts to gain a
70 deeper understanding—to find a definition, if you will—of those four elements that scientists made monumental discoveries in physical and molecular chemistry. Scientists could finally define water, for example, as a compound composed of two hydrogen atoms bonded to a single atom of oxygen. Now,
75 such a straightforward and simple description of so esoteric a concept as life may be unrealistic, but that is a small matter. The process of learning, of hypothesis and experiment, of trial and error, of investigation and observation, all brought to bear in a unified effort to achieve a goal—this is the true aim of
80 science. Perhaps in the end, rather than leading us to an answer, it will be the search itself that brings us closest to understanding what it is to be "alive."

31. The primary purpose of the passage is to:

   A. discuss the reasons for, and the difficulty and complexity of, establishing a definition of life.
   B. analyze the criteria for defining life.
   C. differentiate between definitions that are philosophical and biological in nature.
   D. explain the difference between the Gaia theory and traditional systems of thought.

32. The main function of the second paragraph (lines 13–27) in relation to the passage as a whole is to:

   F. dispute the scientific basis of the search for a definition of life.
   G. offer instances in which specific criteria can be problematic.
   H. provide historical context for the process described in the remainder of the passage.
   J. discuss solutions to the problems scientists encounter defining life.

33. The author mentions humans and mules in the third paragraph (lines 39–47) primarily to:

   A. demonstrate some of the problems that the specific criteria we use for a definition can cause.
   B. establish a means of comparison between the two species.
   C. challenge any definition that would not include both as "alive."
   D. persuade the reader to try to discover a definition of life.

34. According to the passage, all of the following could be considered, in general terms, to be alive EXCEPT:

   F. a forest fire.
   G. a computer virus.
   H. an automobile.
   J. the Earth as a whole

35. According to the passage, what is the primary problem with the term "complexity"?

   A. It is subjective and based on arbitrary criteria.
   B. It may easily be applied to things that are not alive as well.
   C. It has limitations that are philosophical and biochemical in nature.
   D. It can be accepted only by proponents of the Gaia theory.

36. According to the passage, scientists have been seeking a definition of life:

   F. ever since space exploration has been possible.
   G. ever since the time of Aristotle.
   H. to settle finally the debate over the Gaia theory.
   J. with greater intensity now than in the past.

37. As it used in line 37, the phrase *break down* most nearly means:

   A. malfunction.
   B. explain.
   C. weep.
   D. reduce.

38. In the context of the passage, the phrase "what exactly are we looking for?" (line 11–12) most nearly suggests that a definition of life:

   F. is one of many answers biologists are trying to discover.
   G. can be found if the investigation is carried out in a precise manner.
   H. will open up an array of other questions, leading to further investigation and discovery.
   J. is an essential first step towards finding evidence of life on other planets.

39. The passage indicates that the Gaia theory differs from traditional systems of thought in that the Gaia theory:

   A. will bring us closer to finally understanding how to define life.
   B. treats the Earth as a whole as a single living organism.
   C. considers there to be only four elements in the universe.
   D. has led to monumental discoveries such as alternative biochemistries.

40. Suppose a philosopher were to lead an investigation with the aim of finding an objective definition for "love." Based on the passage, the author would most likely describe this undertaking as:

   F. interesting but unrealistic.
   G. pointless and unscholarly.
   H. worthwhile and straightforward.
   J. arbitrary and useful only to philosophers.

END OF TEST 3
STOP! DO NOT TURN THE PAGE UNTIL TOLD TO DO SO.
DO NOT RETURN TO A PREVIOUS TEST.

Chapter 27
Reading Practice
Test 4: Answers and
Explanations

READING PRACTICE TEST 4 ANSWERS

1.	B		21.	D
2.	H		22.	F
3.	B		23.	C
4.	J		24.	H
5.	A		25.	C
6.	H		26.	H
7.	C		27.	A
8.	J		28.	G
9.	D		29.	D
10.	G		30.	H
11.	C		31.	A
12.	F		32.	G
13.	D		33.	A
14.	F		34.	H
15.	D		35.	B
16.	G		36.	G
17.	C		37.	D
18.	F		38.	J
19.	C		39.	B
20.	G		40.	F

SCORE YOUR PRACTICE TEST

Step A

Count the number of correct answers: _____. This is your **raw score**.

Step B

Use the score conversion table below to look up your raw score. The number to the left is your **scale score**: _____.

Reading Scale Conversion Table

Scale Score	Raw Score	Scale Score	Raw Score	Scale Score	Raw Score
36	40	27	30	18	18
35	39	26	29	17	16–17
34	38	25	27–28	16	15
33	37	24	26	15	14
32	36	23	24–25	14	12–13
31	35	22	23	13	11
30	34	21	22	12	9–10
29	32–33	20	20–21	11	8
28	31	19	19	10	6–7

READING PRACTICE TEST 4 EXPLANATIONS

Passage I

1. **B** While a number of other people, including Kealoha's family, customers, and Santos, are all mentioned in the passage, they are all described from Kealoha's point of view, and only as she remembers them.

2. **H** The Moana Hotel is described as *world-famous* (line 28), so it would have been well-known on the island as well, as (F) states. The passage mentions her working there as a chambermaid (lines 32–33) and the variety of people, *from the obscure to the famous*, (line 34) who stayed there. However, the number of rooms at the Moana is never given, making (H) the only choice *not* supported by the passage, and therefore correct.

3. **B** Kealoha worked at her parents' *market stall* (line 8). When Kealoha and Santos listened to radio programs, Pup is described as *sitting and staring at the radio* (lines 64–65), and the passage states that Kealoha met Santos when she began working at the Quartermaster Corps (lines 49–50). The only question of the four *not* answered by the passage is (B); Santos was *raised in Tacoma* (line 67), but no mention is made of the age at which he moved there from the Philippines.

4. **J** The paragraph lists the different jobs she held and relates them each to her personality, but there is no evidence to support the fact that this was due to her growing *bored* with them, as stated in (F). Choice (G) is supported by the passage but only talks about one of the jobs she held, so it's not a main idea. There is no mention of whether Kealoha lost the opportunity to spend holidays with her family, as (H) states, or how she may have felt about it.

5. **A** The third paragraph (lines 32–38) mentions Kealoha working as a chambermaid, seeing famous people, and being promoted for her work, supporting (B), (C), and (D). The fifth paragraph mentions her *cooking meals in their tiny kitchen*, not at the Moana, but in her own home. Since (A) is the choice that is unsupported, it is the correct answer.

6. **H** Kealoha, thinking about the first time she met Santos, remembers that he was *slightly-built and fair-skinned, which made him look even younger than he was* (lines 69–70). There is no dialogue in the passage similar to what is stated in (F) and (G), and there is also no evidence for (J), which states that Santos may have reminded Kealoha of someone she once knew.

7. **C** The fourth paragraph describes Kealoha as *eager to take advantage of the new opportunities citizenship offered* (lines 41–42). Although her *sisters* and *troops* are both mentioned, there is no evidence given for her feeling either *sadness* or *dismay*, as in (A) and (D). There is no mention of the *concern about the loss of her heritage* in (B).

8. **J** The first paragraph describes Kealoha's aspirations *to have enough money to visit the faraway places these visitors would talk about—Los Angeles, Sydney, or even New York* (lines 11–13). Kealoha worked in her parents' market (line 8), but there is no mention in the passage of her wanting to open one of her own or of owning a farm, as in (F) and (G). Kealoha's sisters *chose to go to university on the mainland* (lines 42–43), not Kealoha.

9. **D** Kealoha is described in the third paragraph (lines 32–38) as having been promoted twice while at the Moana Hotel, and there is no evidence to show she was ever given added responsibility or higher pay while working for her parents. The actual number of hours she worked at either her parents' market stall or at the Moana is not given in the passage.

10. **G** When Kealoha first met Santos, *he was terse, but not rude, and called her "Ms. Kealoha." She could tell that he was trying to make his voice sound deeper than it actually was* (lines 73–75) in an effort to appear older. Choices (F) and (H) both involve dialogue, of which the passage has none, and while (J) may seem plausible, there is no evidence given for how Santos may have felt about being promoted.

Passage II

11. **C** Mann accepted the position of First Secretary of Education *despite. . . the lack of any demonstrated interest in public education prior to his appointment* (lines 4–6), and carried out his duties with *an almost unbelievable zeal* (lines 14–15). This contradicts (A) and (B). The passage states that Mann continued his efforts for education reform after his wife's death (lines 58–61), eliminating (D).

12. **F** The *proposal* in lines 52–55 was for *the disuse of corporal punishment*, which *displeased a group of schoolteachers in Boston*, as stated in (F). There is no support in the passage that Mann, his parents, or the biographer Younger disapproved of Mann's proposal.

13. **D** The passage states that the grief Mann felt over the death of his first wife *never wholly left him*, and he not only lost his only brother at about the same time but also *inherited substantial debt*. Nonetheless, his *vision for change continued unabated* (lines 57–60). While he may have been *angry* about these events, there is no support in the passage for his feeling *afraid*, as in (A). Similarly, Mann is never described as *uncaring* or *selfish*, as (B) states; in fact, he is consistently shown to be quite the opposite. There is evidence that Mann was quite *confident* but nothing to support the fact that he may have been *surprised* about either event, making (C) incorrect.

14. **F** The statement in lines 10–13 is talking about the positive effects Mann had on public education after he accepted the role of First Secretary of the Board of Education, not the *folly* of his decision to accept the role, as in (G). Choice (H) refers to his *upbringing* prior to that point, which hadn't prepared him for the position, and there is no evidence for the comparison in (J) between Massachusetts and other places.

15. **D** In the last sentence of the passage, the author states that Mann was an example to others because of his *commitment not only to ideals but also to action*. There is no mention in the passage of him seeking approval, as (A) states. While some of Mann's reforms involved legislation, there is no evidence for the claim in (B) that he thought this was the *only* means of reform. Choice (C) is supported by the passage, but the pursuit of one's own education isn't what the author offers as *an example for others who seek social reform*.

16. **G** Mann's proposal was for the *disuse* of corporal punishment (lines 52–55), so he must have felt it to be *improper*. There is no irony on the ACT, and (F), (H), and (J) are all reasons to keep using corporal punishment.

17. **C** Lines 35–38 refer to Mann's campaign as *unprecedented and daringly progressive*. Duplicating an existing system would not make his campaign *unprecedented*, just as *cautiously instituting small reforms, one at a time* would not be daring, making (A) and (B) incorrect. Choice (D) mentions *cost-saving measures* and *his predecessor*, neither of which are talked about in the passage.

18. **F** Discussing Mann's passion for education reform, the passage refers to *abolition* (lines 41–45) as *a cause Mann would champion with equal fervor upon his election to the U.S. Senate*. This contradicts (G), as *obsessively* would mean he was focused on education only. Choice (H) can be eliminated because Mann's voting record is never mentioned. Mann certainly claimed that education was the responsibility of the state, as (J) states, but he did so as First Secretary, not as a U.S. Senator (lines 38–41). Additionally, there is no evidence offered in the passage to support how articulate or amazing he may have been in doing so.

19. **C** Lines 72–75 state that the reason Mann visited every schoolhouse in the state in the first year of his administration was *to assess personally the condition and quality of each*. There is no mention of Mann's desire to travel being the reason he left the state legislature, as (A) states; the only reason given in the passage was *dependable salary* (lines 7–8). There is no mention of the number of schoolhouses being sufficient or not, so you can eliminate (B). Choice (D) contradicts the passage, which describes Mann as successful primarily because of the energy and personal attention he put into his job.

20. **G** Both accounts use the same general criteria to praise Mann for his reforms and are not *critical* in tone—eliminate (F) and (H). The passage's fourth paragraph (lines 46–61) recounts Mann facing criticism from various sources, making (J) incorrect.

Passage III

21. **D** The narrator does indeed visit a movie studio, as (A) states, but that is not the focus of the story; her meeting with Bergman is. The narrator never mentions wanting to become *an actress like Bergman*, and there is no support for *adjusting to life* in (C)—the narrator merely mentions the fact that they live in California.

22. **F** Speaking as an adult, the narrator feels inspired by Bergman in the final paragraph (lines 78–82). Choices (G), (H), and (J) all occurred when she was a child.

23. **C** The narrator relates Bergman's insistence on calling each other by their first names *just like friends should* (line 63) and remembers her as *smiling* and *friendly* (line 74). Bergman's actions are not *snobbish*, so eliminate (B). The people on the movie studio lot are described as *rushed* (line 41). Choice (D) is contradicted by Bergman's quote, *I have no regrets* (line 76).

24. **H** When she first meets Bergman, the narrator describes her as *so strikingly tall and beautiful that I could barely think to say anything* (lines 47–48). There is no evidence to show she was afraid, as (F) states, or felt *envy* or *jealousy*, as (G) states. The narrator describes herself and her sister as *excited* and *doubtful* (line 22) but not during her meeting with Bergman.

25. **C** The narrator says that she has seen all of Bergman's films (line 70) and goes on to say how one film in particular *makes me remember that day* (lines 72–73). In the final paragraph (lines 78–82), the narrator says she was too young to fully appreciate meeting Bergman, so eliminate (A). There is no evidence in the passage for the sisters being *too busy to think about* meeting Bergman, as stated in (B). Choice (D) is also unsupported since the photos clearly meant a great deal to the narrator and her sister. Additionally, the narrator never expresses a desire to purchase a dress of her own.

26. **H** The narrator mentions that *many of the large buildings looked nearly identical* (lines 35–36) before describing the building they approach as *indistinguishable from the others* (line 38). *A riot of noise and color* in (F) refers to the move studio lot in general, not the buildings specifically. The narrator uses *full of spectacle and wonder* in (G) to describe her memories of the entire visit. Choice (J) is a description of Bergman herself.

27. **A** The narrator compares her memories of meeting Bergman to a scene in a movie, *full of spectacle and wonder and emotion* (lines 68–69). *Performance*, *demonstration*, and *extravaganza* also have similar meanings to *spectacle*, but *marvel* best fits the context of *wonder and emotion*.

28. **G** The comparison being made in the twelfth paragraph is between the tragic character Bergman portrays in the film and *the smiling, friendly, generous woman I met*. There is no evidence for (F), as the narrator is referring to only one movie. Choice (H) is unsupported since Bergman's *appeal to fans of all ages* is never discussed. The narrator describes Bergman as *smiling, friendly,* and *generous*, which disagrees with (J).

29. **D** In the last paragraph, the narrator states *I was only eleven when I met Ingrid Bergman* (line 78).

30. **H** Speaking about the words Bergman used to describe her own life, the narrator states *but as I read those words now. . . I can't help but recognize, and be inspired by, a truly independent spirit.* Choice (F) can be eliminated because it is contradicted by the narrator's statement *I was only eleven when I met Ingrid Bergman and couldn't really understand the magnitude of her accomplishments* (lines 78–79). There is no proof for the claim in (G) that the narrator's aunt and sister had any *influence* regarding her appreciation of Bergman, and no mention is ever made of seeing Bergman in the gown Tìa Elena made—eliminate (J).

Passage IV

31. A The passage as a whole is a discussion of not only how scientists define life and the difficulties they encounter but also the reasons it is important for them to do so. The *criteria* used for defining life are discussed, but that is not the primary purpose of the passage. Similarly, the notions of *philosophical* and *biological* criteria in (C), and the *Gaia theory* and *traditional systems of thought* in (D) are discussed, but they are not the main focus of the passage.

32. G The second paragraph states *with a concept as vastly complex as life itself, the use of simple terms can be problematic* (lines 14–15) and offers some examples of specific criteria, as well as some examples that fit the criteria, but not the definition. However, there is no evidence that the intent is to *dispute the scientific* basis of this definition, as (F) claims. Choices (H) and (J) are incorrect, as there is no *historical context* given nor *solutions* offered in the second paragraph.

33. A In the third paragraph, the author uses humans and mules as two examples of autonomous life forms and questions whether they technically fit that criterion since both species *depend on plants for survival*. While the two species certainly share that trait, there is no proof in the text that a *means of a comparison between the two species* is being established. There is no *challenge* offered in the text, as (C) states, nor is there evidence that author is trying to persuade the reader to take any sort of action— eliminate (D).

34. H The second paragraph (lines 13–27) lists a *forest fire*, which *self-reproduces* and could be said to have a *metabolism*, and a *computer virus*, which *evolves according to its "environment,"* as examples of phenomena that meet at least some of the criteria for life. The *Gaia theory* in the fifth paragraph (lines 48–57) considers *the Earth as a whole* to be a *living organism*. The only example not offered by the passage is (H), *an automobile*, making it the correct answer.

35. B The author uses *the individual cells of our bodies* (line 23) as an example of entities that are complex but may still not be considered strictly to be alive. There is no mention of the term *complexity* being either *subjective* or *arbitrary*, as (A) states, nor is there a discussion of its *limitations*. *Complexity*, as a defining term, is not discussed in connection with the *Gaia theory*, making (D) incorrect.

36. G The passage states that *since the time of Aristotle, there have been any number of definitions of life put forth* (lines 5–6). *Space exploration* is offered as a reason why scientists are so interested in finding a definition (lines 7–11). The debate over the *Gaia theory* (lines 48–57) is described as a result of the search for a definition, not the reason behind it. There is no comparison in the text between the intensity of the present-day search and that of scientists in the past, so (J) can be eliminated.

37. D In lines (35–38), the author uses the phrase *break down* to describe a chemical process. Choices (A), (B), and (C) do not fit this context.

38. **J**   The author poses the question to emphasize his earlier point about space travel and the ability to seek life on other planets (lines 7–11). The author does not mention the *many other answers* sought by biologists in (F), and there is no mention of the *investigation* needing to be carried out with a certain level of precision. In the sixth paragraph (lines 58–82), the author discusses the search for a definition leading to further *investigation and discovery*, but that is a different point from the one he is making in the first paragraph.

39. **B**   The author states that the *Gaia theory is a system of thought that treats the Earth as a whole as a single living organism* and refers to the theory as *a radical departure from traditional systems of thought*, so that must be the difference. The author offers the theory as an example, not a solution, so eliminate (A). The universe being composed of *only four elements* is mentioned later in the passage (line 66), but not in conjunction with the Gaia theory, making (C) incorrect. *Monumental discoveries* (lines 71–72) and *alternative biochemistries* (44–45) are also mentioned in the passage, but also not in connection with the Gaia theory, so (D) is incorrect.

40. **F**   It is reasonable to infer that the author of this passage would attach the same importance of finding a definition for *love* to philosophers as he would that of a definition of *life* to biologists, and anticipate the same benefits, which directly contradicts (G). He gives several examples of the complexities of finding a single definition, saying *the use of simple terms can be problematic* and *the answer . . . won't really be an answer but rather a whole series of new questions*. This is the opposite of *straightforward*, so eliminate (H). There is no support in the passage for the notion that the author would find such an investigation *arbitrary*, which eliminates (J). The author would agree that such an investigation was *interesting*, as (F) states, and he also makes it very clear that an objective definition is *unrealistic* by suggesting several times that a single answer won't be found. *Perhaps in the end, rather than leading us to an answer, it will be the search itself . . .* shows that he doesn't expect there to be a clear answer at the end of the search. Both parts of (F) are supported, leaving it as the best answer.

Chapter 28
The ACT Writing Test

OVERVIEW

The ACT Writing test is a section with one essay prompt. You must pay an additional fee to take this portion of the ACT, and test takers who do write the essay are usually put in a separate room from those who don't. When you take the Writing test, you will receive two additional scores on your score report. First, you'll see the Writing test score, as well as four sub-scores (ideas and analysis, development and support, organization, and language use and conventions). Much like the overall score, these subscores will be scored and reported on a 2–12 scale. Second, you'll get a combined English/Writing/Reading score called the English Language Arts Score. The most important thing for you to know, however, is that Writing test score and sub-scores, and the English Language Arts Score do not factor into your composite. English, Math, Reading, and Science are still the only scores reflected in the composite number.

Essay Scoring

According to ACT, each essay is evaluated on how well it exhibits your ability to do the following:

- analyze different points of view on a complex issue

- develop your position and support your ideas using logical reasoning, prior knowledge, and experience

- organize ideas in a logical way

- use language clearly and effectively according to the rules of standard written English

ACT's scoring guidelines are built around a "holistic" grading system; two graders will read your essay and rate it from 1 (low) to 6 (high) based on their overall impressions of the above criteria. These ratings are then added together to create your Writing subscore, which ranges from 2–12. If the grades assigned by each reader differ by more than a point, a third reader will evaluate the essay to reconcile the difference.

More Great Books

Check out *Cracking the ACT* for in-depth, comprehensive ACT test preparation from your friends at The Princeton Review.

Writing Test Practice

Let's look at a practice Writing Test to get familiar with this new format.

Many societal changes come about as a result of conflict. A single act of persecution or violence towards an individual can spark widespread protests demanding change in an oppressive government. On a smaller scale, students at a school or employees in a workplace may feel dissatisfied with the way things are run and lobby for a change in policies. Many times such conflicts result in positive changes, but is disagreement necessary to evoke change? Given the number of social issues that cause strong emotional reactions from multiple sides, it is worth examining the implications of such conflict.

Read and carefully consider these perspectives. Each suggests a particular way of thinking about the role of conflict in social change.

Perspective One	Perspective Two	Perspective Three
If people are not in some way dissatisfied with their situations in life, change will never happen. Motivation to act for change can come only from righteous indignation.	Heated conflicts rarely result in lasting change. On the contrary, those in charge are more likely to respond to civil and constructive conversation than to attacks.	Much positive change comes about without conflict at all. When people are content, they are better able to work together to further improve society.

Essay Task

Write a unified, coherent essay in which you evaluate multiple perspectives on the role of conflict. In your essay, be sure to:

- analyze and evaluate the perspectives given

- state and develop your own perspective on the issue

- explain the relationship between your perspective and those given

Your perspective may be in full agreement with any of the others, in partial agreement, or wholly different. Whatever the case, support your ideas with logical reasoning and detailed, persuasive examples.

For starters, let's look at the instructions in the prompt. These directions never change, so you'll always need to do the following things:

- analyze and evaluate the perspectives given

- state and develop your own perspective on the issue

- explain the relationship between your perspective and those given

Although there are certainly more facets to a well-written essay than the three points above, we can use these as a springboard for constructing an essay that garners a higher score. Below, you can see a sample essay response that received a score of 4. Let's see how this student addresses the issue of whether or not conflict should be used as an agent of change.

Part I: The Intro

> *I believe that conflict is necessary for change. When a person is satisfied with their position in life, they have no reason to make changes. The most important social changes happen when there is direct conflict with authority; civil conversation often isn't enough. Direct conflict can result in widespread support for an overhaul of the way things are, such as in the Civil Rights movement and the American Revolution.*

Although it may not be the most complete introduction you've ever read, this paragraph accomplishes a few important goals. First, the writer clearly takes a position on the issue and is in agreement with the first perspective given in the prompt. Second, the other two perspectives in the prompt are briefly addressed. Third, the writer tells the reader why direct conflict is necessary. The reasons presented clearly foreshadow what will be discussed in the body paragraphs.

Part II: The Body

> *The idea that conflict is necessary for change can be seen through the example of the Civil Rights movement. Because African Americans were unhappy with the idea of 'separate but equal,' they are able to successfully lobby for a change. When Rosa Parks refused to give up her seat on a bus, her simple act of disobedience sparked a bus boycott that eventually became a landmark case in the struggle for civil rights. If African Americans had never protested against the unfair segregation laws, the Civil Rights Act would never have passed.*

> *Some people believe that violent conflict is counterproductive. This situation was clearly demonstrated in the events leading up the American Revolution. When Great Britain imposed a variety of taxes on the American colonies, many colonists wanted*

to sever all ties with Britain and a series of riots and massacres broke out. However, many colonists did not want to be in direct conflict with Great Britain; instead, they wanted to mend their relationship with King George through compromise and discussion. One view on the role of conflict in change would say that such violence doesn't help any cause and the colonists were worsening their own situation by doing it. But the violence of the riots and the American Revolution eventually led to the creation of the United States, it is now the most powerful nation in the world. The United States would have never become the country it is today if not for that initial conflict.

While it is true that some change, such as increased enforcement of Civil Rights law, happens over time without major conflict, change happens more quickly and more effectively when there is conflict to draw people's attention to the matter at hand. If African Americans in the 50s had not been dissatisfied with segregation, they would not have worked to change it. Similarly, if the American colonists hadn't thought there was a problem with 'taxation without representation,' they wouldn't have started the American Revolution.

The first paragraph supports the writer's position that that conflict is necessary for change by using a specific example. What do you notice about the details given to support this example? The inclusion of a specific act of civil disobedience enhances the general claim by providing some concrete information.

In the second body paragraph, the writer addresses the second perspective included in the prompt, which argues heated conflict rarely causes real change. The author is able to refute this perspective using another concrete example, the American Revolution. Similarly, the third body paragraph discusses the third perspective, which argues change can occur without conflict at all. The writer argues against this perspective by drawing from and expanding upon both of the previous examples.

Overall, however, the body paragraphs are well-structured and use clear transitions to move from one point to the next. You'll notice that this student's grammar is not perfect, but a few errors are considered normal, given the time allotted for drafting the essay. You do want to try to keep your grammar and spelling as clean as possible, but it's not a huge factor in your score. Most of all, it's important for the essay to maintain focus by sticking to the reasons put forth in the introduction, and this essay does a good job of staying on track.

Now let's look at the conclusion:

Part III: The Conclusion

In conclusion, as can be seen through the examples of some landmark moments in the Civil Rights movement, change comes about more effectively as the result of conflict.

Although the conclusion is quite short, it meets the standard the writer needs to earn a to earn a high score. The writer restates his or her position on the issue and mentions the reasons cited in the body paragraphs. If you find yourself with this short of a conclusion, it's likely that you ran out of time. Be sure to outline your essay and stick to the plan before you start writing.

We've done some pretty focused analysis of this essay in order to get an idea of what should be accomplished in each portion of your response. You may not have been awed by the level of detail or rhetorical flourish, but our goal here isn't to win the Pulitzer Prize. Below, we've reproduced the entire essay; pretend you're a holistic grader and read through the essay. Give yourself about two minutes, and think about your overall impression of the writer's response.

I believe that conflict is necessary for change. When a person is satisfied with their position in life, they have no reason to make changes. The most important social changes happen when people rebel against authority, which can result in widespread support for an overhaul of the way things are.

The idea that conflict is necessary for change can be seen through the example of the Civil Rights movement. Because African Americans were unhappy with the idea of 'separate but equal,' they were able to successfully lobby for a change. When Rosa Parks refused to give up her seat on a bus, her simple act of disobedience sparked a bus boycott that eventually became a landmark case in the struggle for civil rights. If African Americans had never protested against the unfair segregation laws, the Civil Rights Act would never have passed.

Some people believe that violent conflict is counterproductive. This situation was clearly demonstrated in the events leading up the American Revolution. When Great Britain imposed a variety of taxes on the American colonies, many colonists wanted to sever all ties with Britain and a series of riots and massacres broke out. However, many colonists did not want to be in direct conflict with Great Britain; instead, they wanted to mend their relationship with King George through compromise and discussion. One view on the role of conflict in change would say that such violence doesn't help any cause and the colonists were worsening their own situation by doing it. But the violence of the riots and the American Revolution eventually led to the creation of the United States, the most powerful nation in the world. The United States would have never become the country it is today if not for that initial conflict.

While it is true that some change, such as increased enforcement of Civil Rights law, happens over time without major conflict, change happens more quickly and more effectively when there is conflict to draw people's attention to the matter at hand. If African Americans in the 50s had not been dissatisfied with segregation, they would not have worked to change it. Similarly, if the American colonists hadn't thought there was a problem with "taxation without representation," they wouldn't have started the American Revolution.

In conclusion, as can be seen through the examples of some landmark moments in the Civil Rights movement, change comes about more effectively as the result of conflict.

Do you think this essay "adequately" responds to the prompt? It is lengthy and well structured; it has a clear introduction and conclusion; the supporting examples are present and have some concrete details; the essay acknowledges the other perspectives and explains how they relate to the writer's position. It uses some transitions; its errors are minimal and do not significantly distract the reader. We could go on, but you get the idea. High scoring essays are considered superior because of what they have, while low scoring essays are considered inferior because of what they lack. As long as you have the basics, your essay should be strong enough to get to get you to your target... target score. After that, it is all a matter of degree. Take a look at the essay below, which received a 6—while all the same components are present, this essay paints a more holistically pleasing picture.

History is replete with examples of the downtrodden rising up against their oppressors to demand change. Rebellions can be bloody, as Nat Turner's slave rebellion was, or peaceful, like India's struggle for independence from Great Britain under Gandhi. While the levels of violence associated with rebellions vary widely, even peaceful revolutions do not take place unless there is some level of conflict or disagreement between different social strata. When people are satisfied with the status quo, they will not work for change.

It may seem on the surface like the two examples given above are wildly different from each other. Nat Turner's slave rebellion lasted only a few days, and while many white slave owners were killed, the rebels failed to improve their situation. Turner himself was gruesomely dismembered after his execution. But while the immediate results of his uprising were to reinforce the power of whites over their slaves, it is harder to quantify what kind of long-term effect it may have had. News of Turner's rebellion and others like it helped to spread the message to blacks and whites that slaves wanted change. It is true that slavery would likely have been abolished whether or not this one event happened, but if there had been no underlying discontent with the institution of slavery, it might still exist today.

Gandhi's struggle, in contrast to Turner's, lasted throughout his life, was characterized by peaceful protest, and resulted change that can be directly attributed to his actions. But it is a mistake to argue that his brand of non-violent revolution happens without conflict. The people of India were unhappy with British rule and were struggling for their freedom in just the same way that slaves in the United States were fighting for theirs.

Even in a situation where it seems that change is taking place because all parties concerned are working together for a better tomorrow, there must be some underlying level of dissatisfaction driving the change. At my school, students in the National Honor Society recently started an after-school peer tutoring program where struggling students can come for extra help. There was no protest or violence of any kind involved in starting this program. But if there were no need for it, which is to say that if all students were getting all the help they needed from the system that was already in place, the program wouldn't have been established.

Change appears with many different faces, from the seemingly innocuous to the unspeakably bloody. Though it may seem hard to compare the opposite ends of the spectrum, what all change has in common is some level of discontent. Without that sense that things could be different, change would never happen.

In all honesty, some people will have more trouble understanding this essay than they will have understanding the essay that received a 4. That's one of the oddities of holistic grading; high scoring essays exhibit a stronger command of language and a rhetorical grasp that allows for complete elaboration of the ideas presented. We're not telling you to be overly florid, but once you're a strong essay writer, you're going to have to hone your delivery to earn a 6. Here are some quick pointers that you can use to develop your essay response further:

- In your introduction, "grab" the reader by opening with an intriguing statement or rhetorical question. An interesting lead-in will engage a holistic reader early.

- Always start with your strongest example first when writing your body paragraphs. If you've gotten the reader's attention in the introduction, a strong first example will further convince him or her that your essay is an effective one.

- Vary your sentence length. Don't overuse long, complex sentences or short, declarative sentences.

- Utilize different transitions—some variety will make your essay flow both logically and stylistically.

- In your conclusion, retain the focus of the essay without restating everything you've discussed verbatim. Refer to your examples without repeating them exactly, and be sure to mention the other perspectives one last time.

Part III
Paying For
College 101

If you're reading this book, you've already made an investment in your education. You may have shelled out some cold, hard cash for this book, and you've definitely invested time in reading it. It's probably even safe to say that this is one of the smaller investments you've made in your future so far. You put in the hours and hard work needed to keep up your GPA. You've paid test fees and applications fees, perhaps even travel expenses. You have probably committed time and effort to a host of extracurricular activities to make sure colleges know that you're a well-rounded student.

But after you get in, there's one more issue to think about: How do you pay for college?

More Great Titles from The Princeton Review
• *Paying for College Without Going Broke, 2018 Edition*
• *The Best 382 Colleges, 2018 Edition*

Let's be honest: College is not cheap. The average tuition for a private four-year college is over $33,000 a year. The average tuition of a four-year public school is about $6,695 a year. And the cost is rising. Every year the sticker price of college education bumps up about 6 percent.

Like many of us, your family may not have 33 grand sitting around in a shoebox. With such a hefty price tag, you might be wondering: "Is a college education really worth it?" The short answer: Yes! No question about it. According to a 2010 report by the College Board, the median earnings of full-time workers with bachelor's degrees were $55,700 in 2008—$21,900 more than those of workers who finished only high school.

Still, the cost of college is no joke. It's said that a college education ultimately pays for itself; however, some pay better than others. It's best to be prudent when determining the amount of debt that is reasonable for you to take on.

Here's the good news. Even in the wake of the current financial crisis, financial aid is available to almost any student who wants it. There is an estimated $177 billion—that's right, billion!—in financial aid offered to students annually. This comes in the form of federal grants, scholarships, state financed aid, loans, and other programs.

We know that financial aid can seem like an overwhelmingly complex issue, but the introductory information in this chapter should help you grasp what's available and get you started in your search.

How Much Does College Really Cost?

When most people think about the price of a college education, they think of one thing and one thing alone: tuition. It's time to get that notion out of your head. While tuition is a significant portion of the cost of a college education, you need to think of all the other things that factor into the final price tag.

Let's break it down.

- Tuition and fees
- Room and board
- Books and supplies
- Personal expenses
- Travel expenses

Collectively, these things contribute to your total Cost of Attendance (COA) for one year at a college or university.

Understanding the distinction between tuition and COA is crucial because it will help you understand this simple equation:

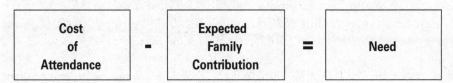

Check Out Our Financial Aid Library
PrincetonReview.com/scholarships-financial-aid.aspx

When you begin the financial aid process, you will see this equation again and again. We've already talked about the COA, so let's talk about the Estimated Family Contribution, or EFC. The EFC simply means, "How much you and your family can afford to pay for college." Sounds obvious right?

Here's the catch: What you think you can afford to pay for college, what the government thinks you can afford to pay for college, and what a college or university thinks you can afford to pay for college are, unfortunately, three different things. Keep that in mind as we discuss financing options later on.

The final term in the equation is self-explanatory. Anything that's left after what you and your family have contributed still needs to be covered. That's where financial aid packages come in.

WHAT'S IN A FINANCIAL AID PACKAGE?

A typical financial aid package contains money—from the school, federal government, or state—in various forms: grants, scholarships, work-study programs, and loans.

Let's look at the non-loan options first. Non-loan options include grants, scholarships, and work-study programs. The crucial thing about them is that they involve monetary assistance that you won't be asked to pay back. They are as close as you'll get to "free money."

Grants

Grants are basically gifts. They are funds given to you by the federal government, state agencies, or individual colleges. They are usually need-based, and you are not required to pay them back.

One of the most important grants is the Pell Grant. Pell Grants are provided by the federal government but administered through individual schools. Amounts can change yearly. The maximum Federal Pell Grant award is $5,775 for the 2015–2016 award year (July 1, 2015, to June 30, 2016). For the 2016–2017 award year (July 1, 2016, to June 30, 2017), the maximum award will be $5,815.

You apply for a Pell Grant by filling out the Free Application for Federal Student Aid (FAFSA). Remember that acronym because you'll be seeing it again. Completing the FAFSA is the first step in applying for any federal aid. The FAFSA can be found online at www.fafsa.ed.gov.

There are several other major federal grant programs that hand out grants ranging from $100 to thousands of dollars annually. Some of these grants are given to students entering a specific field of study and others are need-based, but all of them amount to money that you never have to pay back. Check out the FAFSA website for complete information about qualifying and applying for government grants.

The federal government isn't the only source of grant money. State governments and specific schools also offer grants. Use the Internet, your guidance counselor, and your library to see what non-federal grants you might be eligible for.

Scholarships

Like grants, you never have to pay a scholarship back. But the requirements and terms of a scholarship might vary wildly. Most scholarships are merit- or need-based, but they can be based on almost anything. There are scholarships based on academic performance, athletic achievements, musical or artistic talent, religious affiliation, ethnicity, and so on.

When hunting for scholarships, one great place to start is the U.S. Department of Labor's "Scholarship Search," available at www.careerinfonet.org/scholarshipsearch. It includes over 5,000 scholarships, fellowships, loans, and other opportunities. It's a free service and a great resource.

There is one important caveat about taking scholarship money. Some, but not all, schools think of scholarship money as income and will reduce the amount of aid they offer you accordingly. Know your school's policy on scholarship awards.

Federal Work-Study (FWS)

One of the ways Uncle Sam disperses aid money is by subsidizing part-time jobs, usually on campus, for students who need financial aid. Because your school will administer the money, they get to decide what your work-study job will be. Work-study participants are paid by the hour, and federal law requires that they cannot be paid less than the federal minimum wage.

One of the benefits of a work-study program is that you get a paycheck just like you would at a normal job. The money is intended to go toward school expenses, but there are no controls over exactly how you spend it.

Colleges and universities determine how to administer work-study programs on their own campuses.

Check Out the Scholarship Search Page
PrincetonReview.com/ scholarships.aspx

The Bottom Line? Not So Fast!
It is possible to appeal the amount of the financial aid package a school awards you. To learn more about how to do that, check out "Appealing Your Award Package" at PrincetonReview.com/ appealing-your-award.aspx

LOANS

Most likely, your entire COA won't be covered by scholarships, grants, and work-study income. The next step in gathering the necessary funds is securing a loan. Broadly speaking, there are two routes to go: federal loans and private loans. Once upon a time, which route to choose might be open for debate. But these days the choice is clear: *Always* try to secure federal loans first. Almost without exception, federal loans provide unbeatable low fixed-interest rates; they come with generous repayment terms; and, although they have lending limits, these limits are quite generous and will take you a long way toward your goal. We'll talk about the benefits of private loans later, but they really can't measure up to what the government can provide and should be considered a last resort.

Stafford Loans

The Stafford loan is the primary form of federal student loan. Loans can be subsidized or unsubsidized. Students with demonstrated financial need may qualify for subsidized loans. This means that the government pays interest accumulated during the time the student is in school. Students with unsubsidized Stafford loans are responsible for the interest accumulated while in school. You can qualify for a subsidized Stafford loan, an unsubsidized Stafford loan, or a mixture of the two.

Stafford loans are available to all full-time students and most part-time students. Though the terms of the loan are based on demonstrated financial need, lack of need is not considered grounds for rejection. No payment is expected while the student is attending school. The interest rate on your Stafford loan will depend on when your first disbursement is. The chart below shows the fixed rates set by the government.

The interest rates for Direct Subsidized Loans and Direct Unsubsidized Loans are shown in the chart below.

Loan Type	Borrower Type	Loans first disbursed on or after 7/1/17
Direct Subsidized Loans	Undergraduate	4.45%
Direct Unsubsidized Loans	Undergraduate	4.45%
Direct Unsubsidized Loans	Graduate or Professional	6%

The interest rates above are fixed rates for the life of the loan. As with grants, you must start by completing the Free Application for Federal Student Aid (FAFSA) to apply for a Stafford loan.

PLUS Loans

Another important federal loan is the PLUS loan. This loan is designed to help parents and guardians put dependent students through college. Unlike the Stafford loan, the PLUS has no fixed limits or fixed interest rates. The annual limit on a PLUS loan is equal to your COA minus any other financial aid you are already receiving. It may be used on top of a Stafford loan. The interest rates on PLUS loans are variable though often comparable to, or even lower than, the interest rates on Stafford loans. Your PLUS Loan enters repayment once your loan is fully disbursed (paid out).

To become eligible for a PLUS loan, you need only complete a Free Application for Federal Student Aid (FAFSA). There are no other special requirements or forms to fill out.

Perkins Loans

A third and final federal loan you should be aware of is the Perkins loan. Intended to help out students in extreme need, the Perkins loan is a government-subsidized loan that is administered only through college and university financial aid offices. Under the terms of a Perkins loan, you may borrow up to $5,500 a year of undergraduate study, up to $27,500. The Perkins loan has a fixed interest rate of just 5 percent. Payments against the loan don't start until nine months after you graduate. Apply for Perkins loans through your school's financial aid office.

Private Lenders

We said it before, and we'll say it again: DO NOT get a private loan until you've exhausted all other options.

That said, there are *some* benefits to securing a private loan. First off, many students find that non-loan and federal loan options don't end up covering the entire bill. If that's the case, then private lenders might just save the day. Second, loans from private sources generally offer you greater flexibility with how you use the funds. Third, private loans can be taken out at anytime during your academic career. Unlike most non-loan and government-backed financial options, you can turn to private lenders whenever you need them.

All private lenders are not the same! As the old song says, "You better shop around." Every lender is going to offer you a different package of terms. What you need to do is find the package that best fits your needs and plans. Aside from low interest rates, which are crucially important, there other terms and conditions you will want to look out for.

Low origination fees

Origination fees are fees that lenders charge you for taking out a loan. Usually the fee is simply deducted automatically from your loan checks. Obviously, the lower the origination fee, the better.

Minimal guaranty fees

A guaranty fee is an amount you pay to a third-party who agrees to insure your loan. That way, if the borrower—that is you—can't pay the loan back, the guarantor steps in and pays the difference. Again, if you can minimize or eliminate this fee, all the better.

Interest rate reductions

Some lenders will reduce your interest rates if you're reliable with your payments. Some will even agree to knock a little off the interest rate if you agree to pay your loans through a direct deposit system. When shopping for the best loan, pay careful attention to factors that might help you curb your interest rates.

Flexible payment plans

One of the great things about most federal loans is the fact that you don't have to start paying them off until you leave school. In order to compete, many private lenders have been forced to adopt similarly flexible payment plans. Before saying yes to a private loan, make sure that it comes with a payment timetable you can live with.

IT'S YOUR CALL

No matter what the state of the economy, it is always a good idea to thoroughly research the assortment of low-interest federal assistance programs available to you. Weigh your financing options (loans, grants, scholarships, work study, etc.) against the overall cost of your college education. Remember that this is a personal choice with potentially long-term ramifications, and that what your peers are doing may not be right for you. Talk it over with your parent(s) or guardian(s). With thoughtful planning (and a lot of form-filling!) it's possible to pay your way though school without breaking the bank.

NOTES

NOTES

NOTES

NOTES

NOTES

NOTES

NOTES

NOTES

NOTES

NOTES

NOTES